PAUL IN THE GRIP OF THE PHILOSOPHERS

PAUL IN THE GRIP OF THE PHILOSOPHERS

THE APOSTLE AND CONTEMPORARY CONTINENTAL PHILOSOPHY

PETER FRICK, EDITOR

Fortress Press

Minneapolis

PAUL IN THE GRIP OF THE PHILOSOPHERS

The Apostle and Contemporary Continental Philosophy

Cover design: Tory Herman

Cover image: From *Cities of Paul* by Helmut Koester, copyright © 2005 the President and Fellows of Harvard College. All rights reserved. Used here by permission of Fortress Press.

Library of Congress Cataloging-in-Publication data is available

Print ISBN: 978-0-8006-9912-3

eBook ISBN: 978-1-4514-3865-9

The paper used in this publication meets the minimum requirements of American National Standard for Information Sciences—Permanence of Paper for Printed Library Materials, ANSI Z329.48-1984.

Manufactured in the U.S.A.

This book was produced using PressBooks.com, and PDF rendering was done by PrinceXML.

Tom Maier

φίλος
ἀδελφός
θεόλογος
σύνδουλος

CONTENTS

Paul in the Grip of Continental Philosophers   1
    What is at Stake?
    Peter Frick

1. Nietzsche   15
    The Archetype of Pauline Deconstruction
    Peter Frick

2. Heidegger on the Apostle Paul   39
    Benjamin Crowe

3. Paul of the Gaps   57
    Agamben, Benjamin and the Puppet Player
    Roland Boer

4. Jacob Taubes—Paulinist, Messianist   69
    Larry L. Welborn

5. Circumcising the Word   91
    Derrida as a Reader of Paul
    Hans Ruin

6. Gianni Vattimo and Saint Paul   117
    Ontological Weakening, Kenosis, and Secularity
    Anthony C. Sciglitano Jr.

7. Badiou's Paul   143
    Founder of Universalism and Theoretician of the Militant
    Frederiek Depoortere

8. Agamben's Paul   165
    Thinker of the Messianic
    Alain Gignac

9.   Mad with the Love of Undead Life   193
     Understanding Paul and Žižek
     Ward Blanton

10. The Philosophers' Paul and the Churches   217
     Neil Elliott

Bibliography   239
Index of Subjects   255
Index of Names   259
Index of Biblical References   263

Paul in the Grip of Continental Philosophers

What is at Stake?

Peter Frick

Pauline scholars, theologians, philosophers, historians, Christians—really all persons who have an interest in the apostle Paul—find themselves in the same basic quandary: How to make sense of this man Paul, how to interpret and understand his teaching, and how to determine its significance, then and now? In other words, the reader of Pauline texts is confronted with the perennial hermeneutical question. To be sure, the hermeneutical circle is indeed wide, complex, and multifarious; but there are two basic presuppositions that Paul's interpreters have in common. The first and basic one is that the starting point of an encounter with Paul is the reading of his letters and the attempt to interpret and understand them. In our postmodern context, this once basic proposition—that Paul is an author and that we encounter him through his texts—is now questioned in itself; we will return to this question below. The second presupposition is the fact that each reader has a unique *Sitz im Leben* within which she or he must make sense of Paul. In other words, the contextual location of each Pauline reader is distinct from the location of other Pauline readers. Correspondingly, the presuppositions—though as Gadamer has shown, they are actually "prejudices" and not mere neutral prerequisites—that each interpreter of Paul brings to the text are equally distinct. This is the case not only in terms of social location but also in terms of time. The Pauline interpretations of Augustine, Luther, Bultmann, Barth, or Tillich are evidently different from our own today. They are removed both in time[2] and in social, intellectual location. Our cognizance of these differences should keep us from committing the error of anachronism and open our eyes to the plurality of contexts. Examining how the philosophical interest in Paul developed and

---

1. See Hans-Georg Gadamer, *Wahrheit und Methode*, 5th ed. (Tübingen: J. C. B. Mohr, 1986), 270–95.

2. Ibid., 296–305.

1

how, in this very development, the hermeneutical locations and presuppositions (necessarily and sometimes dramatically) changed will place us in a better position to make intelligible Continental philosophy's interest in, if not fascination with, Paul.

THE FIRST PHILOSOPHY AND CHRISTIAN THEOLOGY

Let us start at the beginning of what we now call the Western intellectual tradition. Here theology and philosophy were more or less compatible friends. Even before Paul had penned one word of his letters, Greek thinkers had already tried to work out a fruitful relationship between theology and philosophy. It was Aristotle—and not a Christian theologian—who introduced the word θεολογία ("theology") into the intellectual discourse of the Occident. He understood theology as the "first philosophy" (πρώτη φιλοσοφία) by virtue of its reflecting on first causes and their Being, ideas that led him to the concept of God.[3] The Greek interweaving of theology and philosophy was taken up in both the Jewish and Christian traditions. The prime example of an early Jewish thinker who embraced the relation between philosophy and theology in positive terms is Philo of Alexandria. As a thinker committed to both the observing of Torah and a Middle-Platonic philosophical outlook, he saw no inherent conflict in employing philosophy as "the handmaid" of theology. In other words, for Philo, philosophical reflection strengthened his theology and made his faith more intelligible to the non-Jewish reader.[4]

When we come to the apostle himself, his own letters and the account of his life in the book of Acts give a rather meager portrait of Paul as a philosopher, or as an apostle interested in philosophical themes. Even though Paul invokes the Stoic Aratus (see *Phaenomena* 5) in his speech in Athens (see Acts 17:28), it seems fair to say that he does so for apologetic and theological reasons rather than for the sake of philosophical discourse. Luke comments that both Stoics and Epicureans were not very impressed with him, most likely because Paul argued for the resurrection of the dead.[5] In the Christian tradition, the interest in the relation between theology and philosophy emerged only after Paul. Thinkers such as Tertullian, Justin Martyr, Origen, the Greek

---

3. See Aristotle, *Metaphysics* 1026a, 1064b, 983a.

4. For Philo's attempt to work out a coherent synthesis between Judaism and Middle Platonism, see my study *Divine Providence in Philo of Alexandria*, Texts and Studies in Ancient Judaism 77 (Tübingen: Mohr Siebeck, 1999).

5. For a positive assessment of Paul's affinity with Greek thought, see Troels Engberg-Pederson, ed., *Paul in His Hellenistic Context* (Minneapolis: Fortress Press, 1995); and Abraham J. Malherbe, *Paul and the Popular Philosophers* (Minneapolis: Fortress Press, 1989).

fathers, Anselm of Canterbury, Thomas Aquinas, Luther, and a host of other thinkers found it nearly impossible to do theology without paying at least a minimal tribute to the influence of philosophy. This is not to claim that all these thinkers enthusiastically embraced philosophy. Tertullian and Luther, for example, did not conceal that they had little use for Greek thought. For Luther, Scripture—including Paul's letters—must be interpreted within the framework of *sola scriptura*, apart from an additional philosophical framework. He therefore made no bones about his distaste for Aristotelian philosophy. By the time of the Reformation, the debate on the relation of theology and philosophy, often couched in the metaphor "Jerusalem versus Athens," was sometimes more divisive for theology than it was unifying.

THE MODERN PERIOD

The next stage of theological-philosophical discourse was the epoch of the modern period. Here we are in the unusual position to demarcate that period by precisely two hundred years: from 1789 to 1989, respectively the fall of La Bastille in Paris and the fall of the Berlin Wall. At the beginning stands the French Revolution, with its program that we today summarize as basic human rights. Not incidentally, the beginning of modernity is also characterized by the definition of "Enlightenment," as in the essays of Mendelssohn and, most famously, Kant. It seems to me that the Enlightenment period arguably has had the most profound philosophical influence on theology. Almost all of the Continental philosophers—Kant, Mendelssohn, Spinoza, Hegel, Kierkegaard, Feuerbach, Nietzsche, Fichte, and Heidegger, to name a few—challenged theology to such an extent that theology, at least in the academy, was not able to ignore philosophy's demands on it. Philosophy's rigorous and relentless questioning of theology's ontological and epistemological premises inevitably led to large fissures and cracks in many theological systems. At the end of the modern period, it was nearly customary to declare the demise of theology and the end of metaphysics.[6] The crisis in theology brought about by Enlightenment philosophies opened up the door, however, for theology's reflection on its own presuppositions of interpretation. Schleiermacher's inaugurating of what we now refer to as the discipline of hermeneutics was definitely a crucial milestone in theology's reconception and clarification of its own foundation and tasks. The interrelatedness of theology and philosophy in

---

6. See, for example, Theodor W. Adorno, *Metaphysics: Concepts and Problems*, trans. Edmund Jephcott, ed. Rolf Tiedemann (Stanford: Stanford University Press, 2000); and Timothy Stanley, *Protestant Metaphysics after Karl Barth and Martin Heidegger* (Eugene, OR: Cascade, 2010).

the sphere of hermeneutics can be seen now, for example, in the fact that no serious hermeneutical reflection by any theology can do so today apart from reference to Gadamer and many others engaged in the field of hermeneutics. We now return to the theme of hermeneutics and Continental philosophy.

Postmodern Thought after the Berlin Wall

The fall of the Berlin Wall in 1989 left a tremor felt in every corner of the globe. The demise of that wall actually signifies the enormous unhinging of one ideology (Cold War Communism) and with it the parousia of a new, apparently incontestable ideology (neoliberal capitalism). Indeed, as is well known, Francis Fukuyama announced that the fall of the Berlin Wall signified "the end of history."[7] By that he did not mean that a particular epoch in history had come to an end (Communism), but rather that humanity as a whole had reached a kind of an end point, ideologically and economically. Ideologically, the only political alternative for all the world was now liberal democracy, and economically, the only viable economic system was that of free-market capitalism (American style). Fukuyama (who studied under Allan Bloom, Roland Barthes, and Jacques Derrida) later revised and modified his views, essentially distancing himself from the neoconservatism of the Bush administration.[8]

Nonetheless, the sentiment that Fukuyama initially expressed after the fall of the Berlin Wall is noteworthy because it serves as a foil to making intelligible—at least in part—the interest and context of Continental philosophy in the apostle Paul. In short, for most of the contemporary philosophers, interest in Paul stems from the fact that they see in him, more or less, an ally in their attempt to deconstruct a world that accords with neoliberal political and economic policies in the new post–Berlin Wall era. Some of the philosophers discussed in this volume have expressed their own underlying philosophical and ideological assumptions openly; others have been more hesitant to articulate them candidly and upfront. (Alain Badiou, for example, has no inhibition to declare his Marxism openly,) while Walter Benjamin—given the imminent danger of the Nazi regime—gave more hints than insights into his own political views. Common to all postmodern thinkers, not only the ones discussed in the essays below but also a host of others, is the conviction that our contemporary

7. See the book by the same title, Francis Fukuyama, *The End of History and the Last Man* (New York: Free Press, 1992).

8. See, for example, Francis Fukuyama, *The Great Disruption: Human Nature and the Reconstitution of Social Order* (New York: Free Press, 1999); *America at the Crossroads* (New Haven: Yale University Press, 2006); *Our Posthuman Future* (New York: Farrar, Strauss and Giroux, 2002).

world is dominated, exploited, and threatened by power structures that breed injustice, inequality, poverty, and reinforce many of the "isms" that devalue human lives individually and collectively. The collapse of Communism in Eastern Europe has opened the floodgates for neoliberal governments and their accomplices in the corporate world (often these become one, as in the case of the Bush administration)[9] to now spread their propaganda and force their (violent) action on many parts of the globe.

The apparent nonexistence of other viable political and economic alternatives has prompted a large number of contemporary European (and, increasingly, non-European) philosophers to expose and deconstruct these neoliberal structures and the apparatuses that support them. Accordingly, postmodern philosophy is always poststructuralist to the extent that philosophic discourse aims at the demise of the structures that enslave humanity. The starting point of many Continental philosophers, namely, the critique of the vestiges of bourgeois hegemony, is thus to be affirmed by any person who is not blind to the realities of our world.

AN UNFORTUNATE DICHOTOMY: LEFT VERSUS RIGHT

Many readers on "the right" may immediately think, however, that Continental philosophy's critique of neoliberal policies is the approach "of the left." While "the left" may have good intentions, such a response continues, it nonetheless misses the mark, because the real predicament of humanity is not the global enslavement brought about by greedy politicians and corporations but the enslavement of the person to the power of sin. This bipolarity of "left" and "right" is in itself a structure that makes genuine dialogue nearly impossible. While labels do have a certain function, namely, to act as a cipher for underlying ideological premises, in our current discussion on Paul, it would be advisable to set them aside. Here is the reason, or more modestly, the attempt to suggest a reason, why students of Paul should give a fair hearing to Continental philosophy vis-à-vis the apostle.

The left-versus-right dichotomy is ineffectual and mostly precludes genuine understanding between the two, exceptions notwithstanding. The "right" needs to listen to the "left" because the left has very clearly discerned that this world is in need of healing. It is wounded by powerful structures that are all too often associated with the name of Christ whom Paul proclaimed. The Pauline message that is meant to be "the good news" has in reality become

---

9. A brilliant analysis of the Bush era and its political perversion for economic gain is Naomi Klein, *The Shock Doctrine: The Rise of Disaster Capitalism* (Toronto: Knopf Canada, 2008).

the news unto oppression and death. Suffice it here to point to the history of Latin America during the last five hundred years, the history of slavery, and the marginalization of women and persons of color. In other words—and as the essay by Neil Elliott at the end of this book makes abundantly clear—the task of identifying human injustice, suffering, and oppression should have been an integral part of the message and action of the Christian church from the moment the apostle to the Gentiles had started to preach the gospel of the risen Christ.

This dichotomy of "left" and "right" is, then, in my view both unfortunate and unnecessary: those on the "left" and the "right" both equally and correctly discern that our world is fundamentally and substantially hurt by injustice. For the former, the answer and the core of this human plight is the preaching of the good news of the risen Messiah by means of the message proclaimed by Paul (personal salvation); for the latter, it is critique and the call for the demise of imperial structures that continue the oppression of the masses by the powerful few (social liberation). If this analysis, however sketchy it is here, is correct, then it follows that both—"left" and "right"—must concede that they possess only a partial truth. Those who wish, as I do, not to downplay the core of Pauline theology and whose objective it is to proclaim good news as a message of personal *and* social liberation can do so only by drawing on the sociological analysis and insights of those who dare to name the evil in our world. Put differently, the student of Paul is not faced with an either/or decision: *either* accept Pauline theology and dismiss the insights and challenges of Continental philosophy *or* embrace Continental philosophy's critique of structural oppression but give up Pauline theology. To express it in the most condensed manner: the one gospel of Jesus Christ announces at the same time the message of liberation for the individual human believer *and* for human communities who suffer injustice and oppression. As a case in point, a movement that has sought to achieve this kind of synthesis of "orthodoxy" and "orthopraxis" is liberation theology. To pit one against the other is a fundamental mistake that goes against the claims of gospel itself. If it is indeed the case that "faith without works is dead," then the artificial dichotomy of "left" versus "right," based on a divisive political fault line, should be given up by Pauline scholars, theologians, and, ideally, all Christians.

THE GREAT HERMENEUTICAL SHIFT

I am not suggesting that a student of Paul, or a biblical scholar or theologian for that matter, can uncritically take over the underlying assumptions of

Continental philosophy without considering the monumental shift in hermeneutics. What is this shift? In nuce, it is this: from the beginning to about the end of the modern period, theological thinking was predicated on a specific hermeneutical assumption, namely, that philosophical thinking will clarify and make more coherent theology's own self-understanding. In relation to Paul, the starting point was the Pauline corpus; theology and philosophy were both employed in tandem to make the meaning of the Pauline letters intelligible. Theology was the queen of the interpretive undertaking and philosophy the handmaid. A good illustration of this dynamic is found in the work of Bultmann and Tillich. By maintaining constant, fruitful dialogue with Heidegger, Bultmann's theology, for example, was shaped by the Heidegger's existential philosophy, albeit in such a way that Bultmann did not forfeit the primacy of theology in favor of philosophy; the latter served as a significant tool to sharpen the former.

But in Continental philosophy, the hermeneutic baseline is the reverse. Some contemporary philosophers, such as Badiou, have no interest in the theology of Paul and, indeed, care absolutely nothing about the good news of the risen Messiah. Their interest in Paul lies outside of the message of Paul, outside his letters, and thereby outside the Scriptures and the demands they make on the Christian. Badiou, for example (as most others as well), already has a philosophy, an ideological system of his own. Their starting point is their own philosophy, and not the Pauline corpus. In their philosophizing, they need Pauline thought only to the extent that it corroborates ideas already articulated in their systems of thought. This applies more or less to all the Continental philosophers. They are not pursuing Pauline studies because they want to discover Pauline theology or how Paul's thought shapes the Christian church. Quite to the contrary, they use Paul as if his thought is a quarry from which they can pick up a few useful stones for their own ideological buildings.

The great hermeneutic reversal can thus be described in these terms: On the one hand, the vast majority of theologians employ philosophy in order to interpret and understand Paul's letters, and correspondingly his theology. They treat Paul as an author and his texts as legitimate sources for speaking about objective realities; they begin with Paul. On the other hand, contemporary philosophers interested in Pauline thought do not begin with Paul and his texts. They have their own ideological structures and therefore employ Paul in the service of those structures. They also do not substantially use theology to clarify their philosophy; the former is hardly ever the handmaid of the latter. What should the student of Paul make of this reversal?

THE DEATH OF THE (OTHER) AUTHOR?

My main critique of Continental philosophy's appropriation of Paul in the name of deconstructing the structural evils of the world is the unavoidable deconstruction of Paul as the "other." To be fair, this critique does not apply equally to all Continental philosophers. And yet, Postmodern thought is predicated—rightfully so—on the recovery of the person who is unlike "us," or in academic jargon, the "other." Readings of history and the contemporary social-political scene are rewritten from the perspective of the marginalized and oppressed, or as Bonhoeffer said, long before liberation theologies and postmodern thought picked up the expression, "from below." In his own words, world history needs to be recast "from the perspective of the outcasts, the suspects, the maltreated, the powerless, the oppressed and reviled, in short from the perspective of the suffering."[10] Another way of expressing the reversal of the voices of world history is to give the "other" his or her voice. As long as the powerful speak on behalf of the "voiceless," the reversal cannot happen. And this is precisely the paradox between Paul and his Continental admirers. Continental philosophy uses the voice of Paul, but does not always give him his own voice. Continental philosophy changes the voice of Paul to say things that Paul may not have been willing to say. In terminology that comes from the pens of Continental thinkers themselves, it seems to me that Paul has suffered "the death of the author."

The idea of the death of the author is the brainchild of Roland Barthes.[11] He suggests that there is in fact no such thing as an "author" and correspondingly no such a thing as a "text." Here, then, is the dilemma for me. Inadvertently, perhaps, but nonetheless ironically, the death or suspension of the author seems to me unavoidably "a murdering" of a person. Erasing an author—and this is to some extent what some of the thinkers examined in these essays cannot avoid—is a kind of taking hostage of the author-person, in our case the life and teaching of Paul.[12] In the words of Emmanuel Levinas: the grandeur of modern antihumanism (his term) "consists in making a clear space for the hostage-subjectivity by sweeping away the notion of the person."[13] The

10. Dietrich Bonhoeffer, *Letters and Papers from Prison*, Dietrich Bonhoeffer Works 8, trans. Isabel Best et al., ed. John W. de Gruchy (Minneapolis: Fortress Press, 2010), 52.

11. See Roland Barthes, "The Death of the Author," in *Image, Music, Text* (Glasgow: Fontana 1977), 142–48.

12. Cf. Seán Burke, *The Death and Return of the Author. Criticism and Subjectivity in Barthes, Foucault and Derrida* (Edinburgh: Edinburgh University Press, third edition 2008).

13. Emmanuel Levinas, *God, Death and Time*, translated by Bettina Bergo (Stanford: Stanford University Press, 2000), 182. For an excellent discussion of Levinas from the point of philosophical

irony lies precisely in the fact that Continental philosophy has, to its credit, created a significant space for "the other." There can be no doubt that Barthes and Foucault wanted to open up new and hitherto unexplored spaces for the other precisely by suspending the idea of author. And yet, is the very space those postmodern thinkers want to open up—namely, more freedom, recognition, and space for being the other—vitiated by the death of the author? In other words, does the death of the author turn out also to be the death of the other? For how is it possible to suspend the notion that Paul is an author without not also suspending the notion that he is our other? There is no point in explaining away Paul's alterity vis-à-vis Continental philosophy's systems. All the more, then, the retrieval of alterity hinges precisely on permitting the other to speak and be heard as the other. There is no such thing as a "dead other." Is it not then the case, to push even further, that an author (irrespective of how much I (dis)like him or her, even if the other is my enemy) is always and necessarily the other? The consequence of the dismissal of the other in the death of the author opens up a wide margin for misuse. If Paul is not really the "other" as the "author," then it is an easy step to create him in one's preferred image, either as traditional *Saulus judaicus*, or as *Paulus theologicus*, or a *Paulus philosophicus* or, today, as the newly celebrated *Paulus politicus*.

CRITICAL AND CONSTRUCTIVE APPRAISAL

Since the essays in this book is are directed at students of Paul and those who are curious about the nature and intent of Continental philosophy's attention to Paul, I would like to conclude with four summative comments that are meant to put into perspective the questions I have raised above and also provide some further pointers for intellectual engagement.

1. The history of the relation between theology and philosophy sketched above is necessarily incomplete. The main function is to show that the emphasis of that relation has changed fundamentally. Throughout much of Western history, theology employed philosophy in order to clarify its own positions with greater coherence, but the focus of that dialogue was, more or less, on theology itself. The collapse of the Berlin Wall symbolized a dramatic shift, however—namely, the apparent triumph of unrestrained capitalism, against which philosophers on the Continent reacted with reinvigorated social and philosophical analysis. In other words, the concrete, actual human situation, and not an abstract new philosophical idea, became the starting point for

hermeneutics, cf. Jens Zimmermann, *Recovering Theological Hermeneutics. An Incarnational-Trinitarian Theory of Interpretation* (Grand Rapids: Baker Academics 2004), 187–229.

their philosophizing. To put it differently, Continental philosophers did not begin (or more accurately, did not exclusively begin) their deliberations with a theoretical analysis of economic systems and only then observe the new danger for human suffering because of the announcement of the triumph of capitalism.[14] To the vexing surprise—or annoyance—of many a Pauline interpreter, the apostle became part of the philosophical solution.

2. Dialogue that leads to understanding requires that both the Pauline interpreter and the Continental philosopher openly acknowledge their respective hermeneutical prejudices and presuppositions. The Pauline scholar and the philosopher are both equally called to a hermeneutically self-conscious reading of Paul. It is not enough simply to make claims on Paul, be they of a biblical-theological or social-philosophical nature. Both have to account for their positions in an intellectually responsible manner. The philosopher has to accept the question of whether a reduction of the apostle to a *Paulus politicus* is nothing but a redeployment and reconceptualization of basic Pauline words and symbols. Is such an exercise in the end nothing but a fancied and intellectualized emptying of these symbols, stripping them of substance and content? The Pauline interpreter, however, must ask whether the claim that Paul is purely a *Paulus theologicus* does not also amount to putting a straitjacket on the apostle that suffocates his message of liberation at the roots. Is it not also an illicit reduction of the gospel the apostle preached when the social, political, and existential questions undoubtedly addressed or implicated in his letters are brushed off as if they merely concern a "few liberals"? Expressed differently, both Pauline theologians and Continental philosophers must be cognizant of the boundary lines their hermeneutical frameworks and prejudices entail.

3. But who can demarcate such boundary lines, and who is presumptuous enough to be the judge? The answer, in short, is implicated in the core conceptions of both the Pauline message and Continental philosophy. In the former, it is the message of unconditional love (ἀγάπη). In the words of Paul, ἡ ἀγάπη ἀνυπόκριτος (Rom. 12:9), ἡ ἀγάπη τῷ πλησίον κακὸν οὐκ ἐργάζεται· πλήρωμα οὖν νόμου ἡ ἀγάπη (Rom. 13:10), πάντα ὑμῶν ἐν ἀγάπῃ γινέσθω (1 Cor. 16:24), to which, of course, we may add 1 Corinthians 13.[15] Paul's view of love as an unconditional power by which the neighbor must

---

14. In the history of theology, the most obvious attempt to correlate the actual human situation of suffering and poverty with a social (Marxist) analysis and the gospel of Jesus Christ was the phenomenon of Latin American liberation theology. For details, see the works by Gustavo Gutiérrez, Leonardo Boff, Jon Sobrino, and many others.

15. In my view, the most theologically penetrating and psychologically freeing reflection of what unconditional love of the other means is that of Dietrich Bonhoeffer, *Life Together*, Dietrich Bonhoeffer

be approached is paralleled in contemporary philosophy in the notion of the "other."

Suffice it here to say that again both the Continental philosopher and the Pauline scholar must ask themselves whether their respective hermeneutical prejudices and presuppositions lead de facto to a violation of the love of neighbor or the suspension of the other. There is no doubt that both—philosopher and theologian—desire that their thinking be a conduit toward life: The former envisions a *real and fulfilling life here on earth* for the oppressed and exploited masses of the poor; the latter assigns priority to an *eternal life*. This division is not to be seen as absolute, but merely as the indicator of priority in the respective forms of thinking for the philosopher and theologian.

In view of life, then, the theologian must be mindful of the fact that Jesus Christ did not live and was not resurrected for a *theology* but for the sake of *life* itself. And this is precisely the challenge of the neighbor, the other, including the enemy. Because the Christian interpreter of Paul has no direct, unmediated, soul-to-soul claim on any other person,[16] and because the path of grace is nothing but a divine mystery, it follows that no Christian person has the right to hold hostage another person, the other, with the gospel. In Bonhoeffer's words, "I must release others from all my attempts to control, coerce, and dominate them with my love."[17] In other words, even the very best of (Christian) intentions may end up violating the neighbor in a move that goes against the very core of Jesus' and Paul's message.

In view of life, the philosopher must be equally mindful of the fact that the suspension of the other is nothing but the destruction of *life, even if only* the life of one person. If our suspicion, that the suspension of the author inevitably entails the death of the other, is correct, then it follows that the Continental philosopher faces a dilemma. Is it legitimate to suspend the author-other of Paul in order to employ his thought as a building block for one's own ideology or philosophy? This critique works only on the assumption that the philosophers have, in fact, misunderstood or (deliberately) misappropriated Paul's thought for their own ends. (To repeat, this does not apply equally across the spectrum of Continental thought.) Nonetheless, I take it that some of the philosophers do

Works 5, trans. D. W. Bloesch and J. H. Burtness, ed. Geffrey Kelly (Minneapolis: Fortress Press, 1996), 27–47. On Bonhoeffer's correlation of theology and philosophy, see also Peter Frick, ed., *Bonhoeffer's Intellectual Formation: Theology and Philosophy in His Thought*, Religion in Philosophy and Theology 29 (Tübingen: Mohr Siebeck, 2008).

16. See Bonhoeffer, *Life Together*, 31, 33, 41, 43–44.

17. Ibid., 44.

agree that their interpretations of Paul are idiosyncratic, at least to the extent that these have nothing to do with a traditional, theological exegesis. Is this kind of appropriation already a violation of the face of the other (Levinas)?

Without presuming to be the judge in this matter, there seems to me a test case that every author can apply to his or her writing. The question is this: How would I respond if my writings were being (mis)used in ways that clearly went against the grain of my intentions? (I do not believe that we write without intentions.) What if, hypothetically (and somewhat absurdly) speaking, future generations would use our very own writings to substantiate ideas and thoughts that would be employed in the service of ideologies we ourselves radically oppose? What if, for example, the corpus of Continental philosophy would one day be discovered as the ideal framework for the ideas of incumbent tyrants, oppressive systems, or intellectual jihadists of all sorts of propaganda that the authors of the philosophical corpus would today vehemently reject? In that case, I presume, the philosophers and we ourselves would insist—rightfully so—on being respected as an author and "other." I do not want to push this comparison too far. But I do want to bring into focus that the question of author and the other is often given little bearing on my discourse until I myself am implicated in its suspension.

Let us return to Paul. The question is whether a purely theological-exegetical reading of Paul and, likewise, a purely political-philosophical reading of Paul are not, more or less, readings that equally suspend Paul as author and other. Since the suspension of a person, even if only metaphorically in relation to a writing, entails some kind of subtraction of life and the disallowance of Being, both are faced with the same challenge: Do their purported theologies and philosophies actually contribute to life, individually and collectively, without at the same time destroying the life of the other? The reader must herself or himself find a path through this complex reality.

4. The purpose of the essays in this volume is to help the student of Paul find an orientation in this vast, complex, and often overwhelming discourse on the apostle vis-à-vis Continental philosophy. With the exception of the last essay, the task of each contributor is to focus on one of the Continental philosophers or their forerunners in such a way that the significance of each philosopher is made relevant in relation to the apostle Paul. Given the intricate nature of this discourse, it goes without saying that this volume as a whole does not presume to present a final analysis or conclusion with regard either to one of the philosophers or to the debate as a whole; rather, this work seeks to function as an invitation and stimulus to pursue this debate in greater detail. Moreover, the essays in this collection are not uniform to the extent that the contributors

share an overarching and unifying position, let alone a consensus, on either Paul or Continental philosophy or the relationship between the two. Just as each author can only speak for himself in these essays,[18] the reader too must form and articulate his or her opinion in dialogue with the apostle Paul, with the Continental philosophers, and with the interpreters speaking in this collection.

18. As editor, I have made a sustained and repeated—but ultimately unsuccessful—attempt to recruit female scholars to participate in this project, not because this is the politically correct step to take, but, in the spirit of these reflections, to be genuinely enriched by the voice of an other. Nonetheless, it is my hope that the voice of women will be heard in this discourse, perhaps as a response to some of the essays presented here.

1

Nietzsche

The Archetype of Pauline Deconstruction

Peter Frick

> *Das Christenthum dagegen*
> *zerdrückte und zerbrach den Menschen*
> *vollständig und versenkte ihn*
> *wie in tiefen Schlamm.*[1]
>
> —NIETZSCHE

INTRODUCTION

In this essay I am discussing the proliferation of interest in Paul, namely the recent and increasing interest of contemporary European philosophers in the thought of the Apostle. Perhaps to the chagrin of Pauline interpreters, there exists a vexing interest in the Pauline corpus by Continental philosophers. Alain Badiou, for example, a French Marxist philosopher employs Paul in the service of his own philosophical interest and project. "Truth be told," says Badiou, "Paul is not an apostle or a saint. I care nothing for the Good News he declares, or the cult dedicated to him. . . . Irreligious by heredity . . . I have never really connected Paul with religion . . . or to any sort of faith"[2] which, for Badiou, is a mere fable. Giorgio Agamben, in contrast

---

1. Friedrich Nietzsche, *Menschliches, Allzumenschliches. Kritische Gesamtausgabe 2,* ed. Giorgio Colli and Mazzino Montinari, 2nd ed. (Berlin/New York: de Gruyter, 2002), 1:114.

2. Alain Badiou, Saint Paul. The Foundation of Universalism (Stanford: Stanford University Press, 2005), 1.

to Badiou, focuses on the first few verses in Paul's Letter to the Romans in which he "proposes to restore Paul's Letters to the status of the fundamental messianic text for the Western tradition."[3] Likewise, continental philosophers such as Slavoj Žižek,[4] Jacques Derrida[5] and Gianni Vattimo[6] and others engage Paul also in their own philosophizing context. To these European avant-garde philosophers, Paul does not so much matter as a first century ambassador of the message of Jesus the Messiah, but rather, he plays the pivotal role as "the indispensable instigator of, and paradigm for, a radical political project aimed at the heart of contemporary imperial capitalism."[7] Since the other essays in this volume examine these Continental philosophers in greater detail, the objective of this essay is a more modest one. I will focus mainly on the philosophical protagonist that the contemporary philosophers often invoke in their own discourse, namely Friedrich Nietzsche.

Nietzsche's Dilemma with Paul

Why Nietzsche? The answer, in short, is that virtually all of these Continental philosophers stand in a tradition that claims Nietzsche, along with Heidegger, as an important forebear for their cause. Nietzsche's critique of Christianity in general—possibly inspired by his reading of Kierkegaard—and of the apostle Paul in particular functions as the invisible spine in many of the discourses in continental philosophy. Following in the footsteps of Martin Heidegger, his teacher, Gianni Vattimo wrote an entire monograph on Nietzsche[8] and frankly

---

3. Giorgio Agamben, *The Time that Remains: A Commentary on the Letter to the Romans*, translated by Patricia Dailey (Stanford: Stanford University Press, 2005), 1. Agamben dedicated this book to Jacob Taubes. On Agamben, see the essay by Alain Gignac below; on Taubes, see Larry Welborn's essay below.

4. Cf. Slavoj Žižek, *The Fragile Absolute, or Why Is the Christian Legacy Worth Fighting For?* (London: Verso, 2000) and also Žižek, *The Puppet and the Dwarf: The Perverse Core of Christianity* (Cambridge: MIT Press, 2003). On Žižek, see the essay below by Ward Blanton.

5. Cf. the work by Theodore W. Jennings Jr., *Reading Derrida/Thinking Paul* (Stanford: Stanford University Press, 2006). On Derrida, see the essay below by Hans Ruin.

6. See, for example, Gianni Vattimo, *Belief* (Stanford: Stanford University Press, 1999); and Vattimo, *After Christianity* (New York: Columbia University Press, 2002). On Vattimo, see the essay below by Anthony Sciglitano.

7. Theodore W. Jennings Jr., "Paul and Sons: (Post-modern) Thinkers Reading Paul," in David Odell-Scott, ed., *Reading Romans with Contemporary Philosophers and Theologians* (New York: T & T Clark International, 2007), 85–114, here 86. On Nietzsche and Paul as political, ideological agents, see the essay by Jan Rehmann, "Nietzsche, Paul and thte Subversion of Empire," in *Union Seminary Quarterly Review* 59 (2005): 147–61.

8. Gianni Vattimo, *Nietzsche: An Introduction* (Stanford: Stanford University Press, 2002).

acknowledges the importance of both thinkers in the re-conception of his own ideas on Christianity: "I have begun to take Christianity seriously again because I have constructed a philosophy inspired by Nietzsche and Heidegger, and have interpreted my experience in the contemporary world in the light of it."[9]

Let us take as a starting point for our discussion a dictum by the philosopher Jacob Taubes. Shortly before his death in 1987, Taubes presented at a colloquium in Heidelberg a series of philosophical lectures on the political theology of Paul.[10] In the course of his lectures he remarked: "Let someone come and really theologically challenge this."[11] The reference to the expression "really theologically challenge this" is to Nietzsche's critique of Christianity, in particular as Taubes sees it, the problematic of sin, conscience, guilt and atonement in the Pauline corpus. Karl Jaspers,[12] like many interpreters before and after him, similarly sees Nietzsche entire philosophical project, including his nihilistic tendencies, as a suffering and tragic response to Christianity in general and, in Vattimo's words, "the biblical account of original sin"[13] in particular. In other words, one of the key dilemmas for Nietzsche was the Pauline understanding of sin. Arguably, the weight of this doctrine, at least how Nietzsche understood the Pauline teaching and observed it in his Lutheran context, was for him the root of many other struggles with Christianity and life in general.[14] As we shall see, Nietzsche lays heavy charges at the feet of the Apostle, charges that are indeed so weighty that nothing less than human existence itself is at stake.

9. Vattimo, *Belief*, 33. On Vattimo relation to Nietzsche and Heidegger, see Thomas G. Guariano, *Vattimo and Theology* (New York/London: T & T Clark International, 2009), 42–44; cf. also, Ola Sigurdson, "Reading Žižek Reading Paul," in *Reading Romans with Contemporary Philosophers and Theologians*, 213–41, the section on Nietzsche, 215–18.

10. Published as Jacob Taubes, *The Political Theology of Paul* (Stanford: Stanford University Press, 2004).

11. Ibid., 87.

12. Cf. Karl Jaspers, *Nietzsche und das Christentum,* 2nd ed. (Munich: R. Piper, 1952).

13. Vattimo, *Nietzsche*, 185. In his *Belief*, 88–90, Vattimo speaks of sin in terms similar to Taubes' when he characterizes sin as "guilt" that may be more properly spoken of in a non-metaphysical sense as a "pity" or "lost opportunity."

14. Nietzsche's critique of Christianity must be placed within the larger context of his rejection of Platonic metaphysics and its hierarchical ontology as it shaped Christianity. For Nietzsche, Christianity is nothing else but a cheap Platonism for the people. In *Götzen-Dämmerung*, he outlines—on a mere two pages and six points—how this "history of falsification" runs from Plato through Kant to the demise of the world; cf. Kritische Gesamtausgabe 6, ed. Giorgio Colli and Mazzino Montinari, (Berlin/New York: de Gruyter, second edition 2002), 80–81. See also Jan Rohls, *Philosophie und Theologie in Geschichte und Gegenwart* (Tübingen: Mohr Siebeck, 2002), 503–5.

This is not to claim that the notion of sin is the only or the exclusive vantage point into our examination of Nietzsche and Paul. Nonetheless, in view of Pauline scholars and theologians who read Paul with passion and are perplexed about the beguiling interest of contemporary European philosophers in their hero, we will take up Taubes' challenge and explore the Nietzschean antagonism against Paul's "entire dialectic"[15] of sin vis-à-vis its exegetical, theological and philosophical nuances. In this way, we can engage both Nietzsche and Paul and open up a larger and more fruitful dialogue for those interpreters interested in this debate. We will address the following issues: What is behind the philosopher's utter rejection of Pauline theology and what has come of it in Christian tradition? In fairness to Paul, we must ask, did Nietzsche correctly understand and interpret what the Apostle wanted to communicate about sin? And in fairness to Nietzsche, are there issues around the Pauline conception of sin that indeed justify the questions and critique that the philosopher launches at the Apostle?

NIETZSCHE ON PAUL

In *Daybreak*, Nietzsche gives aphorism 68 the title "The First Christian."[16] The title of this unusually long aphorism is a violent stab at the life and thought of the Apostle Paul. In a constant tirade of attacks, Nietzsche leaves no doubt as to his utter disdain for this man. The Bible, Nietzsche laments,

> contains the history of one of the most ambitious and importunate souls, of a mind as superstitious as it was cunning, the history of the apostle Paul who, apart from a few scholars, knows that? But without this remarkable history, without the storms and confusions of such a mind, of such a soul, there would be no Christianity; we would hardly have heard of a little Jewish sect whose master died on the cross.[17]

---

15. Cf. Taubes, *Political Theology of Paul*, 87.

16. For a discussion of this aphorism, cf. Hans Hübner, *Nietzsche und das Neue Testament* (Tübingen: Mohr Siebeck, 2000), 159–63.

17. Friedrich Nietzsche, *Daybreak. Thoughts on the Prejudices of Morality*, translated by R. J. Hollingdale. Texts in German Philosophy (Cambridge: Cambridge University Press, 1982), § 68.

So here we have it: Jesus may have been the master of a small, insignificant Jewish sect, but Paul was the founder of that religion we now call "Christianity." How did it happen? Nietzsche continues:

> The ship of Christianity threw overboard a good part of the Jewish ballast . . . it went and was able to go among the heathen—that is a consequence of the history of this one man, of a very tormented, very pitiable, very unpleasant man who also found himself unpleasant.[18]

How does Nietzsche know that Paul was so "very tormented?" According to the same aphorism, Paul

> suffered from a fixed idea, or more clearly from a *fixed question* which was always present to him and would never rest: what is the Jewish *law* really concerned with? and in particular, what is the *fulfilment of this law*?[19]

On the one hand, Nietzsche correctly discerned that the question of the law became one of the central *theological* questions for Paul. But on the other hand, he also merely echoed the nineteenth century *psychological* interpretation current among Pauline scholars, namely that before his calling Paul was personally tormented by his inability to keep the law. In recent Pauline scholarship, however, there is very little support for the view that Paul was psychologically wounded because of the insurmountable demands of Torah—and rightly so.[20] If the law was such a tormenting issue for Paul, how did he overcome it? On this question, Nietzsche once again has his own ideas:

> At last the liberating idea came to him, together with a vision, as was bound to happen in the case of this epileptic: to him, the zealot of the law who was inwardly tired to death of it, there appeared on a lonely

18. Ibid.
19. Ibid.
20. Cf. Hübner, *Nietzsche und das Neue Testament*, 163; Heikki Räisänen, *Paul and the Law* (Tübingen: J.C.B. Mohr, 1983), 229–36; and Krister Stendahl, "The Apostle Paul and the Introspective Conscience of the West," in *Paul among Jews and Gentiles* (Philadelphia: Fortress Press, 1976), 78–96.

road Christ with the light of God shining in his countenance, and Paul heard the words: 'Why persecutes thou *me?*' What essentially happened is this: his *mind* suddenly became clear; 'it is *unreasonable*', he says to himself, 'to persecute precisely this Christ! For here is the way out, here is perfect revenge, here and nowhere else do I have and hold the *destroyer of the law!*' ... The tremendous consequence of this notion, this solution of the riddle, whirl before his eyes, all at once he is the happiest of men—the destiny of the Jews—no, of all mankind—seems to him to be tied to the idea of ideas, the keys of keys, the light of lights; henceforth history revolves around him! For from now on he is the teacher of the *destruction of the law!*[21]

So now we know! Nietzsche tells us unflinchingly: the origin of Christianity amounts to the vision of a tormented man who had an epileptic seizure! "With that the intoxication of Paul is at its height . . . This is the *first Christian*, the inventor of Christianness [*Christlichkeit*]!"[22] The good news about the crucified master was corrupted into the vilest of news, by Paul.[23] The upshot of all this is clear: Nietzsche's inexhaustible disdain of Christianity—with its particular vulgar imprint in the aphorisms of *The Anti-Christ*—is in the first place not so much an attack on Jesus Christ as it is a fierce reckoning with what this despicable character Paul has done with the life and teaching of this Jesus. In other words, we may say that Nietzsche's bone of contention with Christianity is to a large extent an issue of hermeneutics: how does one interpret the life and saying of Jesus of Nazareth? On this matter, Nietzsche and Paul were worlds apart.

The theological consequences that Nietzsche attributes to Paul's misappropriation of the simple message of Jesus are indeed far-reaching. As already mentioned above, for the sake of this essay we will focus on what

21. Nietzsche, *Daybreak*, § 68.

22. Ibid.

23. Cf. Friedrich Nietzsche, *The Anti-Christ, Ecce Home, Twilight of the Idols, and Other Writings*, translated and edited by Judith Norman and Aaron Ridley. Texts in German Philosophy (Cambridge: Cambridge University Press, 2005). Here *The Anti-Christ*, § 42: "Der 'frohen Botschaft' folgte auf dem Fuss die allerschlimmste: die des Paulus." Jörg Salaquarda, "Dionysus versus the Crucified One: Nietzsche's Understanding of the Apostle Paul," in James C. O'Flaherty, Timothy F. Sellner and Robert M. Helm, *Studies in Nietzsche and the Judeo-Christian Tradition* (Chapel Hill: The University of North Carolina Press, 1985), 100-129, argues that "it is not until The Antichrist that Nietzsche achieves an unequivocal differentiation of the roles of Jesus and Paul in the origin of Christianity, and at the same time arrives at an unrestrained opposition to the Apostle" (here 104).

Nietzsche has to say about the notion of sin in the context of Paul's view of
God, life and afterlife, conscience and guilt.

NIETZSCHE ON THE INVENTION OF SIN

At the risk of oversimplification we may say that Nietzsche's view of sin unfolds
within the two poles of Paul's view of God and, related to it, Paul's idea of
an afterlife, or in theological terms, the idea of eschatological transcendence.
In *The Anti-Christ*, Nietzsche reduces Paul's view of God to the formula: *deus,
qualem Paulus creavit, dei negatio* ("the God, whom Paul invented, is the negation
of God").[24] In this context, the full force of Nietzsche's anti-philosophy, that is
to say, his untamed hatred against the Pauline conception of God breaks open
without restraint:

> That we find no God—either in history or in nature or behind
> nature—is not what differentiates *us*, but that we experience what has
> been revered as God, not as 'godlike' but as miserable, as absurd, as
> harmful, not merely an error but a *crime against life*. We deny God as
> God.[25]

The reasons for the denial of (Paul's invented) God[26] is that a God

> who is all-knowing and all-powerful and who does not even make
> sure that his creatures understand his intention . . . who allows
> countless doubts and dubieties to exist . . . who . . . holds out the
> prospect of frightful consequences if any mistake is made as to the
> nature of truth, [how could such a God be said to be] a God of
> goodness?[27]

Or else, Nietzsche keeps on mocking, perhaps God was a God of goodness, but
lacked intelligence and eloquence and was himself in error about his truth. Even

24. *The Anti-Christ*, § 47.

25. Ibid.

26. Hübner, *Nietzsche und das Neue Testament*, 217, suggests that Nietzsche's tragic "no" to the God of
the Bible stems from his false caricature of the biblical God.

27. Nietzsche, *Daybreak*, § 91.

worse, how can we speak of a God of love and holiness and sinlessness when "he creates sin and sinners and eternal damnation and a vast abode of eternal affliction and eternal groaning and sighing!"[28]

Nietzsche's contempt for things eternal is tied to his wholesale rejection of the "state *after* death."[29] It is once again "Paul's invention" and his "method of priestly tyranny," namely "the belief in immortality [*Unsterblichtkeit*]—which is to say the doctrine of the 'judgment' . . ."[30] Again, "Paul himself" taught this "*outrageous* doctrine of personal immortality"[31] and, once more:

> Paul knew of nothing better he could say of his Redeemer than that he had *opened* the gates of immortality to everyone . . . it was only now that immortality had *begun* to open its doors—and in the end only a very few would be selected: as the arrogance of the elect cannot refrain from adding.[32]

Why is Nietzsche so enraged with the Pauline teaching of immortality in the world to come? Arguably, for Nietzsche the reasons for his rejection are not so much theological as they are, so often, psychological in nature. Nietzsche says it best himself: "When the emphasis of life is put on the 'beyond' rather than on life itself—when it is put *on nothingness*—, then the emphasis has been completely removed from life."[33] For Nietzsche, the idea of immortality in a

28. Ibid., § 113. Nietzsche seems to comfort himself when he wonders in the following sentence that "it is not altogether impossible that even Dante, Paul, Calvin and their like may also have penetrated the gruesome secrets of such voluptuousness of power" with regard to God. Hübner, *Nietzsche und das Neue Testament*, 261, argues that the anti-philosophy of Nietzsche is mutually predicated on anti-moralism because of (faith in) God and on anti-theism because of morality.

29. Nietzsche, *The Anti-Christ*, § 41.

30. Ibid., § 42.

31. Ibid., § 41.

32. Nietzsche, *Daybreak*, § 72.

33. Nietzsche, The Anti-Christ, § 43. Curiously, the atheist philosopher Alain Badiou, Saint Paul, 61, comes to rescue Paul from the fangs of Nietzsche in regard to the latter's interpretation of this very passage. "Nietzsche is not precise enough," Badiou argues. For when Paul shifted "the center of gravity of that [Christ's] entire existence beyond this existence" it was in view of a principle "on the basis of which life, affirmative life, was restored and refounded for all. Does not Nietzsche himself want to 'shift the center of gravity' of men's life beyond their contemporary nihilistic decadence? And does he not require for this operation three closely related themes of which Paul is the inventor; to wit, that of the self-legitimating subjective declaration (the character of Zarathustra), the breaking of history in two ("grand politics"), and the new man as the end of the guilty slavery and affirmation of life (the Overman)? If

world "beyond" this world is tantamount to the utter negation of life because it projects life into the realm of the not yet, the realm of nothingness. Elsewhere Nietzsche says the same thing in different words: Christians are so pathetic because they deny life *par excellence*:

> Christianity is called the religion of *pity* [*Religion des Mitleidens*].—Pity is the opposite of the tonic affects that heighten the energy of vital feelings; pity has a depressing effect. You lose strength when you pity . . . Schopenhauer was right here: pity negates life, it makes life *worthy of negation*,—pity is the *practice* of nihilism . . . pity wins people over to nothingness! . . . You do not say 'nothingness': instead you say 'the beyond'; or 'God'; or 'the *true* life.'[34]

At the core of Christianity lies the practice of pity and love of neighbour, a practice which at once denies the vitality of life and thereby postpones "the *true* life" to the realm beyond. In a nutshell, Nietzsche charges that Christians' earthly life is devalued and forfeited for life in the future. Immanence is swallowed up by transcendence.

How is Paul tied into this evil of immortality in the "beyond" of a coming age? Nietzsche leaves also no doubt in this instance. Just as Paul is the inventor of Christianity and the inventor of the idea of immortality, so likewise he is the inventor of the concept of sin. In an aphorism entitled "Belief in the Sickness as Sickness," Nietzsche comes straight to his point: "It was Christianity which first painted the Devil on the world's wall; it was Christianity which first brought sin into the world."[35] Since we already know that Paul invented Christianity, it follows for Nietzsche that he is also the culprit who is responsible for the contrivance of sin. Indeed, Nietzsche says so. Paul, he sneers, "invented the repellent flaunting of sin, it introduced into the world sinfulness *one has lyingly made up*."[36] Elsewhere Nietzsche's scorn knows no limits:

Nietzsche is so violent toward Paul, it is because he is rival far more than his opponent. The result being that he 'falsified' Paul at least as much as, if not more than, Paul 'falsified' Jesus."

34. Nietzsche, *The Anti-Christ*, § 7.

35. Friedrich Nietzsche, *Human all too Human*, translated by R. J. Hollingdale (Cambridge: Cambridge University Press, 1996), § II.2:78.

36. Nietzsche, *Daybreak*, § 29.

> Once more: sin, this supreme form of human self-desecration, was invented to block science, to block culture, to block every elevation and ennoblement of humanity; the priests *rule* through the invention of sin.[37]

Luther, a monk with "all the vindictive instincts of a wounded priest" misunderstood the Renaissance and the Pope in Rome. He "saw the corruption of the papacy when precisely the opposite was palpable: the old corruption (*Verderbnis*), the *peccatum originale*, Christianity, was *not* sitting on the papal seat any more! But rather, life! Rather, the triumph of life!"[38] All of this "imaginary sinfulness"[39] weakens and destroys life rather than celebrating it. Ideally, for Nietzsche, when a person reaches a high level of education (*Bildung*), one moves beyond superstitious, religious concepts (*Begriffe*) and anxieties such as belief in angels, the salvation of the soul, and the belief in original sin.[40] Even though, education alone does not seem to enlighten humanity to the danger of the belief of sin. Nietzsche detects its ramifications in all areas of life, even in the sphere of music. He argues that modern music betrays its "grand tragic-dramatic mode" because of sin. "'For Heaven's sake, however did sin get into music'?" Nietzsche ponders. Music, he claims, is tragically distorted by

> the *great sinner* as Christianity imagines him and desires him to be: the slow pace, the passionate brooding, the agitation through torment of conscience, the terrified praying and pleading, the enraptured grasping and seizing, the halting in despair—and whatever else marks a man as being in a state of great sin. Only . . . Christianity [holds] that all men are great sinners and do nothing but sin.[41]

Nietzsche's aphorisms leave no doubt that he not only thinks the idea of human sinfullness—and consequently also the "need of redemption"[42]—are the invention of Paul, but perhaps even more troubling for him is the fact that its presence is felt ubiquitously. In its most tragic expression, Nietzsche believes,

37. Nietzsche, *The Anti-Christ*, § 49.
38. Ibid., § 61.
39. Nietzsche, *Human all too Human*, § I:141.
40. Cf. Ibid., § I:20.
41. Ibid., § II.2:156.
42. Ibid., § I: 476.

sin is at the core destructive to all positive, vital, cultural and human manifestations of life and largely destroys at the root[43] what it means to become human. Below we will return to these points in our discussion of Paul and Nietzsche, but first we will review Taubes' comments on Nietzsche.

TAUBES ON NIETZSCHE AND SIN

Taubes is interested in Nietzsche because of the latter's recognition that "in Christianity something in the soul has changed profoundly."[44] Then he cites one of Nietzsche's aphorisms from *Daybreak*: "It is not altogether impossible that the souls of Dante, Paul, Calvin and their like may also once have penetrated the gruesome secrets of such voluptuousness of power."[45] In a similar vein, but as Taubes says, even more important for him, is another one of Nietzsche's sayings: "All deeper people—Luther, Augustine, Paul come to mind—agree that our morality and its events are not congruent with our *conscious will*—in short, that an explanation in terms of having goals *is insufficient*."[46] Taubes does not tell his readers that Nietzsche was actually trying to give an answer to the fundamental question: "How deep does morality go? Is it merely part of what is learned for a time? Is it a way we express ourselves?"[47] Commenting on Nietzsche's ponderings, Taubes remarks:

> Whoever has understood this has understood more of Paul and of Augustine and Luther than can be found on this subject in normal exegesis. That is, they all understand that the ego doesn't call the shots in the human beings. That the autonomous human being, the I, doesn't call the shots, but that behind him there are forces at work that undermine the conscious will. They don't overcome it, but undermine. That is, if you want to express it in a formula, that in the I there is a profound powerlessness. And nevertheless Nietzsche maintains the critique of Christianity. For what he finds horrifying, and this is a very humane concern, is the cruelty of the pang of

43. In *Human all too Human*, § I:56, Nietzsche deconstructs the "false idea" that humanity is corrupt and sinful, but admits that "its roots have branched out even into us ourselves and our world."

44. Taubes, *Political Theology of Paul*, 87.

45. Nietzsche, *Daybreak*, § 113.

46. Friedrich Nietzsche, *Writings form the Late Notebooks*, edited by Rüdiger Bittner, translated by Kate Sturge. Texts in German Philosophy (Cambridge: Cambridge University Press, 2003), 59; translation slightly altered.

47. Ibid.

conscience. The conscience that can't be evaded. Romans 7, right? And his second accusation: that Christianity hypostasizes sacrifice rather than abolishing it. Let someone come and really theologically challenge this![48]

Taubes analyzes Romans 7 quite ingenuously. As a philosopher he gives more credit to Paul, Augustine and Luther than to academics who engage in "normal exegesis." For these ancient "deep people," he claims, have understood two major things, namely the issue of the ego and the related matter of conscience. Regarding the issue of the ego, Taubes is unmistakeable: the autonomous human self "doesn't call the shots" since there are "forces at work" that undermine the will. Indeed, even though the I is not entirely incapacitated, it is nonetheless undermined by a "profound powerlessness." Regarding the matter of conscience, Taubes points to something crucial in Nietzsche's entire critique of the Pauline concept of sin. There is "in Nietzsche a deeply humane impulse against the entanglement of guilt and atonement, on which the entire Pauline dialectic . . . is based. This continually self-perpetuating cycle of guilt, sacrifice, and atonement needs to be broken in order to finally yield an innocence of becoming (this is Nietzsche's expression). A becoming, even a being, that is not guilty."[49]

These words make it abundantly clear that the "entire Pauline dialectic" is for Nietzsche (and Taubes?) an insurmountable problem that he encounters on a deeply existential level. The issues hinted at here are fundamental theological questions with inescapable psychological consequences. There is Nietzsche's encounter of this dialectic on a deeply compassionate level; then there is the loss of innocence in the cycle of sin and its attempt to overcome it; and, finally, there is the most lamentable of all, namely the near impossibility of "becoming." How each of these points may be correlated with Paul and within Nietzsche we will discuss below, first in Paul and then in both of them.

PAUL ON SIN AND SINS

Before we are in a position to correlate Paul and Nietzsche on the questions of sin, guilt and conscience, I will first delineate the Pauline concept of sin in its major division into sin and sins. Without attempting to cast either Nietzsche (or Taubes) into a Pauline mould of theological reflection on the

48. Taubes, *Political Theology of Paul*, 87.
49. Ibid., 87–88.

question of sin, in what follows, I am trying to sort out the assumptions, arguments and conclusions they each bring to the table, so to speak. My discussion is predicated on my hermeneutical and theological position of the crucial distinction between sin (in the singular) and sins (in the plural). My argument is that Nietzsche's remarks on the cruel "pangs of conscience" can be placed within a Pauline matrix of the teaching on sin (hamartiology) without emptying the force they have had for Nietzsche himself.

I agree with the comment shared by many Pauline scholars that "Paul nowhere delineates his doctrine of sin, but it is clear enough that he sees it under two aspects: it is both what we do by choice, and voluntary action, and also a power whose grip we cannot escape simply by deciding to."[50] There are two main reasons why it is crucial to uphold the Pauline distinction between sin (in the singular) and sins (in the plural)—one is philological, the other theological. In what follows, I will provide a necessarily succinct sketch based on the Pauline epistles.

In his letters, Paul makes the clear philological distinction between the use of ἁμαρτία and ἁμαρτίαι.[51] The singular ἁμαρτία is typically qualified such as in Rom. 3:9 where the Apostle notes that Ἰουδαίους τε καὶ Ἕλληνας πάντας ὑφ᾽ ἁμαρτίαν εἶναι. In the preopositional phrase ὑφ᾽ ἁμαρτίαν the term ἁμαρτία is best understood in analogy to the expression ὑπὸ νόμον. In both cases, a person is not concidentally or merely temporarily in the sphere of influence of either the Torah or sin, but consistently and without the ability to escape that influence. The specific mentioning of Ἰουδαίους τε καὶ Ἕλληνας in conjunction with the term πάντας leaves no doubt that Paul was thinking inclusively: all people, whether Jew or Greek, are subject to sin. Just as a Jew is obligated to keep all of Torah by virtue of being a child of Abraham, so both Jews and Gentiles are under the power of sin. In Gal. 3:22 he expresses the same thought: συνέκλεισεν ἡ γραφὴ τὰ πάντα ὑπὸ ἁμαρτίαν.

In Rom. 5:12 Paul makes the further connection between Adam's sin and death: δι᾽ ἑνὸς ἀνθρώπου ἡ ἁμαρτία εἰς τὸν κόσμον εἰσῆλθεν καὶ διὰ τῆς ἁμαρτίας ὁ θάνατος. Sin entered the world through one person, but the consequence of death applies to all, because all sinned: καὶ οὕτως εἰς πάντας ἀνθρώπους ὁ θάνατος διῆλθεν, ἐφ᾽ ᾧ πάντες ἥμαρτον. In Rom. 6:17 Paul further concretizes the idea that sin is an enslaving power when he says ἦτε δοῦλοι τῆς ἁμαρτίας (cf. Rom. 6:6: . . . τοῦ μηκέτι δουλεύειν ἡμᾶς τῇ ἁμαρτίᾳ).

---

50. John Ziesler, *Pauline Christianity* (Oxford/New York: Oxford University Press, 1986), 71–72.

51. In my essay, "The Means and Mode of Salvation: A Hermeneutical Proposal for Clarifying Pauline Soteriology," in *Horizons in Biblical Theology* 29 (2007): 203–22, I have discussed the question of sin and sins in greater detail; cf. 205–8.

Evidently, the use of the noun δοῦλος and the verb δουλεύειν in conjunction with the singular ἁμαρτία makes it hermeneutically implausible to interpret Paul's concept of sin as anything else but the conviction that sin constitutes an inescapable power.[52] Moreover, Paul further specifies that Christ himself died to sin (singular) once (Rom. 6:10: ὃ γὰρ ἀπέθανεν, τῇ ἁμαρτίᾳ ἀπέθανεν ἐφάπαξ) and will never die sin a second time. In the same way, Christians must consider themslelves dead to sin. Paul's emphasis that Christ died only once and that Christians die only once to sin is a further crucial dimension of the fact that he distinguishes between the power of sin and the consequences of that power, namely the concrete acts of sin. The first is of an ontological, the second of an ethical nature. In spite of the fact that Christ died for sin—as in his resurrection he overcome and ultimately broke its enslaving power—does not automatically entail that Christians are no longer able to commit deeds of sin. Theologically there is no tension or contradiction between the broken power of sin and the still possible acts of sin. The power of sin is broken, but concrete sins need to be forgiven many times until the return of Jesus Christ.[53]

In this context it is instructive to recognize that Paul never employs the term ἄφεσις. The reason is unambiguously clear: sin cannot ever be forgiven;[54] there is simply no such thing as the forgiveness of sin because for Paul sin amounts to an ontological[55] separation between humanity and God. It is crucial to recognize that from the ontological priority of sin now follows the consequence of the various manifestations of sin—in Pauline terminology, being "in Adam"—namely the various deeds of sin, our sins. The sequence from sin to sins is irreversible. We are sinners, therefore we sin. These various sins are concretized in human experience as the disruptions of life on all levels of existence, that is to say, various spheres such as the ethical, psychological, racial, sexual, economic, ecological, social, structural etc. In other words, sins are the immanent, routinely and unavoidable misdeeds and failures of our existence. It

52. Jürgen Becker, *Paulus. Der Apostel der Völker* (Tübingen: J.C.B. Mohr, 1989), 415, speaks of Paul's singular use of the term "sin" and its "Machtcharakter." In Rom. 7:17 and 20 Paul uses the expression ἡ οἰκοῦσα ἐν ἐμοὶ ἁμαρτία, an idea that has clear ontological dimensions. On this idea of in Stoic philosophy, see Anthony A. Long, *Hellenistic Philosophy. Stoics, Epicureans, Sceptics* (Berkeley and Los Angeles: University of California Press, 1986), 172.

53. The expression ἄφεσις (τῶν) ἁμαρτιῶν is used 11 times in the New Testament: in Matt. 26:28; Mark 1:4; Luke 1:77, 3:3, 24:47; Acts 2:38, 5:31, 10:43, 13:38, 26:18; Col. 1:14

54. The New Testament never employs the expression "forgiveness of sin" (ἄφεσις ἁμαρτίας). On the distinction between sin and sins, see also Paul Tillich, *Systematic Theology* (Chicago: University of Chicago Press, 1957), 2:52.

55. Cf. Jürgen Becker, *Paulus. Der Apostel der Völker*, 411, who raises the question of the "ontologischen Gehalt der Sündenaussagen" in Paul.

is precisely in this realm, in the existential-ontic dimension of life, where we must now locate our discussion with Nietzsche and Paul.

PAUL, NIETZSCHE AND SIN

We are now in a position to examine Nietzsche's critique of the (Pauline) concept of sin vis-à-vis Paul himself. We will begin with a possible common ground, and then move towards a discussion on where and why they diverge.

(1) The one aspect of the Pauline understanding of sin that Nietzsche affirms—albeit implicitly and not as much as a theological insight as a phenomenological description—is the distinction between sin and sins. Even in the midst of his angry rejection of the entire concept of sin, Nietzsche's language betrays that he is indeed somehow an heir to that Pauline distinction. In one and the same aphorism (evocatively entitled "Victory of Knowledge over Radical Evil"), Nietzsche implicitly affirms both sin and sins. It is a false idea, Nietzsche insists, "that mankind is fundamentally evil and corrupt" and hence we should give up the term "sinfulness [*Sündhaftigkeit*]" altogether. Although sinfulness is a false idea, he admits, "its roots have branched out even into us ourselves and our world. To understand *ourselves* we must understand *it*." In the same context he notes that a person may "blunder" or "as the world puts it, sins [*sündigen*],"[56] that is to say: to commit deeds of sin.

The important point to take from this aphorism is that Nietzsche affirms both the existence of sin and its consequence as sins, expressed by him with the verb *sündigen*. It is revealing that he admits that the entire world is marked by such a distinction and that a person's self-knowledge must reckon with this fact, however negative it may be.

(2) Even though we just noted that Nietzsche speaks of both the idea of sin (in the singular) and the various deeds resulting from sin, namely concrete sins (in the plural), the tone of his language does not in any way suggest that he agrees with this central Pauline distinction. Quite to the contrary! In the same aphorism in which he mentions both *Sündhaftigkeit* and *sündigen* in one breath, he is quick to clarify: "the idea that mankind is fundamentally evil and corrupt" is a "false idea" since "there is no such thing as sin in the metaphysical sense."[57]

---

56. Nietzsche, *Human all too Human*, § 1, 56.

Since Nietzsche is convinced that Paul is the inventor of the idea of sin, it is congruent with this view that he also argues that there is no such thing as a metaphysical dimension or reality of sin. In other words, Nietzsche rejects that sin has any supernatural or theological cause, dimension or reality. In one of his sayings he refers to the "metaphysicians" who pronounce "man evil and sinful by nature ... and thus *make* him himself bad."[58] Nietzsche's point is obvious. Since there is—in his view—no such reality and power as sin and the sinfulness of a person as such, the entire scheme of humanity's sinfulness is a clever social-theological *construction*. As he contends, "metaphysicians," i.e. pastors, priests, theologians etc. are the real culprits because *they make* a person believe that s/he is evil by nature. The real human dilemma is therefore not that people *are* sinful but that they *are made into sinners* by Christian metaphysicians.

(3) Given that Nietzsche vehemently rejects humanity's sinfulness as a mere theological invention, it follows that he also rejects what we termed in Paul the understanding of sin as "ontological gap." If the whole idea of sin is invented by Paul and the likes of him, then to say that humanity is separated from God makes no sense to Nietzsche. Correspondingly, the Pauline claim that the correlative of the power of sin is ultimately death finds only contempt in Nietzsche; such a belief is for him the foul root for the Christian devaluation of life and the fantasy of an afterlife.

(4) As Taubes' comment cited above indicates, the most troubling aspect of the Pauline "invention" of sin is for Nietzsche that it has the negative consequence of guilt and a conscience tormented by guilt. This is a deeply troubling issue for Nietzsche that manifests itself in two distinct but interrelated ways: guilt characterizes the human relation to God while bad conscience is primarily a matter of human experience.

On the one hand, the issue of guilt is related to the Christian understanding of God. At one point Nietzsche scoffs that "Christians even begot children with a bad conscience."[59] The reason for bad conscience is that it is "woven together with the concept of God" via the concepts of "guilt [*Schuld*]" and "obligation [*Pflicht*]"[60] In particular, "the advent of the Christian God as the maximal god yet achieved, thus also brought about the appearance of the

57. Ibid.
58. Ibid., § I, 141.
59. Ibid.

greatest feeling of indebtedness [*Maximum des Schuldgefühls*] on earth."[61] The "feeling of indebtedness" to God—empowered by the Christian doctrine of sin[62]—seeks to escape the clutches of a punishing God. For this reason, Nietzsche thinks, even the early Christians took the position that "it is better to *convince* oneself of one's guilt rather than of one's innocence, for one does not quite know how so *mighty* a judge [God] is disposed—but to fear that he hopes to find before him none but those conscious of their guilt!"[63] What Nietzsche is so enraged about, it seems, is that Christians are motivated by the low and base motives of fear, punishment and guilt, rather than by noble ones. The first are a sign of the denial of life, while only the second affirm life. In other words, the problem is that Christians play into the hands of a God who requires the denial of life.

On the other hand, guilt and the experience of guilt feelings are decidedly a matter of human experience. In a series of aphorisms (16-21) in Book Two of his discourse *On the Genealogy of Morality*, Nietzsche delineates his basic understanding of the concept of conscience. At the outset, Nietzsche proclaims: "I look on bad conscience as a serious illness to which man was forced to succumb."[64] When our instincts and unregulated impulses were reduced to "relying on thinking, inference, calculation, and the connecting of cause and effect, that is, to relying on their 'consciousness', that most impoverished and error-prone organ,"[65] the consequences for humanity became enormous. For the restraint of impulses and instincts, Nietzsche maintains, if "not discharged outwardly *turn inwards*—this is what I call the internalization of man: with it there now evolves in man what will later be called his 'soul'."[66] The problem that "in Christianity something in the soul has changed profoundly,"[67] as Nietzsche sees it, is that it has tragic implications for the individual person and for humanity as a whole. "The whole inner world," was changed "to the degree

---

60. *On the Genealogy of Morality*, § II, 21; translation slightly altered, in Friedrich Nietzsche, *On the Genealogy of Morality*, edited by Keith Ansell-Pearson, translated by Carol Diethe. Cambridge Texts in the History of Political Thought (Cambridge: Cambridge University Press, revised edition, 2007).

61. *On the Genealogy of Morality*, § II, 20.

62. On Nietzsche's correlation between sin, guilt and law, cf. *Daybreak*, § 68.

63. Nietzsche, *Daybreak*, § 74. Cf. *On the Genealogy of Morality*, § II, 20: "The feeling of indebtedness [Schuldgefühl] towards a deity continued to grow for several millennia, and indeed always in the same proportion as the concept of and feeling for God grew in the world and was carried aloft."

64. *On the Genealogy of Morality*, § II, 16.

65. Ibid.

66. Ibid.

67. Taubes, *Political Theology of Paul*, 87.

that the external discharge of man's instincts was *obstructed* . . . all those instincts
of the wild, free, roving man were turned backwards, *against man himself* . . .
that is the origin of 'bad conscience'."[68] In the end, this whole "bad-conscience"
tragedy unfolds as the loss of instincts tied to the loss of freedom: "The *instinct of
freedom*, forcibly made latent . . . this instinct of freedom forced back, repressed,
incarcerated within itself and finally able to discharge and unleash itself only
against itself; that, and that alone, is *bad conscience* in its beginnings."[69]

A possible solution for Nietzsche in overcoming the feeling of guilt and
to get rid of a terrible conscience is from moving away from Christian theism
to atheism. Such a movement, Nietzsche claims, may be deduced "from the
unstoppable decline in faith in the Christian God" which is tantamount to
"a considerable decline in the consciousness of human debt [*menschliches
Schuldbewusstsein*]; indeed, the possibility cannot be rejected out of hand that
the complete and definitive victory of atheism might release humanity from this
whole feeling of being indebted towards its beginnings, its *causa prima*. Atheism
and a sort of *second innocence* belong together."[70]

(5) How does Nietzsche's view of sin, guilt and a guilt-ridden conscience
square with Paul's teaching on these ideas?

First, Taubes is correct in discerning that Nietzsche's critique of sin focuses
on the psychological aspect of sin, namely its guilt and its corollary, the feeling
of guilt in the conscience. The question that is crucial in this regard is whether
Nietzsche himself understood the nature of guilt vis-à-vis sin correctly. In
other words, does Nietzsche have an exegetically and theologically proper
understanding of sin and guilt that does justice to Paul? Perhaps unwittingly,
but nonetheless, Nietzsche finds an ally in Ed Sanders who also argues that
Paul "really does *not* deal with sin as *guilt*"[71] and even more so in Krister
Stendahl.[72] And indeed, Sanders and Stendahl are right in that Paul never
explicitly discusses the aspect of guilt and bad conscience in relation to his
otherwise extensive discussion of sin, especially in Romans. Even when Paul

---

68. *On the Genealogy of Morality*, § II, 16.

69. Ibid., § II, 17.

70. Ibid., § II, 20.

71. *Paul and Palestinian Judaism, A Comparison of Patterns of Religion* (Philadelphia: Fortress, 1977),
500.

72. Stendahl, "The Apostle Paul and the Introspective Conscience of the West," 78–96. See also the
critique of this essay by Ernst Käsemann, "Justification and Salvation History in the Epistle to the
Romans," in *Perspectives on Paul* (Philadelphia: Fortress Press, 1971), 60–78; and Stendahl's rejoinder to
the critique in *Paul among Jews and Gentiles*, 125–33.

speaks of Adam's sin as being typical for all humanity and bringing about death, he does not speak of the aspect of guilt and bad conscience. Then where does the correlation between sin, guilt and conscience come from, where does Nietzsche get it from?

As even a brief perusal of the history of Christian theology indicates, the origin of these ideas can be traced to Augustine. Stendahl in particular set up a trajectory that runs from Augustine to Luther: "In Protestant Christianity—which has its roots in Augustine and in the piety of the Middle Ages—the Pauline awareness of sin has been interpreted in the light of Luther's struggle with his conscience."[73] As is well known, in the Pelagian controversy Augustine not only coined expressions such as *peccatum originale, peccatum radicale, non posse non peccare* etc. but also introduced the claim that sin constitutes a person's *reatus* or *culpa* before God by virtue of every person's constitution as a sinner. For Augustine, the forensic aspect of sin is its guilt. We know that Nietzsche read Augustine and was very likely familiar with these fundamental concepts. Moreover, it is also very likely that Nietzsche was influenced, in a negative manner, by Luther and Calvin who embraced the Augustinian teaching on original sin in their own articulation of theology. The issue with Luther, as Stendahl argues, is that he is the culprit who painted the Pauline teaching on sin with the unrecognizable color of bad conscience. Stendahl does not mention Nietzsche at all in his study, but conceptually the portrayal of the former fits the ideas of the latter very well. At any rate, whatever the theological source of Nietzsche's severe critique of sin and guilt, it is clear that he perceived in that doctrine very restrictive if not cruelly destructive psychological effects in relation to the becoming of a person.

Second, Pauline scholarship is split on the question of whether one may speak implicitly of sin as guilt even though there is no explicit terminological evidence in the Pauline writings. One the one hand, as Stendahl champions, Paul does not seem to have been tormented by a bad conscience. In fact, he may have had a "rather 'robust' conscience."[74] Is lack of evidence for a bad conscience in Paul indicative of the lack of guilt in his conception of theology?

Stephen Westerholm, for example, argues that "Paul's concern here is not with human *feelings* of guilt, but with God's overcoming and expunging the (objective) guilt incurred by human sin."[75] Similarly, he remarks that "the drama of sin and atonement in Romans 3 in not just a matter of bringing

73. Stendahl, "The Apostle Paul and the Introspective Conscience of the West," 79.

74. Ibid., 80.

75. Stephen Westerholm, *Understanding Paul. The Early Christian Worldview of the Letter to the Romans*, 2nd ed. (Grand Rapids: Baker Academic, 2004), 74.

peace to a guilt-ridden conscience."[76] In other words, if Paul's position can indeed be interpreted in the sense that sin implicates guilt and the consequence of that guilt is death, then Nietzsche's and Paul's understanding of the term guilt belong to entirely different realms of understanding. Nietzsche—as he says repeatedly himself—looks at guilt from a psychological perspective while Paul is, arguably, concerned with sin as an existential, ontological issue. The problem that is thus making a direct—and hence fair—comparison between Nietzsche and Paul difficult is precisely the confusion between psychological and theological concepts *as if they were operative on the same level.*

Let me be more specific: Nietzsche is certainly correct in observing the psychological effects of the doctrine of sin in his historically conditioned context as anxiety, fear of pleasure, guilt, bad conscience and anything else that amounts to the denial of life. However true these observations may be, they do not necessarily and not logically lead to the conclusion that therefore the Pauline concept of sin must by virtue of its definition include the psychological aspects of guilt, bad conscience and the denial of life. In fact, I suggest the reason why Stendahl does not find any reference in which Paul speaks of his "bad conscience" is precisely because there is no necessary correlation between the sin of guilt—in a forensic and ontological sense—and the psychological response to it. In other words, some Christians acknowledge like Paul that they are sinners, but they are not psychologically incapacitated by a guilt-ridden conscience, while others acknowledge their sin and sins but are plagued by guilt and a bad conscience. The issue is, in my view that Nietzsche seems to think that Christians *uniformly* belong to the second group.

(6) To repeat Taubes' comment once more: in Nietzsche, he says, there is "a deeply humane impulse against the entanglement of guilt and atonement, on which the entire Pauline dialectic . . . is based. This continually self-perpetuating cycle of guilt, sacrifice, and atonement needs to be broken in order to finally yield an innocence of becoming (this is Nietzsche's expression). A becoming, even a being, that is not guilty."[77] Taubes' remarks make it clear that when we speak of Nietzsche's psychological critique of sin and guilt we are not merely comparing a psychological to a theological or philosophical understanding of sin. In other words, Nietzsche is not so much interested in what people believe on these matters, but what their beliefs do to them as human beings in their concrete lives. In his diatribe against bad conscience,

---

76. Ibid.
77. Taubes, *Political Theology of Paul*, 87–88.

Nietzsche calls the human being both a "fool" and "prisoner" by allowing bad conscience to take hold of him/her. With bad conscience "the worst and most insidious illness was introduced, one from which mankind has not yet recovered; man's sickness of *man*, of *himself*."[78] Humanity is sick from sin, guilt and bad conscience. Hence, the fundamental issue for Nietzsche is this: the Pauline-Christian teaching on sin and guilt destroys a person's possibility of truly and genuinely becoming human. How can a person become healthy?

It is decisive in this context to understand the Nietzschean distinction between being and becoming. According to Hatab, Nietzsche seeks to overcome the Western theological and philosophical tradition with its penchant of dividing reality into the binary opposites of "being" and "becoming." Opposites such as good and evil, time and eternity, spirit and nature, reason and passion, truth and appearance etc. are not mutually exclusive and cannot, therefore, be set against each other.[79] The fundamental error of the metaphysicians is precisely that at the expense of "becoming" they focus on "being" as the unchangeable, as grounded in God, as the thing-as-such. Quite to the contrary, Nietzsche asserts, "what constitutes the value of the good and revered things is precisely that they are insidiously related, tied to, and involved with these wicked, seemingly opposite things."[80] Only in "becoming" can the conflicting forces of opposites be harnessed for the affirmation of life. Put differently, the Christian denial of life, which has its roots in the static realm of being, must overcome "being" and embrace "becoming" in the midst of the fluid, dynamic, unstable, and changeable conditions of life. As Hatab puts it, "The innocence of becoming is Nietzsche's alternative to all Western moralistic scripts that portray the life-world as a fallen or flawed condition, which would require reparation according to transcendent or historical forms of transformation."[81] For Nietzsche, it is therefore nearly impossible to create a "becoming" person unless the Western intellectual tradition forfeits its view of the world as "being" in sin, guilt, and full of a bad conscience. And yet, it requires a "new kind [*Gattung*] of philosopher"[82] before a new humanity is

---

78. *On the Genealogy of Morality*, § II, 16.

79. Cf. Larry J. Hatab, *Nietzsche's Life Sentence. Coming to Terms with Eternal Recurrence* (New York: Routledge, 2005), 13.

80. *Beyond Good and Evil*, § 2, in Friedrich Nietzsche, *Beyond Good and Evil*, translated by Rolf-Peter Horstmann and Judith Norman. Cambridge Texts in the History of Philosophy (Cambridge: Cambridge University Press, 2003).

81. Hatab, *Nietzsche's Life Sentence*, 62.

82. Nietzsche, *Beyond Good and Evil*, § 2.

grounded in the flux of "becoming." In the treatise *Thus Spoke Zarathustra*, Nietzsche gives that new kind of person the name *Übermensch.*

(7) For Paul, the central anthropological issue is not how a person can "become" someone different or something more. To a certain extent, Paul would allow for human self-improvement and perhaps self-fulfillment in a Nietzschean sense of the idea of "becoming," but not so much as a psychological than a spiritual reality. Indeed, Paul speaks of the possibility of human "becoming" when he speaks of the fruit of the Spirit in Galatians. This language of the fruit of the Spirit assumes the possibility of human transformation but it also assumes that something else has happened beforehand, and that is central to Paul—and in contradiction to Nietzsche.

Whereas Nietzsche emphasized a person's "becoming," Paul speaks of a person's "new creation." In 2 Cor. 5:17 Paul says that εἴ τις ἐν Χριστῷ, καινὴ κτίσις· τὰ ἀρχαῖα παρῆλθεν, ἰδοὺ γέγονεν καινά. When Paul announces a "new creation," he assumes that two things have already "become" a reality. On the one hand, the person who is a new creation is so only "in Christ" and that means, on the other hand, that the "old things" have been overcome. The reference to the "old things" is for Paul an affirmation that the conditions of the old creation were the conditions under the power of sin and that precisely in Christ that power has been disempowered and definitively defeated. In other words, while Nietzsche's vision for humanity is that of the coming *Übermensch,* as he spells out in *Thus Spoke Zarathustra,* Paul speaks of the "new person" (cf. καινὸς ἄνθρωπος in Eph. 2:15) in Christ. That person is a new being and on that basis is still in the process of becoming.

Conclusion

Any fair assessment of Nietzsche vis-à-vis Paul must take into consideration a certain Nietzschean idiosyncrasy without which a comparison of the two remains inequitable.[83] The peculiarity is this: Nietzsche's critique of everything Christian does not proceed from an "objective" theological understanding of the Christian faith but from his personal observation and experience of those around him—mother, aunts and others like them.[84] The issue that thus comes to the fore is that his devastatingly negative experiences enmeshed him in an

---

83. For a recent excellent study of Nietzsche in relation to major Christian themes, cf. Stephen Williams, *The Shadow of the Antichrist. Nietzsche's Critique of Christianity* (Grand Rapids: Baker Academic, 2006).

awkward logic: if Christians are entangled in the denial of life then it must follow that the Christian doctrine and faith as such must be the underlying problem. In Nietzsche's observation, the real issue was not how Christians thought theologically regarding sin and guilt, but the fact that they were plagued in their everyday lives with psychological fear and guilt because of it. In other words, theology was not the problem—but life.

The ultimate anthropological difference between Nietzsche and Paul rests on their diametrically divergent hamartiological presuppositions. Whereas for Paul and—as Nietzsche has seen correctly—also for most subsequent expressions of Christian doctrines, the overarching dilemma is that of sin and its ensuing deeds, Nietzsche radically rejects the very notion of sin and sins. In other words, while for the Apostle, the core of the Christian life is inextricably linked to the overcoming of the deeds of sin, for Nietzsche the entire doctrine of sin has no other purpose than to violently destroy a person's life. For him, the psychological consequences are so blatantly dehumanizing that one must give up the belief in sin if there is even the slightest possibility for the affirmation of life. Christians must re-evaluate their constant self-devaluation.

Can Christians learn anything from Nietzsche's critique regarding sin? The answer is a qualified "yes." Irrespective of the severity and one-sidedness of Nietzsche's attack, he is right in his observations that Christianity may and does amount to a denial of life. More precisely, in certain historically, ecclesiologically and theologically conditioned forms, Christianity appears as denial of life. In this regard Nietzsche's critique stands, even to this day. And yet, his critique stems from a theologically weak understanding and a historically conditioned observation of Christianity that in the end mitigates the full force of his critique. His charges, though in some sense may be traced to Paul, capture only an aspect of the Apostle's teaching on sin.[85] In this regard, Nietzsche was himself led astray. His psychological interpretation of Paul's theology of sin, while it raises many valid questions, remains ultimately fragmented and imbalanced, even tragic.

84. Cf. Hans Hübner, *Nietzsche und das Neue Testament*, 4, who argues that Nietzsche's upbringing with his mother and two aunts presented him with a warped and distorted conception of the Christian faith; this was surely tragic for an intellectually gifted young man.

85. For Paul, guilt in its forensic sense is vindicated, overcome in the resurrection; the consequence, result of sin in the here and now, in this life, is still felt (psychologically) as guilt, although it need not to. Those in Christ have reason to let go of their guilt, especially their guilt feelings. Here Nietzsche's observations are entirely correct. He encountered too many Christians who were driven by anxiety, beleaguered by guilt feelings and thus committed the crime of denying life. Paul would have to agree with Nietzsche inasmuch as it is psychologically possible to be plagued by guilt even though theologically that guilt has been overcome.

2

Heidegger on the Apostle Paul

Benjamin Crowe

Martin Heidegger (1889–1976) remains one of the most influential and controversial philosophers of the twentieth century.[1] His influence has been pronounced well beyond the confines of philosophy as a discipline, with theology in particular proving to be fertile soil for the reception of his ideas. Raised a Roman Catholic in the Upper Danube River valley in southwestern Germany, Heidegger began his professional life as a student of theology at Albert-Ludwigs-Universität in Freiburg-im-Breisgau. While he distanced himself from the church in 1919, he remained keenly interested in religious and theological issues for the rest of his life. Indeed, in the late 1930's, Heidegger comments on his own work:

> But who could deny that a confrontation with Christianity discreetly accompanied the whole path up to this point?—A confrontation which was not and is not some 'problem' that was latched onto, but rather at *once* the preservation [*Wahrung*] of my own origin—of the parental house, homeland, and youth—and a painful separation from it. Only someone thus rooted in a really vital Catholic world could have an inkling of the necessities that exerted anrily effect on the path

---

1. There is a vast scholarly literature on Heidegger's disastrous involvement with the Nazi regime in the 1930's, an event that remains the single most divisive issue regarding his thought. Some of the best, sober scholarship on this issue includes: Michael E. Zimmerman, *Heidegger's Confrontation with Modernity: Technology, Politics, Art* (Bloomington: Indiana University Press, 1990); Hans Sluga, *Heidegger's Crisis: Philosophy and Politics in Nazi Germany* (Cambridge, MA: Harvard University Press, 1993); Julian Young, *Heidegger, Philosophy, Nazism* (Cambridge: Cambridge University Press, 1998) and Iain Thomson, *Heidegger on Ontotheology: Technology and the Politics of Education* (Cambridge: Cambridge University Press, 2005).

of my questioning up to this point like subterranean earthquakes (G 66:415).[2]

It can hardly be a surprise, then, to learn of Heidegger's contacts with and influence on some of the century's most important theologians. Lutherans like Rudolf Bultmann, Gerhard Ebeling, and Eberhard Jüngel received many of his ideas into their own work. Karl Rahner, himself one of the most influential Roman Catholic thinkers of the century, studied under Heidegger in Freiburg. Pope Benedict XVI has described Heidegger's influence on his intellectual development at the start of his own career. Without a doubt, then, theologians of diverse outlook have found Heidegger's thought to be fruitful.

But what about Heidegger's own theological inquiries, and the influence of religious thinkers on his thought? Scholars have carefully examined Heidegger's appropriations of Augustine, Thomas Aquinas, Luther, Schleiermacher, Kierkegaard, Franz Overbeck, and others.[3] But Heidegger's engagement with the Apostle Paul stands out as a seminal moment in the development of his thought. In this essay, I will provide an overview and brief examination of three of the more important aspects of this encounter.[4]

Heidegger reads Paul's writings as documentary records of the way of life of the primitive church. The first way in which he appropriates these texts is

2. I have followed scholarly convention by citing Heidegger's works parenthetically in the body of the text. The references are given to the German-language original and, where applicable, to the corresponding English translation, using the abbreviations (volume number followed by section/page number) found in the bibliography of this monograph.

3. For two studies of Heidegger's relationship to Aquinas and other scholastics, see John D. Caputo, *Heidegger and Aquinas: An Essay on Overcoming Metaphysics* (New York: Fordham University Press, 1982) and S.J. McGrath, *The Early Heidegger and Medieval Philosophy: Phenomenology for the Godforsaken* (Washington, DC: Catholic University of America Press, 2006). A particularly good discussion of Heidegger's engagement with Schleiermacher is found throughout John Van Buren, *The Young Heidegger: Rumor of the Hidden King* (Bloomington: Indiana University Press, 1994). On Heidegger and Luther, see my *Heidegger's Religious Origins: Destruction and Authenticity* (Bloomington: Indiana University Press, 2006).

4. For other discussions of Heidegger's reading of Paul, see John D. Caputo, "*Sorge* and *Kardia*: The Hermeneutics of Factical Life and the Categories of the Heart," in *Reading Heidegger From the Start: Essays in His Earliest Thought,* ed. Theodore Kisiel and John Van Buren (Albany: SUNY Press, 1994), 327–44; Theodore Kisiel, "Heidegger (1920–1921) on Becoming a Christian: A Conceptual Picture Show," in *Reading Heidegger From the Start*, 175–92; Christopher Rickey, *Revolutionary Saints: Heidegger, National Socialism, and Antinomian Politics* (University Park: Pennsylvania State University Press, 2002); and Thomas Sheehan, "Heidegger's 'Introduction to the Phenomenology of Religion,' 1920–1921," *The Personalist* 60 (1979): 312–24.

as sources for a *phenomenology of religion*, i.e., for a descriptive-analytic account of the fundamental structures that render experience intelligible in religious terms. Second, Heidegger takes the eschatological orientation of the earliest Christians, as reflected by Paul's writings, to be a particularly vivid, intensified, and focused kind of experience. Heidegger's *phenomenological method* commits him to grounding his descriptions and analysis on such "basic experience [*Grunderfahrungen*]," taken to be disclosive of elemental features of human existence in general. Finally, like many of his theological contemporaries, Heidegger maintains that Paul's writings exhibit an uncorrupted "primal Christianity [*Urchristentum*]," supposedly free of the intellectual and institutional accretions of later ages. By engaging closely with this foundational moment of the Christian tradition, Heidegger hoped to develop and appropriate "primal Christianity" as a *counter-cultural possibility* for his own time. Thus, in these three ways, Heidegger's own philosophical agenda shaped the manner in which he reads and appropriates Paul. After discussing each of these three dimensions of Heidegger's engagement, I will provide some considerations regarding the abiding importance of this seminal moment in modern intellectual history. I will conclude with some critical thoughts concerning what Heidegger might have missed in his reading of Paul.

PAUL AND THE PHENOMENOLOGY OF RELIGION

By at least 1917, Heidegger had begun to find his own independent voice as a philosopher. At this early stage, one of his central projects was the development of a *phenomenology of religion*.[5] His mentor, Edmund Husserl (1859–1938), encouraged him in this endeavor, partly by providing him with the posthumous notes of another student, Adolf Reinach (1883–1917), who had been working in a similar area prior to his death in World War I. Thus, during the winter semester of 1920–1921, Heidegger offered a course entitled "Introduction to the Phenomenology of Religion" in Freiburg. Roughly the second half of

5. There is some degree of scholarly controversy surrounding the precise nature of this project and the manner in which it fits with Heidegger's larger philosophical endeavor. On the one hand are those who argue that Heidegger's famous commitment to the "atheism" of philosophy entails that religion *per se* was never really his central interest. See, for example, Theodore Kisiel, "War der frühe Heidegger tatsächlich ein 'christlicher Theologe?" in *Philosophie und Poesie: Otto Pöggeler zum 60. Geburtstag*, ed. Annemarie Gethmann-Siefert (Stuttgart: Frommann-Holzboog, 1988), 59–75. On the other hand are those who maintain that the phenomenology of religion is a free-standing inquiry within Heidegger's larger oeuvre. See, for example, my *Heidegger's Phenomenology of Religion: Realism and Cultural Criticism* (Bloomington: Indiana University Press, 2008).

the semester was devoted to achieving a preliminary "phenomenological understanding" of "primal Christian religiosity" as articulated in Paul's letters. To aid in understanding what Heidegger tries to accomplish by reading Paul in this lecture course, a brief discussion of what a Heideggerian phenomenology of religion amounts to is in order.[6]

Throughout the lecture course of 1920–1921, Heidegger helps articulate the nature of his project partly by way of contrast with other approaches. To take one example that is prominent in the earlier part of the lecture course, he critically engages the (then) recent work of Ernst Troeltsch (1865–1923). In the course of Heidegger's discussion of Troeltsch, it emerges that what fundamentally distinguishes a phenomenology of religion from a "philosophy of religion" in Troeltsch's sense is that the latter tends to treat religion like an "object [Objekt]," which means that it adopts a detached observational or theoretical stance (G 60:35-36; G 60:51).[7] In other words, Heidegger thinks that typical approaches towards religion assume what some contemporary philosophers might call the "view from nowhere" or the "point of view of the universe," i.e., an allegedly standpoint-free position that abstracts away from what Heidegger calls the researcher's own "anxious concern [Bekümmerung]" about existence. Within this point of view, one finds oneself in a relation in which the person doing the relating is never herself brought into question (G 60:82). While this allows for a degree of unbiased objectivity that is both legitimate and useful to certain scientific enterprises, Heidegger challenges the normative hegemony of this point of view. As a phenomenologist, Heidegger is committed to allowing the meaning or intelligibility of experience emerge just as it is constituted in itself, rather than through a prior construction. He further radicalizes this methodological imperative, derived from Husserl, by contending that the meaning of experience (at least in some important cases, such as in religious experience) can only be brought out by putting one's own existence into play. As he puts it in this lecture course, "Phenomenological understanding, on the other hand, is determined from the enactment of the one who is engaging in reflection" (G 60:82).

Heidegger further articulates this project as "bringing to light" the "categories" that are *alive in life itself* in an original way" (G 61-62/47; 88/66).

6. For a considerably more detailed discussion of these issues, see my *Heidegger's Phenomenology of Religion*.

7. In the nomenclature of post-Kantian German philosophy, a distinction is often made between *Objekt* and *Gegenstand*, both of which can be rendered by the single English word 'object.' Roughly, the term *Objekt* indicates an observed fact that figures into scientific inferences and theory, whereas *Gegenstand* is a broader term that encompasses the content of virtually any perceptual state.

This way of putting it reflects what might be called the fundamental assumption of his entire project, namely, that human life is always already *meaningful* or *intelligible*.[8] Understanding life does not require subsuming it under concepts derived from reason, but rather in reading off from life itself the meaningful patterns that are, as it were, built into it. Heidegger expresses this fundamental view in his first lecture course after World War I: "Life as such is *not* irrational (which has nothing whatever to do with 'rationalism'!)" (G 56/57; 219/187). He makes a similar point two semesters later, in the winter of 1919–20: "Life is not a chaotic confusion of dark torrents, not a mute principle of power, not a limitless, all-consuming disorder, rather *it is what it is only as a concrete meaningful shape*" (G 58:148). Thus, when Heidegger is doing phenomenology he is trying to "extract" or uncover the inherent intelligibility of life *as it is lived*. This, in turn, requires that inherited conceptual frameworks be subjected to radical criticism to clear the way for the investigation. It also means that the conceptual vocabulary of phenomenology has to be of a unique kind in order to prevent the kinds of distortions that Heidegger thinks are all too common in other accounts of human experience.[9]

Heidegger's actual execution of this project with respect to Paul's letters is detailed and rich enough that I cannot provide a complete account of it here. Nevertheless, several important elements of his discussion can be brought out in order to give one a good sense for Heideggerian phenomenology of religion. After a rather sketchy discussion of Galatians, Heidegger turns his attention to 1 and 2 Thessalonians. In a loose note later included in the edition of these lectures, Heidegger explains that the content (the "what") of the letters, when looked at phenomenologically, is actually a "how," viz., how it is that Paul and his little community live what Heidegger calls "factical life-experience" (G 60:145). 1 Thessalonians is thus "an *anxiously concerned existential* 'meditation' [*Besinnung*]' on the situation" (G 60:140). At the heart of this "situation" is a shared historical self-understanding on the part of the community. Their identity lies in their "having become" what they now are through the reception of Paul's proclamation (G 60:93-95), which in turn connects them to God in a way that is lived out as a "turn" in their lives away from slavery to idols and towards the liberating service of God (G 60:95). Importantly, this

8. Steven Crowell provides a particularly clear and useful discussion of these fundamental aspects of Heidegger's approach to phenomenology. See the essays collected in *Husserl, Heidegger, and the Space of Meaning: Paths Toward Transcendental Phenomenology* (Evanston: Northwestern University Press, 2001).

9. Heidegger typically refers to this conceptual vocabulary, and the method whereby it is constructed, as "formal indication." For an account of what this involves, see Daniel O. Dahlstrom, *Heidegger's Concept of Truth* (Cambridge: Cambridge University Press, 2001).

relationship to God is not a matter of speculative thought, but, again, of "how" life is actually lived (G 60::97). The direction of this new life is determined by eschatological expectation. Qualitatively, this is a matter of "affliction" that at the same time binds one to God (G 60:97-98). As with the relation to God, the eschatological attitude here is the farthest thing from theoretical detachment. Instead, the community faces a constantly renewed choice of its way of life and a concomitant attitude of "wakefulness" and "sobriety" (G 60:104-105).

Heidegger thus places the community's historical self-understanding, rooted in the reception of Paul's proclamation, at the center of his phenomenological analysis. The subtle but profound shifts in the meaning of existence that this brings about are perhaps most apparent for Heidegger in 1 Cor. 1:26-27 and 7:20, where Paul tells his church that they must live in the world "as if" they did not live in the world (G 60:116-117). For Heidegger, this shows that the very meaning that things have is sensitive to the shift in historical self-understanding that has been actualized. Indeed, this is one of the hallmarks of what he here calls "factical life-experience," i.e., that our self-understanding and our understanding of the world we inhabit are inextricably bound together in such a way that they reciprocally condition one another. In the case of Paul's church, the basic characteristic of things (i.e., that they exist) remains unchanged, as do their objective properties (stones are still hard, water is still wet). But the *significance* that these things have has been altered at a deep, pre-conceptual level; Paul expresses this by saying that it is *as if* they did not really exist (G 60:117). Again, Heidegger connects this back to the self-understanding of the early Christians; unlike their contemporaries, their identity is focused not on "worldly" pursuits, but rather on the "otherwordly" event of the coming of the Lord.

There is much more that can be said about Heidegger's phenomenological reading of Paul and, indeed, of other religious figures like Augustine and Luther. Still, the basic tenor of his project is fairly evident. Heidegger is interested in getting to the heart of ancient Christian religious life while simultaneously avoiding the pitfalls that he regards as inherent in the methods of other philosophers. Crucially, this means that Paul cannot be treated as an "object" of historical analysis; instead, the researcher's own "anxious concern" for existence must be brought into play. This, in turn, reveals deep structures within religious life that are typically opaque to the historian. These structures turn out to be specifications of more universal features of human experience as it gets concretely lived out. It is to this feature of Heidegger's approach to phenomenology that I now turn.

"Primal Christianity" as a "Basic Experience"

Heidegger's interest in developing a phenomenology of religion as a particular area of philosophical inquiry is embedded in a much larger project that he variously calls by names such as "hermeneutics of facticity" and "fundamental ontology." This essentially involves the articulation or explication of the basic structures of our immediate, meaning-laden existence (what Heidegger calls *Dasein* or "being-here" in *Being and Time*), which proves to be the fundamental layer at which all intelligibility is constituted. This fundamental "being-in-the-world" is, crucially, something in which we have a stake. It is, as he famously puts it in *Being and Time*, something that is in each case my own, a matter of "care [*Sorge*]" or "anxious concern [*Bekümmerung*]." This means that the fundamental sense of human existence is lost or distorted when one adopts a detached theoretical attitude towards it. This brings the question of how one is to gain access to existence to the very forefront of Heidegger's concerns, and it is here, once again, that Paul plays a key role in his thought.

The way in is, as Heidegger puts it in *Being and Time*, a "basic experience [*Grunderfahrung*] of the 'object' to be disclosed" (G 2:232/275). The quotation marks around the word 'object' indicate once again Heidegger's concern with avoiding a theoretical stance towards the phenomenon. When the 'object' in question is human existence as it is concretely lived out in "anxious concern," the "basic experience" in question must be one in which a person has a grip on the sense of his or her existence that avoids what Heidegger earlier calls the "de-historicization of the I" (G 56/57; 206/174). In a letter of 1919 to his friend Elisabeth Blochmann, Heidegger explains what he is after in terms of the "graced moments" in life in which "we feel ourselves belonging immediately to the direction in which we live," in which we achieve an "understanding having of ourselves [*verstehende Sichselbsthaben*]."[10] That is, phenomenology starts with an actual moment of experience in which we catch a glimpse of the basic shape of our lives. By analyzing what is thus opened up to view, Heidegger maintains that we can gain a deeper reflective grasp on what it means to be human in general.

It is precisely as such a "basic experience" that Heidegger turns to Christian religiosity in its "primal" or "original" form. In a lecture course given in the winter semester of 1919–1920, Heidegger announces one part of his discussion under the heading "Christianity as the historical paradigm for the shift of

---

10. *Martin Heidegger and Elisabeth Blochmann, Briefwechsel, 1918–1969*, ed. Joachim W. Storck (Marbach am Neckar: Deutsche Schillergesellschaft, 1989), 10. The role of a "basic experience" in Heidegger's project is discussed at more length in my *Heidegger's Religious Origins*, 22–37.

emphasis of factical life to the self-world" (G 58:61). He goes on to clarify the claim being made here:

> The self-world as such enters into life and is lived as such. What is present in the life of the original Christian community signifies a radical inversion of the direction of the tendency of life—one has in mind particularly world-denial and asceticism (*the idea of the Kingdom of God, Paul* (cf. Ritschl)). Herein lives the motive for the development of a totally new context of expression which life itself brings forth and which we today call *history* (G 58:61).

Heidegger's claim is that "primal Christianity" shelters a kind of intensified experience of life in all its "anxious concern," and that it thus affords him access to phenomena within human existence that have been distorted or simply ignored by the dominant philosophical tradition. A good illustration of this move can be had from Heidegger's discussions of the key concept of "world." Famously, in *Being and Time*, Heidegger argues against the Cartesian tradition that human existence is fundamentally a matter of "being-in-the-world."[11] The sense of "world" here is not simply of a collection of objects in space and time. Instead, a world is a network of meaning in which individuals and communities carry out their lives and develop their self-understanding. For Heidegger, this sense of world has been missing from the dominant philosophical tradition. It is present, however, within the life of the primitive church as shaped by and recorded by Paul.

In a loose note titled "On Paul," attached to the manuscript of his lecture course for the summer semester of 1923, which is, incidentally, a crucial milestone on the way to the fully articulated concept of "being-in-the-world" in *Being and Time*, Heidegger writes: "Flesh-*spirit* (see *Religion in History and the Present*): to be in them, a *how* as a 'what' [. . .]" (G 63:111/86). To be "flesh," to be of the "world," is not for Paul a physical condition, but rather a spiritual one. As Heidegger had earlier discussed in 1920–1921, at issue is the "how" of one's life, and Paul calls upon his flock to be "in the world but not of the world." The world is not a collection of things, but rather a context of meaning according to which those outside the church order their lives. This context consists of a

---

11. The classic scholarly account of Heidegger's conception of "world" remains Hubert L. Dreyfus, *Being-in-the-World: A Commentary on Heidegger's* Being and Time, *Division I* (Cambridge, MA: MIT Press, 1991).

largely tacit sense of what matters in life, which in turn allows other things to show up as significant in relation to this. Thus, for example, a person in the ancient Roman "world" might have a largely tacit sense that social advancement is one of the more important matters to attend to in one's life. In the light of this understanding, something else, like a marriage, comes to matter in a particular way. One might imagine that, in such a "world," rather than being an expression of romantic love marriage matters as a means to social advancement. This, in turn, has significant effects on how one pursues a marriage, on which people strike one as marriageable, and on how one considers other people, such as one's own family, in relation to the project.

In a 1929 essay, Heidegger is much more explicit about the importance of primitive Christianity in disclosing this new sense of "world." The world, for Paul, is not an object, but rather is a mode of human existence (G 9:39-40/ 112-113). Heidegger explains the difference at greater length in a lecture course of 1928:

> For example, when Paul in the *First Letter to the Corinthians* and in the *Letter to the Galatians* speaks of *kosmos houtos*, this world, it means this total condition of beings, and not only and in the first instance nature, the 'cosmic,' in our sense. 'This world' means this condition and this situation of human beings, this sort and way of their Dasein, indeed the way they act towards virtues and works, towards nature and everything, their way of evaluating goods. Indeed, *kosmos* is the direct term for the way in which human Dasein is, for its attitude, its way of thinking, *he sophia tou kosmou*. This *kosmos*, this how, is defined by its relation to the *kosmos*, already dawning, to the *aion ho mellon* [age to come]. The condition of all beings is regarded in relation to the *eschaton*, the final situation (G 26:222/173).

As this discussion makes clear, Paul matters for Heidegger because he articulates one of the fundamental phenomena of human existence in a manner that avoids the distorting assumptions of the philosophical tradition. Paul shows Heidegger a sense of "world" that brings out its character as a temporally structured network of meaning within which things and human lives acquire their significance.

PAUL AS POSSIBILITY

Throughout his life, Heidegger maintained the conviction that "primal Christianity" constituted a radical and largely unrealized possibility for human existence, one that had been distorted or compromised by its assimilation into the Western philosophical tradition. For example, in an essay from the late 1940's called "Nietzsche's Word: 'God is Dead'," Heidegger writes:

> For Nietzsche, Christianity [*Christentum*] is the historical, secular-political phenomenon of the Church and its claim to power within the formation of Western humanity and its modern culture. Christianity in this sense and the Christian life of the New Testament faith are not the same. Even a non-Christian life can affirm Christianity and make use of it for the sake of power; conversely, a Christian life is not necessarily in need of Christianity. Therefore, a confrontation with Christianity is by no means an absolute battle against what is Christian, no more than a critique of theology is a critique of the faith for which theology is supposed to be the interpretation (G 5:219-220/164).

One important influence on Heidegger in this respect is Franz Overbeck (1837–1905), an influential early critic of nineteenth-century liberal Protestant theology and colleague of Nietzsche. Theodore Kisiel reports Heidegger's invocation of Overbeck's thought during a talk by Wilhelm Heitmüller, himself an exponent of the liberal "History of Religions" school.[12] In a letter of November 24, 1922, Heidegger acknowledges receipt of Overbeck's posthumous *Christentum und Kultur* from his philosophical comrade-in-arms, Karl Jaspers.[13] Heidegger refers to Overbeck once more in a 1970 preface to his 1927 essay "Phenomenology and Theology":

> Almost one hundred years ago there appeared simultaneously (1873) two writings of two friends: the "first piece" of the "Unfashionable Observations" of Friedrich Nietzsche, wherein the "glorious Hölderlin" is mentioned; and the "little book" *On the Christianness of*

12. See Kisiel, "War der frühe Heidegger tatsächlich ein 'christlicher Theologe'?" 73-75.

13. Martin Heidegger and Karl Jaspers, *Briefwechsel, 1920–1963*, ed. Walter Biemel and Hans Saner (Frankfurt am Main: Vittorio Klostermann, 1990), 37.

Today's Theology, who established the world-denying expectation of the end as the basic characteristic of what is primordially Christian (G 9:45-46/39).

Overbeck's view of the uncompromisingly critical stance towards "culture" exhibited by early Christianity clearly impressed Heidegger deeply. For Heidegger, "primal Christianity" represents not only a historical period in the development of a major world religion, but, more importantly, an unrealized possibility for life in the present. The intensification of life that characterizes the earliest forms of Christianity cuts against the depersonalization and complacency that Heidegger sees as hallmarks of modern culture (e.g., G 58:58-60). Famously, in *Being and Time*, Heidegger articulates the relevant contrast here as between an "inauthentic [*uneigentlich*]" and an "authentic [*eigentlich*]" mode of life. The German words themselves indicate something of what Heidegger is after; an "authentic" life is one that is owned up to, one that is radically individualized.[14]

It is here that Paul once again becomes important for Heidegger. While Heidegger acknowledges that there are many different paradigms of an authentic life, he consistently turns to religious forms of life. Paul's letters, in addition to providing a source for a phenomenology of religion and for a phenomenology of human existence more generally, also provide the outline for what Heidegger takes to be an authentic manner of existence. As noted previously, Heidegger focuses on the way that the historical self-understanding of Paul's church was decisively shaped by the reception of the proclamation [*Verkündigung*]. The content of this proclamation, for Heidegger, is the "scandal of the cross" (G 60:144). Perhaps more important for Heidegger is the "how" of the proclamation, the manner of its being proclaimed: it "breaks in [*einschlägt*]" (G 60:143). It is a "shock [*Anstoß*]" that interrupts the complacent worldliness of Paul's auditors, and so brings about a fundamental reorientation of existence (G 60:144). It is not simply a theory about life that one is to file away, but rather it is something that can only be preserved in "anxious concern" (G 60:137). This,

14. For some differing accounts of the nature of "authenticity" and of other philosophical issues at stake in its articulation, see: Michael E. Zimmerman, *Eclipse of the Self: The Development of Heidegger's Concept of Authenticity* (Athens: Ohio University Press, 1981); Charles Guignon, "Authenticity, Moral Values, and Psychotherapy," in *The Cambridge Companion to Heidegger*, ed. Charles Guignon (Cambridge: Cambridge University Press, 1993), 215–39; and Taylor Carman, *Heidegger's Analytic: Interpretation, Discourse, and Authenticity in* Being and Time (Cambridge: Cambridge University Press, 2003). My own reading of authenticity, reflected here, is articulated in *Heidegger's Religious Origins*, especially in chs. 5–6.

for Heidegger, is what Paul means when he tells the church at Corinth that his message comes in "spirit" and in "power" (G 60:137).

This radical "reversal [*Umwendung*]" of life consists, for Heidegger, in an altered relation to the world, a kind of uncanny position of suspension that undermines the somnolent tranquility of normal life. This "tribulation [*Trübsal*]" or "affliction [*Bedrängnis*]" lies in the fact that the normal patterns of life have been disrupted in an irrevocable manner: "Christian life is not continuous and linear, but is broken up: all the relations to the surrounding world must pass through" this new self-understanding (G 60:120). It is the eschatological expectation of the coming of the Lord that fundamentally magnifies and sustains this transformation (G 60:97-98), despite the tendency of Paul's church to lapse back into "natural idleness." The advent of the Lord presents his church with two radically different possibilities, either complacent "darkness" or vigilant "wakefulness." The former option involves maintaining a basic orientation towards daily, worldly concerns, and the peace and security that such routines bring. As such, those who adopt this attitude "do not possess themselves, they have forgotten the ownmost self [*das eigene Selbst*]" because they "submit themselves to what life offers them, occupy themselves with some of the tasks of life" (G 60:103, 105). Rather than seizing hold of their lives as individuals, they have opted for a kind of self-abdication, which amounts to a failure to work out the meaning and import of their lives. The favored alternative, then, involves the "light" of self-knowledge, in which each individual "stands alone before God" (G 60:112). This is not a once-and-for-all affair, but rather a constantly renewed "distress [*Not*]" (G 60:127-128). Being faithful to the reception of the proclamation requires a kind of intensified concern with oneself, a sort of vigilance in which one fully "owns up [*sich eigen*]" to oneself. Returning again and again to the fundamental commitments of faith, a person is thus called to be "wakeful" at each moment to the manner in which this commitment unfolds over her life.

For Heidegger, human life is perpetually marred by a tendency to "fall" or "decline" into tranquil self-abdication. The dominant cultural features of late modern society (e.g., mass media, the anonymity of the metropolis) exacerbate the problem. Moreover, intellectual discourse is all too often complicit in this tendency. Thus, for Heidegger, the uncompromising insistence of Paul's proclamation, and his continual exhortations to remain "awake" and "sober," take on a new significance. Not only does Paul present a way of life that runs directly counter to the tranquilizing temptations of life, but his writings represent a mode of discourse that admits of no compromise with them.

CRITICAL ASSESSMENT

What is to be made of Heidegger's appropriations of Paul? Does Heidegger offer anything of value for theologians and Biblical scholars today, or, on the contrary, is his reading too tendentious, too driven by his own idiosyncratic philosophical agenda, to be helpful? There is not a straightforward answer, either positive or negative, to this question. Heidegger's engagement with Paul is of such complexity that a comprehensive assessment is simply not possible. All the same, there are a number of points that can be made that bring out both the positive potential in Heidegger's reading as well as some of its palpable limitations.

Heidegger's appropriation of Paul, for both a phenomenology of religion (see above) and for a more general interpretation of the fundamental structures of human existence (see above), are clearly instances of "secularizing" scriptural texts. Like historical criticism, Biblical archaeology, and other modern disciplines, Heidegger does not appropriate scripture as a theological or doctrinal authority. Unlike some of his other intellectual heroes, such as Augustine and Luther, Heidegger does not expound the Bible to develop a doctrinal system or to provide spiritual guidance for the church. At the same time, however, Heidegger's approach is clearly different in important respects from many modern disciplinary approaches to the Bible. Heidegger does not assume anything about the historicity of the events narrated in the texts, and he is not particularly concerned with questions about the authorship of scripture. He seeks neither to verify the witness of scripture nor to debunk it.

What, then, is the value of this uniquely Heideggerian approach to Paul? In suspending judgment on some of the major debates of the modern era regarding the Bible, Heidegger is able to bring scripture into new conversations. Without pronouncing on theological or polemical issues, Heidegger can show how the Bible can be profitably read from a phenomenological point of view. What this ultimately means is that Heidegger shows one way in which the Pauline corpus can inform an inquiry into the basic determinations of human existence, irrespective of the theological commitments of the person undertaking the investigation. The unique features of the life of Paul's community open up aspects of what it means to be human that, at least by Heidegger's lights, are largely overlooked in other sources.

In what ways might such a phenomenological reading serve a theological project? Ultimately, this is for theologians and Biblical scholars to decide. For his part, Heidegger hoped that what he uncovered in his phenomenology might help to revolutionize theology. The work of colleagues like Rudolf Bultmann and students like Karl Rahner certainly gave him some reason to suspect that this might indeed come to pass. At the very least, the findings of a phenomenological investigation of Paul might serve to reorient theology away from some of its traditional concerns (e.g., apologetics and dogmatics) and towards a careful examination of the significance of the Christian message in the lives of individuals, as exemplified by Paul and his church.

Heidegger's appropriation of Pauline Christianity as a paradigm of an "authentic" way of life might also be important for contemporary theologians, particular in our "secular age." His insistence on the radically uncompromising nature of "primal Christianity" provides ample food for thought regarding the place of the church in contemporary culture and society. From a Heideggerian point of view, the withdrawal of Christianity from the public sphere in many places presents an important opportunity, rather than something to regret. Heidegger might argue that, as in its earliest stage of development, Christianity can once again take an uncompromisingly critical stance towards many elements of culture and society in which it was previously complicit.

While this is a positive possibility, there are, to be sure, important limitations attached to Heidegger's interpretation of Paul as a paradigm for an "authentic" life. When the contents of a text are presented in this way as an ideal, it becomes particularly important to consider how the material is being read and interpreted. As I have described above, Heidegger sees in Paul's writings a way of life that is characterized by "anxious concern" for the self, as opposed to complacent self-abdication. This does indeed seem to be the sense of Paul's call to be "wakeful" and "sober." And yet, the vision of life that Paul consistently elaborates in his writings seems to include a great deal more than this. For Paul, owning up to one's life *as a Christian* is the crucial thing. This means that various defining features of a Christian identity must be part of the picture, and some of the most important of these are absent from Heidegger's discussion. In other words, some constitutive features of Paul's conception of a Christian self-understanding, which are absolutely central both to the relations between the members of the community and their relations to God, get left aside. Here, I will briefly discuss four of these: (1) the importance of apostolic tradition and authority; (2) shared liturgical practices and the norms embedded in these; (3) prayer; and, (4) self-emptying love.

Paul's letters are filled with direct and indirect references to the fact that obedience to apostolic authority, both in the form of tradition and of normative custom, is an indispensible aspect of a properly Christian way of life. In Romans, for example, Paul exhorts the recipients of his letter to become "obedient from the heart to the standard of teaching to which you were comitted" (RSV) (Rom. 6:17; cf. Rom. 1:5, 16:17). He is even more direct in 1 Corinthians, where dissention within the community makes obedience to shared tradition particularly salient. Apostolic custom, partly as constituted by Paul's own conduct, is referenced as of paramount authority throughout the letter (1 Cor. 4:17; 11:1, 11:16). Paul directly tells the Corinthian church to "maintain the traditions just as I handed them on to you" (1 Cor. 11:2), a comment that also suggests his own sense of deference to a pre-existing normative tradition. Crucial examples of this tradition include the words of institution at the Lord's Supper (1 Cor. 11:23) and a primitive creedal statement regarding Christ's death and resurrection (1 Cor. 15:3-5). Similarly, Paul elsewhere describes his famous visit to Jerusalem, where he sought the blessing of the original apostles for his mission to the Gentiles (Gal. 2:2; 2:9-10). In addition to these invocations of tradition and of his own apostolic custom, Paul also points to the customs of the church in Judea as paradigmatic (1 Thess. 2:14).

As I have discussed above, Heidegger certainly places Paul's proclamation at center stage in his account of the formation of Christian existence. Yet, his elaboration of just what Paul's message is strikes one as strangely flat. Paul indeed proclaims "Christ crucified," as Heidegger notes, but this proclamation brings with it a whole set of commitments that express just what it means to properly receive this proclamation. These commitments are ramified in the apostolic tradition and in the normative customs of the church. In that he leaves these aside in his own account, Heidegger's depiction of "primal Christianity" as a paradigmatically "authentic" manner of existence risks being vacuous.

Another central element of a Christian life for Paul is intimately bound up with the reception and maintenance of apostolic tradition and the normative customs of the earliest Christian communities, viz., common liturgical practice. This, too, is largely absent from Heidegger's discussion, though he does make reference to the Thessalonians' transfer of allegiance from false idols to the service of God. For all his emphases on the shared historical self-understanding of the ancient church, Heidegger's depiction of Christian existence is largely confined to that of the individual in her "anxious concern." The ideal of authenticity that he lifts out of his reading of Paul is similarly centered on each individual's "ownmost" possibility of existence, on the radically individuated nature of human life and the concomitant requirement that each individual "own up" to her own unique existence. For Paul, however, living a Christian life is scarcely intelligible apart from the shared liturgical practices of baptism and the Lord's Supper. The reception of the proclamation by the single individual is not the sole catalyst of one's entry into the radically new way of life in the church. While he does not seem to regard it as his particular ministry, which was indeed that of proclamation, Paul nevertheless insists that baptism is a defining moment of Christian life (e.g., Rom. 6:1-5; 1 Cor. 12:13). The ritual of baptism and the commitments undertaken in the context of the ritual lie at the heart of the "call" which each Christian receives.

1 Corinthians records Paul's intense concern with the proper observance of another central liturgy in the early church, i.e., the Lord's Supper. It is precisely through this common liturgy that the church's identity is both founded and continually renewed. "The cup of blessing that we bless, is it not a sharing in the blood of Christ? The bread that we break, is it not a sharing in the body of Christ? Because there is one bread, we who are many are one body, for we all partake of the one bread" (1 Cor. 10:16-17). Moreover, the rejection of pagan worship by Gentile Christians is ratified for Paul by participation in the Lord's Supper. "You cannot drink the cup of the Lord and the cup of demons. You cannot partake of the table of the Lord and the table of demons" (1 Cor. 10:21). Later on in the same letter, Paul argues that the proper observance of the Lord's Supper is determined precisely by the degree to which it cements the communal bond (1 Cor. 11:18-22). As a tradition received from directly from Jesus (1 Cor. 11:23), the content of the ritual marks the church as a new community whose identifying characteristic is its allegiance to the life and teachings of Christ. This is why Paul is so emphatic about the observance of due order within the liturgy (1 Cor. 14:26-36).

As with obedience to tradition and the observance of common liturgical practices, Paul places prayer at the very center of a recognizably Christian life. His letters are pervaded with his own prayers for various individuals and for the community to whom he writes, as well as requests for prayers both on his own behalf and on that of other people. In part, prayer is important because it also forges an unbreakable bond that unites small, ethnically diverse communities scattered around the Mediterranean world. For example, Paul writes:

> He who rescued us from so deadly a peril will continue to rescue us; on him we have set our hope that he will rescue us again, as you also join in helping us by your prayers, so that many will give thanks on our behalf for the blessing granted us through the prayers of many (2 Cor. 1:10-11).

Paul seems to envision a kind of invisible network of prayer that not only works for the good of the church but also overcomes or negates physical and social distances. Prayer, in other words, constitutes a bond of love (e.g., Phil. 1:3-4). More than that, however, it is through prayer that each Christian achieves an intimacy with God, something that Heidegger only alludes to in passing. For Paul, this intimacy is precisely what makes a Christian life unique, and which enables one to persevere in this new life.

> Do not worry about anything, but in everything by prayer and supplication with thanksgiving let your requests be made known to God. And the peace of God, which surpasses all understanding, will guard your hearts and your minds in Christ Jesus (Phil. 4:6-7).

Paul even goes so far as to argue that it is not that the individual Christian achieves intimacy with God through her own efforts in prayer, but rather that it is the very Spirit of God that establishes this unbreakable bond. "When we cry, 'Abba! Father!' it is that very Spirit bearing witness with our spirit that we are children of God" (Rom. 8:15). Or again: "Likewise the Spirit helps us in our weakness; for we do not know how to pray as we ought, but that very Spirit intercedes with sighs too deep for words. And God, who searches the heart, knows what is the mind of the Spirit, because the Spirit intercedes for the saints according to the will of God" (Rom. 8:26-27).It is thus no surprise when Paul exhorts the Thessalonians to "pray without ceasing" (1 Thess. 5:17), for it is by prayer that each Christian is united to the others and to God (1 Thess. 5:17).

This brings me to the final defining factor in Paul's vision of a Christian life that is largely absent from Heidegger's appropriation of it. For Paul, it all comes down to responding to God's self-emptying love with love for one's neighbor (Phil. 2:4-11). Echoing the teaching of Jesus, Paul maintains that all the commandments "are summed up in this word, 'Love your neighbor as yourself.' Love does no wrong to a neighbor; therefore, love is the fulfilling of the law" (Rom. 13:9-10). Perhaps one of the most extraordinary and powerful passages in any of Paul's letters is the exuberant hymn to love in 1 Corinthians 13. Here, Paul insists that none of the actions that externally mark out a Christian life are of any significance without love (1 Cor. 13:1-3). He closes this remarkable letter with the exhortation "Let all that you do be done in love" (1 Cor. 16:14). Elsewhere, Paul suggests that the centrality of love to Christian life is almost too obvious to merit comment (1 Thess. 4:9-10).

It is also clear throughout his letters that love for Paul is not a feeling empty of content but a pattern of behavior. Many of his letters demand that their recipients demonstrate the love that defines them as Christians by caring for the poor and needy, particularly in distant congregations. "Contribute to the needs of the saints; extend hospitality to strangers" (Rom. 12:13). He exerts himself to collect funds "for the poor among the saints at Jerusalem" (Rom. 15:16; 1 Cor. 16:1-4), and holds up Christians in Macedonia as exemplars of active love in this regard (2 Cor. 8:2).

In his own account of Paul's message in the 1920–1921 lecture course, Heidegger certainly discusses love as a key feature of Christian life, and he provides a powerful depiction of Paul's fatherly "anxious concern" for the Thessalonians. And yet, his phenomenological rendition of Christian existence simply does not give love the pride of place that it clearly has for Paul. In Paul's vision, the communal identity shaped by tradition and expressed in liturgy and prayer ultimately rests on a bond of love. This bond is inaugurated by God's actions in Christ, enacted and cemented in the life of the community, and expressed in self-sacrifice. Any genuinely Christian ideal quite simply must reflect this radical vision in all of its demanding detail and power.

While these limitations of Heidegger's reading of Paul should give us pause, it is nevertheless the case that this momentous encounter remains an extraordinary fruitful and seminal event in the history of twentieth-century philosophy. The effect of this reading of Paul on Heidegger's thought, and so, less directly, on the generations of thinkers influenced in turn by Heidegger himself, can scarcely be overestimated. For us today, revisiting Heidegger's discussions of Paul can still provide fertile ground for new reflection and, perhaps, for new creative encounters with Paul's ancient texts.

3

Paul of the Gaps

Agamben, Benjamin and the Puppet Player

Roland Boer

In an almost hallucinogenic few pages at the close of *The Time That Remains*, Giorgio Agamben[1] argues that one may trace the deep, if somewhat hidden, effect of the Apostle Paul on Benjamin's texts, texts that never mention Paul explicitly. I propose to offer a close reading of these carefully perverse pages, unpicking Agamben's arguments to see whether a very messianic Paul does indeed emerge from an equally messianic Benjamin, or whether it is an elaborate puppet play. Or, to shift the metaphor, I shall ask whether Agamben has discovered a window into the hidden world of Benjamin's thought, a window that opens up onto Paul himself, or whether the window is frosted, stained glass or perhaps a complex series of mirrors.

Before proceeding, let me recap the basic argument that sets up these final few pages in Agamben's book, an argument with two dimensions: the crucial role of what he calls "pre-law" and the pervasive concern with messianism. For Agamben, the solution to the tension in Paul between faith and law, πίστις and νόμος, may be found in the realm of pre-law, an amorphous moment before the differentiation of law, politics and religion that can be discovered only through linguistic analysis inspired by Émile Benveniste. Further, the messianic is the name for a dual tension, one in terms of time and the other in terms of act. If the first is a suspended moment (καιρός) between an instant of chronological time and its fulfillment, the "time that remains" of the title to the book, then deactivation is the mechanism by which the law is deactivated in order to pump up its potentiality so that it may be fulfilled. To my mind, this resort to the pre-

---

1. Giorgio, *The Time That Remains: A Commentary on the Letter to the Romans*, trans. P. Dailey (Stanford, CA.: Stanford University Press, 2005).

law in order to understand Paul is the major argument of the book, so much so that Agamben sees everything in the Pauline letters through the lens of the law.[2]

On this basis, what does Agamben argue in the final pages of *The Time That Remains*? Hidden in the labyrinthine, if not occult, final text of Benjamin—*Theses on the Philosophy of History*[3]—may be identified four citations of Paul: one from 2 Cor. 12:9-10 concerning messianic weakness; another from Rom. 5:14 on the image; a third, the term *Jetztzeit*, that captures Paul's sense of the "now-time," ὁ νῦν καιρός (even though he does not use the phrase himself); finally, the theme of recapitulation or bringing together (ἀνακεφαλαιώσασθαι), especially in the pseudo-Pauline Eph. 1:10, "all things are recapitulated in the Messiah," which is evoked whenever Benjamin uses *zusammenfassen*. For Agamben, "this should be enough to prove a textual correspondence, and not mere conceptual correspondence, between the theses and the letters." Indeed, he goes on, "the entire vocabulary of the theses appears to be truly stamped Pauline."[4] A rather breathtaking conclusion from the slimmest of evidence, is it not? But Agamben is not averse to hanging vast arguments on the thin threads of linguistic analysis.[5]

---

2. Since I have offered a sustained critique of this argument in *Criticism of Religion: On Marxism and Theology II*, Historical Materialism Book Series (Leiden: Brill, 2009), I will not revisit that critique here.

3. Cf. Walter Benjamin, *Selected Writings*, ed. H. Eiland and M. W. Jennings, vol. 4, 1938–1940 (Cambridge: The Belknap Press of Harvard University Press, 2003), 389–400 .

4. Agamben, *Time that Remains*, 144.

5. Even though the critical literature on Agamben is now voluminous, and even though engagements with the book on Paul increase at a slower pace, specific attention to this last section of the book are noticeably lacking, as may be seen in Mika Ojakangas, "Apostle Paul and the Profanation of the Law," *Distinktion* 18 (2009): 47–68; David Fiorovanti, "Language, Exception, Messianism: The Thematics of Agamben on Derrida," *Bible and Critical Theory* 6 (2010): 1–18; Paul J. Griffiths, "The Cross as the Fulcrum of Politics: Expropriating Agamben on Paul," in *Paul, Philosophy, and the Theopolitical Vision*, ed. Douglas Harink (Eugene, OR: Cascade, 2010)), 179–97; Ryan L. Hansen, "Messianic or Apocalyptic? Engaging Agamben on Paul and Politics," in *Paul, Philosophy, and the Theopolitical Vision*, ed. Harink, 198–223; Grigor Taxacher, "Messianische Geschichte: Kairos und Chronos: Giorgio Agambens Paulus-Auslegung weiter gedacht," *Evangelische Theologie* 7 (2010): 217–33; Colby Dickinson, "Canon as an Act of Creation: Giorgio Agamben and the Extended Logic of the Messianic," *Bijdragen* 71 (2010): 132–58; Matthew Sharpe, "Only Agamben Can Save Us? Against the Messianic Turn Recently Adopted in Critical Theory," *Bible and Critical Theory* 5 (2009): 1–26; Job De Meyere, "The Care for the Present: Giorgio Agamben's Actualisation of the Pauline Messianic Experience," *Bijdragen* 70 (2009): 168–84; and Denis Müller, "Le Christ, relève de la Loi (Romains 10, 4): la possibilité d'une éthique messianique à la suite de Giorgio Agamben," *Studies in Religion/Sciences religieuses* 30 (2001): 51–63.

Surreptitious Quotation

So let us return to the beginning and consider his argument more closely. The opening lines invoke the famous hunchback dwarf in the first of Benjamin's theses, a dwarf who hides inside a chess-playing puppet wearing Turkish attire and who ensures that this puppet wins any game it may be called upon to play. The key is the analogy to philosophy, in which historical materialism becomes the puppet, which can win only if it "enlists the services of theology, which today, as we know, is small and ugly and has to keep out of sight."[6] Not one to spend too much time in the complex tradition of encounters between theology and Marxism,[7] Agamben deftly interprets "theology" in this sentence as a "hidden theologian," who is now "concealed between the lines of the text."[8] Which text? Benjamin's own text, of course. As is his wont, Agamben now claims that he has stumbled upon a secret hidden to all until now, that the "hunchback theologian," who has been carefully hidden by Benjamin, has been flushed out of hiding by the sleuthing of Agamben himself. No prizes for guessing who that hunchback theologian might be.

The problem for Agamben is that Benjamin nowhere mentions the Apostle Paul in his entire and somewhat jumbled opus, let alone the *Theses*. So Agamben must find a key to the secret passage, a key that comes from Benjamin's complex practices of citation—*The Arcades Project*, for instance, is a work of devilishly complex and ultimately uncontrolled citation.[9] But Agamben focuses on a few texts in which Benjamin reflects on his own practice of citation: not only must citations be incognito, drawing together past and present, but they are also done by spacing. How does Agamben know? He cites a brief comment in Benjamin's essay, "What Is the Epic Theatre?"[10] In the midst of a discussion of Brecht's theatrical practice, particularly the gesture which interrupts, Benjamin uses the example of quotation, or rather the "quotable gesture:" not only are plays necessarily interrupted, but interruption

---

6. Benjamin, *1938–1940*, 389.

7. To which is devoted my five-volume series: Criticism of Heaven: On Marxism and Theology, Historical Materialism Book Series (Leiden: E. J. Brill, 2007); Criticism of Religion: On Marxism and Theology II, Historical Materialism Book Series (Leiden: Brill, 2009); Criticism of Theology: On Marxism and Theology III (Leiden: Brill, 2011); Criticism of Earth: On Marx, Engels and Theology, Historical Materialism Book Series (Leiden: Brill, 2012) and In The Vale of Tears: On Marxism and Theology V, Historical Materialism Book Series (Leiden: Brill, 2013).

8. Agamben, *Time that Remains*, 138.

9. See Walter Benjamin, *The Arcades Project*, trans. H. Eiland and K. McLaughlin (Cambridge: The Belknap Press of Harvard University Press, 1999).

10. Benjamin, *1938–1940*, 302–9.

is one "of the fundamental devices of all structuring."[11] So also with quotation, for "interruption is the basis of quotation," so much so—and here we pick up Agamben's own quotations of Benjamin—that "quoting a text entails interrupting its context." In Brecht's plays, this may take the form of an actor quoting his own gestures on stage, gestures that themselves are the specifically quotable features of the play. Then we stumble across a passing comment upon which Agamben seizes: "an actor must be able to space his gestures the way a typesetter spaces type."[12] *Sperren*, spacing, is the word upon which Agamben leaps, except that now he engages in one of his many interpretive sleights of hand. He begins by noting that in older styles of typography, spacing was an alternative mode of providing emphasis for type-setting that was unable to use italics. But now in a brief comment he makes two deft slips: firstly, such spacing entails a double-reading, a reading twice; secondly, this double-reading "may be the palimpsest of citation."[13] The first may be justified by Benjamin's text, where he gives the example in which an actor quotes later in the same play his own earlier gesture, but the second is a stretch. Benjamin's point is that the actor must space out such gestures, such quotations of his own acts, in a fashion analogous to the way words are sometimes spaced within quotations—well-paced, timed so that they do not rush upon one another. That is not the same as saying that the spacing of words is itself a sign of citation, or indeed that Benjamin is leaving occult traces in his texts for private eyes such as Agamben to find. And lest we think that all Benjamin's citations operate incognito, a brief glance at *The Arcades Project* will soon indicate that Benjamin's primary practice was to list his sources openly.

Spaced-Out Paul

Nonetheless, in the spirit of creative misreading, let us grant Agamben his point: when Benjamin uses a typewriter and when he spaces out words, he is quoting an unacknowledged text. The next step of the argument is even more daring, so much so that in the published text of his book, Agamben needs to bolster his argument with a facsimile of Benjamin's type-written and corrected text. Here we find: "*Dann ist uns wie jedem Geschlecht, das vor uns war, eine s c h w a c h e messianische Kraft mitgegeben*," that is, "Then, like every generation that preceded us, we have been endowed with a *w e a k* messianic power."[14] With

11. Ibid., 305.
12. Agamben, *Time that Remains*, 139.
13. Ibid.

that spaced "*s c h w a c h e*" the hunchbacked theologian shows his hand at last; the Turkish puppet with a long pipe (full of hashish) is now Benjamin and the dwarf is none other than Paul. Two further assumptions back up this even larger assumption: one is that Benjamin had the text of Luther's Bible in front of him as he wrote his theses, and the other is that only in Paul do we find such a conjunction of weakness and messiah. The first assumption begins as a "most likely" and soon becomes—in typical scholarly fashion—a certainty. The second relies on a rather creative misreading of Paul in 2 Cor. 12:9-10, where we find the response from none other than God to Paul's request to be relieved of his famous thorn in the flesh: "But he said to me, "My grace is sufficient to you, for my power is made perfect in weakness [ἐν ἀσθενείᾳ]." I will all the more gladly boast of my weaknesses, that the power of Christ may rest upon me. For the sake of Christ, then, I am content with weaknesses, insults, hardships, persecutions, and calamities; for when I am weak, then I am strong." The Christian tradition's dialectic of strength in weakness, perpetually sought after in monastic returns to simplicity and self-flagellation, used as justification for martyrs' eager leaps into the flames, pilloried by Nietzsche as the basis of the slave mentality of Christianity, is interpreted by Agamben earlier in the book in his discussion of the deactivation, preservation, and fulfillment of the law.[15] In this "messianic inversion," the weakness of the law means its power.

Even if we grant Agamben's juridical interpretation, which is highly problematic (as I have argued elsewhere), what relation does all this have to Benjamin's "weak messianic power," specifically the conjunction of weakness and the messiah? Let us begin by looking again at the quotation from Paul (above), which soon reveals no messiah in that text. Indeed, I have deliberately quoted the RSV here, where the word "Christ" appears twice. However, in Agamben's quotation from Paul we read, "for the sake of the Messiah." In this switch lies a distinct problem for Agamben's search for that hunchback theologian, Paul, in the gaps of Benjamin's texts. Earlier in the book, Agamben argues at some length that Χριστός in Paul's letters should bear one of its other meanings as Messiah, for Χριστός is but the Greek translation of the Hebrew *messiach*, both of them meaning "anointed." All of which leads to the rather uncomfortable conclusion that with "weak messianic power" Benjamin also invokes, or even actually means, "weak Christological power"—at least if we follow Agamben's internal logic. And here he cannot rely on the spurious

14. Benjamin, *1938–1940*, 390; Agamben, *Time that Remains*, 139–40.

15. Agamben, *Time that Remains*, 95–99.

assumption that Benjamin was poring over Luther's translation, for there too Christ is present.

It is of course possible that Benjamin was quoting Paul and even that he really meant "weak Christological power," so much so that the fundamental direction of the *Theses* deals with redemption through Christ. However, I am not sure Agamben would want that conclusion, even though his argument pushes very strongly in this direction. As far as Agamben's interpretation of Paul itself is concerned, the trap is that in his very effort to efface Christ from Paul's texts by translating Χριστός as "Messiah," he enables Christ to be more present than ever. Indeed, Agamben is simply unable to produce a theory of the messianic from Paul's texts without the weight of Christianity behind him. It appears in his notion of "the time that remains" (that is, between Jesus' life-death-resurrection and his coming again), in the argument concerning the deactivation of the law, in the designation of "apostle" as "emissary of the Messiah," and above all in his translation of "Jesus Messiah." And if Paul's messianic thought is inescapably Christological, then the Pauline tone of the "entire vocabulary of the theses"[16] must also be Christological. That would entail a theological version of the personality cult entirely at odds with Benjamin's concerns.[17]

Each step of this argument creaks with both the heart-stopping leap of potential insight and the dangers of the thinnest of ropes on which to rely should the leap fail. We need to grant Agamben much leeway to achieve his aim: that Benjamin is quoting when typing in spaced-out fashion, that *s c h w a c h e* does indeed refer to Paul in 2 Cor. 12, that Benjamin has Luther's Bible open before him as he writes the *Theses*, that Christ just means Messiah, and that Benjamin somehow escapes the inescapable Christological nature of Paul's arguments.

IMAGE, NOW-TIME AND RECAPITULATION

Three other purported moments of Pauline quotation also appear in Benjamin's *Theses*—at least in Agamben's eyes. I will spend less time on these, since he uses largely the same approach in each case, albeit with an occasional twist.

16. Ibid., 144.

17. On the crucial role of Christology in the personality cult, see Max Horkheimer and Theodor W. Adorno, *Dialectic of Enlightenment: Philosophical Fragments*, trans. E. Jephcott (Stanford: Stanford University Press, 2002), 206–9, and Roland Boer, *Criticism of Heaven*, 433–35.

1. IMAGE: BILD

a. Benjamin: "The true image [*das wahre Bild*] of the past *f l i t s* by. The past can be seized only as an image that flashes at the moment of its recognisability, and is never seen again … For it is an irretrievable image of the past which threatens to disappear in any present that does not recognize itself as intended in that image."[18]

b. Paul: "Yet death reigned from Adam to Moses, even over those whose sins were not like the transgression of Adam, who was a type of the one who was to come [τύπος τοῦ μέλλοντος]" (Rom. 5:14).

c. Luther: "*welcher ist ein Bilde des der zukunfftig war*" (Agamben's rendition), which translates as "he who was an image of the one who was to come" (Rom. 5:14).

Typos in Paul becomes *Bild* in a text oddly quoted from Luther,[19] from where it then makes its way into Benjamin's text as a mode of relating past and present, indeed of defining messianic time itself. Quite some air has opened up between the Paul-Luther connection and Benjamin's evocation of the (photographic) image, for the connection is by no means obvious.[20] But does Benjamin's hypothetical mode of quotation assist Agamben in this case? No, for the word that is now spaced-out is not "image" but "flit," or "flee" in Agamben's translation of *h u s c h t*. In reply, all Agamben can do is weakly offer – with a couple of tentative "mays"—an allusion to 1 Corinthians 7:31, "For the form of this world is passing away."

18. Benjamin, *1938–1940*, 390–91.

19. The 1545 and 1912 Luther Bibles read '*welcher ist ein Bild des, der zukünftig war.*' I am not entirely sure which "Luther Bible" Benjamin is supposed to have in front of him as he writes the *Theses*. Agamben may be citing the German Luther himself wrote, before standardized spelling, but this is nowhere spelled out by Agamben.

20. Agamben feels called on to assert that Benjamin's fascination with flash photography actually encompasses all art, texts, records and documents. Further, conscious of the large leap to Paul, he suggests that Benjamin's meaning is better conveyed by this text from *The Arcades Project*: "It is not that what is past is casts its light on what is present, or what is present its light on what is past; rather, image is that wherein what has been comes together in a flash with the now to form a constellation. For while the relation of the present to the past is purely temporal (continuous) the relation of what-has-been to the now is dialectical, in leaps and bounds" (Benjamin, *The Arcades Project*, 463).

2. NOW-TIME: JETZTZEIT

a. Benjamin: "History is the subject of a construction whose site is not homogenous, empty time, but time filled full by now-time [*Jetztzeit*]."[21]

b. Paul: ὁ νῦν καιρός; no text of Paul is quoted here, although this phrase is for Agamben a constellation of both Pauline and pseudo-Pauline texts, such as 1 Cor. 7:1, Gal. 6:10, Eph. 5:16 and Col. 4:5.[22]

Luther does not assist us now, nor does a printed text, so Agamben must rely on one hand-written manuscript, in which *Jetztzeit* is encased on its first appearance in quotation marks. Is that enough to secure its derivation from Paul? For Agamben it is, but now a curious twist emerges in his argument: the phrase ὁ νῦν καιρός, "the now-time," does not actually appear anywhere in Paul's texts. Instead, it is a back-translation of *Jetztzeit* into Greek. A very Benjamin-looking Paul, perpetual cigarette in hand, with disheveled hair and crumpled clothes and that slightly vacant stare of the regular dope-head, now appears unheralded in Agamben's text. Or to change the image, the relation between puppet and dwarf has been exchanged, for now Paul is the puppet and Benjamin the hunchback theologian. Agamben would have *liked* Paul to have written ὁ νῦν καιρός, but Paul did not.

3. RECAPITULATION: ZUSAMMENFASSEN

a. Benjamin: "Now-time, which, as a model of messianic time, comprises the entire history of mankind in a tremendous abbreviation, coincides exactly with the figure which the history of mankind describes in the universe."[23]

b. Pseudo-Paul: "A span for the fullness of time [καιρός], to unite [ἀνακεφαλαιώσασθαι] all things in Christ, things in heaven and on earth in him" (Eph 1:10).

c. Luther: "*alle ding zusamen verfasset würde in Christo*," that is, "all things are gathered together in Christ."

d. Agamben: "All things are recapitulated in the Messiah."[24]

---

21. Benjamin, *1938–1940*, 395.

22. See Agamben, *Time that Remains*, 68–70.

23. Benjamin, *1938–1940*, 396.

24. Agamben, *Time that Remains*, 143.

The less "evidence" Agamben has, the more certain he seems to become. Here we have no signal of surreptitious quotation, the text comes from a recognized pseudo-Pauline letter, and the citation of the German is again somewhat curious.[25] A word on pseudo-Paul: almost all Pauline criticism operates with two unquestioned assumptions: at least some of the letters are the *ipsissima verba* of Paul himself, and this slight collection of writings provides an insight into the whole of Paul's thought, much like a drop of water can reflect the sun. Agamben's usage of pseudo-Pauline letters, assuming that they give us an insight into Paul himself, may on the hand be criticized for being an uncritical slip, thereby speaking of the "church's Paul" or perhaps the "conservative Paul" of all the letters attributed to the man. On the other hand, it may also be read as an unwittingly highlighting of the assumptions of authenticity and universality that afflict Pauline scholarship.

To resume: Agamben claims that all of the above "proves" a deep dependency of Benjamin on Paul's letters, that the *Theses* are saturated with a Pauline conceptual framework. So certain is this conclusion from the preceding solid argumentation that Agamben can simply state that Paul's ἀπολύτρωσις, redemption, is thoroughly central—via Luther of course—to *Erlösung* in Benjamin's notion of historical knowledge.

WHIFFS OF EXTERNAL EVIDENCE

But we need not take Agamben word for these connections, for no less than Jacob Taubes and Gershom Scholem support such readings. Or do they? First, Taubes suggests that Rom. 8:19-23 may have influenced Benjamin's brief "Theological-Political Fragment."[26] Not quite the *Theses* and nothing more than a suggested correspondence, so much so that Agamben stresses he differences between the texts of Paul and Benjamin. Yet Taubes' "intuition is certainly on the mark,"[27] even if his actual example misses that mark.

Perhaps Scholem is more helpful … but only if one accepts the most secret of handshakes in the darkest of alleys. As though to clinch his argument, Agamben suggests Scholem gives an occult signal of his troubled knowledge

---

25. Once again, the 1545 and 1912 Luther Bibles read *"alle Dinge zusammengefaßt würden in Christo."* My copy of the 1984 version has *"daß alles zusammengefaßt würde in Christo."*

26. Walter Benjamin, *Reflections: Essays, Aphorisms, Autobiographical Writings*, trans. E. Jephcott (New York: Schocken, 1978), 312–13, and Jacob Taubes, *The Political Theology of Paul*, trans. D. Hollander (Stanford: Stanford University Press, 2004), 70.

27. Agamben, *Time that Remains*, 141.

of Benjamin's dependence on Paul. It comes in a long essay interpreting the role of the angel in Walter Benjamin's thought, in which Scholem argues that the fragment "Agesilaus Santander"[28] is actually autobiographical,[29] and that the title is an anagram—with a superfluous "i"—of *der Angelus Satanas*.[30] Having produced an argument that would have made Agamben jealous for its occult nature, Scholem goes on to suggest possible biblical allusions: Midrash Rabba for Exodus 20 and 2 Cor. 12:7 with its *angelos santanas* (Scholem adds the "s"). Agamben notes the singularity and fleeting nature of the reference, but nevertheless concludes both that the *angelos santana* is also the "thorn in the flesh" (acquired on Paul's journey into the heavens a few verses before perhaps) of the same verse and that Scholem is "implying an identification with Paul on the part of Benjamin."[31] Scholem is doing no such thing; even if we grant all of Scholem's extraordinary argument, he merely suggests a possible biblical connection that may be more Scholem than Benjamin—not a dependence or identification.

CONCLUSION

Agamben closes his argument by deploying a Benjaminian hermeneutic to justify the reading he has undertaken: instead of the assumption that works are infinitely interpretable at any given moment, he suggests each work has a historical index that locates it within a particular time and place, but then that same index also fires it off on a trajectory that will only land and come to fulfillment at another, very specific moment. This is *das Jetzt der Lesbarkeit*, the "now of legibility." Has Paul's prophetic text then realized itself in Benjamin's text, or have they both come to such a messianic moment in Agamben's own text? He claims that they may well have done so: "Whatever the case may be, there is no reason to doubt that these two fundamental messianic texts of our tradition, separated by almost two thousand years, both written in a situation of radical crisis, form a constellation whose time of legibility has finally come today."[32] And I had always assumed that messiah would be marked by the vehement denial of being such.

28. Walter Benjamin, *Selected Writings*, vol. 2, *1927–1934*, trans. R. Livingstone, ed. M. Jennings, H. Eiland and G. Smith (Cambridge, MA: The Belknap Press of Harvard University Press, 1999), 712–16 .

29. There are actually two such fragments.

30. Gershom Scholem, *On Walter Benjamin: Critical Essays and Reflections*, ed G. Smith (Cambridge, MA: MIT Press, 1991), 51–89, here 68.

31. Agamben, *Time that Remains*, 145.

32. Ibid.

Nonetheless, that claim raises one final question: do these hints in Benjamin's *Theses* provide a threshold into the world of Paul? Or do both Paul and Benjamin freely pass back and forth through the threshold, sharing ideas, assumptions, textual references? Threshold is of course the title of this section (as also "*Tornada*," a final stanza that wraps up and disperses in a rhyming poem), alluding to Benjamin's love of thresholds in *The Arcades Project*—whether entrances to arcade, skating rink, pub or tennis court,[33] or the various entries into the "underworld" of the Metro, where we find sewer gods, catacomb fairies, labyrinthine passages with "a dozen blind raging bulls."[34] Bewildering, labyrinthine and occult the argument indeed is in these closing pages.

But I would like to shift the metaphor back to two that have appeared earlier in this discussion: the window and puppet. In the gaps of the spaced-out words do we really find Paul? Are Benjamin's texts a window to Paul, a window that provides new light on Benjamin's confused arguments? Or is that window frosted, diffracting and spreading light so that we can see only a dim silhouette? Or perhaps stained and colored, so that Paul becomes both iconic and strangely hued? Or it is really a mirror, in which Benjamin merely sees himself? Or perhaps it is both, a window-cum-mirror: Agamben looks through a window in which he sees Benjamin peering through a second window to Paul, but to Agamben's dismay, Benjamin is merely peering into a mirror. Little may Agamben realize, but the window into which he looks is also a mirror.

Finally, the much-abused hunchback dwarf and puppet: in my critique of the suggestion that *Jetztzeit* is drawn from the non-existent Pauline phrase ὁ νῦν καιρός, I pointed out that we no longer have Benjamin as the puppet and Paul as the miniature theologian, for now the roles have been reversed: Benjamin has become the dwarf and Paul the puppet. True enough, but with one caveat: Agamben is the one pulling the strings for both.

Or is he merely having us on?

33. *The Arcades Project*, 88–89.
34. Ibid., 85.

4

Jacob Taubes—Paulinist, Messianist

Larry L. Welborn

Jacob Taubes—The Enigma

In an editorial note at the end of *The Political Theology of Paul*, Aleida Assmann relates one of the many Taubes stories that circulated among his students and friends: "In June 1986, Taubes brought a prescription to a pharmacy at the Roseneck in Berlin. The pharmacist deciphered the name and asked, to make sure: 'Is your name Paulus?' Upon which Taubes answered, 'Actually, yes, but on the prescription it says Taubes'."[1] That Taubes' identification with Paul was more than light-hearted is demonstrated by explicit statements in the transcript of his lectures, such as: "Now I of course am a Paulinist, not a Christian, but a Paulinist."[2] What this identification meant to Taubes, and how his identity as a Paulinist related to the other identities that Taubes claimed as a Jew and a philosopher,[3] grants entrée not only to what Taubes said about Paul in his lectures of 1987, but also to what Taubes did not say, yet toward which he gestured, with his concluding exhortation to the theologians: "So: Begin anew to interpret Paul!"[4]

The ambiguities of Taubes' identity have been a cause of ire for his interpreters, both with respect to his politics and his theology. Mark Lilla chafes at the fact that "in New York in the late Forties he taught Talmud to some future neoconservatives," while "in Berlin you will find a photo of him addressing a demonstration of Sixties radicals while Rudi Dutschke and Herbert Marcuse sit admiringly at his side."[5] Christoph Schmidt (of the Hebrew

---

1. "Editorial Note" to Jacob Taubes, *The Political Theology of Paul*, ed. Aleida Assmann with Jan Assmann, in conjunction with Horst Folkers, Wolf-Daniel Hartwich, and Christoph Schulte, trans Dana Hollander (Stanford: Stanford University Press, 2004), 143.

2. Ibid., 88.

3. Ibid., 4: "Why Paul concerns me as a Jew, . . . why Paul concerns me as a philosopher."

4. Ibid., 95.

University of Jerusalem) describes Taubes' book on Paul as "the quintessence of his constant vacillation between Jewish and Christian traditions."[6] Schmidt seeks to expose Taubes' dependence upon "the modern Catholic 'church fathers' of the twentieth century," asserting that Taubes' 1947 doctoral thesis on the eschatology of the West[7] "owes far more than is fitting to the Jesuit Hans Urs von Balthasar's *Apocalypse of the German Soul*,"[8] and that his presentation of Paul's political theology "evidences more than just a deep affinity with the reconstruction of Paul's Epistle to the Romans by the 1929 convert to Catholicism Erik Peterson."[9] With unconcealed animosity, Schmidt observes that, fortunately, neither Taubes' Jewish nor his Protestant readers were aware of his dependence upon these Catholic authors,[10] and so took for a "genius" one who was really a "charlatan."[11] Evidently, Taubes, too, found the no-man's land of his identity a site of combustion: Aleida Assmann quotes a letter in which Taubes writes about his "uneasy Ahasueric lifestyle at the borderline between Jewish and Christian, at which things get so hot that one can only (get) burn(ed)."[12]

Twenty years after the publication of Taubes' Heidelberg seminar,[13] there are useful summaries of Taubes' interpretation of Paul by scholars of the New Testament and Judaism (Alain Gignac, Angela Standhartinger, Elizabeth Castelli, Daniel Langton),[14] alongside the indispensable "Afterword" to Taubes' lectures by Wolf-Daniel Hartwich, Aleida Assmann, and Jan Assmann.[15] More

5. Mark Lilla, "A New, Political Saint Paul?," *The New York Review of Books* (October 23, 2008): 4.

6. Christoph Schmidt, "Review Essay of Jacob Taubes' *The Political Theology of Paul*," *Hebraic Political Studies* 2 (2007): 238.

7. Jacob Taubes, *Abendländische Eschatologie* (Bern: A Francke, 1947).

8. Schmidt, "Review Essay," 239, referencing Hans Urs von Balthasar, *Apokalypse der deutschen Seele: Studien zu einer Lehre von letzten Haltungen* (Salzburg: Anton Pustet, 1937–1939).

9. Ibid., referencing Erik Peterson, *Der Brief an die Römer* (Würzburg: Echter, 1997).

10. Schmidt, "Review Essay," 239–40.

11. Ibid., 241.

12. "Editorial Note" to Taubes, *Political Theology of Paul*, 143. If Assmann is responsible for the parenthetical additions to the sentence that she quotes, then the locus of combustion may have been *within Taubes himself*, rather than in friction between Taubes and his environment.

13. Originally published in German as Jacob Taubes, *Die Politische Theologie des Paulus* (München: Wilhelm Fink Verlag, 1993).

14. Alain Gignac, "Taubes, Badiou, Agamben: Reception of Paul by Non-Christian Philosophers," in *Reading Romans with Contemporary Philosophers and Theologians,* ed. David Odell-Scott (London: T & T Clark, 2007), 155–211; Angela Standhartinger, "Paulus als politischer Denker der Gegenwart: Die Pauluslektüre von Jacob Taubes, Alain Badiou und Giorgio Agamben aus neutestamentlicher Sicht," in *Politische Horizonte des Neuen Testaments*, ed. Eckart Reinmuth (Darmstadt: Wissenschaftliche Buchgesellschaft, 2010), 68–91; Elizabeth A. Castelli, "The Philosophers' Paul in the Frame of the Global:

importantly, Taubes' understanding of Paul has had an impact upon historians of religion such as Daniel Boyarin,[16] and philosophers such as Alain Badiou and Giorgio Agamben.[17] Indeed, Agamben's commentary on Paul's letter to the Romans bears the dedication: "Jacob Taubes *in memoriam*."[18] Agamben asserts that the publication of Taubes' *Political Theology of Paul* "marks an important turning point" in the project of reclaiming Paul as the fundamental messianic thinker in the Western tradition.[19] Thus, the time for introductions to Taubes' thought and overviews of his argument has long passed, and what is called for at the present moment is an assessment of the implications of Taubes' interpretation of Paul and an hypothesis regarding its origin and aims, focused, as indicated above, on the question of Taubes' identity and, more importantly, on the identity of that future community of "Paulinists" whom Taubes sought to summon through his lectures.

TAUBES' THESIS: PAUL, THE FOUNDER OF THE NEW PEOPLE OF GOD

The central thesis of Taubes' interpretation of Romans is that "For Paul, the task at hand is the *establishment and legitimation of a new people of God*."[20] Paul's undertaking is thus an historic instance of what the German constitutional theorist Carl Schmitt called "political theology" with the special meaning which Schmitt gave to that term.[21] In Schmitt, "political theology" discloses the ultimate basis of every constitutional order in a decision made by a "sovereign," a revolutionary act that can be glimpsed whenever the legal order breaks down in a "state of emergency."[22] Taubes attributes to Paul a keen awareness of the

Some Reflections," in *South Atlantic Quarterly* 109 (2010): 653–60; Daniel R. Langton, *The Apostle Paul in the Jewish Imagination* (Cambridge: Cambridge University Press, 2010), 250–64.

15. Taubes, *Political Theology of Paul*, 115–42.

16. Daniel Boyarin, *A Radical Jew: Paul and the Politics of Identity* (Berkeley: University of California Press, 1997).

17. Alain Badiou, *Saint Paul: The Foundation of Universalism* (Stanford: Stanford University Press, 2003), originally published as *Saint Paul: La Foundation de l'universalisme* (Paris: Presses Universitaires de France, 1997); Giorgio Agamben, *The Time That Remains: A Commentary on the Letter to the Romans* (Stanford: Stanford University Press, 2005), originally published as *Il tempo che resta. Un comment alla Lettera ai Romani* (Bollati Boringhieri, 2000). See also Slavoj Žižek, *The Puppet and the Dwarf: The Perverse Core of Christianity* (Cambridge, MA: MIT Press, 2003).

18. Agamben, *The Time That Remains*, 3.

19. Ibid., 1–3.

20. Taubes, *Political Theology of Paul*, 28; original emphasis.

21. Carl Schmitt, *Political Theology: Four Chapters on the Concept of Sovereignty*, trans. George D. Schwab (Cambridge, MA: MIT Press, 1985); originally published as *Politische Theologie. Vier Kapitel zur Lehre von der Souveränität* (1922).

arrival of a "state of emergency" for the Jewish people: "The basis of such an idea is that the *orgē theou*, God's anger, wants to annihilate the people because it has sinned."[23] Hence Paul's "great sorrow" and "unceasing anguish in heart" over his "kinspeople according to the flesh" (Rom. 9:2-3). In the face of this existential danger, Paul's Epistle to the Romans announces the sovereign decision of God to establish and legitimate a new people which includes Gentiles along with Jews.[24] The catalyst for this new congregation is the paradoxical faith in a Messiah "who was nailed to the cross by *nomos*."[25] The νόμος that condemned and crucified the Messiah was not the Torah of Moses, however, but the legal order of the *Imperium Romanum*.[26] Thus, Paul's antinomian gospel, encapsulated in the formula "you are not under law but under grace" (Rom. 6:14), is to be understood as "a political declaration of war on the Caesar,"[27] whose world-wide hegemony threatens the existence of Israel.

In an extended piece of Talmudic exegesis, Taubes compares Paul's announcement of God's sovereign decision to constitute a new people through faith in the Messiah with God's delivery of the Ten Commandments to the Hebrews through Moses on Mount Sinai.[28] The crisis faced by Paul and the Israelites of the first century recapitulates the threat of annihilation experienced by Moses and the wilderness generation who had sinned by worshipping the golden calf, so that God's "wrath waxed hot against them," and God resolved to "destroy them" (Exod. 32:10).[29] Just as Moses "stood up" in the moment of danger and "prayed vigorously and begged for mercy," "taking hold of the Holy One like a man who seizes his fellow by his garment,"[30] so Paul was gripped by a "tremendous fear," not merely at the prospect of "distress or persecution" for "God's elect," but at the possibility of "separation from the love of God."[31] Just as Moses "risked his life for them," praying that God would blot him out of the Book of Life, if He did not show mercy,[32] so Paul pronounced the anathema upon himself, wishing that he were "accursed and cut off from Christ," for the sake of his "kinspeople according to the flesh," should the promises given to

22. Schmitt, *Political Theology*, 5–15.

23. Taubes, *Political Theology of Paul*, 28.

24. Ibid., 38–49.

25. Ibid., 24, 49.

26. Ibid., 23.

27. Ibid., 16.

28. Ibid., 28–32.

29. Ibid., 29.

30. Ibid., citing Berakhot 32a.

31. Ibid., 26–27, citing Rom. 8:38—9:2.

32. Ibid., 30, citing Berakhot 32a.

Israel fail.[33] Just as Moses' prayer elicited "pardon" from the Holy One,[34] so Paul "speaks of nothing other than atonement."[35] And just as God instructed Moses, "Carve two tablets of stone" (Exodus 34) as the constitution of a new people,[36] so Paul depicts the form of life of the new congregation under a single, radical law of love (Rom. 13:8-10).[37]

Taubes suggests that the ground of his Moses-Paul typology is not merely situational, but emerges from a deep experience in which every Jew shares, because it has been ritualized in the Day of Atonement.[38] By way of a lengthy quotation of Franz Rosenzweig's *Star of Redemption*,[39] Taubes opens a perspective on the phenomenology of the Jewish soul, by interpreting the communal experience through its liturgy.[40] Thus, on the evening of Yom Kippur, the whole congregation of Israel is "in the grip of trembling."[41] In solemn prayer, the congregation enters into a "state of exception," in the Schmittian sense, publicly renouncing all vows, oaths and pledges, and declaring them null and void.[42] Then, with formulae taken from the Book of Numbers, the congregation is confronted with the threat of destruction.[43] The liturgy continues with a petition, "May all the people of Israel be forgiven,"[44] and climaxes in a thrice-repeated declaration of divine pardon: "The Lord said: 'I pardon them as you have asked'."[45] Only then is the congregation able to arise, like a man rising from the dead, and begin the circuit of a new year under the covenant of divine mercy.[46] The point of this excursus is not only to prove that the author of the Epistle to the Romans was truly Jewish, "more Jewish," Taubes insists, "than any rabbi I ever heard anywhere,"[47] but rather to argue

33. Ibid., citing Rom. 9:3.
34. Ibid., citing Berakhot 32a.
35. Ibid., 32.
36. Ibid., 37.
37. Ibid., 52–53.
38. Ibid., 32, 38.
39. Ibid., 34–37, citing Franz Rosenzweig, *The Star of Redemption*, trans. William W. Hallo (New York: Holt, Rinehart and Winston, 1970), 325–28.
40. Ibid., 34, 38.
41. Ibid., 32.
42. Ibid., 33.
43. Ibid., 34.
44. Ibid.
45. Ibid.
46. Ibid., 34–37.
47. Ibid., 11.

that the comparison with Moses comes from Paul himself,[48] because Paul shares in the quintessentially Jewish experience of atonement.

In the quest for atonement, Taubes asserts that "Paul understands himself as outbidding Moses."[49] By "outbidding," Taubes means that, in establishing and legitimating a new people of God, Paul did something more than Moses did, indeed, something that Moses would not have done: Paul opened the Jews, God's holy people, to the Gentiles.[50] Taubes acknowledges that the identity of this new, transfigured people of God, and the status of the old people, the Jews, "winds up becoming unclear."[51] Yet the means by which the transformation is effected can be determined: it is the πεῦμα that transforms the people.[52] That is, Paul spiritualizes the concept "Israel" by means of a *sensus allegoricus*, which "is not only textual, but a form of life."[53]

THE TAUBES-SCHMITT DIALOGUE

Up to this point in Taubes' exposition of Romans, it would seem that the model for his interpretation of Paul is taken directly from Carl Schmitt, whose theory of sovereignty and the state of exception furnishes the hermeneutical key to Paul's political theology. Commentators on Taubes generally assume that the context and impetus for Taubes' lectures on Paul was his *Auseinandersetzung* with Schmitt,[54] which stretched over forty years,[55] and that it was from Schmitt that Taubes derived the concept "political theology."[56] Taubes certainly encourages this perception: references to Schmitt are sewn throughout his lectures.[57] The autobiographical introduction relates the story of Taubes' meeting with Schmitt at the latter's home in Plettenberg in 1979.[58] As Taubes tells it, he developed for Schmitt, spontaneously, and on the basis of his reading

48. Ibid., 40, 47.

49. Ibid., 39.

50. Ibid., 41.

51. Ibid.

52. Ibid., 43, 45.

53. Ibid., 44, referring to the theory of allegory in Walter Benjamin's *The Origin of German Tragic Drama* (London: New Left Books, 1977).

54. See Standhartinger, "Paulus als politischer Denker," 70.

55. See Appendix A: "The Jacob Taubes-Carl Schmitt Story" in Taubes, *Political Theology of Paul*, 97–105.

56. So, e.g., Wolf-Daniel Hartwich, Aleida Assmann and Jan Assmann in the "Afterword" to Taubes, *Political Theology of Paul*, 138–42.

57. Ibid., 2–3, 7, 31, 40, 51, 64–70, 75, 85, 92, 97–105, 107–13.

58. Ibid., 2–3.

of Romans 9-11, the entire picture of Paul as "the founder of a people" who "outbids Moses."[59] Indeed, Taubes avers that his Heidelberg lectures of 1987 were commissioned by Schmitt, who said: "Taubes, before you die, you must tell some people about this."[60]

Yet, when one comes to the end of Taubes' discussion of Paul and Moses, and encounters the point on which Taubes claims that he "challenged Schmitt,"[61] the content of the revelation is curiously anti-climactic: that Paul included "all Israel" in the salvation of God (Rom. 11:26); that the Israelites are "beloved as regards election, for the sake of their forefathers" (Rom. 11:28); and that "the gifts and calling of God are irrevocable" (Rom. 11:29).[62] Even if the eminent state law theorist confessed, as Taubes reports, "That I did not know!",[63] the notion that Paul proclaimed the salvation of "all Israel," including the Jewish people, whose covenant had never been revoked (Rom. 9:4; 11:29), was already widespread in 1979, owing to the influence of Karl Barth's discussion of the election of the people of God in volume 2.2 of the *Church Dogmatics* of 1942.[64] Barth emphasized the unshakable faithfulness of God's love for and election of Israel, not only in the past and in an eschatological future, but also in the present.[65] Moreover, Krister Stendahl, with whom Taubes had often been in conversation,[66] published in 1976 the text of lectures that he had delivered in various venues since the early 1960s, in which he argued that "the climax of Romans is actually chapters 9-11, i.e., Paul's reflections on the relation between the church and the synagogue, the church and the Jewish people … their coexistence in the mysterious plan of God."[67] Stendahl insisted: "It should be noted that Paul does not say that when the time of God's kingdom, the consummation, comes, Israel will accept Jesus as the Messiah. He says only

---

59. Ibid., 3.

60. Ibid.

61. Ibid., 51.

62. Ibid.

63. Ibid.

64. Karl Barth, *Die kirchliche Dogmatik*, vol. 2.2 (Zürich: Evangelischer Verlag Zollikon, 1942), 332–35. See the discussion in Joseph Sievers, "'God's Gifts and Call Are Irrevocable': The Reception of Romans 11:29 through the Centuries and Christian Jewish Relations" in *Reading Israel in Romans*, ed. Cristina Grenholm and Daniel Patte (Harrisburg: Trinity Press International, 2000), 127–73, esp. 149–55.

65. Barth, *Die kirchliche Dogmatik*, 2.2, 332–35. For the influence of Barth's interpretation of Romans upon Catholic theology, see Philip J. Rosato, "The Influence of Karl Barth on Catholic Theology," *Gregorianum* 67 (1986): 654–78, esp. 661–67. For echoes of Barth's language in the Vatican II declaration *Nostra Aetate*, see Sievers, "God's Gifts and Call Are Irrevocable," 151–55.

66. Taubes, *Political Theology of Paul*, 41.

67. Krister Stendahl, *Paul Among Jews and Gentiles* (Philadelphia: Fortress Press, 1976) 4.

that the time will come when 'all Israel will be saved' (Rom. 11:26)."[68] Thus, the climactic lesson of the Taubes-Schmitt dialogue would seem to contain little to justify the sense of testamentary revelation that pervades the Heidelberg lectures, or to warrant the assertion with which the seminar concludes: "Only now can an interpretation of Paul be begun—on an entirely new level."[69] If Taubes' *Auseinanderstezung* with Schmitt did not supply the basis for the new interpretation of Paul to which Taubes summoned the theologians, then what did?

BENJAMIN'S "THEOLOGICO-POLITICAL FRAGMENT" AS TAUBES' SUBTEXT

In what follows, we shall endeavor to develop an alternative hypothesis regarding the origin and aim of Taubes' interpretation of Paul, and in consequence, a new understanding of the principle of identity of that transfigured people of God which Paul sought to establish and legitimate, an identity which, for Taubes, still defines the possibility of a redeemed humanity in the future. We will attempt to demonstrate that the document which fueled Taubes' interpretation of Paul was not Schmitt's *Political Theology*, but another essay of the Weimar period bearing a similar title, an essay which happens to be the only text cited and expounded by Taubes in its entirety—Walter Benjamin's "Theologico-Political Fragment."[70]

As is well known, Walter Benjamin was the close friend and constant correspondent of Taubes' teacher, Gershom Scholem,[71] whose *Major Trends in Jewish Mysticism* was dedicated, as Taubes reminded the theologians,[72] "To the memory of Walter Benjamin, the friend of a lifetime."[73] It is to the eighth chapter of Scholem's study of Jewish mysticism, the chapter on Sabbatianism, that Taubes turned for the clue to "the inner logic of the messianic" at work

68. Stendahl, *Paul Among Jews and Gentiles*, 4. Note also the publication in 1983 of the thorough treatment of the subject of Paul and Judaism by Gerd Lüdemann, *Paulus und das Judentum* (München: Kaiser Verlag, 1983).

69. Taubes, *Political Theology of Paul*, 94.

70. The English translation of the essay appears in Walter Benjamin, *Reflections: Essays, Aphorisms, Autobiographical Writings*, ed. Peter Demetz, trans. Edmund Jephcott (New York: Harcourt Brace Jovanovich, 1978), 312–13; the German original is in Walter Benjamin, *Illuminationen: Ausgewählte Schriften* (Frankfurt: Suhrkamp, 1977). Taubes argues that Benjamin's fragmentary essay "dates from around 1921" (*Political Theology of Paul*, 70).

71. Gershom Scholem, *Walter Benjamin: Die Geschichte einer Freundschaft* (Frankfurt: Suhrkamp, 1975).

72. Taubes, *Political Theology of Paul*, 7.

73. Gershom Scholem, *Major Trends in Jewish Mysticism* (Jerusalem: Schocken, 1941).

in Paul's notion of "faith."[74] As Taubes presents it, following Scholem, the seventeenth-century messianic movement known as Sabbatianism was a response to an "external catastrophe" for the Jewish community, namely, the trauma of the Jews' expulsion from Spain.[75] The Jews who passed through this misfortune did so by "reinterpreting" their suffering as an "inner experience of redemption."[76] The crisis demanded "a faith that is paradoxical": a "messianic concentration" of the soul, in "contradiction of the evidence."[77] Thus, Sabbatai Zvi, who according to Scholem was manic-depressive, experienced himself as the Messiah in the euphoric-exalted phase of his illness, while he committed "strange (or paradoxical) acts" against the law in the melancholic-depressed humor.[78] The paradoxical faith required of Sabbatai Zvi's followers was intensified when the latter-day Messiah did the unthinkable, and converted to Islam.[79] Yet, even after Sabbatai Zvi's apostasy, his prophet Nathan of Gaza continued to assert, paradoxically, that his followers might be saved by "pure faith" in the Messiah, citing like Paul the *sola fide* principle of Habakkuk 2:4—"He whose soul is justified by faith shall live."[80] Taubes had little difficulty in drawing out the parallels between Paul's faith in "a son of David hanging on the cross" and Nathan of Gaza's faith in a Messiah who had "descended into the abysses of impurity."[81] In both cases, the soteriological principle at work was a "messianic concentration on the paradoxical."[82]

The language in which Taubes describes "the inner logic of the messianic" in Sabbatianism and Paulinism clearly reflects the influence of Walter Benjamin's essay of 1921.[83] For example, contrasting the inner intensity of the Messianic with the principle of happiness in the order of the profane, Benjamin had written that "the immediate Messianic intensity of the heart, of the inner individual human being, passes through misfortune, as suffering."[84]

---

74. Taubes, *Political Theology of Paul*, 7–11, referencing Scholem, *Major Trends in Jewish Mysticism*, 286–324.

75. Taubes, *Political Theology of Paul*, 9.

76. Ibid.

77. Ibid., 10.

78. Gershom Scholem, *Sabbatai Sevi: The Mystical Messiah, 1626–1676*, trans. R. J. Zwi Werblowsky (Princeton: Princeton University Press, 1973), 128.

79. Scholem, *Sabbatai Sevi*, 282; Taubes, *Political Theology of Paul*, 8–9.

80. Scholem, *Sabbatai Sevi*, 284.

81. Taubes, *Political Theology of Paul*, 9–10.

82. Ibid., 10.

83. To some degree, this is also true of Scholem's account of Sabbatianism, reflecting the intensity of his conversations with Benjamin on the messianic idea in the 1920s.

84. Benjamin, "Theologico-Political Fragment" in *Reflections*, 313.

Our inference regarding the impact of Benjamin's concept of the Messianic upon Taubes is confirmed, when Taubes turns in part II of his seminar ("Effects. Paul and Modernity: Transfigurations of the Messianic") to comment on Benjamin's essay.[85] Thus, Taubes insists: "Romans 8 has its closest parallel in a text that is separated from it by nearly nineteen hundred years, Walter Benjamin's 'Theologico-Political Fragment'.[86] Specifically, Taubes sees Benjamin as the truest exegete of Paul's account of the "subjection of the creation to futility," so that the "whole creation has been groaning in labor pains until now … waiting for redemption" (Rom. 8:20-23).[87] In an "astonishing parallel" to the Pauline notion of the futility and labor pains of creation,[88] Benjamin speaks of "worldly existence" as leading to an "eternity of downfall, transitory in its totality," and related to the Messianic only "by reason of its eternal and total passing away."[89] Taubes also sees a close parallel between Paul's attitude toward the Roman Empire as expressed in Romans 13 and Benjamin's understanding of the task of world politics, whose method Benjamin identified as "nihilism."[90] As the ground of these astonishing parallels, Taubes posited a shared traumatic experience: "This is said out of the same experience, and there are hints in the text that confirm this. These are experiences that shake Paul through and through and that shake Benjamin through and through."[91] In detecting the influence of Paul upon Benjamin, Taubes was the forerunner of Giorgio Agamben, who eventually discovered, and documented, by consultation of the *Handexemplar* of the "Theses on the Philosophy of History," several hidden, and not so hidden, Pauline citations in Benjamin's final statement of his messianic conception of history.[92]

BENJAMIN ON THE MESSIANIC AND THE MUNDANE

The aim of Walter Benjamin's "Theologico-Political Fragment" is to define the relationship of the Messianic Kingdom to the order of the profane. Thus,

85. Taubes, *Political Theology of Paul*, 70–76.

86. Ibid., 70.

87. Ibid., 72–74.

88. Ibid., 72.

89. Benjamin, "Theologico-Political Fragment," 312–13; cited by Taubes, *Political Theology of Paul*, 72.

90. Taubes, *Political Theology of Paul*, 72, citing Benjamin, "Theologico-Political Fragment" in *Reflections*, 313.

91. Ibid., 74.

92. Agamben, *Time That Remains*, 138–45, referencing Taubes as a predecessor in this insight.

like Schmitt, Benjamin is concerned with the relation of divine sovereignty to institutional politics. But, in contradistinction from Schmitt, Benjamin insists that the Messiah does not come to establish a new constitutional order, but to "redeem" and "complete" history: "the Messiah consummates all history."[93] Thus, "the Kingdom of God is not the *telos* of the historical dynamic ... but the end."[94] For this reason, ("theocracy has no political, but only a religious meaning."[95]) "The order of the profane," Benjamin argues, is not created by the decision of a god-like sovereign, but arises naturally out of the human pursuit of "happiness.[96] By "happiness," Benjamin understands the this-worldly experience of good fortune, which is "transient in its totality," and so attains its goal only in "downfall ... by virtue of its eternal and total passing away."[97]

Should we conclude, therefore, that Benjamin strictly distinguished between the spiritual and the political, so that the two orders are related to one another only as limit concepts? In that case, Benjamin's account of the relationship between the Messianic and the profane would hardly seem to qualify as "political theology," whose concept requires the intermingling of the theological and the political. But, in fact, Benjamin *does not* insist upon the separation of the religious and the political, but posits a complex relationship between the two, whose nature is *dialectical*. Employing an allegorical figure, Benjamin pictures the relation between the Messianic and the profane as arrows pointing in opposite directions and augmenting each other through opposing force: "If one arrow points to the goal toward which the profane dynamic acts, and another marks the direction of Messianic intensity, then certainly the quest of free humanity for happiness runs counter to the Messianic direction; but just as a force can, through acting, increase another that is acting in the opposite direction, so the order of the profane assists, through being profane, the coming of the Messianic Kingdom."[98] On this basis, Benjamin is able to conceive of a form of participation in worldly politics by those who strive for the Kingdom of God. The name which Benjamin gives to this dialectical engagement in politics is "nihilism."[99]

---

93. Benjamin, "Theologico-Political Fragment" in *Reflections*, 312.

94. Ibid.

95. Ibid.

96. Ibid.

97. Ibid., 313.

98. Ibid., 312.

99. Ibid., 313.

CORRECTING MISUNDERSTANDINGS OF TAUBES

Recognition of the decisive influence of Benjamin's "Fragment" upon Taubes' conception of Paul's political theology prevents misunderstanding of Taubes' position in two directions: on the one hand, as a "negative" political theology that encourages quietism, and on the other hand, as a "democratic counterpart" to Schmitt's theory of sovereignty that nurtures covenantal theocracy on the ground of Jewish tradition. The former interpretation is offered by Martin Terpstra and Theo de Wit, who argue that Taubes insisted upon "no spiritual investment in the world as it is:" "For Taubes, this is the first and ever-renewing task of political theology: *separating* the spiritual from the secular claims and powers."[100] Accordingly, Taubes did not see any real political potential in messianic thinking.[101] The latter interpretation is put forward by the authors of the "Afterword" to Taubes' lectures, Wolf-Daniel Hartwich, Aleida Assmann and Jan Assmann: "For [Taubes], political theology is first and foremost the doctrine of the formation of a *Ver-Bund* (as he calls it), a union-covenant in the [Jewish] sense of a people of God."[102] According to Hartwich and the Assmanns, this Jewish perspective arose after the destruction of the Kingdom of Judah (in 586 B.C.E.), when the trauma of the loss of political sovereignty was "displaced onto the idea of the Messiah;"[103] "The explosive power of Israel's political theology consists in the fact that here the people replaces the sovereign as the incarnation of divine sovereignty."[104] Hartwich and the Assmanns conclude that "Taubes argues with reference to the Jewish background and takes the political as a question about religious communization and its binding powers."[105]

Misunderstanding of Taubes' conception of political theology is altogether natural, given the elliptical style of communication that resulted from Taubes' awareness "that time was pressing so personally," because of his incurable illness.[106] As Hartwich and the Assmanns observe, even under ordinary circumstances, "Taubes unfortunately did little to adequately secure the preconditions of understanding. His strength lay in speaking always from the absolute interior, that is, concretely, with reference to a certain position and on

---

100. Martin Terpstra and Theo de Wit, "'No Spiritual Investment in the World As It Is': Jacob Taubes' Negative Political Theology" in *Flight of the Gods: Philosophical Perspectives on Negative Theology*, ed. Ilse N. Bulhof and Laurens Ten Kate (New York: Fordham University Press, 2000), 341.

101. Ibid., 342.

102. Taubes, *Political Theology of Paul*, 140–41.

103. Ibid., 141.

104. Ibid., 140.

105. Ibid., 141.

106. Ibid., 1.

the ground of a polemical constellation. Beyond this, he was hardly concerned with marking difference in a generalized discourse."[107] Yet, a reconstruction of the preconditions and interconnections of Taubes' thought is crucial, since upon this depends an understanding of the political theology that Taubes attributes to Paul. Anyone who wishes to sketch the contours of the new interpretation of Paul to which Taubes summoned the theologians must venture to fill in the gaps in Taubes' obscure exposition. Our wager is that Walter Benjamin's dialectical conception of political theology furnishes a surer guide to Taubes' reading of Paul than a negative inference drawn from Taubes' silence, or a speculative reconstruction of the Jewish background of Taubes' position.

THE TASKS OF BENJAMIN'S MESSIANIC HISTORIAN

Because the "Theologico-Political Fragment" is Benjamin's most concentrated text, it is difficult to form an estimation of what kind of acts might have constituted "politics as nihilism." But other documents belonging to the dossier of the Benjamin-Schmitt debate on the concept of political theology provide glimpses of what Benjamin had in mind.[108] In an essay published in 1921 under the title "Zur Kritik der Gewalt,"[109] Benjamin sought to demonstrate the existence of a "power" or "force" (Gewalt) that lies "outside the law," and that is therefore capable of suspending the constant "oscillation of law-making and law-preserving violence" upon which the power of the state depends.[110] Benjamin calls this alternative figure of power "divine violence" or "sovereign violence."[111] Within the human sphere, divine power manifests itself as "pure" or "unalloyed," because it neither makes nor preserves law; it is "immediate" in that it breaks the cycle of violence maintained by ideology and myth; and it is "revolutionary" in that it aims at "the abolition of state power" and thus inaugurates "a new historical epoch."[112]

Benjamin gives two examples of such "pure" or "revolutionary" violence. In retrospect, the examples seem prophetic of events in the latter half of the twentieth century. First, in the arena of the class struggle, Benjamin envisions

107. Ibid., 139–40.

108. On the documents belonging to the Benjamin-Schmitt debate on sovereignty, see Giorgio Agamben, *State of Exception* (Chicago: University of Chicago Press, 2005), 52–64.

109. Walter Benjamin, "Zur Kritik der Gewalt" in *Gesammelte Schriften* I (Frankfurt: Suhrkamp, 1955); translated as "Critique of Violence" in *Reflections*, 277–300.

110. Benjamin, "Critique of Violence" in *Reflections*, 300.

111. Ibid., 297, 298, 300.

112. Ibid., 297, 300.

a "proletarian general strike" that "sets itself the sole task of destroying state power."[113] Such an action is "pure" and "anarchistic," "for it takes place not in readiness to resume work following concessions and this or that modification to working conditions, but in the determination to resume only a wholly transformed work, no longer enforced by the state."[114] Martin Luther King's plan for a "Poor People's Campaign" had such a revolutionary aim, and would have been effected by pure, nonviolent means: he planned to block the bridges of Washington D.C. and occupy the runways of the national airport with a nonviolent army of the poor, until the edifice that produced grinding poverty was dismantled.[115] Benjamin's second example envisions a representative of religious tradition who embodies an "educative power, which in its perfected form stands outside the law."[116] Such a religious educator might seek to extend divine power into the political realm by reiterating the divine commandment "Thou shalt not kill," thus seeking to arrest or annihilate the cycle of violence upon which state power depends.[117] Ominously, Benjamin warned that "such an extension of pure or divine power is sure to provoke, particularly today, the most violent reactions,"[118] a fate which befell Archbishop Oscar Romero, when he directed the divine injunction against the military of El Salvador in his final radio broadcast.[119]

In the "Theses on the Philosophy of History," composed by Benjamin a few months before his death, one catches a final glimpse of the kind of action that might spring open the door between the Messianic and the profane. In the second thesis, Benjamin speaks of "a *weak* Messianic power" with which every generation is endowed that is capable of redeeming what has been lost in the past.[120] Giorgio Agamben demonstrated that in this passage Benjamin was alluding to a Pauline text, 2 Cor. 12:9-10, which reveals the paradoxical weakness of Messianic power.[121] But what is crucial here is Benjamin's assertion that the "historical materialist" has knowledge of this secret—both the weight

113. Ibid., 291.

114. Ibid., 291–92.

115. James M. Washington, *A Testament of Hope: The Essential Writings and Speeches of Martin Luther King* (San Francisco: Harper, 1986), 671–72.

116. Benjamin, "Critique of Violence" in *Reflections*, 297.

117. Ibid., 298.

118. Ibid.

119. James R. Brockman, *Romero: A Life* (Maryknoll, NY: Orbis Books, 2005), 241–42. I thank my Fordham colleague Michael Lee for this reference.

120. Walter Benjamin, "Theses on the Philosophy of History" in *Illuminations*, ed. Hannah Arendt, trans. Harry Zohn (Glasgow: William Collins Sons, 1979), 256.

121. Agamben, *Time That Remains*, 139–40.

of the redeemed past and the weak divine power with which he is gifted.[122] That is, Benjamin attributes to a certain kind of scholar, namely, the historian who experiences "the immediate Messianic intensity of the heart," a role in theological politics.

The "Theses" are directed at scholars such as Jacob Taubes, an address which Taubes registers in what he says about "Benjamin's program."[123] Benjamin aims to disenthrall such scholars from an antiquarian approach to the past "wie es eigentlich gewesen ist,"[124] who content themselves with "establishing a causal connection between various moments in history ... telling the sequence of events like the beads of a rosary."[125] Benjamin insists that so long as the past is approached in this way, the historian remains "ensnared" in the nets of worldly power constructed by the rulers and, whether consciously or unconsciously, experiences "empathy with the victors."[126] Against this, Benjamin seeks to mobilize a cadre of revolutionary historians who are no longer content to be the "tool of the ruling classes," and who are determined to "wrest the tradition away from a conformism that seeks to overpower it."[127] Benjamin's messianic historian seeks to redeem the past. He does so by supplying "a unique experience with the past."[128] Thus, he "seizes hold of a memory that flashes up at a moment of danger."[129] That is, he "grasps the constellation" which his own endangered moment in history forms with a definite, previous one.[130] The sudden recognition that "the same threat hangs over both the tradition and its receivers" provides access to the immediate Messianic intensity of the heart that bears the potential for redemption.[131] The messianic historian then "gives that configuration a shock, by which it crystalizes into a monad. . . . In this structure he recognizes the sign of a Messianic cessation of occurrences, or, put differently, a revolutionary chance in the fight for the oppressed past."[132] If one asks, concretely, what the messianic historian does in this moment, the answer can only be that he writes, or lectures (as Taubes did).[133] Yet, Benjamin describes the writing of such a

122. Benjamin, "Theses" in *Illuminations*, 256.
123. Taubes, *Political Theology of Paul*, 83–84.
124. Benjamin, "Theses" in *Illuminations*, 257, referencing Ranke.
125. Ibid., 265.
126. Ibid., 258, 260.
127. Ibid., 257.
128. Ibid., 264.
129. Ibid., 257.
130. Ibid., 265.
131. Ibid., 257.
132. Ibid., 265.

historian in revolutionary and even violent terms. Such history-writing is "a tiger's leap…in the open air of history";[134] to be sure, it is a "dialectical" leap, but "that is how Marx understood the revolution."[135] Benjamin compares his messianic historians with the revolutionaries in the streets of Paris during the July revolution who fired on the clocks in the towers "in order to stop the day."[136] Completing the picture of the historian as revolutionary, Benjamin identifies those on behalf of whom the messianic historian should write as "the struggling, oppressed class," observing that "In Marx, it appears as the last enslaved class, as the avenger that completes the task of liberation in the name of generations of the downtrodden."[137]

TAUBES' NOTION OF "POLITICAL THEOLOGY"

On the hypothesis that Benjamin's messianic conception of history supplies the key to Taubes' interpretation of Paul, we may now venture to fill in some of the gaps in Taubes' exposition and to project the conclusions that Taubes was prevented from drawing by the pressure of time. First, it is clear that Taubes did not attribute political "quietism" to Paul, as Terpstra and de Wit suggest.[138] Taubes concludes his lengthy quotation of Rom. 8:18-29 with the comment, "this is the anti-Caesar," and exhorts his hearers: "Keep in mind: this is written to Rome, where the aura is the cult of the emperors."[139] In his treatment of Romans 13, Taubes insists, following Barth, that Paul's counsel of subjection to worldly authorities be kept in dialectical tension with his exhortation in Romans 12: "Do not be conformed to this world, but be transformed by the renewing of your mind" (Rom. 12:2) and "Do not be overcome by evil, but overcome evil with good" (Rom. 12:21).[140] Taubes states explicitly that he understands Romans 13, like 1 Cor. 7:29-32 with its account of existence in the ὡς μή ("as if not"), as advocating the practice of "nihilism as world politics."[141] Taubes insists: "I contend that this concept of nihilism, as developed by Benjamin, is the guiding thread also of the *hōs mē* in Corinthians and

133. Ibid., 264.

134. Ibid., 263.

135. Ibid.

136. Ibid., 264.

137. Ibid., 262.

138. Terpstra and de Wit, "Jacob Taubes' Negative Political Theology," 341–42.

139. Taubes, *Political Theology of Paul*, 73.

140. Ibid., 52.

141. Ibid., 74.

Romans ... that behind all this there is a profound nihilism at work, that it is at work as world politics, toward the destruction of the Roman Empire."[142] In his discussion of Paul and Nietzsche on the final day of his seminar, Taubes hints at the revolutionary potential of Paul's political nihilism. Taubes observes that the "wisdom of this world," which Paul counters with his "word of the cross ... is only possible on the basis of other people's labor."[143] The Nietzschean wise man, like the Greek wise man of old, "is dependent upon leisure, and leisure means that others must work for him, namely slavery."[144] Reminding his hearers of Aristotle's belief that "many people are slaves by nature (*physei*)," Taubes asserts that the Pauline gospel, "in Christ, there is neither slave nor free" (Gal. 3:28), aims at the abolition of the law of nature, along with the ideology that sustains it.[145]

Second, it is also clear that Taubes did not credit Paul with an attempt to establish theocracy on a democratic basis, in which the people embody divine sovereignty, as Hartwich and the Assmanns advocate.[146] True to Benjamin, Taubes holds that only the Messiah consummates history, and that only a paradoxical faith in the Messiah is redemptive.[147] Taubes denies that Paul's political theology is "democratic."[148] Taubes implies that the presuppositional basis of theocracy, whether of the autocratic or the democratic sort, was destroyed by Paul through his radical reduction of the dual commandment ("You shall love the Lord your God with all your heart, and with all your soul, and with all your might" and "You shall love your neighbor as yourself") to a single command, "Love your neighbor as yourself," in Rom. 13:8-10. Taubes views this Pauline reduction as "an absolutely revolutionary act,"[149] polemically aimed not only at the primordial core of Jewish tradition,[150] but also at Jesus himself, who reiterates the dual commandment (Mark 12:29-31).[151] Taubes evidently regarded his discovery of Paul's reduction of the dual commandment as his most important exegetical insight, since it is discussed in both parts of the seminar,[152] and resurfaces at the conclusion.[153] Taubes' estimation of

142. Ibid., 72.

143. Ibid., 80.

144. Ibid.

145. Ibid., 81.

146. Ibid., 138–42.

147. Ibid., 41, 70.

148. Ibid., 73.

149. Ibid., 53.

150. Deut. 6:4.

151. Taubes, *Political Theology of Paul*, 52–53.

152. Ibid., 52–53, 55–56.

the importance of his contribution on this point has recently been validated by Kenneth Reinhard.[154] Further attention to the implications of the Pauline reduction of the dual commandment will permit us to complete our sketch of Paul's political theology and will return us to the question of the identity of the new people of God called into existence by Paul's Messiah.

By omitting the commandment to "love God" from his summary of obligations incumbent upon those who are "in Christ," Paul deprives theocracy of its foundation, as Taubes understands it. Theocracy is by definition that form of government in which God rules upon earth through an authorized representative. Whether the representative is a king or a people, authorization depends upon the maintenance of a bond with the deity. Thus, the king promulgates the myth of divine descent, while the people enter into a partnership with the deity in the form of a covenant. Paul's omission of the command to love God from his summary of the whole law in Rom. 13:8-10 cannot, as Taubes argued, be accidental, given its centrality in Jewish tradition, but reflects Paul's conviction that this bond has been lifted from the shoulders of the new people of God in consequence of the Messianic event. How this came about Paul indicates in Romans 5: through divine κένωσις. This is Paul's interpretation of the death of the Messiah for the weak, the ungodly, and enemies: "God commends his love toward us in that while we were still sinners Christ died for us" (Rom. 5:8, cf. 5:6-11). For those who have experienced the Messianic "calling" (κλῆσις), there is now only one imperative: to love the neighbor as oneself, that is, to love the nearest embodiment of the ones for whom the Messiah died, following the kenotic movement of divine love. Thus, the divine κένωσις has sublated the first commandment. As Kenneth Reinhard observes, "we should not read love of God as simply missing or excluded from Romans 13, but as *marked* in its absence."[155] In any case, it seems likely that Taubes was aware of the implications of his discovery about the dual commandment: the basis of theocracy has been destroyed, because the throne is empty. Once again, we may posit the influence of Benjamin's "Theologico-Political Fragment" upon Taubes' interpretation of Paul: the source of Taubes' insight into Paul's reduction of the dual commandment is probably Benjamin's dictum: "Theocracy has no political, but only a religious meaning."[156]

153. Ibid., 92.

154. Kenneth Reinhard, "Paul and the Political Theology of the Neighbor," UCLA Center for Jewish Studies, *soundandsignifier.com*, May, 2007, 1–32, esp. 17–19.

155. Reinhard, "Paul and the Political Theology of the Neighbor," 17.

156. Benjamin, "Theologico-Political Fragment" in *Reflections*, 312.

To his credit, Taubes did not shy away from the theological implications of Paul's sublation of the commandment to love God. By way of a series of lengthy citations from Freud's *Moses and Monotheism*, Taubes reprises Freud's version of the history of religion: "Judaism had been a religion of the father; Christianity became a religion of the son. The old God the Father fell back behind Christ; Christ, the Son, took his place."[157] Taubes comments: "This is also a contribution to the problem of the dual commandment and its radicalization in the love command: the focus on the son, on the human being; the father is no longer included."[158] For Taubes, the assertion that God the Father has been dethroned is not an ontological claim, but a religious way of speaking about a psychological development. Paul's sublation of the commandment to "love God with all your heart and soul and might" lifted the burden of guilt imposed by paternal law. As Paul's spiritual "descendent,"[159] "Freud, so to speak, enters into the role of Paul" and tries to realize Paul's theological vision by a new therapeutic method.[160] Reinhard summarizes Taubes' understanding of the relation between Pauline theology and Freudian psychoanalysis: "Freud … continues Paul's work by striving to liberate us from the burden imposed by the obscenely cruel paternal agency that we harbor within ourselves."[161] Taubes attributes momentous importance to the recognition that God the Father has been dethroned. The final text cited in Taubes' lectures is the passage from *Moses and Monotheism* in which Freud calls for "a special enquiry to discover why it has been impossible for the Jews to join in the forward step which was implied by the admission of having murdered God."[162] Immediately following this citation, Taubes exclaims, "Only now can an interpretation of Paul be begun—on an entirely new level."[163]

THE IDENTITY OF THE NEW PEOPLE OF GOD

What was at stake for Taubes, ultimately, in Paul's radical reduction of the dual commandment was the identity of that new people of God which Paul sought to call into existence through his proclamation of the crucified Messiah. So long as the first commandment remains in force, the group of people covenanted to

157. Taubes, *Political Theology of Paul*, 92.
158. Ibid.
159. Ibid., 82.
160. Ibid., 95.
161. Reinhard, "Paul and the Political Theology of the Neighbor," 21.
162. Taubes, *Political Theology of Paul*, 94.
163. Ibid.

"love God with all your might" is defined in its totality by the exclusivity of this love. Taubes cites Freud to the effect that, owing to the Jews' persistence in this exclusive love, after the promulgation of the new Pauline doctrine, "they have become even more sharply divided from other people than before."[164] But if the first commandment has been sublated into the second, then the commandment to love the neighbor implies (a new) and not fully specified, social relationship that calls into question the social bond established on the basis of love of God," as Reinhard accurately observes.[165] Indeed, the language in which Paul enjoins neighbor-love as the only remaining commandment in Rom. 13:8-10 defines the neighbor as a site of *difference*: "For the one who loves the other (τὸν ἕτερον) fulfills the law" (Rom. 13:8). In the paraenesis of Rom. 14:1—15:13, Paul argues that, since the law is now fulfilled by love of neighbor, there is no longer any basis for judging one another in the Messianic community (Rom. 14:13). Paul summarizes the politics of neighbor-love: "Therefore, welcome one another, just as the Messiah welcomed you" (Rom. 15:7).

Thus, "all Israel," whose salvation the Messiah brings (Rom. 11:26), is not conceived by Paul as a totality, that is, as a group closed upon itself. The command to love the neighbor implies that the new people of God is perpetually incomplete, limited only by the mysterious experience of the Messianic κλῆσις (cf. 1 Cor. 1:24, 26-28). The new people of God, as Taubes puts it, is "a subterranean society, a little bit Jewish, a little bit Gentile."[166] In any case, the new people of God is not Christian, in the sense that the word later acquired in the course of history: as Taubes reminds, "the word 'Christian' doesn't yet exist for Paul."[167] One senses that, had Taubes given Paul's new people of God a name, he would have called them "Messianists." As Taubes insists, the faith of this new people is "*the center of a messianic logic*."[168] This was how Taubes experienced his own identity "at the borderline between Jewish and Christian."[169] Taubes welcomed signs that some of his contemporaries were venturing in the direction of this border of identity. Taubes relates, with obvious excitement, a story about Krister Stendahl, professor of New Testament at Harvard and bishop of Stockholm, who once asked him, with deep concern, "whether he belongs to the 'commonwealth of Israel'."[170] Recalling this

164. Ibid.
165. Reinhard, "Paul and the Political Theology of the Neighbor," 24.
166. Taubes, *Political Theology of Paul*, 54.
167. Ibid., 21.
168. Ibid., 7; original emphasis.
169. Ibid., 143.
170. Ibid., 41.

moment, Taubes exclaims: "There I saw what Paul had done: that someone from the jungles of Sweden—as seen from where I'm standing—is worrying about whether he belongs to the 'commonwealth of Israel,' that's something that's impossible without Paul."[171]

TAUBES AS HERALD OF THE COMING COMMUNITY

In conclusion, it seems likely that Taubes saw himself as a herald of this new Messianic identity and his Heidelberg lectures as a call to awakening.[172] Seeking to fulfill the task that Benjamin assigned to the messianic historian, Taubes tried to grasp the constellation which his own moment in the shadows of the Holocaust formed with a previous moment of existential danger for Israel, and to give this configuration a shock. Taubes summoned his hearers to the "now of a particular knowability," as Benjamin wrote in a late note.[173] In this moment of sudden legibility, Taubes calls: "So: Begin anew to interpret Paul!"[174]

fulfill Benjamin

171. Ibid.

172. For Benjamin's treatment of the concept of "awakening" and the task of the historical materialist, see Convolute K "Dream City" in Walter Benjamin, *The Arcades Project*, trans. Howard Eiland and Kevin McLaughlin (Cambridge: Harvard University Press, 1999), 388–92, with the discussion of Samuel Weber, *Benjamin's – abilities* (Cambridge: Harvard University Press, 2008), 164–75.

173. Benjamin, *The Arcades Project*, 463, with the discussion in Agamben, *Time That Remains*, 145.

174. Taubes, *Political Theology of Paul*, 95.

5

Circumcising the Word

Derrida as a Reader of Paul

Hans Ruin

And we hadn't finished,
I haven't finished with Saint Paul.

–JACQUES DERRIDA, VEILS

INTRODUCTION

In the year 1967 three books were published in Paris by three different publishing houses, but by the same author, Jacques Derrida, a French philosopher of Algerian-Jewish descent, who was then in his mid-thirties.[1] One of the books was a critical analysis of the problem of meaning and language in relation to time in the work of Husserl, with the title *Speech and Phenomena*. Another was a collection of essays devoted to a number of different thinkers, notably Hegel, Freud, Foucault, and Levi-Strauss, entitled *Writing and Difference*. The third book also consisted of a few essays, the longest of

---

1. The books were Le Voix et la Phénomène (Paris: PUF, 1967), in English translation by D. B. Allison as *Speech and Phenomena* (Evanston, IL: Northwestern University Press, 1978);"*L'écriture et différence"* (Paris: Seuil, 1967), in English translation by A. Bass as *Writing and Difference* (London: Routledge, 1978/ 2001); *De la grammatologie* (Paris: Minuit, 1967). Translated by G. Spivak as *Of Grammatology* (Baltimore: Johns Hopkins Press, 1976).

which treated Rousseau and the problem of the origin of language, but it was presented under one general heading, as *Grammatology*. Throughout the different themes and writers treated in the books, the texts were united by a common critical approach that consisted in locating and cleverly undermining the different ways in which the analysed texts sought to secure their own theoretical position by reference to an origin, a system, or a stable method. In the place of the full and final signifier, Derrida posited an original "difference", as a "trace" of what had always already taken place. Throughout the analyses the theoretical hubris of structuralism was questioned from the position of a Nietzschean spirit of play and transgression. It was the birth of "post-structuralism," but also of Derrida as a public intellectual with an approach that would henceforth always be associated with his name: *deconstruction.*

In more restricted philosophical circles Derrida had already made a name for himself as a prodigious young critical phenomenologist. Five years earlier he had published a translation of a late text by Husserl, "The Origin of Geometry", accompanied by an almost two hundred page long "preface".[2] The text amounted to a full-scale survey of the whole project of phenomenology, with a critical edge, centred on the impossibility of maintaining and accessing a non-temporal meaning. In retrospect one can detect already in this early book the main premises for the deconstructive critique, not only of Husserl but of philosophy at large. Still, at this stage there was no declaration of an alternative method. It was only following the publication of *Grammatology* and the parallel deconstructive readings in 1967 that it became clear that here was a thinker who had somehow also taken French phenomenology to another level by questioning the very foundations on which its beliefs in a philosophy of meaning and consciousness rested. This was done not in the form of a full rejection of its basic premises, but rather as a radicalization, using the phenomenological analysis of temporality itself to undermine the very possibility of a stable "presence."

What more exactly Derrida had accomplished in these works, and what the method of deconstruction really consisted of—if indeed it was a method—has been a topic of debate ever since. In the decades that followed, Derrida continued to publish in a high pace, travelling the globe and giving lectures and courses. At the end of his life in 2004 he had published more than fifty books and numerous articles and interviews. After his death it has also become clear how much of his work had remained unpublished, and that will eventually surface in posthumous volumes. Books on Derrida and deconstruction started

2. Trans. by J. P. Leavey, as *Edmund Husserl's Origin of Geometry* (Stonybrook: Nicolas Hays, 1978).

appearing already in the mid-seventies, and since then this literature has grown steadily.

Just to summarize this whole discussion of the role and meaning of deconstruction is today a research task in itself. Here my goal is more modest, namely to try to contribute to an understanding of how Derrida and his work can and should be related to the contemporary philosophical interest in St Paul. At first glance task this ambition may appear misplaced, for the simple reason that Derrida never wrote about Paul. Among the many classical philosophical, literary, and theological writers to which he devoted careful deconstructive analyses—to Heidegger, Celan, Freud, Kafka, Joyce, Husserl, Nietzsche, Kant, Hegel, Rousseau, Descartes, Augustine, and Plato, just to mention his most famous interlocutors—he never devoted a single text specifically to the writings of St. Paul. When he refers to Paul—which he does on a few occasions—it is mostly in passing, and often with a critical edge. Yet, in one of his late essays Paul does emerge as the focus of his interest, if only over a few pages, in the context of analysing the multi-layered phenomenon of the "veil". It is here that he states the words recalled in the motto above: *"We hadn't finished, I haven't finished with Saint Paul."*[3] In order to make sense of the constellation Derrida and Paul we have to disentangle carefully the implications of this statement. We have to learn to trace how what we could call the Pauline problem—or indeed the Pauline problems, including the problem of Paul himself and his following —does indeed reverberate throughout Derrida's writings in more ways than first meets the eye.

In order to do this, we need to follow a series of Pauline themes or tropes, how they travel through Derrida's works, and also how they are transformed and refigured in the course of this journey. To these themes belongs that of circumcision, but also of justice and hope, as well as of the very idea of deconstruction as an intellectual strategy. But they also include the question of universalism, cosmopolitanism, and to the relation between Jewish and Greek spirituality, and ultimately the spiritual as such. It is my hope to show that as we perform this (in part experimental) reading of "Paul in Derrida", we can see how Derrida and deconstruction is not only a theory that is potentially "applicable" to Paul and his epistles, but also how the very project of deconstruction can be seen as to some extent part of a Pauline intellectual legacy. The meaning of "not having finished with Paul" then also comprises not just continuing to deal with Paul, but also continuing to critically explore and confront him and his inheritance.

---

3. Jacques Derrida and Hélène Cixous, *Veils*, trans. J. Bennington (Stanford: Stanford University Press, 2001), 77.

The literature on Derrida and Paul is scant, with one significant exception, Theodore Jennings' monograph *Reading Derrida/Thinking Paul*, from 2006.[4] The basic idea of this study is to explore and to show how Derrida's thinking, in particular on justice and cosmopolitanism, can be used as an interpretative background for a contemporary reading of Paul. In a laudable effort to free Paul from what he calls the "confessional/ecclesiastical ghetto of doctrinal interest", Jennings wants to show how Paul's discussion of justice and righteousness, especially in *Romans*, contains a message of immediate relevance for our contemporary political-philosophical situation. By performing such a reading he also wants to liberate Paul from the accusations of being the originator of Christian antisemitism, as suggested by Levinas and others.

Jenning's approach is not based on an argument about any direct textual relation between Paul and Derrida. He has a good summary of most of the different passages in Derrida's work where he explicitly mentions Paul. But these remarks are at the same time said to be mostly "blind alleys."[5] The study is a useful sourcebook for exploring the relation between Paul and Derrida, and its summary of Derrida's way of thinking about justice, cosmopolitanism, and messianism does a favour to Christian theology by opening up new, more liberal and liberating ways of relating to central tenets of the Pauline message. But as an argument about the inner philosophical relation and dialectics between Paul's letters and Derrida's work it does not contribute much. Even though Derrida's references to Paul are scant, they carry more philosophical weight than what is recognized by Jennings. The relation between their writings is more profound, complex and potentially controversial, both for contemporary theology and political philosophy. Ultimately Jennings is too committed to "saving" Paul, as when he refers approvingly to an interview with Derrida from the mid–eighties, where the latter recognizes the "use" that was already then being made among theologians of "deconstruction not against their faith but in service of their faith."[6] My argument here will take a different path, as I will try to show how we can read Derrida as implicitly thinking in the wake of a Pauline legacy, but also how he should be seen as an important contemporary critic of how this legacy is cultivated in the present, not least by some of Paul's more ingenious philosophical readers.

---

4. *Reading Derrida/Thinking Paul* (Stanford: Stanford University Press, 2006). Besides Jenning's book there are a few articles published on this theme, notably Deborah Madden and David Towsey, "Derrida, Faith and St Paul," *Literature and Theology* 16 (2002): 396–400.

5. *Reading Derrida / Thinking Paul*, 10.

6. Ibid., 158. This interview by James Creech, Peggy Kamuf, and Jane Todd was published in *Critical Exchange* 17 (1985): 1–33.

To some extent Derrida's ambiguous relation to Paul can be traced to two of his most important predecessors, Nietzsche and Heidegger. In Nietzsche's *Antichrist* from 1888 we have what is probably the most fiercely anti-Pauline discourse in the history of philosophy. It is a reading that Derrida seems to endorse when he, at one point and in passing, recommends Nietzsche for his "lucidity concerning Paul".[7] If we turn to Heidegger and his early lectures on religion from 1921 we have instead one of the most productive attempts in modern times to read Paul through the lens of a contemporary philosophical sensibility and problematic, a reading that was seminal not least for the work of the German Lutheran theologian Rudolf Bultmann, with whom Heidegger stayed in close personal friendship throughout his life. These lectures were not published until 1994, but when they came out they contributed significantly to the rise of the new philosophical interest in Paul from the mid-nineties onward in continental philosophy. Their effect was greater than what is often recognized, as can be seen, for example, in the book on Paul by Giorgio Agamben. In *The Time that Remains*, Agamben takes several of its themes directly from Heidegger, yet with minimal references to the published lectures.[8]

In view of the great importance of both Nietzsche and Heidegger for Derrida's own philosophical orientation and for his particular form of deconstructive critique of the tradition of metaphysics, and in view of the specific importance that they both attached to Paul, I will begin by briefly summarizing how they approach Paul. Together they delineate a dialectical space within which Derrida's writings can be situated as partly an explicit but mostly an implicit response to Paul. The most noteworthy such response is the very idea of deconstruction itself, which I will argue can be traced directly to the Pauline idea of destruction, but mediated through Heidegger's creative appropriation of Paul as a thinker of time and history.

This analysis will be followed by a brief survey of Derrida's explicit turning toward religious and theological matters in his later writings. After this we shall explore how his mode of critically reading texts can be followed through a sequence of Pauline themes: notably that of circumcision, and also those of universality, justice, and hope. In the end, Derrida's ambiguous relation to the apostle is focused in a discussion of the "veil," a theme that may first appear marginal, but which turns out to capture the core logic of his critical readings. As a conclusion Derrida will have emerged not just as a philosopher whose

7. The essay "Faith and Knowledge" is included in the volume *Religion*, ed. Jacques Derrida and Gianni Vattimo (Stanford: Stanford University Press, 1998).

8. Girogio Agamben, *The Time That Remains. A Commentary on the Letter to the Romans*, trans. P. Dailey (Stanford: Stanford University Press, 2005).

method one can chose to apply or not to apply to Paul, but rather as a reader and a critic whose work has an urgent significance for us as we try to make sense of Paul and his ethical, political, and theological legacy today.

NIETZSCHE AND HEIDEGGER AS PHILOSOPHICAL PREDECESSORS

In the contemporary discussion of the re-emergence of Paul in continental philosophy, Nietzsche is rarely mentioned. There are many reasons for this lacuna, but one is the simple fact that the bluntness of his rejection of Paul is hard to digest for anyone seeking a more nuanced restoration of the apostle in and for the present. Still it is worth recalling here, if not only for the fact that Derrida at least at one point seems to endorse it, as indicated in the quotation above. In *The Anti-Christ*, written during the very last months before his final collapse, Nietzsche stages his most violent confrontation with Christianity at large. Here he depicts Christianity as "the war to the death against the higher type of man." And in a vitriolic summary of its spiritual character, in a style that borders—as in all of the writings from the last years—on a kind a grotesque parody, he writes that: "Christianity has taken the side of everything weak, base, failed, it has made an ideal out of whatever *contradicts* the preservative instincts of a strong life; it has corrupted the reason even the most spiritual natures by teaching people to see the highest values as sinful, as deceptive, as *temptations.*"[9] In the words of the *Genealogy*, Christianity is here staged as the epitome of a *reactive* value-formation.

The general figure behind this nihilistic evaluation, according to Nietzsche, is the *theologian*, who comes in many shapes, also as idealistic philosopher. "I have found traces of it everywhere," he writes, "anyone with theologian blood in his veins will approach things with a warped and deceitful attitude." And the pathos that develops out of this is what is known as "*faith.*"[10] It is on this type of spirituality that he declares his "war." And the ultimate representative of this attitude is—*Paul*. In Nietzsche's account it is Paul who brings the Epicurean and Stoic Enlightenment of the late Antiquity to an end. "What he guessed," Nietzsche writes, "was how you can use the small, sectarian

---

9. *The Anti-Christ*, § 5 in *The Anti-Christ, Ecce Home, Twilight of the Idols, and Other Writings*, trans. and ed. Judith Norman and Aaron Ridley, Texts in German Philosophy (Cambridge: Cambridge University Press, 2005). Parts of the following analysis of Nietzsche and Heidegger as readers of Paul are based on my essay "Faith, Grace, and the Destruction of Tradition: A Hermeneutic-Genealogical Reading of the Pauline Letters," *Journal for Cultural and Religious Theory* 11 (2010): 16–34.

10. *The Anti-Christ*, § 9.

Christian movement outside Judaism to kindle a 'world-fire', how you can use the symbol of 'God on the cross' to take everything lying below, everything filled with secret rebellion, the whole inheritance of anarchist activities in the empire, and unite them into an incredible power."[11] Paul thus comes forth as a cunning thinker and politician, who with the help of a perverted set of values, infiltrates the Roman Empire. In Nietzsche's interpretation, an entire culture of evaluation thus collapses from within as a result of what he literally speaks of as a process of infection and decay. Paul is the instrument of a kind of self-corruption of the ancient world, whereby nihilistic and reactive instincts come into power.

In the *On the Genealogy of Morality*, written a few years earlier, he is more attentive to how the adoption of ascetic values in a situation characterized by suffering and subjection, can also constitute a kind of heightening of life's power over itself, and how the ascetic priest thus also provides a kind of minimal control over life, as the *"rule over the suffering."*[12] Ascetic values—and their doctrines of sin, punishment, chastity, grace, redemption, and eternal life—are here not only looked upon and analysed as a kind of necessary and useful evil, deployed by the priestly cast to maintain their control over a suffering population. Instead Nietzsche here also recognizes the close, intimate, even inextricable bond between philosophy and a certain asceticism of the spirit. Indeed, he writes here, it was only in the *"leading-rein"* of this ideal that philosophy ever learnt to take its first toddler steps on earth."[13] This also explains why philosophers tend to have such difficulties in assessing the ascetic ideal in a non-prejudiced manner. Ascetic ideals are in the end different ways, not simply of degrading and destroying life, but of *maintaining* it. And Christianity is described as "the great treasure house" of ingenious means of consolation.

Philosophers and scientists often like to think of themselves as the opponents of ascetic-religious values, but in their most critical posture, they too betray their deeper commitment to these ideals, precisely in their conscientious intellectuality and in—even for them—inescapable *belief in truth*. Thus Nietzsche can write: "However, the *compulsion* toward it, that unconditional will to truth, is *faith in the ascetic ideal itself*, even if, as an unconscious imperative, make no mistake about it,—it is the faith of a *metaphysical* value, a *value as such of truth* as vouched for and confirmed by the ideal alone."[14] To summarize Nietzsche's

11. Ibid., § 58.

12. *On the Genealogy of Morality*, § III:15, ed. Keith Ansell-Pearson, trans. Carol Diethe, Cambridge Texts in the History of Political Thought (Cambridge: Cambridge University Press, revised edition, 2007).

13. Ibid., § III:9.

account, we can see how it depicts Paul, not only as a typical priestly type, who transforms suffering into triumph through the adoption of ascetic ideals. In this function he constitutes a breeding ground for the asceticism of the spirit cultivated also by philosophy and metaphysics. Through the belief in absolute normative and epistemic truth, the theologian and the philosopher share a common heritage. Nietzsche's critique of Paul is therefore not only directed toward Christianity, but toward philosophy itself in its basic metaphysical orientation toward a transcendent world of absolute truths.

Heidegger shares Nietzsche's suspicion toward metaphysical truth and his criticism of the philosophical tradition carries many echoes of Nietzschean themes. Late in life Heidegger would publish a monumental two-volume work, entitled simply *Nietzsche*, which testifies to the great importance that Nietzsche had for his thinking.[15] Yet, in relation to Paul, Heidegger takes an entirely different route, one more aligned with Kierkegaard and through him back to Luther. For Heidegger, Paul is not the initiator of a doctrine of metaphysical truth. In stark contrast to Nietzsche's reading, he seeks instead in Paul a precursor to the opposite position, a kind of non- or pre-theoretical and rudimentary life philosophy that affirms the finitude and uncertainty of factical existence, and one that in this respect can even serve as a critical correlate to Greek Aristotelian metaphysics. This takes place first and foremost in a lecture course from 1920–21, entitled "The Phenomenology of Religious Life" that was only published posthumously in 1994.[16] In the introductory remarks to the course, Heidegger emphasizes that the phenomenological question of method is not a question of the appropriate methodological system, but of *access*, how to find the way to a "factical" life experience. A phenomenology of religious life, he writes, should not be a theory *about* the religious, conceived of as an *object* of study in the standard mode of a science of religion, but rather as *a way of entering in understanding* the religious as a form of meaning-fulfilment or *enactment*.

The course is partly centred on an interpretation of the letters to the Galatians and the Thessalonians. Heidegger seeks to retrieve an understanding not only of what he described as a supposedly "original" articulation of Christian life experience, but also of human facticity as such. Thereby he integrates his reading of Paul into the core of his so-called "analytic of facticity",

14. Ibid., § III:24.

15. Published in 1961 in Germany as *Nietzsche I-II* (Pfullingen: Neske), and in English as *Nietzsche*, trans. David Farrell Krell (San Fransisco: Harper & Row, 1979–87).

16. Martin Heidegger *Gesamtaugabe*, vol. 60, *Phänomenologie des religiösen Lebens* (Klostermann: Frankfurt am Main, 1995). Translated by M. Fritsch as *Phenomenology of Religious Life* (Bloomington: Indiana University Press, 2004).

his theory of human existence, which was then in the making. At the focus of his interest in Paul is a peculiar mode of temporality and historicity that he sees articulated in the letters, a kind of open and indeterminate conception of time, a time somehow outside ordinary chronology. It is from within this existential *situation* that Paul supposedly speaks to his congregation in the making. It is a discourse animated by a heightened sense of risk, a life without certainty, and in relation to which it is even more important to open oneself to hope, wakefulness, resolve, etc. In this way Heidegger tries to work himself towards a basic existential *meaning* of the Pauline discourse, as characterized by a temporal horizon of the coming of Christ, of the παρουσία not primarily understood in the context of a theological-metaphysical dogma, but as an open horizon of lived meaning.

Heidegger's reading of the letters could be described as a secular-philosophical "de-mythologizing" interpretation, as later developed by Rudolf Bultmann, partly in direct inspiration from Heidegger. But it is not only interesting as an early attempt to read Paul as an existential thinker. It is also decisive for the development of Heidegger's own philosophical itinerary. His reading of Paul is part of a larger reorientation that also includes extensive studies of Luther and Kierkegaard. At the heart of this philosophical interpretation of Christian-Lutheran theology is the peculiar temporal-historical sense of *living in a disjointed time*, a time of wakefulness and resolve. It is a *kairological* time, from the Greek καιρός, to which Paul also refers as "the decisive moment," which in both Kierkegaard and Heidegger is rendered as "the moment of vision", the *Augenblick*.[17] In response to such an historical predicament one can no longer simply rely on one's tradition, for this tradition has come to an end, partly through a kind of inner self-corruption and self-forgetfulness. Thus it is necessary to dismantle its claim on us in the present and reopen the question of its possibly more original levels of meaning. This experience of a cut or cesura in the very fabric of history and tradition can be clearly sensed in Paul's own discourse, where we read repeatedly that the law in its old form has come to an end, and that it is now time to live in and through the spirit.

Heidegger's radical appropriation of the epistles merges at this point with his own sense of how the tradition of philosophy has reached an impasse, and that there is a need of a "destruction" of the very legacy of Western metaphysics. This transformation of his historical-hermeneutical thinking takes place during

---

17. For a more extensive analysis of this concept, its historical context, and also its role in Heidegger's existential hermeneutics, see chapter 8 in my *Enigmatic Origins* (Stockholm: Almqvist and Wiksell, 1994).

the same time as he approaches Lutheran theology and through it Paul. It is now that he also begins to elaborate a new form of critical approach to history, that would later be fully expounded in the opening sections of his magnum opus *Being and Time*, where it is stated that in order to clear access to the question of being, we must practice a destruction of the history of ontology.[18] There are multiple motives behind this drastic imagery. But it is Paul who first states that in relation to the previous tradition it must be "destroyed," or as he literally says in 2 Cor. 10:4: "I destroy buildings of thought"—λογισμοὺς καθαιροῦντες, in the Latin translation *concilia destruentes*.[19] This sense of a crisis in tradition, and the necessity of somehow starting anew, also motivates the program of "destruction" in Heidegger thinking. And it leads to a deepened sense of urgency in the interpretation and cultivation of tradition that he also expresses and practices in his own critical reading from this time onward. It is a project that is at once destructive, critical, and constructive, since its ultimate purpose is not negative, but positive. It seeks to retrieve lost and un-thought possibilities in previous philosophical systems, and ultimately to access that very same tradition, as for the very first time.

The Heideggerian program of a destructive-constructive hermeneutics is an essential inspiration for Derrida when he, forty years later, develops his own program for a "deconstruction" of metaphysics. It is widely recognized that the term itself is an adaption of Heidegger's earlier coinage. In one of the articles in *Writing and Difference* Derrida lists as his main predecessors in his critique of metaphysics Nietzsche, Freud, and "more radically so Heidegger".[20] It is, however, not simply a translation into French of the same term. Derrida would always insist that *deconstruction* in the end amounts to something different than *Destruktion*. In the same passage he says of all his forerunners that they remain trapped in a "circle," since they do not see sufficiently the circle in which they already stand. The hope to get outside or beyond metaphysics is nourished by an idea that we could do without the inherited language. Yet, this is precisely the metaphysical illusion, and one that produces various false attempts to break out, which again generates new myths of origins.

18. See *Being and Time*, trans. John Mcquarrie and Edward Robinson (New York: Harper & Row, 1962), § 6.

19. After the publication of lectures on religion and on Paul in 1994, a number of studies have appeared which explore the extent to which the very formation of existential ontology during the early twenties must be seen as interwoven with Heidegger's turning toward Luther and early Christianity. See, for example, Benjamin Crowe, *Heidegger's Religious Origins* (Bloomington: Indiana University Press, 2006).

20. "Structure, Sign, and Play," in *Writing and Difference*, 354.

One can debate if this criticism really applies to Heidegger, who always insisted that even in the "destruction" of metaphysics we operate within the space of that same tradition. Here it is not essential to determine exactly to what extent Derrida is correct in his criticism of Heidegger (which also varies over time). What is more important is to see how the very issue of the meaning of "deconstruction" confronts us in the end with the fundamental question of what it means to belong to a tradition, both as a question if and how we can really understand it, and also if there is a way of breaking free from it and creating something genuinely new. Once we take this same question back to Paul—which neither Heidegger nor Derrida ever do explicitly—then it obtains a world-historical importance, since it concerns the very meaning of the new faith. Does Christianity constitute something entirely "new," or is it to be understood as the critical elaboration of the "old"?[21]

For Derrida, it is clear that the deconstructive critic must work within the system. Yet, he or she must at the same time be open to an incalculable otherness that can manifest itself as the system is short-circuited, an event that also carries a potential ethical and political significance. Derrida does not—unlike what many of his critics have said—condemn man to a "prison-house of language". What he criticizes is rather what he takes to be naïve aspirations simply to step outside tradition, time, and language. Instead, his method suggests the possibility of opening the cognitive and linguistic system to its own inner otherness. There is thus a promise of liberation and a kind of transcendence at work also in deconstruction, but it is essential that it is incalculable, and that it can never be fully mastered.

The more distant roots of the idea of deconstruction in the messianic and apocalyptic temporality of Paul is, as said, never explicitly recognized or discussed by Derrida. But from an early point he articulates the necessity of reflecting on the dual inheritance of Jewish and Greek intellectual culture. This is especially the case in the longest and earliest of the essays in *Writing*

21. One can also phrase the question as to what extent it is even possible or meaningful to break free once and for all from one's cultural inheritance. Related to this issue is a larger question of to what extent the kind of critical hermeneutics that both Heidegger and Derrida develop stand in a longer line of prophetic Judaic scriptural hermeneutics. To explore this longer history, in order to situate both Paul and his modern readers, would be a very worthwhile task, but it is not one that I will try to address further here. For a classic introduction to this topic, see Susan A. Handelman, *The Slayers of Moses: The Emergence of Rabbinic Interpretation in Modern Literary Theory* (Albany: State University of New York Press, 1982). Another important study in this regard is Marlène Zarader's *La dette impensé. Heidegger et l'héritage hébraique* (Paris: Seuil, 1990), that deals with Heidegger and Judaism, and which argues that there is a hidden and suppressed indebtedness to Judaic thought in Heidegger. This is a study that Derrida mentions with appreciation on a few occasions.

and Difference, that deals with Levinas, and his aspiration to move beyond the monolithic Greek philosophy of the same, in favour of the other, which is implicitly identified with Judaism. In his careful critical study of Levinas' philosophical project, Derrida speaks of the irreducible ambiguity of the Greek logos, how it at once captures all difference in sameness, but in doing so also reveals its own exteriority. "Are we Jews? Are we Greeks?" he asks here. And he responds that we live the "difference between the Jew and the Greek, which is perhaps the unity of what is called history. We live in and of difference"[22] This history is and will always be tainted with violence. But hoping to escape all violence will necessarily result in a greater violence, since history "is violence."[23] For this reason the best we can hope for is "the least violence." Paul is not explicitly mentioned here, but Paul is in many ways emblematic for how this fateful constellation has been articulated and enacted, most poignantly so in Gal. 3:28, which speaks of how there is now neither Greek nor Jew, but all are one in Jesus Christ. In Paul we have the idea of both the inclusion of differences, and the transcendence of all difference. His is a voice presumably outside the Greek metaphysical logos, coming from a radical Jewish messianic sense of the end of time. Yet it speaks in favour of a metaphysical identity that is meant to transcend all differences and initiate a new history.

From our reading of Nietzsche and Heidegger as key philosophical predecessors, and also as paradigmatic philosophical readers of Paul, we can thus begin to sense a territory where Paul can be situated in the work of Derrida, as both an important background, but also as a critical contrast. The program of deconstruction is connected to a Pauline sense of time and history as articulated by Heidegger with an inspiration from Kierkegaard. But as such it is also connected to the question of what it means to stand within and at the same time rebel against a tradition, to questions of belonging, inclusion, and exclusion, to the alternatives of revolution and restoration.

DERRIDA ON RELIGION

Nietzsche and Heidegger do not only provide two distinct and, at least on the surface, fundamentally incompatible ways of approaching Paul. Against Nietzsche's uncompromising critique of Paul as a cunning spiritual seducer, stands Heidegger attempt to reinstate Paul as a kind of proto-existentialist thinker of temporality and historicity.[24] Also in relation to religion in general, Nietzsche and Heidegger could seem to represent two extremes. Whereas

---

22. "Violence and Metaphysics," in *Writing and Difference*, 191–92.

23. Ibid., 146.

Nietzsche anticipates Freud in his attempt to discharge the religious impulse at its root, by portraying it as a kind of malady of the soul, Heidegger appears instead to seek a secular-philosophical articulation of the religious and the sacred. He could even be seen as aiming beyond the very dichotomy of the secular and the sacred, through a thinking of Being as event and as gift, in a way that comes to the fore even more in his later writings.[25]

Where does Derrida belong on this territory? In the earlier writings there is little talk of religion. Generally Derrida was perceived as an atheist thinker with no religious commitment or agenda. In a recent and much debated study by Martin Hägglund, deconstruction is even labelled as "Radical Atheism," implying that its conception of difference, finitude and critique of metaphysics even commits it to a radically non-confessional standpoint.[26] This particular book, however, was written as an explicit attempt to criticize a strong tendency among some of Derrida's followers in recent years precisely to re-engage in a discussion with theology and religion. The starting point for this particular development and re-orientation in deconstruction was a conference on religion that took place on the island of Capri in 1994, organized by Derrida and Gianni Vattimo. There he gave the talk "Faith and Knowledge," which was later published in the conference volume.[27] This experimental and wide-ranging essay was to have an enormous importance for the rise of interest in religion in contemporary continental philosophy. Already at the time of its composition, in the early nineties, there was much talk of a "return to religion", and this was also the explicit motivation behind the organizing of the meeting. But what was

24. The problematic politics underlying such a reformatory reading of Paul on Heidegger's part is not something I will go further into here, but it is analyzed in a thoughtful way by Ward Blanton in his *Displacing Christian Origins. Philosophy, Secularity, and the New Testament* (Chicago: University of Chicago Press, 2007).

25. The literature on Heidegger and religion is large and growing. See, for example, Ben Vedder, *Heidegger's Philosophy of Religion* (Pittsburgh: Duquesne University Press, 2007), and Benjamin Crowe, *Heidegger's Phenomenology of Religion* (Bloomington: Indiana University Press, 2008). For the general question of phenomenology as a way to transcend the border between the sacred and the secular, see my *The Ambiguity of the Sacred*, edited with Jonna Bornemark (Stockholm: Södertörn Philosophical Studies, 2012). The question of Nietzsche and religion is of course much more complex, especially if one takes into considerations the later writings where he seems to be searching for not just the abolishing of religion, but for a new Dionysian religion. For a recent study on this topic, see Bruce Benson, *Pious Nietzsche: Decadence and Dionysian Faith* (Bloomington: Indiana University Press, 2008).

26. See Martin Hägglund, *Radical Atheism: Derrida and the Time of Life* (Stanford: Stanford University Press, 2008).

27. Derrida and Vattimo, *Religion*. See also Jacques Derrida, *Acts of Religion*, ed. Gil Anidjar (London: Routledge, 2002), which contains most of the essays by Derrida that deal with religion, including "Faith and Reason."

new in Derrida's approach was his way of breaching again the question of faith and reason, showing from the presumably "atheist" viewpoint of deconstruction how the distinction itself was unstable, and that we should instead think of faith and reason as perhaps sharing a common source.

In the essay Derrida declares his commitment to an "Enlightenment tradition," and a good part of his discussion is concerned with Kant and his 1792 essay "Religion within the boundary of mere reason." But partly through a meditation on the very metaphor of the Enlightenment—the light and the shining—he shows how we as "enlightened" have also already committed ourselves to a space where shining and appearing takes place, and thus in the vicinity of the religious. Consequently, a central point of the analysis is that "faith" is not restricted to the sphere of religion, but signifies a more general comportment, that also manifests itself in rationality. Derrida also identifies what he takes to be two principal sources of the religious, namely the "messianic," or a "messianicity without messianism," and the "chora" as a name (from Plato) designating a region "beyond being," a non-being or ontological middle-ground as also the place of an "infinite resistance."

Another important theme in this essay, and one that appears also in other later essays, is that of "auto-immunity", a concept originally from biology and medicine, designating when an organism fails to recognize itself, and develops immunity in relation to its own tissue. For Derrida, auto-immunity can also take on a more general cultural significance. In a later interview he describes it as when "a living being, in a quasi-*suicidal* fashion, 'itself' works to destroy its own protection, to immunize itself *against* its 'own' immunity [...] Autoimmunitary movements are what produce, invent and feed the very monstrosity they claim to overcome." [28] This model is then used to interpret the inner dynamic of both secularist and theist discourses that tend to produce precisely their own destructive counterparts.

In the essay "Faith and Reason" Derrida refers to Paul only in passing, and then to give recognition to Nietzsche's critique of the apostle, as already quoted earlier. But in its general orientation it is nevertheless much closer to Heidegger's approach in its overall method than to the Nietzschean genealogical critique. It seeks to show how deconstruction and its form of interpretation and critique can in fact be used to open up a discussion about issues that are normally relegated to matters of faith. By questioning the very distinction between the secular and the religious, it outlines a new discursive

28. In Giovanna Borradori, *Philosophy in a Time of Terror: Dialogues with Jürgen Habermas and Jacques Derrida* (Chicago: University of Chicago Press, 2003), 94, 97.

space, a kind of middle-ground similar to Heidegger's methodological neutrality in his early lectures. In the introductory remarks to the essay Derrida also recalls the shared background for many of the people who had gathered for the seminar, namely a broadly understood phenomenological inheritance.

The impact and importance of this essay for the subsequent development of a kind of deconstructive turn in theology has been monumental. It has been most visibly elaborated by scholars such as Hent de Vries, John Caputo, and Yvonne Sherwood who have all published extensively on Derrida and religion, but who have also tried to make use of this theoretical orientation to open new avenues for contemporary theology.[29] Jennings' aforementioned book belongs to some extent to this whole movement, as it tries to make use of Derrida and deconstruction for a new interpretation of Paul and his legacy in the present.

I will not go deeper into this larger problematic of deconstruction and religion, which has contributed to changing the shape of the debate both in theology and in continental philosophy, making again issues of religion and of faith into respectable and urgent topics also for non-believers. It suffices here to be aware of the impact of his intervention. More important for our present purpose, is to see that as far as Paul is concerned, Derrida's "turn toward religion" did not—unlike in the case of Heidegger—lead to any explicit attempt to return to Paul. In order to locate more specifically the position and effect of Paul in the topology of Derrida's thinking we therefore need to look elsewhere, namely to specific themes in his work that carry a Pauline echo. It is to such a theme that we shall now turn, namely to the exemplary problem of circumcision.

CIRCUMCISING PAUL

The ancient Hebrew word "shibboleth" literally means "river" or "stream." In most modern languages it also denotes a "token" or "distinguishing mark." This secondary meaning has its origin from a story in the book of *Judges* (12:6) that recounts how Jephthah and the Gileadites had encircled their enemies, the Ephraimites, along one of the passages across the Jordan river. In order to pass everyone was required to say the word *schibboleth*. The Ephraimites, who spoke the same language as their foes, could not pronounce it in the same way. In their

29. See John Caputo, *The Prayers and Tears of Jacques Derrida: Religion without Religion* (Bloomington: Indiana University Press, 1997); Hent de Vries, *Philosophy and the Turn to Religion* (Baltimore: Johns Hopkins University Press, 1999); and *Derrida and Religion: Other Testaments*, ed. Kevin Hart and Yvonne Sherwood (New York: Routledge, 2005).

mouths, or tongues, it came out as *sibboleth*. Their tongue gave them away, and thus they were killed, all in all over forty thousand according to *Judges*.

Derrida recalls the famous story of this brutal event in an essay on another Paul, his friend the Jewish Romanian-German poet Paul Celan, entitled "Shibboleth for Paul Celan" written in 1984.[30] Celan mentions the word "shibboleth" in one of his poems. For Derrida, however, the theme and the problem evoked by the story from *Judges* of the lethal password obtains a greater significance as an entrance word, not only to Celan's poetry, but to the poetic experience and ultimately to the experience of language as such. To have a language, is always to be part of a community, and thus to belong to and be open to communication. But it is also, and inversely, to be excluded from community and communication, and thus vulnerable. This differentiation takes place not only between different groups, but also between the individual and the community. Language is the expression of an individual experience, which it both preserves and betrays.

In his beautifully crafted interpretation, Derrida shows to what extent Celan was preoccupied with the problem of witnessing, with the date, and with the possibility of giving poetic voice to the singular human event and experience. In his reading of Celan's often enigmatic poems—which are full of dates and vaguely indicated references to historical events—they come forth not only as ciphers of hidden meanings and experiences to be unpacked by the skilled interpreter. They also bear witness of a more general poetic-linguistic predicament, as speaking from within the singular individual experience, from which they seek to establish an uncertain and incalculable pact with the other.

Throughout this interpretation one word and one theme returns repeatedly: "circumcision." It is both the first and last word of the texts, which itself also moves in a kind of circle, encircling its theme, tracing and cutting around it. Through its fundamental ambiguity it is a word and a theme that attracts the critical, philosophical, and also poetic interest of Derrida. In a somewhat later and partly autobiographical text, written in the wake of the death of his mother, and construed as a long commentary on St. Augustine, he even declares that "Circumcision, that's all I've ever talked about.[31] One need not necessarily take at face value this somewhat hyperbolic confession, but it testifies to the importance of this complex cultural practice, which in his

---

30. The text was first presented as a lecture in 1984, and then published in English translation, in S. Budick and J. Hartmann, eds., *Midrash and Literature* (New Haven: Yale University Press, 1986).

31. Derrida, Jacques, "Circumfession," in Jeffrey Bennington and Jacques Derrida, *Jacques Derrida* (Chicago: Chicago University Press, 1996), 70.

thought works as a symbol for a more general predicament, as has also been pointed out in several recent commentaries.[32]

The ancient practice of male circumcision has been documented in many different cultures and religions, from classical Egypt onward. According to Jewish myth it was issued as a command from God to Abraham (Gen 17:10) in order to seal the covenant: "ye shall circumcise the flesh of your foreskin; and it shall be a token of the covenant betwixt me and you" (KJV). To be circumcised is to be part of a chosen community, it is a sign cut into the body, to confirm a pact. In the next passage, God declares that whoever is not circumcised in his body shall have his soul "cut off from his people." In this ominous legend the connection is thus established between individual and community, flesh and spirit, sign and pact. The circumcision is what establishes and enables community, but also what initiates exclusion and violence. We can thereby sense how it recalls a similar logic as in the story of the password. It is a sign, sealed in the body, which gives one away, and that is part of the constitution of community. For a thinker like Derrida, who throughout his writing career was preoccupied with analysing and questioning limits, borders, and distinctions, it is a word that captures the tragic logic of community and communication, as both belonging and exclusion, always both.

A special background resonance for the philosophical significance of circumcision is found in Paul. It is in Romans that we read the famous line: "For he is not a Jew, which is one outwardly; neither is that circumcision, which is outward in the flesh. But he is a Jew, which is one inwardly; and circumcision is that of the heart, in the spirit, and not in the letter" (Rom. 2:25 KJV). This image concentrates the force and logic of Paul's message in all its ambiguity, both in respect to the Law and to the possibility of a universal bond between God and mankind. The privilege of the special covenant between God, Abraham, and the Jewish people, is here both problematized and expanded. The physical circumcision does not guarantee lawfulness, for in order to take part in the law, and thus in righteousness, one needs to pay tribute not to outer signs but to let one's heart and soul be circumcised. Later in Romans Paul writes that also in the original case of Abraham his justification in the face of God did not come about through his circumcision. "And he received the sign of circumcision, a seal of the righteousness of the faith which he had yet being uncircumcised" (Rom. 4:11 KJV).

32. For a good introductory discussion about the significance of this theme in Derrida's thought, see Inge-Birgitte Siegumfeldt's essay "Secrets and Sacrifices of Scission," in Hart and Sherwood, ed., *Derrida and Religion*, 283–93. See also the section on "Circumcision" in Caputo's *The Prayers and Tears of Jacques Derrida*, 250–62.

Even though the letter implies that Abraham was also justified through his inner circumcision, not through this outer sign, Paul's interpretation of the event of Christ establishes the new faith as a new and more radical inscription and internalization of the law in the body of man. The insistence on the circumcision of the human heart rather than that of the male sex contributes metaphorically and concretely to carving out a specific Christian ethos in the making. But in doing so, it also, ingenuously, lays the conceptual cornerstone for a theologically motivated anti-Judaism. As a religion of the law of a closed community, represented by the outer bond—the circumcised penis—Judaism will eventually be set against the supposedly more universal comportment of Christianity, based on inner sentiment—or the circumcised heart. As an eminent post-holocaust poet, Paul Celan is also a witness of where this logic would lead. In view of the disaster of the Christian-Jewish constellation in modernity Derrida's choice of circumcision as his main interpretative scheme for reading Celan is in this respect not incidental.

When discussing the extension of the metaphor of circumcision in *Shibboleth*, Derrida also explicitly recalls Paul. He remarks that the extension of the circumcision beyond the surgical act to a more spiritual sense of circumcision "does not date to Paul". He then mentions several examples of how circumcision is used as a metaphor already in Exdous (6:12, 30). At one point Moses worries that Pharaoh will not listen to him, since his lips are "uncircumcised," and also in Leviticus (6:41) there is a passage that mentions "uncircumcised hearts." Already at this stage circumcision is used to designate a more general token of community, understanding, and communication. Derrida then goes on to specify different meanings of circumcision, as also the sign or shibboleth of a covenant, and an experience of salvation and purification. All of this is developed around the line from Celan in the motto: "for him circumcise the word."

Following Celan's own remark in his "Meridian" lecture which declared that "every poet is a Jew," Derrida writes that in some sense the Jew is found in "every human being circumcised by language or called to circumcise a language." Derrida's point here brings out a dialectic of particular and universal, which resonates in profound ways with how the logic of circumcision operates in Paul. To be circumcised by language is to be part of language. There is no way to have a language without also being circumcised by that language, in the sense of having one's body shaped by a particular practice. By shaping the body, its vocal organs, and its gestures, as well as its cognitive organs, language guarantees the individual its participation in a specific community. Yet, in doing so it also brings about the exclusion from other possible communities.

This is what it means when he says that to be part of language is also to be circumcised by language.

After having first been circumcised by language, there is also the possibility of performing a circumcision on language. When Derrida elaborates the metaphor in this direction he is referring to the impulse of making one's language into one's own, of bending and marking the general and shared medium of language so as to make it speak from within the unique circle of one's singular experience. This aspiration takes place in the most paradigmatic form in the work of the poet. But the poet is here also a universal witness of a human predicament, in which we are always both shaped by our language and called to shape it. Yet, this human universal predicament cannot be equated with a simple generality, applicable to everyone. It is universal in being singular, and in its singularity it is universal. This is the logic that Derrida brings out from his reading of Celan's poetry, and which he choses to stage in the form of a discourse on circumcision. His only explicit mention of Paul here is the remark that it is not only in Paul that we find the metaphorical use of circumcision. But the presence of Paul and his new universalism is everywhere in this argument. For Paul, the idea of the circumcised heart and soul opens the possibility of a new shape of humanity, where the previous particular community is expanded and opened up towards a limitless universality, accessible to everyone. This Greek and Stoic element in Paul, which he combines in such an effective way with Jewish messianism, creates the conceptual space for Christianity as a potentially limitless universal community and communication, and thus the idea of global circumcised subject.

In his reflection on circumcision Derrida can also be said to seek the articulation of a universal human predicament. Still he performs it through an implicit and subtle reversal of the Pauline metaphorical logic. According to Paul the singular event of Christ opens the possibility of a universal community of circumcised subjects. For Derrida, the circumcision of the subject has always already taken place, as the creation of an inside and an outside, of belonging and exclusion Yet, in this universal—and at the same time always singular—predicament, there lies a possibility of a global recognition. It is then not the recognition of a global sameness, of being part of one singular humanity, but the recognition of how in our universality we are singular, or to use a phrase later coined by Derrida's close friend and interlocutor Jean-Luc Nancy, "being singular plural."[33]

33. Jean-Luc Nancy, *Being Singular Plural*, trans. R. Richardson (Stanford: Stanford University Press, 2000).

It would, however, be misleading to characterize Derrida's position as an argument in favour of a certain liberalism opposed to a Pauline communism. Derrida does not build his argument on the basis of an abstract reference to personhood or individuality, or even less so to universal human rights, as in traditional liberalism. His concept of the singular here is more complex, as he understands the individual as constituted in the very intersection of belonging and exclusion, an intersection that is thus polemic and violent from the very start. Paul's logic of circumcision is metaphysical in the sense that it places its hope in a final transcendence of all strife, in a perfect unified humanity under God. In its place Derrida opts for a solution that does not claim to be entirely outside violence, but one that opts for the lesser violence, to recall again his early essay on Levinas and Heidegger. In commenting on Celan's imperative to "circumcise the word" Derrida brings out the sad beauty of this logic, as it lets us experience that also in the most intimate and profound moment of communication there is always a necessity of doing violence, of creating circles, of establishing limits.[34]

To criticise the potential and real violence in metaphysical and Pauline-Christian universalism is of course not unique to Derrida. But what makes him into such a uniquely relevant writer in this particular context, is the fact that he performs this critical and deconstructive argument explicitly through a rehearsal of the very same metaphorical and thematic resources—that of circumcision – by means of which Paul first forges his concept of a new universalism.[35]

Un/veiling Paul

We have seen how in *Shibboleth for Paul Celan* Derrida uses St. Paul's own metaphors of circumcision in order to rethink and transform the Pauline thematic of singularity and universality. He enters the poetic conceptuality of Paul, and opens it to its own inner otherness by linking it with the poetry of Celan, which here serves as a liberating resonance chamber. Ten years later he composes another text for another Jewish friend, the French-Algerian writer and feminist philosopher Hélène Cixous, entitled *Veils*, as a response to an essay that he had received from her entitled.[36] Again we are talking about a marginal

34. See in particular the last sections of *Shibboleth*, where Derrida ties together his whole argument, also with some explicit references to Paul.

35. For an excellent overview of how this universalism in its later Enlightenment form could also serve as a basis of excluding the "particularism" of Judaism, see Jayne Svennungson's article "Enlightened Prejudices: Anti-Jewish Tropes in Modern Philosophy," in *Rethinking Time: Essays on History, Memory, and Representation*, ed. Hans Ruin & Andrus Ers (Stockholm: Södertörn Philosophical Studies, 2011), 279–90.

text in the corpus of Derrida, where its philosophical thematic is interwoven into a meandering meditation on veiling, that combines literary, philosophical, and religious themes, with private recollections. And again the name "Paul" serves as a node and as a kind of shibboleth that unites and secures access between the different layers of the text. "Paul" is here the name not only of the apostle, but also of Celan, who again is cited on the title page of chapter 3. This page is also dated, like a letter, an *epistle*: "Sao Paolo, December 4-8, 1995", since it was during his visit to this city that Derrida wrote the essay. Thus the text in itself is literally a letter from St Paul. Finally there is also a mention of a Paul Moses here, who turns out to have been Derrida's own early deceased brother. Through the constellation of all these Pauls, the text builds an argument, that continues and gathers Derrida's philosophical confrontation with the apostle.

The "veil" is a philosophical metaphor with extraordinarily rich implications. To seek the truth was often equated with seeking to tear apart the veil, in order to "uncover" the nature hidden behind it. To have the veil torn from one's eyes is also a common image for enlightenment. Indeed, the Enlightenment is a philosophy of un-veiling, of coming out of darkness and obscurity, into what is open, lit, and freely exposed. Also in Paul we find a discourse of the veil and the unveiling, as when he speaks in 1 Corinthians of how man in prayer should unveil himself before God: "any man who prays or prophesies with his head covered [veiled], dishonors his head" (11:4 RSV). Paul's discourse too is one of leaving darkness, night, and obscurity, in order to step into the day, in full awaken-ness, uncovered before the truth.

Veiling and unveiling are not only metaphors by means of which the operation of truth is poetically described. In designating truth and knowledge they also invite us to think what truth is. In his famous critical examination of the concept of truth in *Being and Time*, Heidegger criticised the familiar conception of truth as "correspondence", insisting instead that we should understand truth from the viewpoint of the Greek concept of ἀλήθεια, disclosure.[37] As a metaphor "disclosure" aligns itself with a discourse of un-veiling. Yet, it also opens the way toward a deeper critical engagement with the very way that we think about so called "objective truth," a truth presumably already out there, only for man to un-veil or disclose. For Heidegger dis-closure is a finite projection, enacted by human existence, whereby it steps into the lit-up space of an event. But in its dependency on finite existence it can never be final and complete. Thus truth also in its un-covering will preserve its relation

---

36. Derrida and Cixous, *Veils.*

37. *Being and Time*, §44.

to un-truth and to withdrawal. No final unveiling is therefore possible. As we unveil, we also, inevitably, veil. In the somewhat later essay "On the Origin of the Work of Art" Heidegger elaborates this conception, arguing that truth should be seen as a setting into work of an opening, but as an opening bound to a deeper and prevailing strife between earth and sky, darkness and light.[38]

For Derrida, this aspect of Heidegger's thinking was always of fundamental importance. He can be seen struggling with it throughout many of his texts, in ways that we cannot recount here.[39] But it is important to be aware of the philosophical stakes involved, lest the somewhat light-footed and fleeting reflections in a text like *Veils* are not to be misunderstood. When he here addresses the problem of veiling and unveiling, he is activating a metaphysical inheritance that concerns the way in which the philosophical nature of truth has been understood. To put it succinctly: when truth is understood simply as un-veiling and en-lightening, it veils the necessity of veils, the very fact of our facticity, that we inhabit our finite bodies, our destinies, and our relations. In Derrida's essay this other aspect of the veil is conveyed by the story of his *tallith*, the Jewish prayer shawl that he inherited from his family, a cover that covers nothing, and yet a veil that serves to preserve the relation to his own particular past. It is in the name of this both secular and non-secular relation to his Jewish tradition that he calls into question a certain traditional metaphysical logic of the veil, the pretention to know what to veil and what to expose, not least in Paul. For it is Paul who says not only that men must stand unveiled before their God, but also, and in the same passage as quoted above, that the women must keep themselves veiled. In a remarkable formulation that brings out the paradoxical ambiguity of the veil, Paul writes in 1 Cor. 11:5 that whereas men are dishonoured by veiling themselves, "any women who prays or prophesies with her head unveiled dishonors her head—itis the same as if her head were shaven" (RSV).

The veil here operates according to a similar pattern as circumcision, as it conveys the urge to separate a true from a false relation and covenant, while at the same time disclosing in its very metaphor the collapse of this strict logic. It is also at this particular point in his work that Derrida takes on Paul explicitly, first by repeating an argument from *Shibboleth*, that Paul wrongly claimed to "distinguish, for the first time ... the circumcision of the heart ... from the

---

38. See Martin Heidegger, "The Origin of the Work of Art," in *Poetry, Language, and Thought*, trans. A. Hofstadter (New York: Perennical Classics, 2001).

39. See in particular *The Truth in Painting*, trans. J. Bennington (Chicago: Chicago University Press, 1987), which is partly a defence of Heidegger's understanding of art and truth in the face of some of his critics.

circumcision of the body."[40] It is this same Paul, he continues, who "attacked the literal circumcision of men, that same one wanted to veil woman and un-veil man." For Derrida the voice of Paul is deeply ambiguous. In the same gesture as he invites everyone to take part in the new community, he also closes it, to the traditionalists who refuse the new doctrine, and to the women. It is for this reason that the very figure of Paul, as Derrida writes here, is both "very mild" and yet "terrible," someone whose "monstrous progeny" is our history and culture, as he says in the next paragraph.

It is in these passages that we come closest to the heart of Derrida's engagement with Paul, in the very problem of how to handle his troublesome and militant universalism. It is a question of coming to terms with the promise and the violence at once that originates from the idea of a united humanity under one creed. In order to highlight the difficulty that he has with this inheritance, Derrida here opens his text to an inner dialogue, creating a kind of Socratic irony by addressing his own discourse. The whole passage is worth quoting, as it brings out so much of his style, wit, and philosophical character.

> Your epistle against Saint Paul is double-edged, like what you say about circumcision. In everything you're suggesting, with little airs of elliptical reticence, it's as though you were against circumcision but also against those who are against circumcision, you ought to make your mind up. You're against everything… Like what you say against the veil, in your Penelopean discourse, make your mind up… Make your mind up and develop a coherent comparatist hypothesis, with as its key a politics of the tallith, of the veil, the *chador* or the *kipa*, in a secular and democratic school system.[41]

To this critical voice, which he directs to himself, Derrida then responds, in something that grows into an improvised ethical and political credo of his philosophical legacy, combining a reading of Paul—that is, the issue of univeralism and the politics of universal truths—with the current political debates around the veil in France and elsewhere.

40. Derrida and Cixous, *Veils*, 75–76.
41. Ibid., 77.

Not in a hurry. Yes, I'm against, yes, yes, I am. Against those who
prescribe the veil and other such things, against those who forbid
it too, and who think they can forbid it, imagining that this is
good, that it is possible and that it is meaningful. Not in a hurry:
the scholarly, the secular, and the democratic belong through and
through to cultures of the tallith and the veil, etc., people don't even
realize any longer… Contamination is everywhere. And we hadn't
finished, I haven't finished with Saint Paul.

The passage then depicts Paul as one who wanted to veil the heads of women
and unveil those of the men, and one who denounced Moses and the children
of Israel, accusing them of having given in to the veil, of not having known
how to lift the veil, and finally it depicts the doubly resurrected Christ as
"the great Unveiler". One misunderstands this passage if one sees here only a
common accusation of Paul for being an antisemite. Paul is a Jewish preacher,
coming from within the Jewish tradition. And he is as ambiguous as this
tradition itself from the start. Just as the clean break with tradition that Paul is
holding out as a promise is a metaphysical illusion with violent implications,
there is no clean tradition in relation to which Paul can be criticised. His
discourse in its very aspiration to speak from the position of an absolute revealed
truth, is fundamentally "contaminated". Just as "our" Enlightenment tradition
is contaminated when it believes that it can—as in the ruling of the French
parliament—that it can decide about who should be permitted to veil her/
himself, and when it claims to have the moral truth about veiling.

In the end, enlightenment discourse is characterized by a logic of veiling/
unveiling from its very inception, in ways that are by no means innocent, and
that mostly remain unseen. It is for this reason that the deconstructive thinker
will also risk looking vague and irresponsible as the imagined critic portrays
him/her in Derrida's own dialogue ("You ought to make up your mind"). For a
thinking preoccupied with ambiguities, standing on the threshold of an outside/
inside of language, culture and metaphysics, and also preoccupied with the
existentially and politically explosive issue of the relation between the singular/
universal, this imperative is both a source of anxiety and of strength.

In relation to a writer like Paul, this deconstructive swerving between
impossible alternatives becomes even more acute, since Paul himself seems to
be so certain of how to handle all differences. But precisely in relation to
the deconstructive critic a text like the Pauline letters can also be opened up
in its inner metaphoricity and historicity. It can happen not just in virtue of

some clever methodological device, applied randomly from the outside. On the contrary, it is possible because deconstruction, in its very ethos and practice, is already situated in the space opened up by the Pauline letters. This is the space of an uncertain tradition, of a tradition in crisis, where a new ethical universality in the making is articulated by means of violent metaphors of exclusion and inclusion at once. It is a space that in itself gathers the hope of redemption and the threat of violence and extermination.

Seen from this angle, Derrida and deconstruction appears not just as one possible tool for interpreting Paul, but as an unavoidable challenge for any contemporary philosophical–theological reading of the Pauline epistles.

And we hadn't finished with Paul.

6

Gianni Vattimo and Saint Paul
Ontological Weakening, Kenosis, and Secularity

Anthony C. Sciglitano Jr.

The question on the table is "why Saint Paul"? And it is to be specified as "why Saint Paul for Gianni Vattimo," a late-modern philosopher in an age when it is by no means *pro forma* for philosophers to take a positive interest in religious figures. One approach to this question suggests an inquiry as to warrants, that is, historical, sociological, and philosophical reasons for a *philosophical* appeal to an ostensibly religious and Christian form of thought rooted not in discursive rationality, but rather in revelation and the response of faith. In fact, Vattimo contends that stark contrasts drawn by modern thinkers between faith and reason are no longer tenable, and thus religious materials can become available to philosophers as potentially revelatory or disclosive. A second and specifying question then follows: given that religious figures can now be included in philosophical discourse, why *this* religious figure, why Saint Paul? Moreover, in Vattimo's case, we need to ask why a nearly exclusive emphasis on Saint Paul and why not others? What does Paul offer the philosopher that one might not find in other important figures? Certainly a philosopher interested in foregrounding love, as Vattimo clearly is, would find ample resources in Saint John. Finally, we might ask what role the honorific, "saint," plays in Vattimo's thought and what Vattimo might recognize as qualifying marks for this title. I will suggest that the honorific does function in interesting if not ecclesially thick ways for him.

The questions, then, are complex. They are made more so in that Vattimo's writings always have a multifocal orientation. They seek to address pressing practical questions of European political and social culture, the relation of the Catholic Church to secularization, the intellectual convergence of secularization, nihilism, and relativism, the onset of modernity and the "return" of religion, and the nature of philosophical discourse in a technocratic and scientifically oriented society. He writes about none of these items from a distance. Originally from Turin, and a professor in philosophy there for many years, he is an openly gay Catholic thinker, a former member of the European parliament who professes a kind of democratic communism (albeit with important criticisms of Marx), and a prolific editorialist. His political involvements, personal and moral concerns, and desire for European unity play an important role in his thinking about Christianity, the Catholic Church and Europe. It takes Vattimo only a page of *A Farewell to Truth*, for instance, to reveal his thoughts about "Bush and Blair" and "the way that the United States thinks that it can solve this problem [security for an open society] for itself and for the rest of the world, which it doesn't even bother to consult."[1] How, then, does Saint Paul come into all of this?

In one sense, not much. If one is seeking from Vattimo swaths of detailed exegesis, his texts will surely disappoint. To the typical scripture scholar or theologian, his reading will appear impressionistic at best, a kind of post-modern poaching at worst: at once episodic and illicit. Yet in another sense, that is, in terms of the significance of Paul to his major themes, including secularization, weak thought, nihilism, tolerance and even the European Union, the twin Pauline tropes of κένωσις and ἀγάπη (*caritas*), if not determinative, are absolutely central. So, the importance of Paul to Vattimo's thought far outdistances the range of Pauline texts to which he appeals. This makes our task at once simple and difficult: simple because it limits what we need to address in terms of Paul's texts and theology; difficult because essentially all of Vattimo's thought lies in relation to the themes of κένωσις and ἀγάπη. This means that we will need to provide a basic resume of his thought prior to engaging his relation to Saint Paul. Part one will do this by centering the discussion on two sorts of history we find in Vattimo's work, namely, exoteric history and esoteric history. Part two addresses Vattimo's theologically inflected work. While theological themes show up throughout his work, it is nevertheless the case that his works fall broadly into two categories, works of philosophy and works of religion. The focus in this section is on the latter and will show precisely how Vattimo brings the Pauline themes of κένωσις and ἀγάπη into conversation with issues of nihilism, secularization and with the twelfth century

1. Gianni Vattimo, *A Farewell to Truth*, trans. by William McCuaig (New York: Columbia University Press, 2011), xxvi. The most extensive Catholic engagement with Vattimo's thought to this point is the superb work of Thomas G. Guarino, *Vattimo and Theology* (New York, London: T&T Clark International, 2009).

Calabrian abbot, Joachim di Fiore. Section three is brief, and investigates some of Vattimo's remarks about Paul on love and justice. Here I will address the issue of the relation between love and justice and whether concern for one requires, for him, concession of the other. The issue here is whether we return, in Vattimo, to something like a Marcionite form of thought and, relatedly, whether such a form of thought can avoid an anti-Jewish bias. I will argue that anti-Judaism is not avoided and that Vattimo ushers in a kind of apocalyptic form of Marcionism. Finally, I will attempt some assessment as to twentieth century Catholic theologians who might be suitable conversation partners for Vattimo and his work.

EXOTERIC AND ESOTERIC HISTORY

Given Vattimo's many political involvements, it will come as no surprise that he peppers his texts with references to and evaluative comments on historical and political events. Behind these historical events, he thinks, lies a more hidden story, namely, the history of Being (*Seinsgeschichte*). We will call these, respectively, Vattimo's exoteric and esoteric histories. While exoteric history can seem like a jumble of particular events, Vattimo's esoteric history helps reveal or announce a deeper pattern that provides a hermeneutical key for the modern period. This key, which he calls "hermeneutical ontology" and "weak thought," joins esoteric to exoteric history much like the incarnation joins eternity to time. In other words, just as the incarnation reveals the meaning of time, so for Vattimo hermeneutical ontology reveals the philosophical meaning of modernity. Theologically, "weak thought" shows up as the event (*Ereignis*) of κένωσις that eventually fulfills itself in secular, pluralistic culture named by Vattimo as the surprising and nihilistic essence of Christian proclamation. We will begin with a discussion of Vattimo's exoteric history, then discuss his esoteric history and then finish this first section with the hermeneutical key as a linkage between the two. The focus in this first part will be on Vattimo's historical and philosophical observations. Vattimo's explicit treatment of the Pauline motifs of κένωσις and ἀγάπη, and the importance of Joachim di Fiore in relation to these, will be discussed in parts two and three.

Now Vattimo never gives anything like a sustained treatment of historical phenomena, so we must draw from his episodic comments a basic line of thought. For Vattimo, exoteric history witnesses a gradual decline of ecclesiastical authority and, indeed, a decline in the authority of monarchs, emperors, and even the national state. Ecclesiastical authority in the political, moral and economic realms recedes into the realm of the private. The Church resists this marginalization under the banner of anti-modernism,[2] which includes antipathy to Galileo, to Kant's Copernican revolution in philosophy[3], and to freedom of religion (modernist crisis). Galileo,[4] along with Luther, threaten the hierarchy's monopoly on scriptural interpretation; Kant subjects Catholicism's trust in reason's ability to know God to stringent critique; freedom of religion lets society loose from obligations to Catholic belief and practice. Ecclesiastical anti-modernism, Vattimo thinks, led it to also support a variety of extra-ecclesial authoritarian movements in the modern period, whether a French monarch (Louis XIV), Fascism, or contemporary anti-gay, anti-science agendas.[5] The Church's dogmatic insistence on its own rights and the truth of its doctrines—and moral and theological dogmatism more broadly—gave rise to the "wars of religion"[6] which ended up further depleting the Church's authority. Thus, Vattimo associates dogmatism, "fundamentalism,"[7] and metaphysics with violence.

Vattimo is not so blinded by ecclesial-Italian politics, however, that he fails to notice other sites where authority is de-authorized. Marxist Communism, Nationalism[8] and the free market offer targets that he does not resist. All three make claims to non-perspectival knowledge, and require allegiances based upon those claims, that cannot be justified. He is particularly critical, in his work *Farewell to Truth*, of Britain, the United States, and Israel[9] and suggests

2. Vattimo writes, "Christian thought may struggle to remain current, and even the Catholic hierarchy may strive to read the signs of the times and speak to those living in the present. But there is no doubt that, deep down, it sees modernity as the enemy" (*Farewell to Truth*, 49); "Its [the Church's] resistance to modernity is reaching such extremes that it will inevitably lead to a backlash" (Ibid., 52); "Christianity as a core of dogma cannot constitute the cultural basis of Europe's modern identity" (Ibid., 83; cf. 82). I am not clear, however, why Vattimo seems to think the Church teaches creationism (cf. Ibid., 50–51). He seems to confuse this issue with the issue of a profession of God as Creator. These are not the same kinds of issue. He also seems to think that the Church thinks of God as a non-interventionist clockmaker who gives the world its laws from outside; this confuses Deism and Theism (Ibid., 51).

3. *Farewell to Truth*, 35: "Who was it that always thundered against Kant and his perverse subjectivism? It was the Catholic Church, and often monarchs and governments too."

4. Ibid., 50–51.

5. Ibid., 59.

6. Ibid., 82, 83.

7. Vattimo uses this term to designate not so much biblical fundamentalism—although he includes this—as claims that seek to ground anthropological, moral and political claims in a divine foundation or in foundational ideas of human nature or the nature of society (see *Farewell to Truth*, 48–52). He observes that these ideas are tied to "biblical anthropology to which the laws of the state must conform if human nature is not to be violated" (Ibid., 50).

8. Ibid., 80.

9. Ibid., 112.

that the difficulties in who is or is not a terrorist are often elided by appeals to the foundational certitudes of nationalism that in fact are perspectival and contingent.[10] It also seems that the sovereign subject of liberalism would be rife for the weakening of authority that Vattimo envisions for all "essentialist" metaphysics, but he does not focus on this as much in his comments on exoteric history. In any event, Vattimo thinks that democracy rooted in consensus, rather than any politics oriented to strong truth claims, better fits the contemporary *Zeitgeist* which, with its hyper-pluralism of perspectives and paradigms resists all strong truth claims. Instead, for Vattimo, the exoteric legacy is that of a society that makes or produces truth through consensus building rather than discovering truth as a structural component of the world. Here, we have begun to broach our esoteric history.

Complementing this exoteric story of gradual, if agonistic,[11] emancipation is for Vattimo an esoteric story of metaphysical weakening, what he labels "hermeneutical ontology"[12] and "weak thought" (*pensiero debole*). This now relatively famous label indicates the gradual but intrepid de-authorization of atemporal, ahistorical, non-contingent, objectivist metaphysical concepts and modes of reasoning that seek to provide sure foundations for substantive moral, political, and cultural claims. Thus, the end of metaphysics and the onset of Being's withdrawal or Being as the modern event of withdrawal. That which withdraws is the credibility attached to all foundational claims of certainty, including proofs of God's existence, natural law morality, objectivist epistemologies, and the human subject as indubitable foundation. In this context, Kant becomes an interesting figure for Vattimo. Catholic resistance to Kantianism symbolizes for him Catholic anti-modern sentiment and Catholic

---

10. So, for example, Vattimo thinks that the judgments of Nuremberg ought to be endorsed, but not on the basis of an absolute knowledge of good and evil, true and false, but "Rather as a matter of keeping faith with our determinate historical situation: it is our duty to resist the temptation to feel ourselves allied with Truth" (*Farewell to Truth,* 112). Vattimo thinks that the logic of truth is what often leads one to support violence. The Nazi issue, then, is not that they were false or evil so much as that they thought their party was the whole, the Truth, the Good and everyone else was impure, evil, etc. It is their commitment to the logic of absolute truth that is the problem and that remains a problem today in other areas of geo-political affairs. Their sin and error lies, then, not so much in the matter of their convictions, it seems, but in their believing their convictions were absolute certainties. Can we not say, however, that part of the problem with Nazi ideology was that some of their claims were simply and horribly wrong, perhaps because they were so conditioned by self-interest?

11. Vattimo thinks that genuine and meaningful dialogue is and will most often be preceded by conflict. See Ibid., 116.

12. Gianni Vattimo, *The Adventure of Difference*, trans. Cyprian Blamires (Baltimore: Johns Hopkins University Press, 1993), 18–20.

commitment to natural law over against the formalism of Kantian ethics. In this sense, Kant functions as an axiological bellweather for the modern and anti-modern. Yet Kant himself stands on the line between the modern and late or post-modern. Vattimo extols Kant's subject centered account of knowledge congruent with post-modern critiques of putatively disinterested, objectivist accounts of knowing. Yet Kant remains stuck in assumptions of invariant epistemological structures and therefore lapses into metaphysics: "the subject is not the bearer of the Kantian a priori, but the heir to a finite-historical language that makes possible and conditions the access of the subject to itself and to the world."[13] Kant, then, receives plaudits for his focus on the knowing subject and his consideration of the conditions for the possibility of knowledge, but these very conditions need to be radicalized in the direction of hermeneutics or the "interpretive essence of truth."[14]

For Vattimo, Nietzsche and Heidegger prove to be the key figures who perform this radicalization in the direction of a nihilistic hermeneutic ontology. Nietzsche famously proclaims the undoing of all divine grounding for the world: its meaning, value, purpose. For him, there are no atemporal structures or hierarchy of values to be discovered, but only interpretations, perspectives and values to be imparted. Heidegger remembers or recalls Being grasped as eventful emergence against what he considers the reification of Being understood as static essence in the Western tradition since Plato, in his view the historical onset of the forgetfulness of Being.[15] Vattimo follows both: all is

---

13. Gianni Vattimo, *Beyond Interpretation: The Meaning of Hermeneutics for Philosophy,* trans. by David Webb (Stanford, CA: Stanford University Press, 1997), 8. Elsewhere, Vattimo writes, "Overall, though, Kant and many neo-Kantian philosophers have always taken it for granted that reason was unvarying" (*Farewell to Truth,* 65; cf. 66).

14. Vattimo, *Beyond Interpretation,* 9.

15. Vattimo thinks Heidegger's epochalism has been largely occluded in the phenomenological literature for a blander version of Heidegger's work: "But Heidegger's hermeneutical followers generally tend to pick up only the blander and less provocative aspects of this discourse. For them, the universality of hermeneutics and the historicity of knowledge signify merely that history grows as a perpetual interpretative process. To know is to interpret, but to interpret is also to produce new history. In this 'eirenic' perspective, all the dramatic force of the Heideggerian idea of metaphysics is lost. *Truth and Method,* for example, betrays little sign of Heidegger's dramatic vision of the history of western civilization" (*Adventure of Difference,* 22). Counter-examples, I believe, would include John Caputo's *Heidegger and Aquinas: An Essay on Overcoming Metaphysics* (New York, NY: Fordham University Press, 1982) and Hans Urs von Balthasar's wrestling with the Heideggerian "forgetfulness of Being" thesis in *Glory of the Lord,* volumes 4 and 5 (San Francisco: Ignatius Press, 1989, 1991). See also, Cyril O'Regan, "Von Balthasar's Valorization and Critique of Heidegger's Genealogy of Modernity," in *Christian Spirituality and the Culture of Modernity,* 123–58.

interpretation; Being is event (φύσις; *Ereignis*); truth (ἀλήθεια) is the opening up or disclosedness of particular historical-linguistic horizons or epochs, as event. The post or late-modern epoch emerges as one of ungrounding, that is, as a historical period that consistently issues in a "no" to foundational certainties. The history of Being (*Seinsgeschichte*) brings us to a position of weak thought and to what Vattimo calls an "ontology of actuality."[16] In other words, rather than searching for unchanging ideas, reason negotiates to produce consensus for what works best given contemporary views of what is needed or what is good in a particular context.[17] But even this context must never be thought as definitive.[18]

For Vattimo, however, hermeneutics also needs to submit to historicization: "there are no facts, only interpretations, and of course this too is an interpretation".[19] In other words, if hermeneutics promotes the Nietzschean line that "all is interpretation," then it must recognize itself in this proclamation as merely the best interpretation of the historical epoch called modernity, and not settle on metaphysical claims regarding the interpretative nature of human being. Vattimo strives to interpret hermeneutics as the realization of a particular epochal, ontological or horizonal opening (ἀλήθεια). That opening can be named modernity and nihilism understood as the 'essence' and thus τέλος of modern critical reasoning coming to self-knowledge regarding its interpretative, finite and historical character. Here we can broach the issue of section two for the sake of clarity: hermeneutics is that philosophical form derived from and suited to modernity or late modernity grasped as the secularization of Christianity. In this case, all strong ontological-natural claims empty themselves or weaken in a nihilistic vector. Here, κένωσις will serve for Vattimo as an onto-theological symbol to name the "emptying" of non-contingent ontological and moral claims in deference to interpretation and historicization. Moreover, in contrast to Nietzsche, Vattimo contends that

---

16. Vattimo, *Farewell to Truth,* 22.

17. See Ibid., 22–33. Vattimo turns from phenomenology because he believes that much of contemporary European discourse that is inspired by phenomenology has turned toward a kind of realism that he abjures (Ibid., 25). Also, "The only way to try to remember Being in its difference from beings is to suspend the claim to validity of the order of beings as it is given, in fact, in our historical condition" (Ibid., 31). There appears to be a tension in Vattimo's thought here that he recognizes. On the one hand, he wishes to speak of "actuality" or the "situation," but he wants such categories to be primarily philosophical and not sociological because the latter can be a kind of concession to whatever is *au courant* and can also suggest the objectivism inherent to much work in social sciences. Yet he does not want to be an idealist either and restrict philosophical concerns to ideas (See *Farewell to Truth,* 23–24).

18. Ibid., 31.

19. Vattimo, *Beyond Interpretation,* 6.

124 of the Philosophers

charity and not power (save for the power of interpretation) is the most significant interpretation of this nihilistic vector of modernity-Christianity. We will investigate what he means by charity and precisely how κένωσις functions in his onto-theological vision, but here it is important to note that charity operates as the check to unmitigated interpretation and one that he thinks sensible give our particular social-historical epoch.

The term *Seinsgeschichte* (history of Being) serves to draw together esoteric and exoteric history in Vattimo's thought and provides the hermeneutical key for both. In his view, the history of Being is such that at this particular time, Being opens up as hermeneutical ontology, "weak thought" or an "ontology of actuality:" "Ontology is nothing other than the interpretation of our condition or situation, since Being is nothing apart from its 'event', which occurs when it historicizes itself and when we historicize ourselves."[20] If Vattimo follows Nietzsche and Heidegger in thinking Being as event, then ontology will call for "the negation of stable structures of Being, to which thought must necessarily have recourse if it is to 'found' itself upon solid certainties."[21] This form of negation does not apply merely to what Heidegger had in mind when he contested the forgetfulness of Being as φύσις (emergent reality) and its conversion in Western culture to reified and static *essentia*, οὐσία, and *natura* as conceptions that think all Being as product.[22] Vattimo argues that this critique suggests an "end of modernity" insofar as modernity holds to a progressive view of history that assumes a unitary, progressive and teleological notion of history where the new is always held to be superior to the old and thus demands consistent overcoming.[23] The Nietzschean and Heideggerian insistence that Being is "event" suggests the end of such foundational and conceptions of history often laced with a kind of teleological necessity.[24] Being is not on its way to a particular point of arrival that one can know and employ as an evaluative standard. Instead, the "end of history" becomes for him an interpretive destruction of the modern notion that historical change is grasped best as a new stage of progress and thus as a new metaphysical foundation

---

20. Gianni Vattimo, *The End of Modernity. Nihilism and Hermeneutics in Postmodern Culture* (Baltimore: Johns Hopkins University Press, 1991), 3. In Kierkegaardian terms, Vattimo is opting for an episodic and aesthetic view of history rather than an ethical and teleological one.

21. Ibid.

22. For these themes in Heidegger, see *Introduction to Metaphysics* (New Haven: Yale University Press, 2000), 13, 46–49, 63, and 182.

23. Vattimo, *End of Modernity*, 2.

24. See ibid., 3 and 8–13.

for valuation. History too must undergo the Nietzschean and Heideggerian deconstruction and submit to weakening.

Two issues remain that we can broach prior to discussing Vattimo's more direct relation to Saint Paul and to theological themes. First, we need to engage the issue of warrants at the level of genus. If Saint Paul is a religious person and his writings are religious writings, then what does Vattimo think are the philosophical warrants for the appearance of religious writings within philosophical discourse? Second, I want to more systematically expand upon Vattimo's notion of truth and the philosopher's relation to it as it appears in some of his texts.

1. RELIGIOUS WRITINGS IN PHILOSOPHICAL DISCOURSE

Like many contemporary philosophers, Vattimo believes that the end of modern epistemological strictures that restrict knowledge to the quantifiable and reductively materialistic is good for religious forms of thought. Insofar as putative atheistic proofs that belief in God is irrational have failed to persuade, there is nothing to prevent religious insight coming back onto the scene, especially as aids to interpretation of a particular epoch. This is not to say that Vattimo thinks hermeneutics can take the place of the *praeambula fidei* or that proofs of God actually work. Rather, he thinks that attempts to rule religious discourse out of court based upon certain foundational principles have been undermined by the undercutting of such foundational certitudes in modern and post-modern philosophy.[25] Reason itself has undercut the certainties that previously would have been thought to rule out revelation. Or, perhaps better, the difference between truth from reason alone and truth rooted in interpretation of religious and mythological narratives is not nearly so far apart as philosophers once assumed. He will, in fact, go further and at least partly follow Dilthey to claim that hermeneutics itself is rooted in the Judaeo-Christian tradition and, more precisely, in Saint Paul. Here, however, we must restrict ourselves to the generic. The "contamination" of philosophical discourse by religious discourse is based upon his assessment that the critique leveled by hermeneutics against the "idea of truth as verifiable conformity between proposition and thing undermines the rationalist, empiricist, positivist and even idealist and Marxist negations of the possibility of religious experience."[26]

---

25. Vattimo, *Beyond Interpretation*, 45.

2. TRUTH AS OPENING

If Nietzsche is central for Vattimo here, Heidegger is no less so. Heidegger helps him move beyond the notion of truth as correspondence [27] to the idea of truth as *aletheia* or, in Vattimo's words, truth as aperture. The question, for Vattimo, is not how the knowing subject's mental image can correspond to an external world whether finite or eternal, but rather what are the philosophical contours or agreed upon assumptions—political, social, moral—of the present epoch and what, then, is called for as a response. The truth of Being is the truth of the historical/cultural context in which persons find themselves and to which they must respond. Truth, then, is *Ereignis* (event) and ἀλήθεια (opening, disclosure, aperture), the ontological and eventful opening of a particular historical context in which one is thrown.[28]

In more recent work, Vattimo has addressed the issue of truth more expansively. Vattimo follows Heidegger in his critique of correspondence theories of truth. In *Being and Time*, Heidegger argued that the conditions for making particular judgments are a given set of circumstances and assumptions—an epoch—that makes Being present in a particular mode. Science and social science, for instance, are beholden to a quantifiable notion of being and thus limited by that particular mode in which Being shows itself. Vattimo shows his disdain for what he considers a naïve correspondence theory in his attacks on Tarski[29]—more rhetorical than argumentative—in a Heideggerian informed analysis. He does, however, seem to want to endorse a context-specific form of correspondence theory.[30] The truth of Being, in this sense, shows itself in particular epochal contexts within which one can make more and less true statements based on general cultural expectations and consensus. Thus correspondence is not entirely evicted, but modified and given a more

---

26. Ibid., 44–45. Vattimo is quite concerned and aware that this opening up to myth and religion can result in a Hegelian future reduction of all to a concept. We will address his attempt to address this possibility in the next section as it directly calls upon Saint Paul.

27. Vattimo focuses on § 44 of *Being and Time* for Heidegger's critique of correspondence/*adequatio*/agreement theory such that epochal disclosure always pre-exists and conditions particular kinds of putatively objective knowing and allows for interpretations that discover agreements between mind and object. See *Adventure of Difference*, 21. In § 44 of *Being and Time*, Heidegger makes the critique of Kant that Vattimo will follow. See Martin Heidegger, *Being and Time*, trans. John Macquarrie and Edward Robinson (New York: Harper and Row, 1962), 256.

28. Vattimo, *Beyond Interpretation*, 11–12. Cf. Gianni Vattimo, *After Christianity*, trans. Luca D'Isanto (New York: Columbia University Press, 2002), 6.

29. Vattimo, *Farewell to Truth*, 33–36.

30. See Ibid., 9.

humble—because historical and contextual—condition. Truth has the characteristics of event, aperture, and, to a limited extent, correspondence. It is important to further specify the limits here. For instance, Vattimo does not think truth can ever speak of natural being or "essence" except in a historically provisional way. In addition, even if one does describe a state of affairs in its "isness," description does not grant evaluative judgments or "oughts." As in his description of deism, so in his recitation of the is-ought fallacy, Vattimo is convinced by David Hume.[31] This means that Being and the Good are not convertible, at least not in traditional terms. Indeed, "nature" may be the enemy.[32] Insofar as truth is correspondence, the terms of correspondence are set by a particular epoch and consensus within that epoch about both the conditions for true statements and particular judgments. It is in this sense that Vattimo says truth is more nearly produced than discovered. Finally, and almost as an aside, Vattimo brings in Saint Paul's use of truth as ἀληθεύοντες ("truth-speaking"; Eph. 4:15-16).[33] In this case, he conceives of the notion of truth in relational terms. Not an attempt to correspond to an object, but fidelity to a friendship or set of relations or community sets up the desire for truth-telling. Perhaps something like Levinas' discursive notion of truth as justice or as doing justice to an other's discourse can be brought to bear here, though Vattimo will tend more in his later work toward Richard Rorty's pragmatism. Truth-telling will be more or less helpful depending upon the epochal context in which one finds oneself.[34] The philosopher inhabits such a context as a self-conscious interpreter of the present historical epoch and an announcer and prophet of the times and the response to which we are called. The philosopher is the interpreter par excellence; not the interpreter of what is atemporally the case, but rather the interpreter of the future. The philosopher must also be a prophet.

---

31. Ibid., 58; cf. Ibid., 25 where he gestures to Hume against Habermas and especially the Vatican. Hume is an odd bedfellow for Vattimo as Vattimo's entire oeuvre is opposed to "objectivism," a philosophical critique one would think eighteenth centure thought in general, and Hume in particular, would find a difficult challenge to overcome. On Hume, see also, *After Christianity,* 114.

32. Vattimo, *Farewell to Truth,* 59: "Nihilism equals Christianity because Jesus came into the world not to demonstrate what the "natural" order was but to demolish it in the name of charity."

33. Ibid., xxxvi and 10. Vattimo cites the Vulgate edition, which reads, "veritatem facientes in caritate," which he translates "making truth in lovingness."

34. Science is not immune to Vattimo's views here. He doubts that scientists are after truth in a correspondence sense so much as results that make life better for human living (*Farewell to Truth,* 63).

Hermeneutical (Dis)Incarnation: Kenosis, Secularization, and Caritas

Logically prior to our question, "why Saint Paul," is the question, "why the Bible at all?" Why not simply speak of hermeneutic ontology? For Vattimo, however, to put the question this way is to think that reality is interpretable outside of particular textual histories in which we are ineluctably embedded. And the textual history of the West is deeply informed by the biblical writings: "If I reflect on my existence, I am forced to acknowledge that without biblical textuality, I wouldn't possess instruments for thinking and speaking. . . . We cannot speak ourselves otherwise than as Christians, because we are unable to formulate a discourse within our culture without accepting certain premises."[35] More particularly, to speak of hermeneutics is to speak of interpretation with its roots in the biblical traditions of Judaism and Christianity. This is to agree with Wilhelm Dilthey that Jewish and Christian traditions lie at the root of hermeneutics, but to disagree with why this is the case. For Dilthey, hermeneutics arises because of the prominence in Western culture of religions of the book, which leads from Luther's *sola scriptura* to the radical exegesis of Spinoza that ends up in the "liberation of exegesis from dogma."[36] That is to say, interpretation is what is at issue. Elsewhere, he notes that Dilthey posits that Christianity turns philosophy towards subjectivity (and away from objectivity) and thus makes Kant's notion that truth lies within the human individual possible.[37] Thus the emphasis on reason and reasoning processes rather than objects allows for the later move to hermeneutics. Interestingly, he suggests that Thomas Aquinas refuses the Aristotelian doctrine of the eternity of the world (and thus, "objectivity") on the basis of a Christian hermeneutic of divine freedom against more "reasonable" views articulated, for instance, by neo-Platonism's doctrines of *creatio ex deo* and divine necessity.[38] Finally, he notes that interpretation is rooted in the very fabric of scriptural traditions, that is, in Judaism's re-interpretation of itself, in New Testament redaction

35. Ibid., 71. As an example, he notes that while Italian literature is unimaginable without Dante, Dante is impossible to understand without knowing the Bible. We should note that Gadamer's notion of "history of effects" (*Wirkungsgeschichte*) is thus a bedrock assumption for Vattimo.

36. *Beyond Interpretation,* 42, quoting Dilthey's "The Origins of Hermeneutics" (orig. Wilhelm Dilthey, Gesammelte Schriften, vol. 5: *Die geistige Welt* (Leipzig-Berlin: Teubner, 1914). Vattimo accepts the aspect of Dilthey that sees hermeneutics as part of a secularization of the Christian metanarrative of Creation-sin-redemption, but believes that Dilthey's formulation remains too marked by a progressive-style Enlightenment historiography that he wants to challenge (ibid., 43).

37. Vattimo, *Farewell to Truth,* 66–67. See also Vattimo, *After Christianity*, 106–7.

38. Vattimo, *Farewell to Truth,* 69.

history, and in the Johannine affirmation of interpretation (John 14:25-26), which Vattimo reads as a justification for a hermeneutical and non-metaphysical form of Christian faith.[39] The circle, then, is complete: the roots of hermeneutics lie in the biblical traditions; the biblical traditions mark Christianity out as a fundamentally hermeneutical tradition.

Of course this is a generic response to a special question. What contingently warrants the honorific, "Saint," is that Paul's writings form an important part of biblical literature which is so central a part of Western consciousness. Materially and specifically, however, Saint Paul offers three key ideas for Vattimo that he thinks can help reconcile Christianity with modern, secular and pluralistic culture while simultaneously offering a critical norm for engaging discourse in the pluralistic public square. The three ideas are the ineluctable plurivocity of interpretation, κένωσις and ἀγάπη.[40]

We saw in the prior section that Vattimo thinks religious discourse now has a legitimate existence within philosophical discourse. The insights of myth, poetry, religion and other genres affect the very fabric of our self-knowledge thus showing pure reason at best an illusion.[41] Even being in its reifying and quantifiable modern forms shows itself as but one ontological mode rather than Being as such. In working through these issues, Vattimo looks to support a multi-vocal, dialogical and pluralistic approach to truth consistent with truth-building through consensus.[42] The difficulty for hermeneutics lies in the temptation to always lapse back into some foundational and substantial unity (Aristotle) or lurch forward to a teleological and conceptual solution (Hegel). In either case, the plurality of interpretation appears as an allegorical epiphenomenon to a more substantial unity underlying and eventually undoing plurality.[43] Instead, for Vattimo, Heb. 1:1-2[44] and Phil. 2:5-11 provide the keys to an interpretative historicization that he thinks lies at the root of hermeneutics

39. Ibid., 69–70. The passage from John's Gospel: "I have said these things to you while still with you; but the Advocate, the Holy Spirit, whom the Father will send in my name, will teach you everything and remind you of all I have said to you."

40. We have adverted to the importance of the Johannine literature to Vattimo as well and will expand on this below with regard to a Joachimite interpretation of the passage cited above.

41. See Vattimo, *Belief*, 86–87.

42. Vattimo, *Farewell to Truth*, 9: "But if truth is conceived in the hermeneutic terms proposed by many twentieth-century philosophers, truth in politics will be sought above all in the construction of consensus and civic friendship; it is these that make truth, in the descriptive sense of the term, possible."

43. See Vattimo, *Beyond Interpretation*, 52–54. Both, he thinks, fall back into "metaphysical objectivism," whether of substance or subject.

44. Vattimo does not worry about "authentic" writings of Paul and "inauthentic" writings. He reads Hebrews as if written by Saint Paul.

and provides for an epoch of true plurality that can resist the Aristotelian and Hegelian pulls respectively.[45]

On the formal issue of plurality, Vattimo thinks the Hebrews passage speaks to the "interpretative character of every experience of truth"[46] in a way different from the objectivist metaphysics of substance manner of Aristotle. This does not indicate agreement with ecclesial interpretations of Heb. 1:1-2 that envision the fulfillment of Old Testament prophecy in the Incarnation. Vattimo explicitly challenges an interpretation that, he thinks, either ends interpretation or places interpretation in the hands of the hierarchy (or both).[47] Instead, the "many ways" in which God has spoken through the prophets continues in an onto-theological sense when the Incarnation takes on its full and humble intensity as κένωσις. The interesting hermeneutical move is to bring these two passages together along with a Joachimite "history" of salvation.

Vattimo reads κένωσις in a metaphysical-hermeneutic key as the death of the God of the philosophers and of natural religion. In other words, κένωσις is the event (Ereignis) that signs the end of a transcendent deity, the God of alterity, and gives divinity over to the human community in terms of its emancipation from metaphysical violence. κένωσις begins the "dissolution of divine transcendence."[48] Using Vattimo's terms, κένωσις signals the "ontological weakening" of the transcendent ground for theism,[49] natural law morality, and natural religion such that this central Christian proclamation dovetails with the onset of secularity, the ontological weakening of power structures, assumptions of cultural progress and superiority, racist categories, etc. Indeed, secularity can be envisioned as the essence of Christian proclamation once the centrality of κένωσις is announced.[50] The interpretative event of κένωσις comes to fruition in modernity and late modern nihilistic hermeneutics and serves to undermine the violence he thinks inheres in metaphysics. It might also be argued that Vattimo extends Pauline moral

45. Vattimo, *Beyond Interpretation,* 48.

46. Ibid., 47.

47. Ibid., 48; Vattimo, *Belief,* 79. This claim fails to address the remarkable plurality-in-unity discoverable within Christian tradition and its varied interpretations of the scriptural witness. In recognizing this, the Church has refused, for instance, to choose for Thomas and against Bonaventure, or for Ignatius of Loyola and against Theresa of Avila. Having said this, the temptation to a reduction of the tradition to a particular form of thought is a real one both in official circles and, at times, among theological schools.

48. Vattimo, *After Christianity,* 27.

49. Ibid., 133; Vattimo, *Belief,* 39 and 49.

50. Vattimo, *Belief,* 50; cf. Vattimo, *After Christianity,* 36.

exhortation (*paraenesis*) beyond the behavior of Christians within their community to de-commission the hubris embedded in worldviews and institutional presumption. In this sense, secularism and democracy are the vehicles by which the message of κένωσις becomes real in the world. Saint Paul's κένωσις speaks to the ontological weakening Vattimo discovers in the history of philosophy and in our present cultural epoch.

In his *After Christianity* (2002), Vattimo drew heavily upon Joachim di Fiore's three stage view of salvation history and joined this to death of God theology that emphasized divine immanence and the end of divine transcendence.[51] Vattimo's rendition of Joachimite soteriology is a kind of metanarrative familiar to earlier writers such as Gotthold Lessing and Ludwig Feuerbach and to twentieth century radical theologians such as Thomas Altizer.[52] On this view, salvation history moves from an externalist, metaphysical, law-giving God to the revelation of God as Love in the form of a particular person, Jesus Christ, to a stage beyond the particularity of Jesus's revelation and consequent institutional-sacramental structures to the diffusion of Spirit in the community wherein the Kingdom is located, if not fully realized.[53] Secularization is the third age that does away with distinctions between sacred and profane history such that secularity can now become the main locus of divine engagement and interpretation.[54] Existence in this third age, the age of spirit, helps legitimize a "spiritual sense" reading of scripture and doctrine[55] and supports Vattimo's ontological weakening thesis in that the third age, congruent with the philosophical *Zeitgeist*, puts us beyond strong metaphysical systems. If κένωσις has to do with the incarnation, and especially with the death of God, then Vattimo reads this κένωσις in Nietzschean terms

51. See Vattimo, *After Christianity*, 25–41. Indeed, Joachim is a presence in most, if not all, of his texts. *After Christianity* gives the most extensive discussion.

52. See Anthony Sciglitano, "Contesting the World and the Divine: Hans Urs von Balthasar's Trinitarian 'Response' to Gianni Vattimo's Secular Christianity," *Modern Theology* 23 (2007): 536–37 for a discussion of Vattimo and Lessing; See ibid., 535–536 for the discussion of Thomas Altizer and Vattimo. Especially important for the connection with Gotthold E. Lessing is his essay, "The Education of the Human Race," in *Lessing's Theological Writings*, trans. Henry Chadwick (Stanford, CA: Stanford University Press, 1957). For Altizer, see his *The Gospel of Christian Atheism* (Philadelphia, PA: Westminster Press, 1966). For Ludwig Feuerbach, see his *The Essence of Christianity*, trans. George Eliot (New York: Harper, 1957); for the relevant passages, see esp. 32 and 35. Much of the metanarrative that Vattimo finds in Dilthey can also be found in Feuerbach, that is, a movement from heteronomous Israel to the interiority of Christianity and to genuine freedom and reconciliation in atheism.

53. Vattimo, *After Christianity*, 45.

54. Ibid.

55. Ibid., 44, 45 and 47.

as the death of any transcendent divine and/or metaphysical ground for ontological-moral structures and the advent of the possibility of conceiving God as friend.[56] Indeed, in *After Christianity*, this linear and univocal reading of Joachim issues in stark contrasts: "However, Joachim's text can still be our guide because of the general meaning of the age of spirit, which stresses not the letter but the spirit of revelation; no longer servants but friends; no longer awe or faith but charity; and perhaps also not action but contemplation."[57]

It is worth observing, however, that *Beyond Interpretation* and *Farewell to Truth (2007)*, while certainly adverting to Joachim, soft pedal both the Joachimite metanarrative and death of God theology. We might ask why this is the case. A first candidate for an answer would be that Vattimo's *Farewell to Truth* is a philosophical treatment of issues addressed in religious terms elsewhere. And certainly this response does have some credentials in that Vattimo's books evidence a distinction along these grounds. *Beyond Interpretation*, *Adventure of Difference*, and *End of Modernity* are more directly philosophical discussions; *After Christianity* and *Belief* are more theologically inflected or informed discussions. However, this answer does not get us very far. First, all of Vattimo's texts, including *A Farewell to Truth*, regularly mix philosophical, theological and ecclesial issues. Second, as a matter of systematic principle, Vattimo holds that no such scrubbing of the religious from philosophical discourse is legitimate in a late-modern context. This is clear from even a cursory examination of his texts. The distinction never becomes a separation and is more a point about emphasis than generic purity. Equally implausible is the idea that Vattimo has lessened his commitment to a non-violent form of hermeneutical thought. This commitment remains ubiquitous in his work.

One real possibility has to do with Vattimo's dialogue with John Caputo, *After the Death of God* (2007), held between *After Christianity* (2002) and *Farewell to Truth* (2009, Italian edition). It is in this discussion that Caputo points out that death of God theology usually institutes a metanarrative in which supersession is a prominent feature. Moreover, the supersessionist aspect of death of God metanarratives generally consign Judaism to a stage that is irretrievably past and juxtapose Pauline love to Jewish legalism or some form of heteronomy. The use of Joachim, of course, is not unique to Vattimo,

56. Ibid., 27: "Natural and historical symbols . . . really symbolize God only because God has become a human being in Jesus, disclosing that he is akin to finitude and nature and—I would say—inaugurating the dissolution of divine transcendence."

57. Ibid., 31.

and Caputo is aware of this. But Joachimite soteriology makes an epochal interpretation into a metanarrative of three fundamental epochs, each of which sublates and frequently negates the former stage. If former epochs are associated with metaphysics, legalism (whether natural, statutory or both), and violence, then it begins to look like Vattimo reads salvation history as a progressive departing from a violent "Judaic" brand of religion for an immanentist Christian secularism that promotes human autonomy, flourishing, and "friendship" with God.[58] In other words, Vattimo's reading of salvation history not only marginalizes the sacramental structures of Christian life and practice, but also juxtaposes the Pauline kenotic God to the Jewish transcendent God in ways that suggest anti-Judaism and Marcionism. There are certainly grounds in both *After Christianity* and *Belief* for this view.

In *After Christianity* and in *Belief*, Vattimo juxtaposes the God of the Bible to the *causa sui* of the philosophers and contends that it is the latter metaphysical-moral deity to which Nietzsche objected and not the God of the Bible.[59] The juxtaposition was unstable in these texts as it was clear that his particular version of Joachimite salvation history also located metaphysical violence in biblical religion anywhere outside Paul's proclamation of love figured as κένωσις. The instability becomes clear in two ways. On the one hand, Vattimo wants to argue that Nietzsche's declaration of God's death refers to the death of the moral ground of the philosophers and not the biblical God; on the other hand, Vattimo clearly thinks that divine transcendence ends through Pauline κένωσις and that this κένωσις moves interpretation definitively beyond the Old Testament. The God who is friend is *not* the God who is sovereign and decisively not the God of the Old Testament. Vattimo is explicit on the point when he comments on versions of Christian theology that secularize by way of divine alterity:

58. This is Caputo's critique of "theologies of the death of God" in general, and Vattimo's in particular in their dialogue, *After the Death of God* (New York: Columbia University Press, 2007), 66–82, esp. 74–82. Caputo rightly points out that Derrida's *Glas* is written precisely against this kind of Hegelian anti-Jewish pull in death of God philosophical and theological thought. If civil, Caputo's critique is also trenchant. His analysis fundamentally agrees with my own "Contesting the World and the Divine." Caputo raises the specter of Marcionite return in Vattimo. I will affirm this judgment below.

59. "However, in light of our postmodern experience, this [Nietzsche's proclamation of the death of God] means: since God can no longer be upheld as ultimate foundation, as the absolute metaphysical structure of the real, it is possible, once again, to believe in God. True, it is not the God of metaphysics or of medieval scholasticism. But that is not the God of the Bible, of the Book that was dissolved and dismissed by modern rationalist and absolutist metaphysics" (Vattimo, *After Christianity*, 6). Also, ibid., 104: "The God who has been killed by his followers is only—and rightly—the moral God."

In a certain sense, the God who at the end of the secularization process is recovered as wholly other is the God of the Old Testament (let me say this without any anti-Semitic implication), and not the God incarnate in Jesus Christ, of the New Testament revelation, and even less the God understood as spirit in the third age prophesied by Joachim of Fiore.[60]

The God of the Old Testament, on this reading, is what is definitively past and in conflict with the self-emptying God of Philippians that finds its τέλος in secularity. The Marcionite implications are rather obvious. Divine otherness offers only a tragic, Judaizing, and also metaphysical view of Christian revelation, while a thoroughgoing Pauline and kenotic form of thought, consistent with and perhaps driven by a reading of the history of Being (*Seinsgeschichte*), offers a non-violent religiosity functional for a pluralistic secular culture. The contrast, then, between the God of the Bible and the God of metaphysics is not a stable one. Vattimo is every bit as dismissive of swaths of the bible as he is of any metaphysical system of divine attributes. We will see that the issues Caputo raises with Vattimo's construction return when Vattimo speaks of ἀγάπη (*caritas*) and justice, key elements of Marcionite juxtaposition, in the same two texts. First, however, a brief examination of *A Farewell to Truth* on the same issue can suggest that Vattimo's position vis-à-vis Joachimite metanarrative, or at least the strength with which he formulates his position, has itself undergone attenuation.

The first thing to note is that Vattimo in no way reneges on his notion of a "spiritual age," a need to allegorically interpret scripture according to his doctrine of weakening, or the importance of friendship and love. In addition, Joachim does at least make an appearance. Moreover, he thinks Joachim was right to think that "the history of salvation passes through moments and phases."[61] What is of interest is what we do not find in this text. Nowhere that I can find does Vattimo propose here a definite three-stage structure to history that moves from transcendence to immanence, legalism and sovereignty

---

60. Ibid., 37. He makes a similar claim in *Belief* when commenting on John Paul II and what he calls "tragic Christianity: "However, these implications are only the most visible signs of tragic Christianity's overall regressive character, which is inspired primarily by the Old Testament faith, and which tends to undervalue the meaning of Christ's incarnation itself. . . . There is a sort of predominance of Judaic religiosity in the return of religion into contemporary thought (let me make clear that this observation has no anti-Semitic intention whatsoever)" (Vattimo, *Belief*, 83–84).

61. Vattimo, *Farewell to Truth*, 59; cf. 60.

to love. Once Joachim is read at this level of generality, we can notice that both Augustine and Bonaventure, among others, thought that salvation history passed through "moments and phases." This is not to say that the implications of Vattimo's prior commitments are absent; but they are not articulated as such in this text, which gives rise to the possibility that though he wants to emphasize divine love – certainly not a fault! – he no longer feels the need to juxtapose Judaic and Christian elements. Indeed, in *Farewell to Truth*, he hyphenates Judeo-Christian: "The Judeo-Christian revelation lies in the announcement that God is not violence but love, which is a scandalous announcement, so much so that Jesus was put to death for it."[62] There is still a juxtaposition in this text, namely, between *caritas* and *veritas,* but this is no longer a clear juxtaposition between Old Testament and New, Judaism and Christianity. Two questions remain: what is *caritas*, for Vattimo, and precisely how does Pauline thought function hermeneutically for him in terms of Christian existence?

Love (Caritas) and Historicity

The commandment of love, for Vattimo, serves as the center of Christian proclamation, a brake upon the more egregious possibilities open to nihilism, and, joined with κένωσις, a critique of all metaphysical systems. It is the essence and reductive center of all revelation.[63] Charity (ἀγάπη), however, is not a substantive notion that corresponds to a particular set of truths or ethical-natural requirements. Instead, the love commandment is a "'formal' commandment, not unlike Kant's categorical imperative, which does not command something specific once and for all, but rather applications that must be 'invented' in dialogue with specific situations and in light of what the holy Scriptures have revealed."[64] Indeed, the "essence of revelation is reduced to charity, while all the rest is left to the non-finality of diverse historical experiences, even of mythologies that at the time appeared to be binding to particular historical humanities."[65] It is here that he thinks Pauline Christianity must call into question a pure Nietzschean or Heideggerian vision, even when Nietzsche is read, as Vattimo sometimes reads him, as objecting primarily to a moralistic and thus metaphysically violent God rather than the God of Jesus Christ.

---

62. Ibid., 85. He uses the hyphenated form in *After Christianity* as well; this alone does not help his case for, as Caputo points out, the hyphenation itself usually points to a supersessionist system; nor does it suggest anything positive to Islam in the West. The key point here is the lack of emphasis on the other Joachimite elements without change to the importance of love.

63. Vattimo, *Belief*, 78–80.

64. Ibid. 66.

65. Ibid., 77.

Vattimo is aware that nihilism can itself turn into something metaphysical, and thus violent. His warrant for reading love as the essence of his nihilistic vision is that the hermeneutical age, of which nihilism is an aspect, is itself inspired by Christian revelation, as we saw earlier. Thus, a "reduction to love" is not a reduction of either hermeneutics or Christianity from the outside, as it were, but rather serves simultaneously as a secular and Christian hermeneutic principle. Only this, Vattimo thinks, can prevent nihilism, Heidegger's phenomenology, or secularism from turning metaphysical.[66]

If κένωσις and ἀγάπη (caritas) serve to humble a nihilism that can turn metaphysical, it also helps reconfigure particular versions of theological and moral doctrine and forms a matrix for secular cultural practice in an age of pluralism and multiculturalism. "Sin," for instance, becomes a way in which relationships of friendship get broken or damaged, whether relationships among people or between persons and God.[67] Vattimo juxtaposes this relational view of sin to a view related to violating a metaphysical norm or law.[68] "Salvation" becomes the liberating unmasking by way of kenosis and a spiritual sense reading of scripture of metaphysically violent structures that captivate both individuals and societies.[69] On the theological plane proper, salvation unmasks a judging, law-giving God who demands sacrifice to appease his wrath and suggests a God who is or has become "friend."[70] On the anthropological plane, salvation indicates this same relationship the other way around: human beings no longer need look to God in fear, but in friendship. Moreover, caritas indicates that the particular is liberated from its confines within the essential. In other words, an ontology of actuality refuses to judge the individual based upon a putative essence, rather than on what shows itself to be. For Vattimo, caritas and kenosis are also politically and socially relevant. Religious and moral differences should be considered weak interpretations rather than atemporal constants. This will allow one to greet others with hospitality and care as a "foundation" for the necessary tolerance of a multi-cultural, democratic society. It is not entirely clear why those who do not subscribe to Christianity would need to

66. Vattimo believes that charity is the norm for the secular. See Belief, 66 and 88 and After Christianity, 111, where he contends that Heidegger and Nietzsche "remain captive to Greek objectivism and refuse to develop fully the implications of Christianity's antimetaphysical revolution. These cannot be fully developed without recourse to charity."

67. Vattimo, Belief, 90.

68. Ibid.

69. Vattimo, Belief, 66.

70. Vattimo, After Christianity, 39.

do likewise, but for Vattimo κένωσις—and not particular dogmatic, moral or political claims – is the genuine foundation of "Christian" Europe.

Towards the end of *Belief*, Vattimo wrestles with the relation between divine justice and mercy. He suggests that the Old Testament has far more to do with divine justice than the New Testament while realizing elements of justice are certainly to be found in the latter. Divine justice shows remnants of a violent deity and should be de-mythicized not on the basis of extra-Christian reason, but rather on the basis of the love commandment. Of course Caputo is right to point out that this de-mythification will target "Judaic" religiosity and thus Judaic religiosity will be somewhat conflated with the natural sacred and its violence. Unlike Marcion, Vattimo does not juxtapose two gods here. Instead, he contrasts stages of "revelation," that is, stages of interpretation that move away from righteousness and towards love with some cultural baggage leftover along the way. Again, there are complications in his story. In *Belief*, he considers κένωσις as the meaning of creation and redemption.[71] Creation can still function here as a good insofar as its meaning is κένωσις. The context is Vattimo's working out of his death of God theology in relation to more existentialist forms in which divine alterity is emphasized. He labels these other forms "apocalyptic" and "tragic" and argues that their lack of confidence in human goodness allows them to support authoritarian structures.[72] It is interesting here that, on the one hand, *caritas* (ἀγάπη) and κένωσις serve to regulate the possibility of a violent nihilism,[73] but Vattimo sees those authors who would contend for divine alterity as overly concerned about human malevolence. It would seem to be the case that his own emphasis on ἀγάπη and κένωσις is precisely ordered to a lack of confidence that an empty secularism or nihilism can rely upon intrinsic human decency whether in terms of ecclesiastical, secular, and metaphysical power structures. By the time of *After Christianity*, however, it is no longer clear that Creation can carry this positive sense and in *Farewell to Truth* "creation" comes to denote a kind of metaphysical fundamentalism at the root of Catholic doctrines. Moreover, it is clear that divine love and justice cannot abide one another in Vattimo's

71. See Vattimo, *Belief*, 83–84.

72. Vattimo consistently strives to read modernity in a Christian vein without succumbing to what he loosely calls "apocalyptic" views, by which he means tragic or overly negative views. Of course his entire thought is apocalyptic in the sense of *apocalypsis* or revelation.

73. See Vattimo, *Belief*, 63 and 64. Vattimo writes: "If one thinks of nihilism as an infinite history in terms of the religious 'text' that is its basis and inspiration, it will speak of kenosis as guided, limited and endowed with meaning, by God's love." Cf. ibid., 69.

hermeneutic. Vattimo exhibits a deep distrust, in *Belief*, in the notion of a just God:

> I have the impression . . . that there are far fewer pages in the New Testament regarding 'justice' than 'mercy'; this leads me to my belief that the relation between the two faces of God [righteous and merciful] in fact constitutes a relation between different moments of the history of salvation, and that divine justice is an attribute that is rather close to the natural conception of the sacred, which must be "secularized" precisely in the name of the commandment of love.[74]

The Marcionite strand of Vattimo's thought—and it is the dominant strand—is here to the fore. In fact, we should point out that while Joachim thinks of a divine pedagogy that moves from one stage of revelation to another precisely because humanity needs such an education, it is not clear that Vattimo's association of Old Testament revelation and also divine justice with violence can be redeemed in terms of divine pedagogy. Too often, the oppositional and binary language with which he approaches his material suggests not a light or weakened interpretative stance, but rather strong declarations of evil and good.

Finally, we can say a word about Vattimo's Heideggerian-Pauline interpretation of existence that he advances near the end of *After Christianity*. The focus here is on *The Phenomenology of Religious Life*, Heidegger's 1920–21 lecture course in Freiburg.[75] We can take account of four factors concerning Christian existence: temporality, "waiting" understood as watchfulness, affliction and the Antichrist. The first thing to notice in Vattimo's treatment is that, unlike many readers of Heidegger, Vattimo notices Heidegger's debts in *Being and Time* to his reading of Christian revelation.[76] Authentic temporality, in this sense, involves not linear time, and not an event in linear time, but Paul's eschatology as read off of 1 Thess. 1:5-7 where Paul uses the term ἐγένετο to express the strange temporality of the eschatological "already." Vattimo believes that Heidegger is making essentially two points. First, he may be

---

74. Ibid., 89–90.

75. Martin Heidegger, *The Phenomenology of Religious Life*, trans. by Matthias Fritsch and Jennifer Anna Gosetti-Ferencei (Bloomington: Indiana University Press, 2004).

76. See, for examples, *After Christianity*, 123–26 and 131. That these connections are not allowed to become explicit in *Being and Time* speaks to a discursive decontamination that Vattimo might have been more critical of in his discussion.

connecting Paul's contention that what he preaches is not unknown to the Thessalonians, but that the Gospel had come upon them already in the power of the Spirit. In Vattimo's terms, then, the announcement was already part of their historicity, of who they were. Secondly, this coming upon the Thessalonians also involves "turning to God from idols . . . and to await his Son" (1 Thess. 1:9-10). Vattimo reads these passages to suggest that Western historicity is caught up in this announcement, the announcement that western culture has already heard and which forms a part of its self-understanding. In addition, this announcement involves a θλῖψσις (1 Thess. 1:6) an affliction, which Vattimo interprets as a kind of waiting and watchfulness, not for a temporal event, but for the παρουσία, which itself marks Christian existence as addressing itself to uncertainty. It is living in this uncertainty, then, that marks Christian affliction, and it is a waiting rather than accepting idols as if they were the Lord, that is the thorn in Paul's flesh. Here, perhaps surprisingly in an author who decries apocalyptic thought, we come upon the figure of the Antichrist through 2 Thessalonians. For Vattimo, Heidegger's thoughts on the Antichrist in 2 Thessalonians reflect the *Seinsgeschichte* of forgetting and concealing the ontological difference. That is to say, just as Heidegger reads Western metaphysics as descending from an early Greek encounter with Being as emergence to the reification of Being as beings, so Christian dogmatic history reflects a forgetting and concealing of the original eschatological waiting for a descent into metaphysical or "Greek" thinking and dogmatic definition. The Antichrist, in this reading, is the metaphysical lie that promises certainty and power, where only in weakness is there genuine strength. *Caritas*, in this case, is the waiting that withholds judgment of others on "metaphysical" bases that refuses to do violence, that seeks not substantive Christian truth claims, but rather to reduce the violence in the world. Of course, such "weakness," in Vattimo's terms, is a powerful interpretation and destruction of much of the Christian theological tradition and, we must admit, renders a Paul in stark opposition to his Jewish heritage. One hopes, then, that at the root of such weakness does not, in fact, stand the impotent potency of *ressentiment*.

Conclusion: Apocalyptic Marcionism

This essay has shown that Vattimo contends for a philosophical rendition of Christian revelation that, he thinks, is also a Christian rendition of hermeneutic ontology suited to the pluralistic and democratic world in which we live. Vattimo argues that given our contemporary philosophical and ideological climate, rationalist proscriptions against discourses of disclosure, whether mythical or poetic or both, fail to compel consent. The undermining of foundational certitudes also undermines the bases upon which such proscriptions rested. Such certitudes, of course, are not the only ones to fall in Vattimian thought. All foundations must crack under the pressure of a history of Being that leads to a notion of Being as the weakening or emptying (κένωσις) of metaphysical claims, correspondence theories of truth, and putatively objective forms of knowledge. All is interpretation, hermeneutics included.

The history of Being meets salvation history, for Vattimo, in the three-part story of Joachim di Fiore, who envisions a movement from heteronomous law to incarnation and to the age of spirit through the Pauline trope of κένωσις. Secularization, then, gets viewed as part and parcel of a Christian impetus and its very essence in the current age. In the secular space, for peace to reign, all must agree to weak renditions of their convictions; but, we should note, all must agree to this on the basis of a Christian and Pauline claim that the Son of God emptied himself for our sake. The limit to Vattimo's nihilistic secularism finds itself in charity: love that refuses violence, withholds judgment, and seeks friendship. In his fascinating reading of Heidegger towards the end of *After Christianity*, Vattimo tries to show how Heidegger's reading of Paul contributes to his ontology of weakening thesis. It is fascinating because Vattimo suggests that not only is Heidegger reading Paul, but that to read Heidegger, we must recall that, even where he fails to mention it, Christian and especially Pauline themes permeate his thought. More interesting still is the Apocalyptic rendition of this thought. There is no doubt, despite his contentions to the contrary, that Vattimo is a profoundly apocalyptic philosopher. ἀποκάλυψις means disclosure, unveiling, and Vattimo's entire thought is conditioned by the idea that epochal disclosures have priority over any notion of truth as correspondence; he has a vision of the Christian life that, in the end, is clearly agonistic in its struggle against any and all metaphysical foundations, what he is willing to name the Antichrist; if there is an Antichrist, then there is also a good angel, namely, the doctrine of ontological weakening itself to which the Christian ought to respond by waiting, watching, and loving. One must pick a side.

We also suggested throughout that Marcionism is a genuine temptation for Vattimo that he mostly, but not always, fails to successfully address. The Joachimite metanarrative plays too strong a role in his thought to overcome what to Jews can only appear as an ironclad and systematic supersessionism that associates their religion with justice and even violence as opposed to love. We noted a possible shift in emphasis in *A Farewell to Truth*, but to this point at least, Marcionite oppositions remain the dominant drift in his thought. Such a metanarrative fits uncomfortably with what Vattimo otherwise seeks to accomplish. What we have in Vattimo, then, is something akin to what I am calling here apocalyptic marcionism.

Let us return to our original question: "Why Saint Paul?" It seems the honorific sets Paul apart for Vattimo because Saint Paul gives him the gifts of κένωσις and ἀγάπη, the central interpretive keys to a system of thought intended to support a non-violent, friendly secular order. Paul becomes, for him, the anti-metaphysical prophet who counsels a weak rendition of thought such that commitments to truth never obtrude the desire for friendship. It goes without saying, of course, that this is not a full reading of Paul, much less the Christian Bible. Moreover, we should certainly ask whether other theological thinkers have embraced issues of the historical contingency of judgements or thought through the biblical teaching on κένωσις and love as fully, or more so, than Vattimo. One might suggest, for instance, that Bernard Lonergan would be an excellent interlocutor on the philosophical side of things, while Hans Urs von Balthasar would be at least an equal with respect to the themes of κένωσις and ἀγάπη. Nevertheless, we can see that the questions Vattimo raises are pointed ones, that the challenges he issues both to a philosophy that would like to think itself pure of Christian entanglements and a Christian theology that would like to hand itself easy victories over contingency while appealing to hermeneutics, must address themselves to the historicity of their relationship and always to the echoes of love that haunt their musings.

7

Badiou's Paul

Founder of Universalism and Theoretician of the Militant

Frederiek Depoortere

INTRODUCING ALAIN BADIOU AND HIS READING OF PAUL

Alain Badiou was born in Rabat, Morocco, in 1937 and was trained as both a mathematician and a philosopher. Badiou began his intellectual career as a disciple of Louis Althusser (1918–1990), the famous French Marxist philosopher, who taught at the Ecole normale supérieure in Paris when Badiou was a student there. In that early phase of his career, Badiou was working on the development of a materialist epistemology. He was particularly interested in the issue of how to think of change in scientific knowledge. A decisive break in Badiou's intellectual development occurred with the student revolt of May 1968, an event that Badiou would a few years later describe as "a genuine road-to-Damascus experience."[1] On that occasion, Badiou discovered Maoism, lost his interest in epistemological issues, and began to develop a Maoist systematic philosophy. However, the collapse of Maoism by the end of the 1970s forced Badiou to move beyond the confines of Maoism. The first fruit of that new phase in Badiou's intellectual career was the 1985 book *Peut-on penser la politique?* ("Can politics be thought?"). In that book, Badiou attributes the failure of Maoism (and Marxism in general) to the fact that it did not sufficiently distinguish between truth and knowledge, between "subjective will" and "historical necessity."[2] It is precisely this distinction that has become the foundation for all of Badiou's mature work,[3] and it is on the basis of this

---

1. Peter Hallward, *Badiou: A Subject to Truth* (Minneapolis: University of Minnesota Press, 2003), 33.

2. See Ibid., 39–40. This opposition between truth and knowledge shows that, for Badiou, truth is not a characteristic of knowledge. This implies, as noted by Hallward, that truth is in Badiou's view not what

distinction that he revised his previous understanding of Marxist notions such as class, the state, and the party. In this way, Peter Hallward explains, Badiou's mature philosophy is to be understood "as a reaction to the failed promise of Maoism," "a response to . . . the defeat of the revolutionary inspiration of Europe's most violent century."[4] Or, to put it differently, Badiou's work since the mid-1980s is an attempt to remain faithful to the events of May 1968 in the changed and changing circumstances of post-Communist Europe.[5]

It is against this background that we can now introduce Badiou's reading of Paul. In 1997, Badiou published a book on the apostle, titled *Saint Paul: La fondation de l'universalisme* (translated into English in 2003 as *Saint Paul: The Foundation of Universalism*).[6] Yet Badiou's interest in the figure of Paul predates the work of that book. He begins the prologue of *Saint Paul* by noting that the figure of the apostle had already inspired him for quite some time. And as further evidence for his long-standing interest in the figure of Paul, Badiou also mentions that in 1982 he had written a play titled *L'incident d'Antioche* ("The incident at Antioch"), in which he reimagines Paul as a female character (named Paula) (*Saint Paul*, 1).[7] However, it would be a grave error to consider Badiou's interest in Paul as betraying a religious sentiment of some sort or as testifying

the classic theories of truth in (analytic) philosophy have made of it: truth is neither correspondence nor coherence; it is also not what is useful or can be verified (see Ibid., 153–54).

3. This can also be derived from the title of Badiou's major book *Being and Event*, trans. Oliver Feltham (London: Continuum, 2005). As this title indicates, the distinction between knowledge and truth also coincides with a distinction between the order of being and that which is not of the order of being, the event. This also suggests a close link between the event and truth. It of course remains to be seen, however, what the event is for Badiou and how it is linked to truth. We will return to this question below.

4. See Hallward, *Badiou*, 31.

5. For further details on Badiou's intellectual itinerary, see Ibid., ch. 2; and Oliver Feltham, *Alain Badiou: Live Theory* (London: Continuum, 2008).

6. The play has remained unpublished until now and was not even yet performed in its entirety. On February 13–14, 2009, a conference based on this play, titled "Paul, Political Fidelity and the Philosophy of Alain Badiou," was organized by Ward Blanton at the University of Glasgow. During this conference a few fragments of the play were presented in English translation (translation by Susan Spitzer). Since the material was unavailable at the time of writing, I could not draw on it. See now Alain Badiou, *The Incident at Antioch*, trans. Susan Spitzer (New York: Columbia University Press, 2012).

7. The play has remained unpublished until now and was not even yet performed in its entirety. On February 13–14, 2009, a conference based on this play, titled "Paul, Political Fidelity and the Philosophy of Alain Badiou," was organized by Ward Blanton at the University of Glasgow. During this conference a few fragments of the play were presented in English translation (translation by Susan Spitzer). Since the material was unavailable at the time of writing, I could not draw on it. See now Alain Badiou, *The Incident at Antioch*, trans. Susan Spitzer (New York: Columbia University Press, 2012).

to some kind of turn to religion in his work. On the contrary, Badiou makes it very clear from the outset that he does not care at all about Paul as a religious figure. "For me," he writes, "Paul is not an apostle or a saint. I care nothing for the Good News he declares, or the cult dedicated to him" (*Saint Paul*, 1). And, to underscore that his interest in Paul is not inspired by religious motives, Badiou even characterizes himself as anticlerical and "irreligious by heredity" (*Saint Paul*, 1).

But why turn to Paul, if not for religious reasons? What is the importance of this figure for somebody like Badiou, who has no affinity with Christianity and even explicitly calls himself irreligious and anticlerical? The answer to this question is that Paul offers to Badiou what Marxism and Maoism are no longer able to offer: a figure of the militant subject. As Badiou explains, Lenin and the Bolsheviks had founded a particular type of militant subject, namely, the party militant. However, with the collapse of Marxism, this particular type of militant subject became obsolete and we are now in need of a new type of militant subject; and this is why Badiou turns to Paul. According to Badiou, Paul "practices and states the invariant traits of . . . the militant figure" (*Saint Paul*, 2). Or, to put it differently: Paul offers us an example of a prototypical militant subject, and that is why he is, in Badiou's view, of interest for us today. Badiou, seemingly aware of the fact that his use of Paul is still in need of further justification, again takes up the question of, Why Saint Paul? at the outset of the first chapter of his book (*Saint Paul*, 4). Here, Badiou once more takes pains to distance himself from Christianity, and he makes it clear that for him the *content* of the Christian proclamation (which Paul, in Badiou's view, reduces to nothing but the proclamation of the resurrection of the Crucified) is completely fabulous. Or, as Badiou puts it: "Let us say that so far as we are concerned it is rigorously impossible to believe in the resurrection of the crucified" (*Saint Paul*, 5). Thus, according to Badiou, we should forget about *what* Paul declares and merely focus on *how he does* this. For, in this way, we will be able to discover "the foundation for the possibility of a universal teaching within history itself," the *formal* structure of a universal truth, a truth that is not dependent on a community or a historical context (*Saint Paul*, 5–6).

Thus what is at stake in Badiou's reading of Paul is the possibility of universal truths in the contemporary world. This interest in the possibility of universal truths is of course closely linked to the interest to reinvent the militant subject. For, is a militant not precisely somebody who is battling for "a universal teaching within history"? (*Saint Paul*, 5). Given his interest in the possibility of universal truths in today's world, it may seem remarkable, certainly at first sight, that Badiou offers in his *Saint Paul* hardly any systematic reflections on truth and that within the book there is no discussion of the way Paul uses the term "truth" (ἀλήθεια) in his letters. The most systematic treatment of the question of truth is at the end of the first chapter of the book, but that is still before Badiou begins to discuss the content of Paul's letters in any detail. There Badiou states that truth "consists in declaring [an event] and then in being faithful to this declaration" (*Saint Paul*, 14). This suggests that understanding the notion of truth in Badiou's work requires insight into his understanding of the event, and we will have to return to this notion of the event further on in this chapter. From the "eventual" character of truth, Badiou draws the conclusion that truth is both singular and universal. He explains this twofold characterization of truth as follows:

> First, since truth is evental, or of the order of what occurs, it is singular. It is neither structural, nor axiomatic, nor legal. No available generality can account for it, nor structure the subject who claims to follow in its wake. Consequently, there cannot be a law of truth. Second, truth being inscribed on the basis of a declaration that is in essence subjective, no preconstituted subset can support it; nothing communitarian or historically established can lend its substance to the process of truth. Truth is diagonal relative to every communitarian subset; it neither claims authority from, nor (this is obviously the most delicate point) constitutes any identity. It is offered to everyone, without a condition of belonging being able to limit this offer, or this address. (*Saint Paul*, 14)[8]

Put differently, truth is "a *universal singularity*" (*Saint Paul*, 13). This allows us to rephrase the issue at stake in Badiou's *Saint Paul* as follows: the question he intends to answer is the question, "What are the conditions for a *universal singularity*?" (*Saint Paul*, 13). According to Badiou, the question of how a truth qua universal singularity is possible is precisely Paul's question. In Badiou's

8. To avoid misunderstanding, it is important to distinguish clearly between "singular" and "particular." "Particular" is for Badiou "whatever can be discerned in knowledge by means of descriptive predicates"; "singular," in contrast, is something that is "subtracted from every predicative description." See Alain Badiou, "Eight Theses on the Universal," http://www.lacan.com/badeight.htm. Thus in the opposition between knowledge/being and truth/the event, particularity is at the side of knowledge and being, while singularity is at the side of truth and the event.

view, Paul wants to liberate the gospel from any possible communitarian confinement, but without submitting it to the generalities available at the time. Expressed differently: for Paul, the gospel is not something of merely local or particular importance (it does not only concern the Jews), but should be addressed to all human beings, regardless of whether they are Jew or Greek, slave or free, male or female (to repeat Paul's famous distinctions in Gal. 3:28). Yet the gospel is neither a new abstract and general philosophy nor a doctrine. What Paul is therefore rejecting, in Badiou's view, is both the empty abstraction (of Roman legalism and Greek philosophy) as well as any form of communitarianism and particularism (*Saint Paul*, 13–14).

This explains why, according to Badiou, Paul is truly our contemporary, as he puts it in the title of the first chapter of his book. For just as Paul was confronted with the impasse between empty abstraction and communitarianism/particularism, so we are confronted with the same impasse today; Paul's way of dealing with it may teach us how we can also deal with it. This leads us to the analysis of the contemporary situation that Badiou offers in the first chapter of his *Saint Paul* (for it is precisely because of that situation that Paul is important for us today). Remarkably, Badiou's analysis of the contemporary situation is very much in line with the one offered by the Leuven theologian Lieven Boeve in his *Interrupting Tradition*.[9] In what follows, I will now first read Badiou and Boeve side-by-side in order to show that the former's analysis of the contemporary situation is not that idiosyncratic and that it is shared by at least one author that cannot be suspected of aiming at reinventing the militant subject. In this way, I also intend to show that Badiou's concerns may appeal to a wider audience than only those who consider themselves to be heirs of Marxism or Maoism. Indeed, is the problem of the universal not an issue that concerns us all?

According to Badiou, our contemporary situation is characterized by two processes, which, to use Boeve's terms, can be described as "pluralisation" and "marketisation." According to Boeve, "radical plurality" is one of the most fundamental characteristics of the contemporary, so-called postmodern, context.

> *Radical plurality* is a basic characteristic of our times. Indeed, the basic premise that the same information can be considered from a variety of completely different perspectives with equal justification

9. Lieven Boeve, *Interrupting Tradition: An Essay on Christian Faith in a Postmodern Context*, Louvain Theological and Pastoral Monographs 30 (Leuven: Peeters, 2003).

is fundamental to postmodernity. Every perspective is understood to have value in itself even if mutual incompatibility as well as occasional conflict are evident. Universal and uniform perspectives no longer hold sway; the master narratives have given up the ghost … Given the fact that plurality as such persists as a presupposition of every kind of thought and deed, one is left with the inevitable conclusion that no one still has the right to claim to be in possession of "the" truth. Postmodern critical consciousness resists in principle every claim to hegemony. Every form of universalistic pretention is critically unmasked as an absolutisation of one particular standpoint.[10]

In Boeve's view, this growing awareness of radical plurality should, at least in principle, lead to more awareness of and a growing respect for the other qua irreducibly other. This suggests that Boeve considers the process of pluralization to be largely arbitrary. Badiou, in contrast, is more negative about the prospects of what Boeve describes as pluralization when he speaks about it as "a process of fragmentation into closed identities, and the culturalist and relativist ideology that accompanies this fragmentation" (*Saint Paul*, 10). Of course, Boeve is also aware of the fact that pluralization can result in either the restoration of self-enclosed identities, a position he labels as "fundamentalism" and "traditionalism," or "radical relativism" and "indifferentism," but he denies that these positions are the necessary outcomes of the process of pluralization – rather, these are for him responses that fail to take postmodernity's radical plurality seriously (respectively by rejecting or disempowering it) and that therefore do not succeed in respecting the other qua other.[11] Thus Boeve is aware that true respect for otherness is difficult, and it is in his view made even more difficult by the "concealed streamlining" or uniformization that results from the "marketisation" or economization of the world, which "reduces diversity in various domains to the diversity of the market whereby monetary value is more important than content." As a result, Boeve notes, "The subject becomes a consumer in the game of supply and demand, both of which are generated by the process itself."[12] Badiou, for his part, points to the same process when he writes about "abstract homogenization" (*Saint Paul*, 10), which is the

10. Ibid., 54–55.
11. Ibid., 69–71.
12. Ibid., 73.

outcome of the ever-increasing "extension of the automatisms of capital" and the configuration of the world as a world market (*Saint Paul*, 9).

In today's world, the realities of pluralization or fragmentation, on the one hand, and uniformization or homogenization (resulting from economization), on the other hand, are found together. It is even the case that the former serves as a kind of motor for the latter. Or, as Boeve puts it: "On closer inspection, therefore, pluralisation would appear to be an *objective ally* of marketisation. In fact the discovery of irreducible plurality opens up an inexhaustible source of possibilities for the market. The diversity of cultural patterns, lifestyles, ideologies and customs etc., provides the narrative of marketisation with a multitude of new opportunities for expansion: new markets, new needs, new products."[13] Similarly, Badiou also identifies a close link between fragmentation and homogenization when he speaks about ever more complex identities as the material used by capital to extend itself (*Saint Paul*, 10–11). Or, to put it differently, for both Boeve and Badiou, pluralization and uniformization are the two sides of the same process, the "extension of the automatisms of capital" (to use Badiou's expression).

Thus to sum up: the problem in today's world is that the universal is always abstract, empty, and without content (everything is reduced to a commodity on the marketplace, possessing a certain monetary value), while concrete content is never universal and is always limited to a particular community or historical context (and therefore, ultimately, simply a matter of contingency, of taste, of like and dislike). In this way, Badiou concludes, there is in today's world nothing that can sustain a universal truth. For a truth can neither be abstract, empty, and without content, nor can it be particular and contextual. Therefore, Badiou contends,argues that there is no truth to be found in the expansion of capital (and its abstract, empty universality) or in communitarian identities (because these are never universal but always particular and limited to a certain time and place). Rather, truth consists in that what is ruled out by today's situation; it consists in an overlap of universality and something concrete. (This is what I take Badiou's description of a truth as being a universal singularity to be about.) And this leads). These insights lead me to propose that the question at the heart of Badiou's reading of Paul (and his philosophy in general) is the question of how truth qua universal singularity is possible: how can we have a universality that is not abstract and empty, a concrete content that is not merely particular and local, not restricted to a particular community or historical situation?

13. Ibid., 75.

Now that we have answered the question of why Paul has come to be of interest for Badiou and described the problems he aims to solve by turning to the apostle, let us continue by taking a closer look at the answer to the issue of the possibility of truth in today's world that Badiou discovered in the letters of Paul and examine in which way he understands the apostle to be the founder of universalism.

Reading Paul with Badiou as the Founder of Universalism

As we have already seen in the previous section, Badiou understands Paul as rejecting both empty abstraction and communitarian confinement of the gospel. Badiou sees this rejection concretized in Paul's rejection of two "regimes of discourse"—namely, "Greek" discourse and "Jewish" discourse. To explain the difference between these two types of discourse, Badiou opposes the main figure on which each of the discourses centers. Greek discourse centers on the figure of the philosopher, the wise man. It is "the discourse of totality," of cosmic order and the rational whole. Jewish discourse, in contrast, centers on the figure of the prophet: it is the discourse of the miracle, the exception, which is read and interpreted as a sign of divine transcendence and power (*Saint Paul*, 41). According to Badiou, both discourses presuppose each other. This can most easily be shown for Jewish discourse. There can only be an exceptional sign when there is a cosmic order that can be interrupted by the exception. Thus Jewish discourse presupposes Greek discourse. But Greek discourse also presupposes Jewish discourse since there can only be a totality when there is a constitutive exception, a "point of incoherence which the cosmic totality requires in order to sustain itself" (*Saint Paul*, 42). Badiou mentions this idea—that a totality always presupposes something that is not part of the totality, but without which that totality would not be possible—merely in passing, and he does not bother to explain it any further. It is worthwhile to take a closer look into the reason why Greek discourse presupposes Jewish discourse since the Jewish-Greek couple plays such an important role in Badiou's reading of Paul.

We can answer the question of why there is no totality without a constitutive exception by taking a look at the question of how a totality or whole comes into being. This question can be rephrased, in terms of Badiou's ontology, as the question of how a situation or set—a "presented multiplicity"—comes into being. According to Badiou, a set or situation is always the outcome of a "count-as-one" according to a certain structure or regime, which, insofar as it prescribes how the count-as-one for that situation is to be performed, can also be characterized as the *law* of the situation.[14] Now, it is important to keep in mind that the count-as-one *as such* is not itself counted as one. Or, to put it differently, a set or situation (a totality, a Whole) always requires something that is in excess of it (a law or rule that determines what counts as a one in that situation). To illustrate this, we can fall back on a scene from Salman Rushdie's *Midnight's Children*. Slovenian philosopher Alenka Zupančič summarizes the scene in question as follows:

> Aadam Aziz has just come back to India from Germany, where he studied to be a doctor. He is called upon to examine a landowner's daughter. When he arrives at the house and asks to see the daughter, her father explains to him that she is a decent girl who does not flaunt her body under the noses of strange men. The young doctor is led to a room where two women, built like professional wrestlers, stand stiffly, each holding one corner of an enormous white sheet. In the very centre of the sheet there is a hole cut, a circle about seven inches in diameter. The doctor is told that he can examine the patient only through this perforated sheet, and he is asked kindly to specify which portion of the girl he wants to inspect . . . During [a period of three years], the landowner's daughter contracts an extraordinary number of minor illnesses, and Doctor Aziz's visits become almost weekly events. On each occasion, he is vouchsafed a glimpse, through the perforated sheet of the young woman's body. There is probably no need to stress . . . that Doctor Aziz develops a strong desire for the daughter whom he only knows *partes extra partes*.[15]

This fragment illustrates how a totality or Whole comes into being. The totality in question here is the set of all that is worthy of Aziz's desire. In the fragment, all that becomes visible through the hole in the perforated sheet becomes desirable for Aziz. Thus, as Zupančič puts it, "The all is specified by its falling under a certain function."[16] Or, as she further explains:

14. Badiou, *Being and Event*, 24–25.

15. Alenka Zupančič, "The Case of the Perforated Sheet," in *Sexuation*, ed. Renata Salecl, Sic 3 (Durham:, N.C.: Duke University Press, 2000), 282–96 (here 282–83).

16. Ibid., 284.

Aziz will find all parts of [the landowner's daughter] desirable, *provided that* he sees them through the hole in the sheet. The back or hidden side of the all ... is always some form of "*provided that*." The reason for this lies in the fact that the all is constituted (or is in process of being endlessly constituted) through the hole of the exception. It is also important not to confound the notion of exception with that of exclusion. The exception *is not* that which is excluded from the series, but that which sets off the mechanism of exclusion (or differentiation), thus creating a set of all that comes under a certain condition.[17]

Thus to answer the question of why Greek discourse qua the discourse of totality presupposes Jewish discourse qua the discourse of the exception: the former always presupposes the latter because a whole can only come into being on the basis of a count-as-one, on the basis of the operation of a function or condition (which necessarily remains outside the whole that is brought about by it). Moreover, the fact that a totality requires a count-as-one on the basis of a condition also sheds fresh light on the character of the empty and abstract universality of capital, of which we spoke in the previous section. In light of what has been said in the present section, that universality can now be characterized as "conditional."[18] Indeed, as Badiou explains, what can circulate freely (or universally) under capitalism is that which can be counted (what has monetary value); while that which cannot be counted (does not possess monetary value) cannot circulate freely/universally. That this is the case, Badiou argues, is confirmed by the fact that, in our age of the free and inhibited circulation of capital, there are ever more laws that prevent the free circulation of human persons (*Saint Paul*, 10). This suggests, furthermore, that the empty and abstract universality of capital is not a true universality at all: precisely because it is conditional, it remains contaminated by something that remains, in the end, particular and is therefore excluding, because only those elements that satisfy the condition of possessing a certain monetary value enter the whole of capitalism.

17. Ibid., 285.
18. See Ibid.

After having explored how Greek discourse presupposes Jewish discourse, let us continue by examining what both discourses have in common. According to Badiou, each of them is a discourse of mastery, either of "philosophical mastery" or "prophetic mastery" (*Saint Paul*, 43). The former refers to the attempt to reach salvation "through direct mastery of the totality [of the universe]"; the latter wants to reach the goal of salvation "through mastery of a literal tradition and the deciphering of signs" (*Saint Paul*, 42). What both discourses have in common, however, is the conviction that the access to salvation is possible through something that is available *within* the universe. Both Greek and Jewish discourse are also discourses of the law (of the cosmic law, which "ties thought to the cosmos," in the case of Greek discourse and of the law of Moses, which "fixes the effects of an exceptional election," in the case of Jewish discourse), and they are discourses of the Father (because they are discourses of obedience, obedience that is to either the cosmos and the empire or to God and the law) (*Saint Paul*, 42). Another way to characterize Greek and Jewish discourse is to describe them as discourses in which there are masters and disciples. To explain this, we can fall back on Paul's statement that "Jews demand signs and Greeks desire wisdom" (1 Cor. 1:22). Somebody, Badiou explains, who performs miracles (a prophet) becomes a master for those demanding to see, just as somebody who is able to offer wisdom (a philosopher) becomes a master for those desiring to know (*Saint Paul*, 58–59). Moreover, neither Greek nor Jewish discourse is truly universal, not only because the one presupposes the other (see above), but also because they divide humankind in two (we have "Greeks" vs. "Jews") (*Saint Paul*, 42).

Thus true universality is possible on the basis of neither the whole nor the exception, but requires that the division between Greek and Jewish discourse and the dialectic between the whole and the exception be overcome. In Badiou's view, this overcoming is realized in Paul's own "Christian" discourse, which for Badiou is *not* to be understood as a synthesis of Greek and Jewish discourse, but is precisely "absolutely *new*" and "equidistant" from both (*Saint Paul*, 43). Or, to put it in terms of the central figures of both discourses, Paul is neither a philosopher (a Greek master) nor a prophet (a Jewish master) (*Saint Paul*, 44)—he is an apostle, that is: somebody who *declares* an event, *in casu*: the "unheard-of possibility" of the resurrection of the Crucified (*Saint Paul*, 45). This Christ event, Badiou contends, is characterized by a twofold exemption: it is both acosmic and illegal. That it is acosmic means that it does not have a place in the cosmic whole and that it cannot function as a sign (*Saint Paul*, 42, see also 56); that it is illegal means that it "is heterogeneous to the law, pure excess over every prescription, grace without concept or appropriate rite" (*Saint Paul*, 57). The declaration of the resurrection undoes the distinction between Greek and Jewish discourse and establishes a truly universal discourse, a discourse in which there are no longer masters and disciples (an apostle is not a master), but all become equal in being sons of the event (*Saint Paul*, 59). And, moreover, insofar as Greek and Jewish discourse are discourses of knowledge ("the philosopher *knows* eternal truths; the prophet *knows* the univocal sense of what will come [*Saint Paul*, 45; emphases added]), Paul's "Christian" discourse is exempted from knowledge as well. The event the apostle declares cannot be known, and the apostle knows nothing. In this respect, Badiou even speaks about "an evental disappearance of the virtues of knowledge" (*Saint Paul*, 45), something which he sees culminating in the following passage from Paul's first letter to the Corinthians.

> For Jews demand signs and Greeks desire wisdom, but we proclaim Christ crucified, a stumbling block to Jews and foolishness to Gentiles, but to those who are the called, both Jews and Greeks, Christ the power of God and the wisdom of God. For God's foolishness is wiser than human wisdom, and God's weakness is stronger than human strength. . . .
>
> God chose what is foolish in the world to shame the wise; God chose what is weak in the world to shame the strong; God chose what is low and despised in the world, things that are not, to reduce to nothing things that are, so that no one might boast in the presence of God. (1:22–29 NRSV)

This fragment is a clear example of the twofold exemption mentioned above. A crucified Christ has no place in the two established discourses: For Greek discourse, which is the discourse of wisdom, a crucified Christ amounts to a "folly" (μωρία); while for Jewish discourse, which is the discourse of the signs that testify to God's power, it is a "stumbling block" (σκάνδαλον). Or, to put it differently, the event brings about a reversal: what was deemed important by the two established discourses (wisdom, power) turned out to be nothing, while what was deemed nothing in the eyes of the world (and was rejected as foolishness and weakness) is what really matters. This also suggests one more way in which Greek and Jewish discourse differ from Christian discourse:

Greek and Jewish discourse are both discourses of being, of "things that are," while Christian discourse is a discourse of nonbeing, of "things that are not." The eminent example of such a thing that is not is precisely the event at the heart of Paul's proclamation, the resurrection. The resurrection is not because it has no place in the established situation (it is acosmic and illegal). It is unheard of and unthinkable, something radically new and different, which also means that it cannot be deduced. It cannot be proven and does not prove anything; it can only be *declared* (see *Saint Paul*, 49).

Let us now return to the problem that inspired Badiou's turn to Paul, the issue of how a universal truth is possible or the problem of how we can have a truth that is neither abstract and empty nor merely particular and local. As was suggested in the previous paragraph, Badiou solves the problem by saying that a truth cannot be sustained by anything that is, by anything that belongs to the established situation, but only by something that is *not*, namely, an event, which is, as we have seen, something that does not have a place in the current situation and cannot be inscribed in it. Or, to put it differently: *only a singularity makes true universality possible*—precisely because a singularity is something that does not belong to any particularity.[19] This of course raises the question of how, on the basis of a singularity, true universality can come about. This brings us back to the other aspect of Badiou's "definition" of truth as it was mentioned in the previous section: truth is not merely a declaration of an event (a singularity), it also consists in being faithful to this declaration. Or, to put it differently: truth is not something that comes about instantaneously, it is a process; true universality is in becoming. This suggests that a truth always requires bearers of that truth, militants that relentlessly work for it. In this way, we are led back to the issue of the militant subject, the issue Badiou raises in the prologue of his *Saint Paul*. Let us now continue by exploring in which way the letters of Paul can be of help in tackling this problem too.

BADIOU'S PAUL AS THEORETICIAN OF THE MILITANT SUBJECT

As we have discussed in the previous section, Paul's "Christian" discourse overcomes, in Badiou's reading of the apostle, the division between "Greek" and "Jewish" discourse. However, it also reveals a new division. This time a division *within* the subject is at stake, a division between "two subjective paths." These two paths are the path of "the flesh" (σάρξ) and the path of "the spirit" (πνεῦμα),

---

19. See note no. 8 above.

and each of them has its own "thought" (*Saint Paul*, 55). In this regard, Badiou refers to Rom. 8:6, offering the following translation of that verse: "The thought of the flesh is death [θάνατος]; the thought of the spirit is life [ζωή]."[20] Badiou is emphatic in underscoring that the distinction between the flesh and the spirit at stake in this verse has nothing whatsoever to do with the distinction between the body and the soul (a distinction that is Platonic in origin and was later adopted by post-Pauline Christianity) (*Saint Paul*, 55–56).[21] It is also important to keep in mind that death and life are here not meant as biological realities, but precisely as two types of thought (*Saint Paul*, 68, 70) and two dimensions of the subject (*Saint Paul*, 73). Badiou further develops the division between flesh/death and spirit/life by linking the former with "law" (νόμος) and "works" (ἔργα), and the latter with "grace" (*charis*χάρις) and "faith" (or "pure conviction," as Badiou prefers to translate Paul's πίστις) (*Saint Paul*, 75). Badiou justifies the link between the law and death on the basis of the particularity of the law and its works. In this regard, Badiou refers to Rom. 3:29–30, where Paul argues on the basis of the unicity of God ("God is one" and is therefore the God of both Jews and Gentiles) for the fact that both Jews and Gentiles are justified on the ground of faith. For Badiou, this link between "the One" (God) and "the 'for all,' or the 'without exception'" is of utmost importance. It explains why Paul rejects the law (and it is of course the law of Moses that is at stake here) as the means of justification: the law cannot be that means because it is addressed to what is only a subset of humankind, and in this way the law divides humankind into two parts ("circumcised" vs. "uncircumcised," as Paul puts it in Rom 3:30) (*Saint Paul*, 75–76).

But granting Paul's point that the law of Moses cannot serve as the universal means of justification because it is too particular (and excludes the Gentiles), why connect the law to the path of the flesh and the thought of death? To make this link, Badiou falls back on the issue of "desire" (ἐπιθυμία). His basic insight is that the law calls desire into being: it "gives life to desire" and

---

20. The NRSV offers the following translation of Rom. 8:6: "To set the mind on the flesh is death, but to set the mind on the Spirit is life and peace."

21. Unfortunately, Badiou is less clear on how we are to understand the opposition between flesh and spirit if they cannot be taken as referring to the body and the soul. My suggestion is that this opposition can be understood in light of Badiou's fundamental distinction between the order of being and the event (see n3 above): "flesh" stands for the order of being, for what *is*; while "spirit" stands for what is *not*, the event. This suggests that a subject can live according to what *is* (that is, follow the path of the flesh) or live according to what is *not* (that is, follow the path of the spirit). It remains to be seen, however, why a life according to what *is* results in the death of the subject while a subject can only be (truly) alive when it lives according to what is *not*. We return to this in what follows.

"unleash[es] the automatic life of desire, the automatism of repetition" (*Saint Paul*, 79). This automatism of desire is, according to Badiou, what "sin" is for Paul. Now that Badiou has introduced sin as the automatism of desire, he can link the law, desire, sin, and death together. In this regard, we can refer to Rom 7:8b–11, where Paul writes the following: "Apart from the law sin lies dead. I was once alive apart from the law, but when the commandment came, sin revived and I died, and the very commandment that promised life proved to be death to me. For sin, seizing an opportunity in the commandment, deceived me and through it killed me" (NRSV). In this passage, Paul distinguishes between the state of the subject before and under the law. Before the law, the subject was alive, and sin (the automatism of desire) was dead; under the law, in contrast, the subject is now dead and sin is alive.[22]

But what does it mean to say that the subject is dead and sin alive? What is the result of this? Paul's answer is that the intervention of the law has resulted in a gap between the subject's will/thought and his deeds. Or, as the apostle puts it:

> I do not understand my own actions. For I do not do what I want, but I do the very thing I hate. Now if I do what I do not want, I agree that the law is good. But in fact it is no longer I that do it, but sin that dwells within me. For I know that nothing good dwells within me, that is, in my flesh. I can will what is right, but I cannot do it. For I do not do the good I want, but the evil I do not want is what I do. Now if I do what I do not want, it is no longer I that do it, but sin that dwells within me. (Rom 7:15–20 NRSV)

Thus in other words: under the law, the subject is no longer master of its own actions, but it is lived by sin, which is, so to speak, an alien power occupying the subject. This leads us to Badiou's interpretation of what "salvation" (σωτηρία) means for Paul. It consists in undoing the separation of will/thought and action. The subject has to come back to life, and sin has to die. But, as sin qua the automatism of desire is the outcome of the intervention of the law, the subject can only "resurrect" when it is separated from the law because, as Paul explains

---

22. Thus, according to Badiou, Paul states that a life according to the law results in death (the death of the subject). This suggests that "the law" functions in Badiou's reading of Paul as another name for "the order being" and "the flesh." Or, to put it differently: Badiou suggests that "living according to the law" and "living according to the flesh" are the same.

in Rom 7:8, "apart from the law sin lies dead." This also explains why, in Badiou's reading of Paul, the law cannot be a means of justification or salvation, and this not even for the Jews. The law is precisely the reason why the subject is inhabited by the alien power of sin and is no longer the master of its own actions. There is therefore no way in which works according to the law can lead to a closing of the gap between will/thought and action that characterizes the subject under the law. Salvation can never be of the order of "what is due"; it "cannot take the form of a reward or wage" but is "the granting of a gift, *kharisma*" (*Saint Paul*, 77).

This has brought us to the topic of grace. As was explained in the first section, Badiou rejects the *content* of Paul's proclamation as fabulous: the resurrection of the Crucified never occurred. Similarly, he has no place in his thought for grace in terms of an intervention by or gift from God. In contrast, he contends, we should secularize the notion of grace and liberate it from any religious confinement. In this respect, Badiou speaks about "a materialism of grace," which amounts to "the strong, simple idea that every existence can one day be seized by what happens to it [that is: by an event] and subsequently devote itself to that which is valid for all" (*Saint Paul*, 66). Or, to put it differently, we don't need to retain the idea of the divine or the supernatural in order to have a concept of grace. This materialist understanding of grace leads us back to the topic of the militant subject because it enables us to sketch the contours of the subject that Badiou descries in Paul's letters. In normal circumstances (that is, under the law, on the path of the flesh), the militant subject lies dead. It is lived by alien powers; its desires are automatically generated by mechanisms and processes beyond its control; its "thought [has] disintegrate[d] into powerlessness and endless cogitation" and is unable "to prescribe action" (*Saint Paul*, 83). Is this not the situation of the individual under global capitalism? Indeed, is today's individual not reduced, as Boeve puts it, to "a consumer in the game of supply and demand, both of which are generated by the process itself"?[23] And is sin therefore not an appropriate term to describe the predicament of the individual under capitalism? According to Badiou's reading of Paul, however, the subject can return to life, fall over to the side of life again (that is, it can "resurrect"), at the occasion of an event. An event is something that happens to the subject, something unheard of and radically new that befalls it. In fact, as we have already seen, an event is *not*; it has no place in the current state of things; it is illegal and acosmic, cannot be proved and does not prove anything. Again, the event is grace: "pure beginning" (*Saint Paul*, 49), "a pure

23. Boeve, *Interrupting Tradition*, 73.

gift," "without cause" (*Saint Paul*, 77). In this way, the event is an opportunity, "the indication of a possibility" (*Saint Paul*, 91). The subject resurrects when it takes this opportunity. The subject that is seized by an event and responds to it by faith (although Badiou prefers, as we have already mentioned, to translate Paul's term πίστις as "conviction"), can be liberated from the alien power that inhabits it and can return to the side of life.[24] In this way, Badiou also secularizes the traditional link between grace and faith. In his materialist or secularized theory of grace, faith/conviction means that the subject "accords" with grace (*Saint Paul*, 87) by declaring or confessing the event (*Saint Paul*, 88). However, faith/conviction as such is not enough. It has to be completed through "love" (ἀγάπη) or, as Badiou puts it quoting Gal 5:6, "faith works only through love" (*Saint Paul*, 89). It is obvious that the love at stake here is not to be confused with some feeling of like or attraction; rather, it is faith/conviction in action, the work of fidelity to the event.[25] Finally, Badiou also rehabilitates the third of the so-called theological virtues, hope. "Hope," he writes, "is 'enduring fidelity,'

24. However, it is questionable whether this return to life implies a return to the life that was experienced by the subject in the state of innocence "before the law." At least according to Zupančič, this is not the case. Rather, the subject undergoes a second decentering instead. Or, as Zupančič puts it: the event "does not imply that life and death now find their 'proper' place and simply coincide with themselves. In other words, it is not that the subject now (re)appropriates life" (Zupančič, "The Case of the Perforated Sheet," 287). In this regard, she refers to Paul's letter to the Galatians, where the apostle writes that "it is no longer I who live, but Christ who lives in me" (2:20). Badiou himself also refers to this verse (*Saint Paul*, 86), and this suggests that the new life in which the subject can participate in the wake of the event is not so much its own life regained, but the life of the event. (Maybe this "life of the event" offers us a way to understand Badiou's use of the term *spirit*.)

25. Badiou also describes this love qua "evental fidelity" (*Saint Paul*, 90) as a law (*Saint Paul*, 88), a "transliteral law, a law of the spirit," "a law raised up by faith, which belongs to the spirit and to life," "a non-literal law" (*Saint Paul*, 87), a "law beyond law" (*Saint Paul*, 88). At first sight, it may seem bizarre that Badiou reintroduces the concept of law, after earlier dismissing it so completely. However, this becomes less strange if we take into account that Paul himself is also less univocal about the law than the passages from Romans 7 quoted above seem to suggest. In this regard, Badiou refers, among others, to Rom. 7:12, where Paul writes that "the law is holy, and the commandment is holy and just and good," and to Rom. 7:14a, where the apostle speaks about the law as "spiritual" (πνευματικός). Badiou also refers to Rom. 13:10, where love is said to be fulfilling the law. Badiou explains this positive use of the law in Paul as pointing to a return of the law qua love. Or, to put it differently: love becomes the law of the subject seized by the event of the resurrection. It is love (in the sense of evental fidelity) that serves as a law to the postevental subject. Or, as Badiou puts it: "Love . . . functions as principle and consistency for the subjective energy initiated by the declaration of faith. For the new man, love is the fulfillment of the break that he accomplishes with the law; it is law of the break with law, law of the truth of law" (*Saint Paul*, 89). This new law cannot implicate the subject in the automatism of desire, because it does not imply any prohibition (and can thus not arouse the desire to what is forbidden), but is purely affirmative (what is prescribed is precisely nothing but evental fidelity, or love) (*Saint Paul*, 89).

tenacity of love through the ordeal, and in no way vision of a reward or punishment. Hope is the subjectivity of a victorious fidelity, fidelity to fidelity, and not the representation of its future outcome" (*Saint Paul*, 95). Thus to sum up: the militant figure suggested by Paul (in Badiou's reading) is somebody who responds with faith/conviction, love, and hope to the grace of an event.

Let us now, to conclude the present section, return to the question of how, on the basis of a singularity, true universality can come about. As explained above, truth does not merely consist in a declaration of an event (faith, conviction), but also in the work of faith (love). It is this love qua work of faith that drives a truth qua process and enables true universality, which is a universality that cannot be contained within any particularity. As we have already mentioned, the event undoes differences between people: in light of the event, all become equalized, all are sons and daughters of the event. Thus what makes a universal truth *possible* is the occurrence of a singularity (an event, something that cannot be inscribed in the established order because it cannot be confined to any existent particularity) and what realizes this possibility is the universal *application* of that event. In Paul's case, this universal application takes the form of a proclamation of the gospel that addressed all. The universality of the Christ event is the universality of a *universal* address. Or, as we have already put it with the help of Badiou: "[Truth] is offered to all, or addressed to everyone, without a condition of belonging being able to limit this offer, or this address" (*Saint Paul*, 14). In this way, existent distinctions among people (Jew vs. Greek, slave vs. free, male vs. female) are traversed, and all are made equal as sons and daughters of the event (see Gal. 3:28: "all of you are one in Christ Jesus"). This does not imply that differences are undone. These differences are still there (in Paul's case: there are still Jews and Greeks, slaves and free persons, males and females); but in light of the event, these differences lose their importance, they become irrelevant. In this regard, Badiou speaks about the event as resulting in "*an indifference that tolerates differences*" (*Saint Paul*, 99 emphasis original).

CRITICAL EVALUATION

In the preceding pages, we have explored the interpretation of Paul that Badiou offers in his 1997 book on the apostle. We have focused on the issues and concerns that motivated Badiou's interest in the figure and the letters of Paul, and we have examined how Badiou sees Paul solving these issues. I do not claim to have offered an exhaustive presentation of the content of Badiou's *Saint Paul*, which remains after all a very dense and difficult text that raises more issues than could be tackled within the scope of the present chapter. For instance, I have left out Badiou's discussion of the meaning of Christ's death in chapter 6 and how what he writes in this regard resonates with radical theology or so-called death-of-God theology.[26] Moreover, I opted for a close reading of *Saint Paul* instead of discussing it in the context of Badiou's other works. Yet I do hope to have succeeded in offering a good impression of what is at issue in Badiou's book on Paul, why the apostle has entered into the oeuvre of this self-proclaimed atheist and anticlerical philosopher, and how he uses Paul's letters. In my discussion of Badiou's reading of Paul as presented here, I have limited myself to trying to understand what he writes about the apostle, leaving aside possible criticisms of what he does with him. Here at the end of this chapter, I now want to offer two possible criticisms. I do not claim these to be original. Indeed, what follows has, in some form or another, already been formulated by other scholars.

A first possible criticism of Badiou's interpretation of Paul concerns its dependence on the distinction between "Jewish" and "Greek" discourse. As has become clear in our discussion above, the idea that Paul establishes a new discourse ("Christian" discourse) that overcomes two established discourses (Greek and Jewish discourse) plays a pivotal role in what Badiou writes about the apostle. Yet precisely this distinction between Greek and Jewish discourse as well as the idea that Paul establishes a new discourse are highly problematic. First of all, it is questionable whether Paul really intended to offer any theory of discourses when he used the Greek-Jewish couple. Indeed, as noted by the American-Israeli philosopher and historian of religion Daniel Boyarin, it is more likely that he considered the terms *Greek* and *Jewish* as referring to different "religious identifications and religio-ethnic practices." Or, to put it simply: for him, *Greek* simply meant "not-Jewish" or "pagan."[27] Moreover, it is probably also incorrect to consider Paul as establishing something new that then can be labeled "Christian" (be it a discourse, a religion, or a people). In this regard, we can refer to the New Testament scholar Dale Martin, who explains that what is at stake in the letters of Paul is *not* that the Christ event allows for the creation of a new people (a "nonethnic universal people" consisting of Gentiles that stop to be Gentiles and of Jews that stop to be

26. This resonance is also noted in John D. Caputo, "Introduction: Postcards from Paul," in *St. Paul among the Philosophers*, ed. John D. Caputo and Linda Martín Alcoff, Indiana Series in the Philosophy of Religion (Bloomington: Indiana University Press, 2009), 1–23 (here 9); although it is not explored further in the book (as noted by Caputo on p. 18).

27. Daniel Boyarin, "Paul among the Antiphilosophers; or, Saul among the Sophists," in Caputo and Alcoff, eds., *St. Paul among the Philosophers*, 109–41 (here 116–17).

Jewish), but that it allows for the Gentiles' being included in Israel, a "grafting of the nations *into the people of Israel.*"[28] This does not mean that it is not justified to see Paul as being "a great universalizer,"[29] but it does question the particular way in which Badiou reconstructs Paul's thought. Moreover, according to John Caputo, this idea of "grafting" shows that Paul is actually offering an alternative to Badiou's subtractive understanding of universality, a model of universality that understands it as consisting in opening up one's own particularity to include others. "Pauline universality," Caputo contends, is about "the universal extension of the Jew to include everyone," "the universality of the inclusion of the Greek in the Jew."[30] A second important problem with Badiou's interpretation of Paul is his understanding of the law. As noted by Swedish theologian Jayne Svenungsson, Badiou's understanding of Paul seems to presuppose "a quasi-Christian dialectic of Law and Grace which carries problematic anti-Jewish undertones."[31] This quasi-Christian (or should we say, quasi-Lutheran) understanding of the relationship between law and grace to which Svenungsson refers understands law and grace as being in complete mutual exclusion. The "problematic anti-Jewish undertones" that come with this kind of position imply (implicitly or explicitly) that the (messianic) event of grace abolished the law and that it is therefore, from now on, no longer justified to still observe the law (or, to put it differently, to remain an observing Jew). As has become clear above, Badiou shares this kind of understanding of the relationship between law and grace. As we have seen, law stands for him for the order of being, the flesh, and leads to the death of the subject; grace is linked to the event, that which does not belong to the order of being, and just as the event is in his view completely disconnected from the order of being, grace is completely disconnected from the law. It is highly questionable, however, whether any Jew (Paul included) could ever accept such a sharp opposition between law and grace. Or, in the words of Svenungsson, a Jewish believer would not understand the messianic event as resulting in "a liberation from the Law," but as enabling "a liberation *to* the Law"[32]—which implies that the law is not opposed to grace, but is already part of it. Hence, it can be argued that Badiou is not interested at all in the law of Moses as a religious given and

28. Dale B. Martin, "Teleology, Epistemology, and Universal Vision in Paul," in Caputo and Alcoff, eds., *St. Paul among the Philosophers*, 91–108 (here 100–101).

29. Ibid., 93.

30. Caputo, "Introduction," 3.

31. Jayne Svenungsson, "Wrestling with Angels: Or How to Avoid Decisionist Messianic Romances," *International Journal of Žižek Studies* 4 (2010): 1–16, here 2.

32. Ibid., 3.

speaks about the law in general (as a synonym for the established order). But maybe that's precisely the problem: that he uses the example of the Mosaic law to theorize about the law in general and does this from the perspective of what Svenungsson characterizes as the "modern European" and "notably Protestant" negative understanding of the law as "static, prohibitive, condemning."[33]

These two examples show that biblical scholars and theologians cannot but make serious objections to Badiou's philosophical reading of Paul. But does this mean that Badiou's Paul lacks all legitimacy? Not necessarily, American historian Paula Fredriksen argues, as long as we do not take Badiou to be a historian who is interested in understanding and formulating as exactly as possible what Paul meant to his first-century context, but as somebody who stands in the long tradition of thinkers who appropriated and shaped Paul to solve their contemporary problems. Such appropriations of foundational texts (like Paul's letters), Fredriksen adds, are necessarily "anachronistic" and "false to the original author"—and there is nothing wrong with that (as long as we remain aware of it and do not try to sell our anachronistic interpretations as historically accurate).[34] But is Badiou *merely* shaping Paul in his own image? At least according to Boyarin, this is not the case. For him, "Badiou's language of event and militance captures something about Paul's texts (and especially Galatians) that more properly theological language misses."[35] Thus anachronistic interpretations of Paul's letters can shed fresh light on these all-too-familiar texts. It is a basic insight of hermeneutics that the meaning of a text cannot be limited to the intention of its author or the way it was understood by its first readers. When a text is read in a new context, the tension between the old text and the new context can produce new and unheard-of meanings. What happens in Badiou's *Saint Paul* is an example of this: old texts (the letters of Paul) enter a new context, a context in which they have until now never been read (the context of Badiou's thought), and they reveal a new meaning, a meaning that was hitherto unthinkable. And this shows that Badiou's *Saint Paul* deserves a place in the long tradition of reappropriating the letters of Paul in ever-new contexts. That this has until recently been a business that was dominated by theologians is no argument against having an irreligious and self-proclaimed anticlerical philosopher like Badiou contributing to it as well. Thus, in the end, Badiou's Paul matters more for systematic theologians[36] engaging

33. Ibid., 1, 12.

34. Paula Fredriksen, "Historical Integrity, Interpretive Freedom," in *St. Paul among the Philosophers*, 61–73 (here 62, 71, and 72).

35. Boyarin, "Paul among the Antiphilosophers; or, Saul among the Sophists," 112.

36. Cf. my *Badiou and Theology*, Philosophy and Theology (New York/London: Continuum, 2009).

contemporary culture and present-day philosophical debates on universality, militancy, subjectivity, and truth than for biblical scholars; but the former would do well to stay in touch with what the latter write in order not to forget that Badiou is not presenting the historical Paul, but his own version of the apostle.

8

Agamben's Paul
Thinker of the Messianic

Alain Gignac

Intellectual bombshell or dud? However wary one must be of fads, Giorgio Agamben has had an undeniable impact that makes him more than just a passing trend. Eclectic, erudite, original, and a tad recondite, he is a virtuoso of paradoxes and subtleties. He displays a train of political thought that, if perplexing and challenging, is always deeply provocative. He proposes a Pauline interpretation that steers off the beaten track and confronts commonly held opinions.

As an exegete of the Pauline corpus, but not being a specialist of Agamben's entire body of work—and not being adequately equipped to verify all his references to philosophical tradition—I seek to achieve here a twofold objective. First, to give an account of Agamben's position regarding Paul within the overall coherence of Agamben's thought; and second, to identify the points where this reading can stimulate and even renew exegetic and theological thought. I will present this in three steps: First, a synthesis of his thought; second, a presentation of his recourse to Paul—particularly in his major work *The Time That Remains*;[1] and third, the identification of several Pauline themes from the perspective both of exegesis and theology (the temporality of salvation, Christian commitment, community as ἐκκλησία, law disabled, Christology). The aim is not so much to critique Agamben in detail as it is to provide an introduction to his thought. First, it is best to take the bull by the

---

1. Giorgio Agamben, *The Time That Remains: A Commentary on the Letter to the Romans*, trans. P. Dailey (Stanford: Stanford University Press, 2005 [Italian 2000]). Henceforth cited in the text as *Time That Remains,* followed by the page number.

horns: for the theologian, is Agamben's position truly significant? Better yet, is it at all relevant?

(Ir)relavance?

Let us be clear from the outset: his is a *philosophical* reading in which the epistles of Paul are treated in the same way as the texts of Aristotle. More specifically, it is a metaphysical reading, relying on abstraction and formalism, far removed from any concrete sociological consideration. Agamben's position is to consider the epistles of Paul as a *classical* work from an agnostic point of view; his is not a Christian reading but rather an approach more in line with Jewish scholars (Walter Benjamin, Gershom Scholem, Jacob Taubes), nor is it a canonical or even a faith-based reading: "What interests me in the texts of Paul is not so much religion, but that other, more specific field, messianism, which is closely related to the political. It is another author, here, that has been pivotal for me, and who is not at all religious: Walter Benjamin. He construes the messianic as a paradigm of the political, or in other words, of historical time. This is more the issue for me."[2] It has been rightly noted that this was messianism without a messiah[3]—as we shall see, what interests Agamben is Paul's enunciative structure and his ethical-political stance rather than his spiritual message or experience. In Agamben's view, Christ is not a proper name, but a title, quite independent of the personality of the person who bears it. Agamben in his book *The Time That Remains,* does not seek to know Christ, but "more modestly and more philosophically, it seeks to understand the meaning of the word *christos,* that is, 'Messiah'" (*Time That Remains,* 18).

Opinions differ, however, on the legitimacy of Agamben's theologico-political thought. On the philosophical level, he has been challenged as being indifferent to personal commitment and corporeal reality, as too ontological and abstract, and especially as pessimistic in the extreme.[4] Yet, without being an activist, Agamben has not been afraid to air his views on current issues in newspapers.[5] He also refused, for example, an invitation as guest lecturer

2. Stany Grelet, Mathieu Potte-Bonneville, and Giorgio Agamben, "Une biopolitique mineure. Un entretien avec Giorgio Agamben," *Vacarme* 10 (1999): 4–10 (consulted online http://www.vacarme.org/article255.html). Our translation.

3. Paul Ricoeur, "Paul apôtre. Proclamation et argumentation. Lectures récentes," *Esprit* (2003): 85–112.

4. Philippe Mesnard and Claudine Kahan, *Giorgio Agamben à l'épreuve d'Auschwitz témoignages, interprétations* (Paris: Éd. Kimé, 2001); Matthew Sharpe, "Only Agamben Can Save Us? Against the Messianic Turn Recently Adopted in Critical Theory," *Bible and Critical Theory* 5 (2009): 40.1–40.20.

at New York University as a protest against the new antiterrorist biometric techniques put in place by the Bush administration—a procedure he refused to submit to.[6] In a feminist perspective, it has been noted that, like in Greek philosophy, women were not taken into account by Agambenian political thought.[7] As for hermeneutics, some have radically invalidated Agamben's positions because of his rejection of faith and of transcendence, which would preclude a fusion of the author's (Paul) and the reader's (Agamben) horizons, since, according to Gadamer, it is impossible to understand Paul unless one accepts his presuppositions—and therefore he cannot contribute to one's self-understanding.[8] And yet another, last critique, but not the least: Agamben appears to fail to take into account the fruit of late twentieth-century biblical studies, specifically the apocalyptic dimension of Paul's worldview.[9] There are, to be sure, some shortcomings in Agamben's works, which I have myself brought to light in a previous article.[10] For example, the importance of charisms is not discussed; the circumstances and historical context of the writings are ignored; Paul's all-important apocalyptic structure is completely eschewed; the soteriological significance of Jesus' death is watered down; Paul's Christocentric stance is made irrelevant; and the concrete politico-religious articulation of Pauline political thought is entirely discounted—whereas Paul opposes the Imperial cult (Romans 13) with a logical faith that emerges as a veritable challenge to established authority (Rom. 12:1-2). And finally, Agamben

5. Giorgio Agamben, "Terrorisme ou tragi-Comédie," *Libération*, November 19, 2008; Agamben, "Non à la Biométrie," *Le Monde diplomatique*, December 6, 2005.

6. Giorgio Agamben, "Non au tatouage biopolitique," *Le Monde diplomatique*, January 10, 2004.

7. Nichole E. Miller, "The Sexual Politics of Pain: Hannah Arendt Meets Shakespeare's Shrew," *Journal for Cultural and Religious Theory* 7 (2006): 18–32; William Robert, "Human, Life, and Other Sacred Stuff," *Journal for Cultural and Religious Theory* 10 (2009): 1–23.

8. Jens Zimmermann, "Hermeneutics of Unbelief: Philosophical Readings," in *Paul, Philosophy, and the Theopolitical Vision*, ed. Douglas Harink (Eugene, OR: Cascade, 2010), 227–53. Indeed, by his "hermeneutics of the present," Agamben proposes an interpretative framework far removed from Gadamer's: Job de Meyere, "The Care for the Present: Giorgio Agamben's Actualisation of the Pauline Messianic Experience," *Bijdr* 70, no. 2 (2009): 168–84 (here 181).

9. Ryan L. Hansen, "Messianic or Apocalyptic? Engaging Agamben on Paul and Politics," in Harink, ed., *Paul, Philosophy, and the Theopolitical Vision*, 198–223. However, there is a possible misunderstanding here since for Agamben, apocalyptic is synonymous with eschatological (a conception of messianic time he rejects). But there is perhaps little difference between the intuition of the sudden advent of the messianic and the belief that in Christ, a new age had already come.

10. Alain Gignac, "Taubes, Badiou, Agamben: Reception of Paul by Non-Christian Philosophers Today," in *Reading Romans with Contemporary Philosophers and Theologians*, ed. David Odell-Scott, Romans Through History and Cultures 7 (New York: T&T Clark, 2007), 155–211.

generally has a tendency to select those passages in Paul that suit him best and to ignore the passages that could temper or counterbalance his analyses.

To the contrary, others liken Agamben's brave vision to that of Martin Luther or Karl Barth, who, having dared to contest the established opinions of their time, were able to open up new vistas.[11] Accordingly, Agamben's posture corresponds to the current uneasiness between the religious and the secular. It calls for a redefining of their interrelation and would better favor the resistance to neoliberal imperialism than does the communitarianism of Christians in the United States—while at the same time toppling Luther's monochromatic Paul![12] In other words, the Italian philosopher would help us rethink the relation of Christians to the world,[13] and redefine once again the ecclesial community.[14] As far as exegesis is concerned, Agamben has undeniably, despite his shortfalls, brought to light new questions (the importance of the subject, the manner of experiencing the "as not," the radical political and ethical perspective), has revived some old ones (messianism, the temporality of the "already/not yet"), or has wrenched us from their grip (for example, the opposition law and faith-gospel).[15] I must admit that, as an exegete, reading such a philosopher who seeks to grasp some of Paul's essential points is a real breath of fresh air. Sometimes it seems that Pauline exegesis goes round in circles. It is often content with merely describing the rhetorical workings of the epistles without engaging theology.[16] The same old debates constantly resurface: between the tenants of the more traditional perspective (Luther, Bultmann) and those of the "new perspective";[17] around Paul's coherence concerning the Torah; on the meaning of πίστις Χριστοῦ (faith in Christ or faithfulness of Christ, Rom. 3:22; Gal. 2:16);[18] concerning the focus of Pauline theology and the manner in which it

11. Paul J. Griffiths, "The Cross as the Fulcrum of Politics: Expropriating Agamben on Paul," in Harink, ed., *Paul, Philosophy, and the Theopolitical Vision*, 179–97.

12. Ward Blanton, "Disturbing Politics: Neo-Paulinism and the Scrambling of Religious and Secular Identities," *Dialog* 46 (2007): 3–13.

13. P. Travis Kroeker, "Whither Messianic Ethics? Paul as Political Theorist," *Journal of the Society of Christian Ethics* 25 (2005): 37–58.

14. Gordon Zerbe, "On the Exigency of a Messianic Ecclesia: an Engagement with Philosophical Readers of Paul," in Harink, ed., Paul, Philosophy, and the Theopolitical Vision, 254–81.

15. Michel Berder et al, "Saint Paul au croisement de la philosophie et de la théologie aujourd'hui: table ronde," *Transversalités* 114 (2010): 67–90.

16. See Robert Jewett, Roy David Kotansky, and Eldon Jay Epp, *Romans: A Commentary*, Hermeneia (Minneapolis: Fortress Press, 2007).

17. See E. P. Sanders, *Paul and Palestinian Judaism: A Comparison of Patterns of Religion* (Minneapolis: Fortress Press, 1977) and James D. G. Dunn, "The New Perspective on Paul," *Bulletin of the John Rylands Liberary* 65 (1983): 95–122.

is developed.[19] But Agamben, in reading Paul from the outside in, confers to it renewed relevance. He reminds us that justification by faith alone does not exhaust the riches of Paul's epistles and that they are a classic of the Western world.

Be that as it may, as one author concludes: "The single most important result of this fascination with Paul is that it contests the claims of church members, theologians, and historians to be the real bearers of the Pauline legacy."[20] A sign of the times, perhaps: on March 8, 2009, Agamben gave a lecture at the famous *Conférences du Carême* at Notre Dame Cathedral in Paris. He raised this question: "What has become of the experience of messianic time in today's Church? That is the question I have come to submit here and now to God's Church in residence in Paris . . . : will the Church take this historic opportunity to rekindle its messianic calling?"[21]

PHILOSOPHICAL VISION

The career of Giorgio Agamben (born in 1942) can be divided into two periods, the turning point being the fall of the Berlin Wall in 1989. Between May 1968 (the Parisian "revolution" and its international repercussions) and 1989, Agamben was part of the Italian and European Marxist intellectual circle—a friend of the filmmaker Pier Paolo Pasolini, he portrayed the role of the apostle Philip in his film *The Gospel according to St. Matthew* (1964). Agamben's main preoccupation then was the anthropological meaning of language. What is the meaning of "I speak"?[22] The aesthetical, literary, and linguistic issues he

18. Michael F. Bird and Preston M. Sprinkle, eds., *The Faith of Jesus Christ: Exegetical, Biblical, and Theological Studies* (Peabody, MA: Hendrickson, 2010); Richard B. Hays, "PISTIS and Pauline Christology: What Is at Stake?," in *Pauline Theology*, vol. 4, *Looking Back, Pressing On*, ed. David M. Hay and E. Elizabeth Johnson (Atlanta: Scholars Press; Minneapolis: Fortress Press, 1997), 35–60; James D. G. Dunn, "Once More, PISTIS CRISTOU," in Hay and Johnson, eds., *Looking Back, Pressing On*, 61–81.

19. Jouette M. Bassler, ed., *Pauline Theology*, vol. 1, *Thessalonians, Philippians, Galatians, Philemon* (Minneapolis: Fortress Press, 1991); David M. Hay, ed., *Pauline Theology*, vol. 2, *1 and 2 Corinthians* (Minneapolis: Fortress Press, 1993); David M. Hay and E. Elizabeth Johnson, eds., *Pauline Theology*, vol. 3, *Romans* (Minneapolis: Fortress Press, 1995); Hay and Johnson, eds., *Looking Back, Pressing On*.

20. Blanton, "Disturbing Politics," 4b.

21. Giorgio Agamben, "L'Église et le Royaume" (paper given at Notre Dame Cathedral in Paris on March 8, 2009), http://www.paris.catholique.fr/Conference-de-M-Giorgio-Agamben-et.html (our translation).

22. See Giorgio Agamben, *Language and Death: The Place of Negativity*, trans. K. E. Pinkus and M. Hardt (Minneapolis: University of Minnesota Press, 1991 [Italian 1982]); Agamben, *Infancy and History: The Destruction of Experience*, trans. L. Heron (New York: Verso, 1993 [Italian 1978]); Agamben, *Stanzas:*

developed during this period would later be used in his second, post-1989 period, which will be more the center of our focus here.[23] Around the middle of the 1990s, the Italian philosopher's output emerged and imposed itself as a coherent oeuvre—his writings have henceforth systematically been translated into French, English, and German. The impasse of the Marxist utopia, but also of the neoliberal economic model of globalization, has stimulated him into shaping a more radical political vision. This is the framework in which Agamben revisits Paul in search of a solution to the insoluble problems of modernity. In short, Agamben's recent work is the culmination of an entire life of thinking, and he uses the figure of Paul to recapitulate this reflection.

In an interview with the French daily *Libération*, Agamben described himself as "an epigone . . . attempting to complete, to bring to fruition what others, far superior to himself, had left unfinished."[24] Five major influences have left their mark on *Time That Remains*,: Martin Heidegger (with whom Agamben studied in the 1960s), Walter Benjamin (whom he published), Carl Schmitt (Benjamin's principal interlocutor and philosophical opponent), Michel Foucault (whose biopolitical analysis Agamben alleges to complete[25]), and Jacob Taubes (to whom Agamben dedicated *Time That Remains* and from whom he borrowed several key concepts: the ὡς μή of 1 Cor. 7:29, the Paul-Benjamin relationship, the κατέχων of 2 Thessalonian. Beyond their differences, it is significant that Agamben should use and reconfigure the intuitions of Benjamin (a Marxist) and Schmitt (a conservative), since both of them think in *theologico-political* terms.

Since Agamben has given much thought to aesthetics and literature, it is relevant to take into account his discursive style, which finds its source in his oral presentations[26]—*Time That Remains* is even subdivided into the six days of a seminar. Like a bee bustling from flower to flower to make its own honey,

Word and Phantasm in Western Culture, trans. R. L. Martinez (Minneapolis: University of Minnesota Press, 1993 [Italian 1977]); Agamben, *Idea of Prose*, trans. M. Sullivan and S. Whitsitt (Albany: State University of New York Press, 1995 [Italian 1995]).

23. Such considerations on language can also be found in his purely theologico-political works: Giorgio Agamben, *Remnants of Auschwitz: The Witness and the Archive (Homo Sacer III)*,, trans. D. Heller-Roazen (New York: Zone, 1999 [Italian 1998]), §3.13–3.18; §4.1–4.3); Agamben, *The Sacrament of Language: An Archaeology of the Oath (Homo Sacer II, 3)*, trans. Adam Kotsko (Stanford: Stanford University Press, 2011 [Italian 2008]).

24. Jean-Baptiste Marongiu and Giorgio Agamben, "Agamben, le chercheur d'homme (entrevue)," *Libération*, Thursday, April 1, 1999. Our translation.

25. "Biopower's supreme ambition is to produce, in a human body, the absolute separation of the living being and the speaking being, ζωή and βίος, the inhuman and the human—survival," Agamben, *Homo Sacer 3*, 156.

Agamben borrows from several sources and in appearance digresses abundantly, gradually constructing an impressionistic argumentation. Progressively, and often in the most unusual ways, he associates texts, concepts, and even works of art that are sometimes years apart in time, thus creating his own collage of sorts. There is something playful in Agamben's approach, as if philosophical activity itself was an illustration of "idleness" and of the "happy life," that is, of the posture that allows the deactivation of the politico-judicial system, its neutralization. I will come back to this later on.

One could qualify the Agambenian method as an archeology of concepts:[27] for instance, in *Time That Remains*, he unpacks the etymology of various terms in the opening of Romans, and charts their semantic shifts in history. He shows that the great thinkers of modern political philosophy have refined their concepts by secularizing Paul's messianism: the puritan ethos of Weber's *profession* (*Time That Remains*, 19–22), Marx's *class* (*Time That Remains*, 29–33), Heidegger's appropriation of the *improper* (*Time That Remains*, 33–34), Hegel's *Aufhebung* (*Time That Remains*, 99–104), and especially Benjamin's *conception of history* (*Time That Remains*, 138–45).

In short, through classical figures from the past (including Paul), Agamben seeks paradigms that reveal the hidden face of the present. To be sure, this is disconcerting for the Bible scholar, the more so that twentieth-century exegesis was more focused on historicity, attempting to discover what the texts meant in the first century rather than what they mean today.

Where should one begin to summarize such a profuse body of work? To oversimplify, one could say that *Time That Remains* is the answer to, or even the solution to the problem presented in, the "trilogy" *Homo Sacer* (which along the way has become a tetralogy, in seven volumes!), but that the Agambenian commentary on Romans was prefigured as early as *The Coming Community* (Italian 1990).[28] Here is the current state of *Homo Sacer*:[29]

---

26. There are several of Agamben's seminars available on YouTube.com, both in English and in French, which give a better idea of the man and his style.

27. Agamben theorized his approach "after the fact," in *The Signature of All Things: On Method*, trans. L. D'Isanto and K. Attell (New York: Zone, 2009 [Italian 2008]).

28. Giorgio Agamben, *The Coming Community*, trans. Michael Hardt (Minneapolis: University of Minnesota Press, 1993 [Italian 1990]).

29. Giorgio Agamben, *Homo Sacer 1: Sovereign Power and Bare Life*, trans. D. Heller-Roazen (Stanford: Stanford University Press, 1998 [Italian 1995]); Agamben, *The Kingdom and the Glory: For a Theological Genealogy of Economy and Government*, trans. L. Chiesa and M. Mandarini (Stanford: Stanford University Press, 2011 [Italian 2007]); Agamben, *The Sacrament of Language: An Archaeology of the Oath (Homo Sacer II, 3)*; Agamben, *Opus Dei : archeologia dell'ufficio: Homo sacer, II, 5* (Temi; Torino: Bollati Boringhieri,

I. *Homo Sacer: Sovereign Power and Bare Life* (Italian 1995)
II.1. *State of Exception* (Italian 2003)
II.2. *The Kingdom and the Glory* (Italian 2007)
II.3. *The Sacrament of Language* (Italian 2008)
II.5. *Opus Dei : archeologia dell'ufficio* (2012)
III. *Remnants of Auschwitz* (Italian 1998)
IV.1 *Altissima povertà* (on "form of life" or "happy life")

The Greeks made a distinction between natural life (ζωή), shared by all living beings and confined to the private sphere (the domestic οἶκος), and qualified life, described also as "good life" (βίος), shared by a particular group and relating to the public sphere (the πόλις). Human βίος distinguished itself from ζωή especially through language—through deliberative and ethical speech. Modernity, however, has brought about a shift in this distinction: the political is no longer concerned with βίος but instead with ζωή which, in deserting the private sphere, has altered the public sphere. As a result, there is a shift from the political (the organization of life as society) to the economic (the law of the οἶκος extended to the public sphere).[30] In this manner, the concepts of βίος and ζωή are both distorted and the citizen is reduced to mere "bare life"—which is no longer either ζωή or βίος! Paradoxically, natural life, in becoming the object of the political, loses its sacred character and destroys the political.

The management of ζωή in the public sphere is called—after Foucault, but with a certain risk of semantic confusion—"biopolitics," that is, the politics of biology. The expression *homo sacer*, "sacred man," is borrowed from Roman law to designate the *object* of this biopolitics, veritable modern antipolitics. In Roman antiquity, the convict became a *sacer*, an outlaw, an exile, bereft of identity, whether religious (he could not be sacrificed) or civil (he could be summarily executed).[31] Paradoxically, even if he is an outlaw, the *homo sacer* must still submit to the law, which can either banish an individual from the civic community or let him stay. The law creates the division between those on the inside and those on the outside.

2012); Agamben, *Homo Sacer 3*; Agamben, *Altissima povertà: regole monastiche e forma di vita: Homo sacer, IV, I* (La quarta prosa; Vicenza: N. Pozza, 2011).

30. That is the thesis in Agamben, *The Kingdom and the Glory*.

31. O. Custer, "Une mise à nu du politique," *Critique* 53, no. 598 (1997): 216–20 (here 217). Note the very Agambenian ambiguity of *sacer*: this living being regarded as sacred can no longer be sacrificed.

Homo sacer thus comes to describe the modern human being: "We are all virtually *homines sacri*."[32] Authority is no longer exercised by citizen subjects, but is exercised on an object, "*bare life* and reduced to the silence of refugees, deportees or the banished: that of a '*homo sacer*' whose biological body is exposed, without mediation, to the action of a force of correction, of imprisonment, and of death."[33] The *homo sacer* reveals the true nature of political authority, which manifests itself when the rule of law is suspended or when the individual is arbitrarily stripped of citizenship. The possibility of suspending constitutional rights determines the source of authority as well as the relative importance of those same rights. Yet it is the exception that today "becomes the rule,"[34] even in times of peace. Since ζωή, the object of political management, is no longer sacred, human rights become arbitrary and are subjected to the whims of those in power—an enemy soldier is no longer considered as such but as a terrorist, and so is not protected by the Geneva Convention; an illegal immigrant will be stopped at the border or deported back to his own country even though his security (his ζωή) may be at risk.

To use an extreme comparison: like in concentration (or death) camps, the modern state deliberately and continually subjects each "citizen" to a de-subjectification, followed by a re-subjectification in order to provoke the subjection of the people, who are no longer persons, but bare lives—their social security numbers having replaced the numbers tattooed on arms but serving the same symbolic purpose. People are "human resources," consumers of mass production and culture, health-care beneficiaries, and so on—they survive but are kept from the fullness of their humanity because they are unable to assume their nature as subjects capable of exercising freedom of expression.[35] Examples that jump to mind are the public health response to the alleged 2009 flu pandemic (and ensuing psychosis), or the exhibitionist presentation of obesity on the NBC network reality show *The Biggest Loser*, or yet again the undue predominance of the economy in newscasts and the all-out commodification of goods and people.

Agamben, it is important to insist, carries his analysis to extremes because he hopes to expose modern (pseudo-)politics for what it truly is—a system whose paradigm is not the city-state (πόλις), i.e. a state founded on the rule

32. Agamben, *Homo Sacer 1*, 115.

33. Grelet, Potte-Bonneville, and Agamben, "Une biopolitique mineure." Our translation.

34. Agamben, *Homo Sacer 1*, 20.

35. "Biopower's supreme ambition is to produce, in a human body, the absolute separation of the living being and the speaking being, ζωή and βίος, the inhuman and the human—survival," Agamben, *Homo Sacer 3*, 156.

of law and on discussion—but rather the concentration camp—that is, a state founded on exception and the suspension of the rule of law.[36] From this perspective, democracy seems no better than totalitarianism: Auschwitz only revealed the logical workings of a system that has been perfected even more since World War II: "In Hitler's Germany, an unprecedented absolutization of the biopower to *make live* intersects with an equally absolute generalization of the sovereign power to *make die*, such that biopolitics coincides immediately with thanatopolitics."[37] Furthermore, in a controversial allusion to Guantanamo: "Indeed, the state of exception has today reached its maximum worldwide deployment. The normative aspect of law can thus be obliterated and contradicted with impunity by a governmental violence that—while ignoring international law externally and producing a permanent state of exception internally—nevertheless still claims to be applying the law."[38] Is there a way out of this dead end? "Agamben sees messianism in Romans as revealing a 'form of life' only possible through including ζωή (the natural) and βίος (the political) within the creation of the biopolitical subject, thus creating a politico-philosophical idea of *life*. Agamben's aim with messianism, or the 'form of life' it creates, is to overturn contemporary nihilism by redefining the themes of the subject, life and biopower."[39] This "form of life," or its equivalent, the "happy life," is hard to understand—it will be the topic of the forthcoming (and last?) volume of *Homo Sacer*—but there is already a glimpse of an explanation in *Time That Remains*. To be sure, though, Paul's messianism is a remedy to the incurable disease of modernity. Agamben hopes for the birth of a messianic community with no identity and no institution, a community that is answerable to singularities that owe it nothing in return, a community that does not yet exist and still needs to be invented, which could at last rebuild the political on new foundations and would no longer dissociate ζωή and βίος,[40] a community

36. "From this perspective, the camp—as the pure, absolute, and impassable biopolitical space (insofar as it is founded solely on the state of exception) will appear as the hidden paradigm of the political space of modernity, whose metamorphoses and disguises we will have to learn to recognize." Agamben, *Homo Sacer 1*, 123. On the state of exception and the suspension of civil rights as a manifestation of a true supreme power (as discussed with Carl Schmitt), see Agamben, *State of Exception*. Where Schmitt had theorized the "state of exception" (which was the legal constitutional framework of the Nazi regime!) before legitimizing the *Führerprinzip*, Agamben essentially endorses the same theory . . . in order to denounce the arbitrariness of modern liberal democracy. See a summary in *Time that Remains*, 104–8.

37. Agamben, *Homo Sacer 3*, 83.

38. Agamben, *State of Exception*, 87.

39. David Fiorovanti, "Language, Exception, Messianism: the Thematics of Agamben on Derrida," *Bible and Critical Theory* 6 (2010): 5.1–5.12 (here 5.5)

that would once again allow free and subjective expression. The attitude of such a community would be an "inoperativity" (*desoeuvrement*) susceptible of "deactivating" the "acts" of law and of the biopolitical system, as if the answer to nihilism were a renewed anarchy.[41]

THE TIME THAT REMAINS

The Time That Remains speaks of urgency, and of Paul as the prototype of the messianic thinker. "What does it mean to live in the Messiah, and what is the messianic life? What is the structure of messianic time? These questions, meaning Paul's questions, *must also* be ours" (*Time That Remains*, 18; emphasis mine)—because, we are meant to understand, the sick stranded in the labyrinths of a bureaucratic health system, AIDS sufferers, illegal immigrants, the elderly, among others, are prisoners in a vast concentration camp, and citizens identified as such today could at any moment be branded as outcasts. In other words, Agamben suggests that Paul's time structure can help us undermine the political alienation we are subjected to.

Let us begin by summarizing the proposition of *The Time That Remains*. According to Agamben, the "possibility of understanding the Pauline message coincides with the experience of such a [messianic] time; without this, it runs the risk of remaining a dead letter.[42] The restoration of Paul to his messianic context therefore suggests, above all, that we attempt to understand the meaning and internal form of the time he defines as ὁ νῦν καιρός, the 'time of the now.' Only after this can we raise the question of how something like a messianic community is in fact possible" (*Time That Remains*, 2). Paul is the most challenging messianic thinker—but Christianity and Judaism have abandoned both the concept and its thinker. (Here, Agamben shows his debt to Benjamin and Taubes.) Inversely, it is impossible to understand Paul the messianic thinker without experimenting messianic time ourselves—which is something our age is in dire need of.

---

40. Agamben, *The Coming Community*. The French edition bears the subtitle "Theory of whatever singularities."

41. Many see in the Occupy Movement(s) an illustration of Agamben's political insight.

42. Note the subtlety or irony of the expression in regard to 2 Cor. 3:6–7: Paul runs the risk of remaining unheeded if messianism is overlooked.

STRUCTURE OF THE BOOK

Agamben sees his book as "a commentary *ad litteram*, in every sense of the word, on the first ten words of the first verse of the Letter to the Romans" (*Time That Remains*, ix). The titles of the six chapters—corresponding to the six days of the seminar—recall the words of Rom. 1:1, which contract and recapitulate the entire epistle:[43] Παῦλος δοῦλος Χριστοῦ Ἰησοῦ / κλητὸς / ἀφωρισμένος / ἀπόστολος / εἰς εὐαγγέλιον θεοῦ. In reality, though, all the epistles are in fact called into play (*particularly* 1 Cor. 7:20-29).[44]

If the title and approach of the book give a sense of urgency—there is too little time left to comment on the entire epistle!—it becomes apparent along the way that its structure in six "days" plus a conclusion titled "Tornada" is also related to temporality. On the one hand, the biblical arithmetic of "6 + 1" alludes to the time of creation plus the time of Shabbat—which is the time of rest, in the double meaning of repose and remnant, and so offers the opportunity, as if from a distance, to consider the whole of the time of creation. "Saturday is not considered to be homogeneous to others. Rather, it is the recapitulation and messianic abbreviation of the story of creation" (*Time That Remains*, 83). Or yet again "8 – 1": the eighth day of the new creation, which will be the end (*eschaton*), is preceded by the day of the Shabbat, which is the time it takes for time to end. A subtle analogy emerges between Agamben's commentary and the biblical story of creation.

On the other hand, this structure also corresponds to a redundant poetic form analyzed by Agamben and meant to serve as the model for messianic time (*Time That Remains*, 78–87). This strict poetic form, the sestina, is composed of six stanzas of six lines each, followed by a final stanza of three lines, the *tornada*, which though it is set a little apart from the rest, recapitulates the whole. Six words only can end each line, these words reappearing once every stanza but always in a different order, following a complex but regular permutation. They also all appear in the final *tornada*. *In the course of reading the poem, the reader already knows the vocabulary of the last stanza, which stanza refers to the reading of the past.* "The sestina . . . is a soteriological device which, th[r]ough [*sic*]

43. Following an Agambenian logic, the *incipit* to the epistle (Rom. 1:1) is yet another parable of messianic time, which *recapitulates* and *contracts* χρόνος (that is, the rest of the epistle).

44. See the passages used throughout *Time That Remains*, for which Agamben supplies his own interlinear translations at the end of the book (*Time That Remains*, 147–85): Rom. 1:1-7, 14-17; 2:9-16, 25-29; 3:9-12, 19-24, 27-31; 4:2-3, 10-22; 5:12-14, 19-21; 7:7-24; 8:19-25; 9:3-9, 24-28; 10:2-12; 11:1-16, 25-26; 13:8-10; 1 Cor. 1:22-29; 2:1-5; 7:17-24, 29-32; 9:19-22; 10:1-6, 11; 13:1-13; 15:7-9, 20-28; 2 Cor. 3:1-3, 12-18; 5:16-17; 12:1-10; Gal. 1:11-17; 2:1-14; 3:10-14; 4:21-26; Eph. 1:9-10; Phil. 2:5-11; 3:3-14; 4:13-17; 5:1-3; 2 Thess. 2:3-11; Philem. 1:15-16.

the sophisticated *mēchanē* of the announcement and retrieval of rhyming end words (which correspond to typological relations between past and present), transforms chronological time into messianic time" (*Time That Remains*, 82). In other words, the linear chronological reading of the poem (36 + 3 lines), that is, the time it takes for the poem to come to an end, is transformed in the process of reading into a time apart, a remnant—that of the three lines of the *tornada*—by recapitulating its own structure; the repetition of these words at the end of lines constantly refers to what comes before and after in the poem.

THE CONCLUSION TO THE BOOK: THRESHOLD

The conclusion (and seventh part) of the book, titled "Threshold or *Tornada*," is consequently very important. This should be the first to be read, for two reasons: first, the chapter's title refers to the book's temporal messianic structure we have just described—the seventh day recapitulates the first six; second, this is where Agamben, as if confiding to the reader, exposes and justifies his initial thesis through an exegesis that also offers a glimpse into his method: a study of the intertextuality between Paul and Benjamin based on unpublished manuscripts Agamben had access to while preparing a new edition of the German philosopher's complete works.[45] These manuscripts apparently reveal some of Benjamin's key concepts, which allude to Paul via Luther's translation of the Bible: *weakness* of messianic power (2 Cor. 12:1–10), image (*Bild*, Rom. 5:14; 1 Cor. 10:6; cf. 1 Cor. 7:31), redemption, recapitulation (Eph. 1:10), and the now (*Jetztzeit*, Rom. 3:21). Referring to the parable in Benjamin's first thesis from *On the Concept of History*, where a puppet (Marxism) playing chess is manipulated by a dwarf hidden under the table (theology), Agamben suggests that Benjamin identifies with Paul and that the dwarf in the parable represents the apostle. Benjamin alone has understood Paul—in fact, no one till now has understood Paul (!). Benjamin's ally—the source of his political philosophy and consequently of Agamben's—is none other than the apostle.

AN OUTLINE OF THE "SIX DAYS"

In order to better examine the theological impact of Agamben's commentary, I will begin by presenting a summary of the book's six chapters, which describe the various aspects of the messianic.[46]

---

45. Brian Britt, "The Schmittian Messiah in Agamben's The Time That Remains," *Critical Inquiry* 36 (2010): 262–87, critiques Agamben's assessment of Benjamin (especially 263, 272–73).

46. I draw here, with substantial modifications, on what I have previously written in Gignac, "Taubes, Badiou, Agamben," 187–94.

The first day: The messianic perspective does away with identity. Paul the apostle experienced this transformation. The free man Σαῦλος (who bore the name of the first king of Israel) became a slave to the Messiah; he lost his identity, his proper name. He was left only with a messianic nickname, Παῦλος (small, in Latin), a nickname that is doubly fitting for a slave (δοῦλος), at the bottom of the social ladder and bereft of a personal identity (a slave being the thing of his Lord and master).[47] Paul has sunk from royalty to insignificance—a reference to Benjamin's "messianic weakness." δοῦλος thus becomes the paradoxical image of the messianic witness. Agamben even goes so far as translating the expression ὑπὲρ δοῦλον (Phlm 1:16) not as "no longer as a slave but as *more than a slave*, a beloved brother" (NRSV), but "as a hyper-slave" (*Time That Remains*, 13). Onesimus loses his condition as a slave only to assume the messianic nonidentity of hyper-slave, which simultaneously repeals and confirms his primary identity as slave. What follows is in a sense merely a further development of this main idea.

The second day: "The messianic vocation is the revocation of every vocation" (*Time That Remains*, 23). The word κλητός, at the core of Rom. 1:1, is also the crux of Agamben's interpretation. He analyzes in detail the workings of the κλῆσις in 1 Cor. 7:17-32, particularly in the final verses (vv. 29-32), which repeat the expression ὡς μή five times. This, Agamben at length insists, he translates as "as not," instead of as "as if."[48] Playing on the meaning of the word "profession,"[49] the idea is to "profess" (in the sense of showing) one's messianic calling without, however, abandoning one's "profession" (in the sense of a competency that defines an identity or a social position), thus nullifying any "professional identity." In Paul's own words:

47. Agamben is well acquainted with the sociology of the Roman Empire. Although to my knowledge the philosopher does not bring it up, there is an analogy to be made between the slave and *homo sacer*, since the law excludes the slave from the sphere of βίος (citizenship); the slave is equally rejected, though less radically, in the area of ζωή.

48. Note that most versions translate ὡς μή by "as though" or "as if," as does 1 Cor. 7:29-32 NSRV. Yet for Agamben (*Time That Remains*, 35–39), to act "as if" is not an option, because messianic time is not a meaningless hiatus but rather a very real posture in a real world—it "is therefore not a matter of eschatological indifference, but of change, almost an internal shifting of each and every single worldly condition by virtue of being 'called'" (*Time That Remains*, 22). The rabbinic origin of the idea of a slight shifting had already been described in aphorism no. 13 in Agamben, *The Coming Community*, 53.

49. I develop here, I believe, on Agamben's thoughts on Weber's double definition of *Beruf* as (religious) vocation and (secular) profession, in *Time That Remains*, 19–23. For a more in-depth analysis, see Christiane Frey, "Klēsis/Beruf: Luther, Weber, Agamben," *New German Critique* 35 (2008): 35–56.

Was anyone *at the time of his call* already circumcised? *Let him not seek to remove the marks* of circumcision. Was anyone at the time of his call uncircumcised? Let him not seek circumcision. Circumcision is *nothing*, and uncircumcision is nothing; but obeying the commandments of God is everything. *Let each of you remain in the condition in which you were called.* Were you a slave when called? *Do not be concerned about it.* Even if you can gain your freedom, *make use of your present condition now* more than ever. (1 Cor. 7:18-21 NRSV; emphasis mine)

Or, in Agamben's words: "To be messianic, to live in the Messiah, signifies the expropriation of each and every juridical-factical property (circumcised/uncircumcised; free/slave; man/woman) under the form of the *as not*. This expropriation does not, however, found a new identity; the 'new creature' is none other than the use and messianic vocation of the old (2 Cor 5:17 . . .)" (*Time That Remains*, 26). "No, the [messianic] vocation calls the [secular] vocation itself, as though it were an urgency that works it from within and hollows it out, nullifying it in the very gesture of maintaining and dwelling in it" (*Time That Remains*, 24). Even though it is presented as a digression, the example of the mendicant orders of the Middle Ages is significant, at least for the prime ideal of poverty as desired and practiced by Francis of Assisi. Even without any worldly belongings, but without retiring from the world, a disciple of Saint Francis could make use of worldly things so as to "create a space that escaped the grasp of power and its laws, without entering into conflicts with them yet rendering them inoperative" (*Time That Remains*, 27). Or, after Yves de Maeseneer's deft formulation, the "messianic world is not another world than the secular world, but the same put under messianic tension."[50] To a certain extent, the entire book is there in a nutshell: the messianic posture defuses the formidable clockwork revealed in *Homo Sacer*, like a standpoint that enables the radical opposition to the existing state of affairs. A male, francophone, academic exegete, therefore, remains so, even though he may conduct his life as a nonmale, nonfrancophone, nonacademic, and nonexegete. Such an individual can still make use of these attributes while refusing to succumb to their pretenses

50. Yves de Maeseneer, "Truth as Performance? History, Transcendence and the 'As If,'" in *Orthodoxy, Process and Product*, ed. Mathijs Lamberigts et al. (Leuven: Peeters, 2009), 277–97 (here 294).

and to the power struggles that underlie them. This demands the lingering question: What is the true meaning of such a posture, and does it not boil down to a contrived utopic concept?

The third day: the messianic vocation creates a remnant (a messianic community) that, paradoxically, does not constitute a new identity. This remnant "is therefore neither the all, nor a part of the all, but the impossibility for the part and the all to coincide with themselves or with each other. *At a decisive instant, the elected people, every people, will necessarily situate itself as a remnant, as not-all*" (*Time That Remains*, 55; emphasis mine). The Torah, through inclusion/exclusion, created a rift between Jews and Gentiles—according to the analysis in *Homo Sacer*, this is how the law always operates. But far from repealing this division, the messianic experience divides it yet again, to the second power, so to speak. In other words, the "division of the law into Jew/non-Jew, in the law/without the law, now leaves a remnant on either side, which cannot be defined either as a Jew, or as a non-Jew. He who dwells in the law of the Messiah is the non-non-Jew" (*Time That Remains*, 51).

Agamben uses three images to clarify his intuition. First, somewhat playfully, he remarks that Paul himself, from the Pharisee (= separate) he was, became an apostle set apart (ἀφωρισμένος): his own experience is also the division of a division. As a Pharisee and an apostle, Paul is doubly estranged, set apart to the second degree. Second, Agamben evokes the story of the Greek painter Apelles, who had succeeded in halving, with a single stroke of his brush, the already ultrafine line painted by Protogenes. Third, playing on words, the philosopher reminds us that every division, in mathematics, leaves a remainder. He refers to Rom. 2:28-29 (the Jew according to the flesh and the Jew according to the spirit) and Romans 9 (Israel and Israel) to assert that there exists "something like a remnant between every people and itself, between every identity and itself" (*Time That Remains*, 52). Finally, the following excerpt is a good illustration of Agamben's method and of his concept of remnant:

> In Romans 11:11-26, Paul describes the remnant's soteriological dialectic with clarity. The "diminution" (*hēttēma*) that makes Israel a "*part*" and a *remnant* is produced for the salvation of the *ethnē*, the *non-Jews*, and foreshadows its *plērōma*, its fullness as the *all*, since, in the end, when the *plērōma* of the people will have come, then "all of Israel will be saved." The remnant is therefore both *an excess* of the *all* with regard to the *part*, and of the part with regard to the *all*. It functions as a very peculiar kind of soteriological machine. As such,

it only concerns messianic time and only exists therein. In the *telos*, when God will be "all in all," the messianic remnant will not harbor any particular privilege and will have exhausted its meaning in losing itself in the *plērōma* (1 Thess. 4:15 . . .). But in the *time of the now*, the only real time, there is nothing other than the remnant.[51] (*Time That Remains*, 56, emphasis mine)

The fourth day: messianic time is a νῦν καιρός – that moment of infinite quality which, removed and withdrawn from historical χρόνος, enables one to grasp it and give it meaning.[52] We are clearly now at the heart of Agamben's thesis. Philosophically, he proposes nothing less than a new philosophy of time. καιρός is a contraction of χρόνος, in accordance with the literal translation of 1 Cor. 7:29 (NRSV): "the appointed time has *grown short*" (emphasis mine). It is the time that time takes to end, "*the time that is left us*," "the time *that* we ourselves are" (*Time That Remains*, 67–68), the time in which our history touches upon eternity without ever attaining it—here again, Agamben uses the metaphor of division, of fracture.

The two ends of the *olam hazzeh* [duration of the world from creation to end] and the *olam babba* [atemporal eternity that comes after the end of the world] contract into each other without coinciding; this face to face, this contraction, is messianic time, and nothing else. Once again, for Paul, the messianic is not a third eon situated between two times; but rather, it is a caesura that divides the division between the times and introduces a remnant, a zone of undecidability, in which the past is dislocated into the present and the present is extended into the past. (*Time That Remains*, 74; see also 62)

51. The Pauline idea of remnant is explicitly applied to the witnesses of Auschwitz in Agamben, *Homo Sacer 3*, 162–64 (§4.12)

52. Agamben had already described "cairological time" in *Infancy and History*, 101–5. For two more detailed and very evocative presentations of messianic time, see Meyere, "The Care for the Present," 175–80, and Griffiths, "Cross as the Fulcrum of Politics," 184–89.

In order to picture messianic time, it is important first to mark the boundary between human time and the "time" of eternity, and then imagine that this boundary is itself cut in two, thus opening a lapse of time encroaching on both times already distinguished. As minute as it may be, this lapse of messianic time helps us get a grip on time and understand the urgency that beckons (the messianic vocation!). In his aforementioned conference at Notre Dame Cathedral, Agamben gives a good description of messianic time and the existential consequences of this qualitative transformation of the "lived experience of time."

> [Messianic time is] on the one hand, the time that time takes to end, but on the other, the time that is left us, the time we need to make time end, to overcome, to free ourselves from the chronological representation of time. Whereas this representation of *time in which* we believe we are separates us from ourselves and transforms us into impotent spectators of ourselves, messianic time, as an *operational time* (*kairos*) in which we for the very first time take hold of time (*chronos*), is the time *that we ourselves are*. It is clear that this time is not another time, which would take place in an improbable and future elsewhere. It is, on the contrary, the only real time, the only time we have. *And to experience this time entails a complete transformation of ourselves and of our* way of life.[53]

As a corollary to all this: "The time in which the apostle lives is, however, not the *eschaton*, it is not the end of time. . . . What interests the apostle is not the last day, it is not the instant in which time ends, but the time that contracts itself and *begins to end*" (*Time That Remains*, 62; emphasis mine). The point is not to wait for the end and the παρουσία (second coming of the Messiah), but to live the present to the fullest, "*par-ous*ia" literally signifying: to be next to; in this way: being beside being, "being . . . beside itself in the present" (*Time That Remains*, 70).

The fifth day: it is through faith that the power of the gospel is realized in weakness and that the Torah is at once accomplished and deactivated (*Time That Remains*,

---

53. Agamben, "L'Église et le Royaume" (emphasis mine; translation ours).

97). Agamben's reading of Paul here uses three models he amply describes elsewhere in his works and that we have touched on earlier. First, he retrojects on Paul the Aristotelian binomial potentiality (δύναμις) / actuality (ἐνέργεια)," particularly on Rom. 1:16 (NRSV): "The gospel is the *power* of God for *salvation* to everyone who has *faith*" (*Time That Remains*, 90, 96–97). God's salvific potential is actualized, but paradoxically, in a messianic faith marked by weakness. Agamben finds more examples of this in Eph. 3:7; Phil. 3:21; 2 Cor. 12:9; as well as in Gal. 3:5; 5:6; and Col. 1:29, where faith is a principle of action. Second, the subjectification that marks the voicing of an idea, where the enunciation is more important than the utterance, sheds light on the workings of faith, which is not chiefly a message but the act of a confessing subject. "The *euaggelion* is therefore not merely a discourse, a *logos* that says something about something independent of the site of its enunciation and the subject who hears it. . . . The announcement is not a *logos* empty in-itself but that may nevertheless be believed and verified: it is born—*egenēthē*—in the faith of the one who utters it and who hears and lives in it exclusively" (*Time That Remains*, 91).[54]

Third, the Torah is to the gospel (and to faith) what the law is to the state of exception (*Time That Remains*, 104–8). Just as the state of exception simultaneously suspends and justifies the law, so also the gospel deactivates the Torah and fulfills it.[55] Agamben comments on Rom. 3:27-31, especially the last verse: "Do we then overthrow the law by this faith? By no means! On the contrary, we uphold the law" (NRSV). He also has an eye on Rom. 10:4, "Christ is the end of the law." The Torah is not destroyed or invalidated, but rather deactivated (καταργεῖν, cf. Rom. 7:6; 1 Cor. 1:28; 15:24), and so is validated—like the exception that proves the rule.[56] The messianic allows for a usage beyond any law. "The law can be brought to fulfillment only if it is first restored to the inoperativity of power. . . . That which is deactivated, taken out of *energeia*, is not annulled, but conserved and held onto for its fulfillment"

---

54. See also Agamben, *Homo Sacer 3*, 140.

55. Note the added paradox: the messianic condition meant to be the antidote to the state of exception that characterizes biopolitics is analogous to it. The crucial difference is that the state of exception is guided by force, whereas the messianic condition is guided by weakness. In other words, the "Messiah's call to slavery, on this reading, is like the state of exception in establishing a sphere without the law; but it is profoundly unlike it because its sphere, the sphere of the church, is one in which vocations are . . . made available for use in a reconfigured temporal order." Griffiths, "The Cross as the Fulcrum of Politics," 185.

56. Note again the paradox and the play on words: if in modern politics the exception has become the rule, in the messianic condition, the exception (the Messiah) proves the rule—which no longer needs to be applied.

(*Time That Remains*, 98). Here we find a "potentiality / actuality" binomial, but in inverse order. The law attains a more advanced state of perfection by going from actuality to simple potentiality.[57] "Paul calls this paradoxical figure of the law in the state of messianic exception *nomos pisteōs*, 'the law of faith' (Rom 3:27), as it can no longer be defined through works . . . , but as a manifestation of 'justice without law' (*dikaiosynē chōris nomou*, Rom 3:21)" (*Time That Remains*, 107). This perfection of the law, this state of exception that recapitulates everything in a messianic perspective, is love (*Time That Remains*, 108, quoting Rom. 13:8-9).

The sixth day: a new relation is established between faith and law, opening up a space of gratuitousness called grace. In this somewhat diffuse chapter, Agamben proposes three ideas recapping those of the fifth day. First, the "messianic is therefore the historical process whereby the archaic link between law and religion (which finds its magical paradigm in *horkos*, oath)[58] reaches a crises [*sic*] and the element of *pistis*, of faith in the pact, tends paradoxically to emancipate itself from any obligatory conduct and from positive law (from works fulfilled in carrying out the pact)" (*Time That Remains*, 119). Hitherto inseparable, the covenant and the commandments are no longer linked; all that remains is the gratuitousness of love. In this sense only can we speak of the new covenant—of a new structure of the covenant. Like messianic time, which is a time apart that allows us to grasp the meaning of χρόνος acutely, so grace is a space where faith and law are no longer indivisible, yet not totally separated. Second, contrary to Martin Buber, who made a distinction between Jewish biblical faith (*emuna*) and the Greek belief in truth (πίστις), and contrary also to the dogma of the institutionalized church, Paul conceived faith as an "I trust" rather than as an "I believe." That is why Paul never affirms (except in Rom. 10:6-10) that Jesus *is* Messiah and Lord, but instead bears witness that he follows Jesus, Christ and Lord, in whom he has complete faith. It is the same with love: we love someone; we are not in love with his merits or his actions. Third, faith is an experience of the word (Rom. 10:6-10), near you, performative, "an experience of a pure event of the word that exceeds every signification" (*Time That Remains*, 134). Once again,

---

57. Elsewhere, Agamben speaks of potentiality, of actuality, and of impotentiality: Giorgio Agamben, *Potentialities: Collected Essays in Philosophy*, trans. D. Heller-Roazen (Stanford: Stanford University Press, 1999); Clayton Crockett, "Piety, Power, and Bare Life: What in the World Is Going On in the Name of Religion?," *Journal for Cultural and Religious Theory* 4 (2003): 1–8 (especially 6).

58. See Agamben, *The Sacrament of Language*.

the Agambenian theory of language is illustrated by Pauline discourse, as it also helps enlighten our understanding of it.

We observe here several characteristics of the "happy life" touched on at the end of the first section: a new theologico-political structure "beyond" law; deactivation of the law; subjective expression; gratuitousness and inoperativity of action (beyond "works" or identities). The end of this chapter comes full circle by affording a glimpse of what the happy life could be, and consequently, of a possible solution to the aporia of the biopolitical.

> "Messianic and weak" is therefore that potentiality of saying which, in dwelling near the word not only exceeds all that is said, but also exceeds the act of saying itself. . . . If this remnant of potentiality is thus weak, if it cannot impose itself as a law, it does not follow that it is passive or inert. To the contrary, it acts in its own weakness, rendering the word of law inoperative, in de-creating and dismantling the states of fact or of the law, making them freely available for use. (*Time That Remains*, 137)

A Provocative Reading

If Agamben's reading of Paul warrants a critical assessment, then it equally puts to the test several established theological certainties. Let us examine five examples.

TEMPORALITY OF SALVATION: ESCHATOLOGY AND KAIROS

Current exegesis approaches the question of Pauline temporality from the standpoint of the history of salvation (under the rarely admitted influence of Hegel) and of the stereotyped formula "already/not yet." Agamben challenges, or rather clarifies, this paradigm. He goes beyond the uninterrupted continuum of χρόνος by insisting on the importance of καιρός, that moment of grace where messianic time unfolds. This partiality to the "now" of decision-making seems curiously tainted by Bultmannian influences. Christ operates a scansion, or a suspension of time, in effect restructuring it and lending it a new dimension. Here and now, someone suddenly appears out of nowhere to meet us and to call to us.

This challenges the usual reading of salvation in terms of a master narrative[59] in which the resurrection is paradoxically relegated to the past and the Christian individual awaits the ἔσχατον, even though he or she is uncomfortably stuck in this prolonged gap, with its many attendant problems: indeterminate deferment of παρουσία, mythological vocabulary, institutionalization, and liability. Agamben reminds us, however, that messianic time is not an interval but a window of opportunity, a time that we cannot settle into. The resurrection, that messianic effect, is not a reality of the past, but an event that can be experienced in the present and that transforms from within, that "messianizes" the world in which we live: "a time within time—not ulterior but interior—which only measures my disconnection with regard to it, my being out of synch and in noncoincidence with regard to my presentation of time" (*Time That Remains*, 67); an "operational time pressing within the chronological time, *working and transforming it from within*" (*Time That Remains*, 67–68; emphasis mine). This approach, in my opinion, renews the meaning of the already/not yet. Salvation is not something in the distant future; it is already nascent at the heart of our world. The kingdom of heaven is not something to wait for indefinitely but to be actively fostered. Nor is salvation an unachievable and ineffectual utopia, which requires us to live "as if" the world will be saved. Salvation is not a speculative hypothesis, but an "operative" fact. In short, the Messiah is not the culmination of history or its accomplishment, but its center.[60]

This also prompts a rethinking of typology, a return to a patristic "economy of salvation,"[61] separate from the history of salvation. "Through the concept of *typos*, Paul establishes a relation, which we may from this point on call a typological relation, between every event from a past time and *ho nyn kairos*, messianic time" (*Time That Remains*, 74). Against a narrative reading that sees in Christ the culmination and pinnacle of the covenant in an unfolding story that begins with Adam and continues with Abraham, Moses, and David, it is important instead to see how the figure of Christ "recapitulates" each figure, each path set down by the Old Testament. In other words, Agamben's proposed structure enables us to reconsider the relationship between Old and New Testament: one is not the sequel to the other but rather its interruption, just as καιρός helps to understand χρόνος without being added to it or replacing it.[62] It also allows us to revisit Saint Augustine's old adage: "The New Testament lies

---

59. For instance, N.T. Wright, *The Climax of the Covenant: Christ and the Law in Pauline Theology* (Minneapolis: Fortress Press, 1992).

60. See also Agamben, *Homo Sacer 3*, 158–59.

61. Economy of salvation is a concept revisited by Agamben in *The Kingdom and the Glory*.

hidden in the Old, and the Old is unveiled in the New," as well as considering a new "Christology of the Old Testament."

CHRISTIAN COMMITMENT AND THE POSTURE OF THE "AS NOT"

We have seen that messianic time compels the politico-ethical posture of the "as not" (in contrast to that of the "as if"). Like the "happy life" Agamben sees as an antidote to modern biopolitics, this posture of the "as not" is hard to circumscribe,[63] but *it clearly raises the question of the role of Christians in society.* It is certainly not a radicalism that in reality merely seeks to control (as in gaining the kingdom of heaven by force), nor is it a blind acceptance or a collusion with the current state of affairs—radicalism and resignation being two extremes of the same nihilism. Nor yet again is it a mental reservation or a comedy in which one acts "as if" the world were saved . . . since… when it is not. The "messianic subject does not contemplate the world as though it were saved. In Benjamin's words, he contemplates salvation only to the extent that he loses himself in what cannot be saved; this is how difficult it is to dwell in the calling" (*Time That Remains*, 42).

So what can be said, or rather, what can be done? Is it a kind of quietism, as suggested by Paul Griffiths, "acting politically without interest in the outcome of such action"?[64] I am not sure. I prefer the reading put forward by Mike Grimshaw, for whom—within the paradox of the weakness and of our awareness of a world that is not saved (where God is absent)—the "messianic" would mobilize us and call us to action.

> To reconsider messianic time in this way exposes our fallacy of expecting the train to come when we well know it will not come as long as we situate ourselves in waiting. To live focused on the arrival of the train, to live focused on the arrival of messiah means we do not engage with what is happening around us. We become so focused on *what* we wish to occur, *when* we wish it to occur, that

62. Jean Calloud, "Ses Écritures qui devaient s'accomplir," in *"Christ est mort pour nous." Études sémiotiques, féministes et sotériologiques en l'honneur d'Olivette Genest*, ed. Anne Fortin and Alain Gignac, Sciences bibliques (Montréal: Médiaspaul, 2005), 107–25.

63. "The solution of resistance to biopolitics is scattered throughout Agamben's writings. It is only actually referred to in the last lines of *Homo Sacer*," Genel, "Le biopouvoir chez Foucault et Agamben," §51 (our translation).

64. Griffiths, "The Cross as the Fulcrum of Politics," 189–97 (especially 196–97).

we forget the world in which we live; we retreat from the world of shared experience. In short, we become sectarian not secular.[65]

In other words, the "remnant therefore is not the possessive object of salvation so much as its instrument in the ministry of reconciliation, and it is precisely the kenotic movement toward the 'unsavable' that effects salvation."[66]

All this compels us to reconsider the tension between Rom. 13:1-7 (obedience to authority[67]) and Rom. 12:1-2. The messianic posture seems neatly described in Rom. 12:2 (not quoted by Agamben): "Do not be conformed to this world, but be transformed by the renewing of your minds" (Rom. 12:2 NRSV). In other words, one is engaged *in* our world; it is, however, an engagement *from a different perspective*. Within the world, but set apart from the world (on the sidelines, so to speak), Christians assume a new posture by forming a remnant that acts fully for the advent of the kingdom of heaven. But how, then, can those plunged in messianic time (the Time That Remains, before the end) live at the edge, as though apart, a remnant as regards a system in which they must continue living while radically contesting it? Is there a middle ground between the sectarian posture and the triumphalism of Christendom?

COMMUNITY AS 'ΕΚΚΛΗΣΙΑ: CHRISTIAN IDENTITY

Summoned by God, the ἐκκλησία is a messianic and political community that must take its place without imposing itself, like a remnant.[68] Agamben impels us to rediscover this intuition and to reinvent a theology of the calling (κλῆσις).

This brings up the question of identity, a hackneyed concept that has come to be watered down. The very fact that it is clichéd, however, reflects a political malaise. The world, while increasingly uniform, is yet full of conflicting values, so the question of identity has become an obsession, with a twofold impact on the religious. On the one hand, there is the temptation to have religion

---

65. Mike Grimshaw, "Ruptured Romans: A Theological Meditation on Paul, Cultural Theory, and the Cosmopolitan Rupture of Grace," *Stimulus* 17 (2009): 32–40 (here 36); P. Travis Kroeker, "Living 'As If Not': Messianic Becoming or the Practice of Nihilism?," in Harink, ed., *Paul, Philosophy, and the Theopolitical Vision*, 37–63 (here 60).

66. Kroeker, "Living 'As If Not,'" 62.

67. For an overview of the history of the interpretation of Rom. 13:1-7, see Mark Reasoner, *Romans in Full Circle: A History of Interpretation* (Louisville: Westminster John Knox, 2005), 129–42.

68. For a critical analysis of Agambenian "ecclesiology," see Zerbe, "On the Exigency," 257–68.

once again become the main element of identity. On the other hand, immersed in a modernity that relegates religion to the private sphere, the faithful no longer know how to define their own identity. By focusing the subject on the messianic καιρός, Agamben revitalizes the fundamental experience of the calling and the transcending of particularisms: *being a Christian cannot represent, apart from this calling, a new identity*. It is rather adopting a position, a different attitude toward primary identities that enables one to transcend them by deactivating them. Moreover, this "suspension" of identity creates a new, divided relationship with oneself and with the law.

According to the French theologian and psychoanalyst Jean-Daniel Causse, Agamben's analysis is in keeping with "the manner of being Christianity proposes," in that "Christian identity has the particularity of emanating from the grace of God who has revealed Himself, through Jesus Christ, as the God who loves and recognizes each human being irrespective of his or her qualities, properties, or actions."[69] The issue at stake in the Christian journey is the appropriation of a coherent subjective "identity," "which eludes any attempt to qualify it. Its outward sign, moreover, is Baptism, a mark of grace of course, but precisely of an *invisible* grace."[70] This appropriation concerns faithfulness to the baptismal sign and the apprenticeship of liberty.

Again, such an outlook challenges the (bimillenary) institutionalizing of Christianity into church(es), as well as the sectarian recoiling of communitarianism. The Agambenian notion of remnant, characterized by the transitory, by weakness, and by inoperativity, challenges any triumphalist conception of election. Whether in the minority or the majority, Christians are not everything—the remnant does not exist for itself, for its own salvation, but to save the world, or perhaps only to bear witness that it is in need of salvation.

LAW DISABLED

For the past twenty years, Pauline exegesis has endeavored to find some consistency in Paul's contradictory assertions concerning the law—or at least when it does not declare it mission impossible.[71] The law causes a curse (Gal. 3:10), is nothing but a disciplinarian (Gal. 3:24), is not ordained directly by God (Gal. 3:19), reveals sin (Rom. 3:20), and arouses covetousness (Rom. 7:7). And yet, the law is holy and good (Rom. 7:12), it is not disabled but upheld

---

69. Jean-Daniel Causse, "Communauté, singularité et pluralité éthique," *Transversalités* no 108 (2008): 101-9 (here 104, our translation).

70. Ibid., 105 (emphasis mine).

71. Heikki Räisänen, *Paul and the Law*, 2nd ed. (Tübingen: Mohr, 1987).

by the gospel (Rom. 3:31), and the law does not justify, but attests to God's righteousness (Rom. 3:21). Agamben does not examine all these texts, *but he finds a philosophical solution to these aporia by importing concepts from outside the texts*. He is not interested in Paul's consistency, but in the role Paul attributes to the law—which is perhaps ultimately more fruitful. The *rule* of the law finds its proof only in *exception*. The coming of the Messiah is like a coup d'état that renders the law inoperative (good works are no longer necessary) but confers on it its potentiality. The norm can no longer be observed or transgressed, since the law has been suspended. Of all the solutions I have examined, Agamben's may well be the most complex, but, I dare say, it is in my view the most satisfactory.

CHRISTOLOGY

There remains the formidable problem of Christology. In showing (apparently) no interest in Christ, Agamben has perhaps paved the way for a *negative Christology*. The focus has up till now been mainly on a Christology "from below," which has sought to map the route that led the disciples from the trust they put in a Galilean rabbi to their realization of the messianic nature of the risen Jesus. There has also been the inventory of "christological titles" (Lord, Son of David, Son of Man, Christ, and so on), as well as hints of implicit messianic pretension within evangelic episodes[72]—not to mention the Jesus Seminar. Here again, Agamben shifts our focus. What is the most important question: "Who is Christ?" or "Who *do you say* that I am?" Must we make Christ our own, or must we be made his own (Phil. 3:12).)? Is there not actually a distinction—the realization of which is fundamental to the messianic experience—between the Christ and Christ, the attributes of the Messiah and the events of Easter?[73] If faith is not dependent on the message or on dogma, but rather on the confession of Christ and the relation to him, how, then, to write a true Christo-logy that is no longer a "science of Christ" (knowledge), but a reading of the New Testament that is sensitive to an enunciation which constantly seeks to express the inexpressible—the path of faith? For the "discourse on Christ" (λόγος τοῦ Χριστοῦ) must specify "how to receive salvation in a discourse that does not convey an object to grasp, but shows a path to follow, a path of words in a body [permeated and marked by] words."[74]

---

72. Walter Kasper, *Jesus the Christ* (New York: Paulist Press, 1976).

73. Guy-Robert St-Arnaud, "Le paradigme du messie, l'Oint est-il près?," in *Faut-il attendre le messie? Études sur le messianisme*, ed. R. David, Sciences bibliques 5 (Montréal: Médiaspaul, 1998), 137–71.

74. Anne Fortin, *L'annonce de la bonne nouvelle aux pauvres: une théologie de la grâce et du Verbe fait chair* (Montréal: Médiaspaul, 2005), 106 (our translation).

It has been said that Agamben has neglected the cruciformity of the Pauline discourse, that this is a blind spot in his thinking. This is partly unfair since messianic weakness, both on behalf of the Messiah and of his disciples, is extremely important. Yet to my knowledge, Agamben does not develop the idea that Christ crucified, long before Paul and Onesimus, is the model of the δοῦλος, of messianic humbling (Phil. 2:5-11, which Agamben yet quotes). Even more so, is it not possible to see in the figure of Christ crucified the *homo sacer*, accursed by the law, excluded from Israel, stripped of his right to speak—whose life no longer has any value, who cannot therefore be "sacrificed" (outlaw cursed by the law, outside of the religious sphere, Gal. 3:13) but who can be slain without the protection of the law? A Messiah reduced to a bare life without political rights? In the words of John Milbank,

> He died as three times excluded: by the Jewish law of its tribal nation; by the Roman universal law of empire; by the democratic will of the mob. In the whole history of human polity—the tribe, the absolute state, the democratic consensus—God found no place. He became *homo sacer*, cast outside the camp, abandoned on all sides, so that in the end he died almost accidentally. He died the death of all of us—since he died the death that proves and exemplifies sovereignty in its arbitrariness.[75]

* * *

Other theological notions, which we have not touched on here, are collected by Agamben in the course of his readings, and they in turn, transformed by the Agambenian "interpretative machine," nourish and provoke our theology.[76] The objective of this introduction has merely been to offer a glimpse into the wealth of possible interactions between theology and Agambenian philosophy. Ideally, readers will be persuaded to immerse themselves further in Agamben's prose.[77]

75. John Milbank, "The Christ Exception," *New Blackfriars* 82 (2001): 541–56, (here 549–50).

76. For example, it is remarkable that the glossolalia in 1 Corinthians 12 and 14 illustrates the process of desubjectification/subjectification that occurs during the enunciation, in Agamben, *Homo Sacer 3,* 114–17 (§3.14–15).

77. I wish to thank Jacques-André Houle for the translation of this paper from the original French.

9

Mad with the Love of Undead Life
Understanding Paul and Žižek

Ward Blanton

*This, then, is the limit of common sense.
What lies beyond involves a Leap of Faith,
faith in lost Causes, Causes that, from
within the space of sceptical wisdom, cannot
but appear as crazy. And the present book
speaks from within this Leap of Faith—but
why? The problem, of course, is that, in
a time of crisis and ruptures, sceptical
empirical wisdom itself, constrained to the
horizon of the dominant form of common
sense, cannot provide the answers, so one
must risk a Leap of Faith.[1]*

–SLAVOJ ŽIŽEK

*We preach Christ crucified, a scandal to
Jews and stupidity to Greeks.*

–PAUL

---

1. Slavoj Žižek, *In Defense of Lost Causes* (New York: Verso, 2008), 2.

Payment Passed Due (Final Notice)

To think with Paul and Žižek—or anyone else worth thinking about—is to articulate or inflect them in such a way that an excess of matters, or an excess of significance and signification, starts to churn itself into existence in and through the process. One should declare such a thing out loud and at the very start, as it is important to clarify how one stands, particularly as the end result of our comparative labor will repeat and reinforce the assumptions with which we begin.[2] Are we, in fact, committed to the comparative encounter as simultaneously a productive and a surprising labor, one that will yield new thinking, not only about each of the two poles in our comparative enterprise but also about the enterprise itself, about what we are doing when we compare? This basic hermeneutical question about the very stakes of our questioning is not a trick question. Nor do we need to pretend that it is an opaquely difficult one. Nevertheless, as that hermeneutic philosopher Martin Heidegger once said about language, show me how you stand on this question and I will tell you who you are.

---

2. Here I present the hermeneutical or philosophical issues—which are profoundly important, particularly for thinking about Paul and the philosophers—in a very simple way for an undergraduate audience. I discuss why I think the hermeneutic tradition, conceptualized through the radicality of a young G. W. F. Hegel and a young Martin Heidegger, respectively, is profoundly important *now* for understanding biblical studies and interdisciplinary research in much more detail in chs. 1 and 2 of Ward Blanton, *Displacing Christian Origins: Philosophy, Secularity, and the New Testament*, Religion and Postmodernism (Chicago: University of Chicago Press, 2007). See also my Introduction to Ward Blanton and Hent de Vries, eds., *Paul and the Philosophers* (New York: Fordham University Press, 2012). To mention only three additional readings, note the excellent work of John D. Caputo, *More Radical Hermeneutics: On Not Knowing Who We Are*, Studies in Continental Thought (Bloomington: Indiana University Press, 2000); Stanley Rosen, *Hermeneutics as Politics* (New Haven: Yale University Press, 2003). The elaboration of hermeneutics as politics can also be found in the recent work of Gianni Vattimo and Santiago Zabala, *Hermeneutic Communism: From Heidegger to Marx* (New York: Columbia University Press, 2011). Slavoj Žižek himself often presents "hermeneutics" as a conservative or traditional form of metaphysical grounding, and his comments are for me apropos of important criticisms we should make of what passes now for "hermeneutical" reflection on, say, the Christian or biblical legacies, which can sometimes be a very staid form of edifying discourse intended primarily for some ecclesiastical in-group or other. However, as Žižek would be the first to recognize, there is also to be found in the "hermeneutic" phenomenology of the young Hegel and the young Heidegger a sense of the constitutive *ruptures* with tradition that Žižek tends to associate with psychoanalysis rather than hermeneutics. Similarly, much more technical and expansive encounters between Paul and materialist philosophers like Žižek are to be found in Ward Blanton, *A Materialism for the Masses: Saint Paul and Other Philosophers of Undying Life*, Insurrections: Critical Studies in Religion, Politics, and Culture (New York: Columbia University Press, 2012).

If this little question is demanding, it is because it is simple in the sense of basic or elemental, and perhaps because it opens us to an elemental experience of "not knowing who we are" (as John Caputo once described it excellently), the experience of realizing that we may not turn out to be what we thought we were.[3] Such an experience can be disconcerting. Žižek, in fact, articulates the relevant problem as a psychoanalytic topic that raises questions of ownership of selfhood, identity as property, and also the uncanny or awkwardly disconcerting return of the repressed.[4] Discussing doctrines of the poststructural psychoanalyst Jacques Lacan in relation to Hollywood classics, Žižek describes the issues this way: "'There is no metalanguage' insofar as the speaking subject is always already spoken, i.e., insofar as he cannot master the effects of what he is saying: he always says more than he 'intended to say,' and this surplus of what is effectively said over the intended meaning puts into words the repressed content—in it, 'the repressed returns.'"[5] To invite others to think about Paul and Žižek in this mode, of course, carries with it a strong critique of some recent interdisciplinary discussions of Paul and the Continental philosophers. As Lacan often discussed, there is only one typical way to counter the disconcerting relationship to an excess of matters that haunts all of our assertions as a "repressed" obverse of our own positions on any issue. This way necessitates a *brute assertion of mastery* over against the haunting openness or ungovernable excess of significance itself, an excess of information that always threatens to undo, reverse, or hollow out what we say, think, and feel on a given topic.[6] And while I do not intend to be harsh or overly critical, many recent

3. See Caputo's excellent book *More Radical Hermeneutics*.

4. I discuss some of the ways the Pauline philosophical reflections of Stanislas Breton also constitute a critique of private property—and the identity politics premised on it—in my introduction (titled "Dispossessed Life") to Stanislas Breton, *A Radical Philosophy of Saint Paul*, Insurrections: Critical Studies in Religion, Politics, and Culture (New York: Columbia University Press, 2011).

5. Slavoj Žižek, *Enjoy Your Symptom! Jacques Lacan in Hollywood and Out* (New York: Routledge, 1992), 14. This section is a good example of the way Lacan, like Alain Badiou, often distinguishes psychoanalytic from hermeneutic theories of interpretation. Žižek develops here the idea that the horizon of meaning, or "frame" of reference, for psychoanalysis always itself appears *in* the framed content, a kind of hyperinvested or fetishized phenomenon whose presence actually founds the frame, rather than the other way around. The distinction between these two theories of enframing functions to politicize hermeneutics inasmuch as it forces us to question more radically two modes of being "in" a tradition. Avital Ronell once described herself as the offspring of an intensive but short-lived affair between hermeneutics and deconstruction, two theories with important similarities that nonetheless could not make the relationship last (to my knowledge, not yet published in print; see Ronell's 2010 lecture for the European Graduate School, "Media Technology and Scholarship," online at http://www.egs.edu/faculty/avital-ronell/videos/media-technology-and-scholarship/). I mention the nice description, as the same could be said of Žižek's Lacanian relationship to the early Heidegger and to hermeneutics.

discussions within biblical studies about the Continental philosophers exemplify this Lacanian point very clearly. Consider, for example, that a great many self-styled historians have had surprisingly little to say when it comes to staging a thoughtful exploration of Paul in relation to contemporary critical theory or philosophy (see below). As Lacan might lead us to expect, these figures say their bit of very-little *with a great deal of authority*, however, as if trying to baptize the scarcity of their thoughts or to justify or exonerate readily felt limits of the (multidisciplinary) significance of their few words about, precisely, Paul and the philosophers.[7] Count on it: the more someone bangs on in these debates about being an exemplar of this or that discipline over against another one, the more one asserts disciplinary property rights, the more anxiety and powerlessness such speakers are experiencing in relation to a larger field of intellectual and social possibilities. Such reactions are the best indication that these disciplinarians neither understand nor control the matters at issue.

The important point to make is that we do not need to repeat such an approach. In fact, against the *justification* or *authority* of "mastery," that mask to cover a failure or refusal of real interdisciplinary thinking, we could start—once more—with Heidegger's basic question: *What are we doing when we engage in such a show of disciplinary limits?* Is anything worthy of thinking, worthy of our time or our lives, *happening* here at all? Or have we become rather uncreative accountants of ready-made products from such easily recognized disciplines, as if all that remains to be done is to assert property rights in legal disputes over appropriate academic territories? The problem with some of the early statements of biblical scholars about the evident fascination with Paulinism

6. For those interested in the political implications of this Lacanian axiom, see first of all Bruno Bosteels, *Badiou and Politics*, Post-contemporary Interventions (Durham: Duke University Press, 2011), esp. chs. 1 and 2. Alain Badiou develops these loosely in relation to readings of Paul in *Saint Paul: The Foundation of Universalism* (Stanford: Stanford University Press, 2003), 40-54. Closely related are the excellent philosophical studies of the empty place of power in Slavoj Žižek, *Tarrying with the Negative: Kant, Hegel, and the Critique of Ideology* (Durham: Duke University Press, 1993). Related are Žižek's studies on the way "ideology" or—in the lingo of Lacan—the *objet petit a*, functions as the supplemental stand-in for the absent ground of political life (see Žižek, *The Sublime Object of Ideology* (New York: Verso, 1989).

7. Specifics to follow below. I do not want to be harsh, particularly with important icons of my field. But I do not think it is useful for the intellectual enterprise for, precisely, the *limits of knowledge* among the biblical scholars in relation to the philosophers to become rhetorically inflated and valorized as a virtue. That, in this case, the limits *were* invested with value *rather* than encountered as a perplexing *spur* that drives a quest for further understanding is *just what a radical hermeneutic tradition, particularly one inflected by psychoanalysis*, would have us expect. This is another reason I begin this piece with a nod to this important tradition of philosophical reflection.

among philosophers was not that biblical scholars were incorrect. They were in fact much worse than this—they were, rather, failing to ask the fundamental hermeneutic question: What am I doing here? What is happening here? Is anything, actually, happening at all?

Standing on Hollowed Ground: Žižek's "Originary" Paulinism

To this initial Žižekian invitation, we need to add a Pauline twist, which may have begun to be hinted at already. Note that Žižek thinks that *just* this "hermeneutic" state of affairs is *also another name for a Paulinist story* in which there is no discourse of mastery that is able to manage completely a constitutive "stupidity" or the "scandalous" symptoms of (all) power's *lack* of power. Here we begin to sense *how* there is no metalanguage that could stand outside our conversations about Paul and Žižek as their stable frame or unquestionable master, because the psychoanalytic invitation to a new and improved multidisciplinary conversation about Paul and the philosophers as imagined by Žižek is *already* both philosophical *and* Pauline. *You* are the interpreter being challenged by way of a Pauline theologoumenon, interpreted through Hegel, hermeneutics, and Lacan: truth appears *only as* a form of stupidity or as the emptying out of power and authority (see 1 Corinthians 1; 15).

This Pauline twist is essential. It is the Pauline inflection of the loss of philosophical foundationalisms of all sorts—whether a foundational materialism, rationality, humanism, or theology—which allows Žižek to claim that a radically politicized atheism (another name for the absent center of thought and identity) is the most profound form of faithfulness to the legacy of Paul[8]: "My claim is not merely that I am a materialist through and through, and that the subversive kernel of Christianity is accessible also to a materialist approach; my thesis is much stronger: this kernel is accessible *only* to a materialist approach—and vice versa: to become a dialectical materialist, one should go through the Christian experience."[9] As we will see, Žižek's Paul—in a very

8. No doubt because he, too, inherits Paul by way of German philosophical traditions, Alain Badiou's work on Paul makes a similar gesture. Some of our questions about this topic appear in the transcript of a public interview Susan Spitzer and I held with Badiou about his remarkable piece of Paulinist political theater. See Alain Badiou, *The Incident at Antioch*, trans. Susan Spitzer (New York: Columbia University Press, 2012).

9. Slavoj Žižek, *The Puppet and the Dwarf: the Perverse Core of Christianity* (Cambridge, MA: MIT Press, 2003), 6.

traditional fashion—is interchangeable with his radical "kernel" of "Christianity." The gesture is a classic component of older "Christian origins" stories, narratives that want to find something in Jesus or Paul that somehow explains and justifies the eventual development of two distinctly separate identities, Jewish and Christian.[10] For the moment, note that with assertions like this, Žižek follows an august tradition of understanding early Christianity as a kind of antiphilosophical undoing of rational foundations, a tradition that emerges in Continental philosophical contexts from Luther, Hegel, and Heidegger.[11] The tradition—especially as Hegel and Heidegger develop it—asserts that it is ironically the *loss* of God as a foundational, owned, or knowable master which paves the way for modern thought to radically repeat the "originary" gesture of Jesus or Paul.

This, I think, is the great illumination of the dialogue that Creston Davis established over the years between Žižek and the "radical orthodox" theologian John Milbank, eventually published as *The Monstrosity of Christ*.[12] The real breakthrough of the interaction is that both seemed to realize at some point that theirs was not a dialogue between a Christian and an atheist so much as between two forms of Christian theology: "Our difference is not the one between (his) Christian orthodoxy and (my) atheist heterodoxym since his basic position does not really allow for what [G. K.] Chesterton called 'a matter

10. Žižek's Paul is taken primarily from a philosophical tradition in which such a story would have been theorized and formalized, but not really questioned at this narrative or historiographic level. The same could be said of the Paul of Alain Badiou, with the question remaining about what one could say from more up-to-date historical renderings of someone like Paul, which might push the conversation forward. I make some suggestions about where to go in my lengthy introduction to Blanton and de Vries, eds., *Paul and the Philosophers*. Of all the historical gaffs one finds in this interdisciplinary literature, my favorite is when Žižek wonders about Paul's conversion into an apostle from his position "as a tax collector." The converted tax collector has of course became a stock classic in Western literature, but Paul was not one (see the very useful set of interviews in Slavoj Žižek and Glyn Daly, *Conversations with Žižek* (London: Polity, 2003), 24.

11. I limit myself to mentioning five excellent books: Slavoj Žižek, *Less than Zero: Hegel and the Shadow of Dialectical Materialism* (New York: Verso, 2012); Didier Franck, *Nietzsche and the Shadow of God*, Studies in Phenomenology and Existential Philosophy, trans. Bettina Bergo (Bloomington: Indiana University Press, 2012); Christian Somner, *Heidegger, Aristotle, Luther. Les sources aristotéliciennes et néotestamentaire d'être et temps* (Paris: Presses Universitaires de France, 2005). For those who do not read French, comparably useful information may be found in the learned book of Theodore Kisiel, *The Genesis of Heidegger's* Being and Time (Berkeley: University of California Press, 1995). For more global reflections on the Lutheran legacy in Continental thought, see Mark C. Taylor, *After God*, Religion and Postmodernism (Chicago: University of Chicago Press, 2007).

12. See Slavoj Žižek and John Milbank, *The Monstrosity of Christ: Paradox or Dialectic?*, ed. Creston Davis (Cambridge, MA: MIT Press, 2009).

more dark and awful than it is easy to discuss,' the traumatic *skandalon* of the Christian experience. To put it even more bluntly: my claim is that it is Milbank who is in effect guilty of heterodoxy, ultimately a regression to paganism: in my atheism, I am more Christian than Milbank."[13] That is, the wholisms, the sureties, the teleologies, the conservationist urges all seem to Žižek to smack of a failure of "Christianity," a Christianity that has forgotten the Pauline notion that truth emerges only via scandal and countercultural subversion. Žižek's Paulinism therefore stands in line with the radical revolutionism of a Luther or a Kierkegaard, in light of which even Milbank's Augustinian providentialism seems to Žižek only like the baptism of power.[14]

In part, the tradition works because it follows Luther in imagining the stark dualisms of a text like Paul's letter to the Galatians (e.g., works and faith, wages and gift, law and grace) as indicating *the difference between Christianity and Judaism*, rather than, say, polemical rhetoric aimed primarily at Paul's Christian counterparts in Jerusalem who disagreed with him about the need to circumcise Gentiles. So the distinction between someone who lives, thinks, and believes in the everyday processes of life, calculating causes and effects and proposing various reasonable projects in such an economy was always in this tradition able to be presented as the retrograde, "legalistic" other to the true Paulinist, who was capable of seeing in things something new, something unexpected, something unjustified or gracious. The Lutheran intellectual tradition within which thinkers like Hegel, Heidegger, and Bultmann were steeped was a tradition attuned to the logics and rhetorics of the radical break and the new start.

Against this backdrop, G. W. F. Hegel (1770–1831) and Heidegger (1889-1976) asserted more specifically that philosophy was a better mode of access to the sphere of gracious or unjustified freedom (above, Žižek speaks of the freedom of a Leap of Faith) than historical study or popular and overly concrete religious belief, because only philosophy—they argued—allowed one to stand in the emptied or politically open space of thought itself, a space as it were *before* its population by ready-made objects as we tend to understand them.[15] Philosophy, in other words, was that part of the tradition *best* attuned to the logic and rhetoric of the transformative break with the past. In a tradition

---

13. Ibid., 248.

14. In that respect, Žižek's Christianity—here opposed to the Augustinian providentialism of Milbank—is worth comparing to Cornel West's efforts to reclaim a "prophetic" rather than an "empire" Christianity. See West, *Democracy Matters: Winning the Fight against Imperialism* (New York: Penguin, 2005). To my knowledge not yet in print, a public conversation from 2005 at Princeton University between Žižek and West is readily available on YouTube.

where "originary" Christianity, radical politics, and the allure of radical philosophy are all wound together, of course, this meant that for Hegel, Heidegger, and Žižek, modern philosophy most effectively inhabits the space of "originary" Paulinism. In other words, in this tradition it is philosophy's "lostness," its sense of the openness of possibilities without ground and guarantee, that constitutes it as the best challenge to theology, which it imagines to be about, ultimately, God as the ground or justification or guarantee of reality. The irony, of course, is that this tradition would merge with the "Christian origins" story in a way that often left Hegel, Heidegger, or Slavoj Žižek, feeling that it is precisely the a-theology of modern philosophy which makes it the best *repetition* of the original Pauline moment.[16]

One question astute readers of modern theology and biblical studies may have at this point is whether Žižek's Paul is therefore simply a rehash of the way a New Testament scholar like Rudolf Bultmann (a close ally of the young Heidegger) imagined Jesus or Paul as "original" Christians, Christians imagined in a tableau of those staging a break with received models of the "good life" in order to risk the invention of something new.[17] At one level, yes, like Badiou, the Paulinism of Žižek is very close to the Paulinism imagined by someone like Bultmann, from its assertion that only a "secularized" Christianity remains faithful to Paulinism, to its sense that what "originary" (or repeatable) Paulinism might be is simply to break with the past in order to risk participation in the countercultural invention of something new.

Like Bultmann (or the early Heidegger), Žižek ontologizes *a gap* between the beings of everyday life and their *ground or authorization* in being.[18] In

15. With strong awareness of the important religious genealogy of the cultural question, see Timothy Bewes, *Reification: Or the Anxiety of Late Capitalism* (New York: Verso, 2002). Several years after exploring Paul as an indication of authentic existence, Heidegger's *Being and Time* calls the person who lives stupidly in a reified existence a "Pharisee," something I discuss in the chapter "Paul's Secretary," in *Displacing Christian Origins*. For another link between the profound philosophical critiques of "reified" reality in Heidegger, Georg Lukacs, and the religious tradition, see Lucien Goldmann, *Lukacs and Heidegger: Toward a New Philosophy* (New York: Routledge, 2009).

16. A classic example would be the early Heidegger's identification of a phenomenological stance toward reality with a *type* of Pauline attention to time. In both cases, it is commitment in the *absence of objective support* that links the two. See Martin Heidegger, *The Phenomenology of Religious Life* (Bloomington: Indiana University Press, 2003); discussed in ch. 3 of my *Displacing Christian Origins*.

17. Note the comparability of Bultmann to Heidegger and Georg Lukacs in Breton, *A Radical Philosophy of Saint Paul*, 16–32.

18. See Žižek's discussion of Heidegger in *The Ticklish Subject: the Absent Centre of Political Ontology* (New York: Verso, 1999), 1–69. More recently, Žižek suggests that Heidegger's notions of a political collective were shaped (though not strongly enough) by a model of "the revolutionary collective, a

Heidegger or Bultmann's thought, humanity is constitutively separated, displaced, even expelled from its ground (or, in traditional theological metaphysics, separated, displaced, or expelled from God). And, being ontologically constitutive of humanity, this exteriority in relation to ground must remain without the possibility of reconciliation. As you might expect, this ontological map in both Bultmann and Žižek is itself overlaid onto a story about "originary" Paulinism, whereby the authentic Pauline moment is that moment of action which happens, precisely, *without* ready-made guarantee, orienting knowledge, or simple repetition of the past. Seamlessly woven together, therefore, are a philosophical postfoundationalism, a story of "Christian origins" as a break with "law" and inherited forms of life, and a revolutionary theory of historical change. In this, Žižek's "Christianity" remains very close to Heidegger, Bultmann, Hegel, and Luther.

On the other hand, it must also be said that Žižek's Lutheran Bultmannianism (as it were) adds important new twists onto this old three-stranded narrative of Christian origins. For example, it should be added that Žižek's philosophy is generally much less individualistic than Bultmann's existentialized Paulinism tended to be. Žižek's focus is indeed on κρίσις or an excruciatingly significant life moment of decision-without-guarantee (a topic Bultmann appropriated from this Greek word for "judgment"). But Žižek's crises are less for individuals than for cultures or collective political paradigms. By the same token, also characteristic of the philosophy of Žižek as opposed to Bultmann is that Žižek's work affords much more elaborate analyses of how collective hopes, loves, or political causes emerge into existence even when, in strict ontological terms, these emergences may not be explained by any natural rapports or relationships between these events and any rational, structured, ground. One might even risk the comparative summary that Žižek's Paul might be read as an effort to reclaim for a more structured leftist political movement the radical openness of the synthetic readings of Paul and modern philosophy hit on by a young Bultmann and Heidegger. The open-endedness, or constitutive lostness, of freedom is maintained, but with renewed attention both to the emergence of new collective aspirations and to the organizational or systematic requirements of a really existing political movement. One of the ways Žižek moves ahead on this front is through the topic of enjoyment.

Pauline collective of believers"; see Slavoj Žižek, *The Parallax View*, Short Circuits (Cambridge, MA: MIT Press, 2006), 278. For Bultmann, note the very commons distinctions between the existent and extant throughout essays like those in *New Testament and Mythology* (Minneapolis: Augsburg Fortress, 1984) or entries like "The Law," "Grace as Event," and "Faith as Eschatological Occurrence" in *Theology of the New Testament* (Waco: Baylor University Press, 2007).

A Žižekian New Perspective: From Enjoyment to Solution!

Consider Žižek's appropriation of Jacques Lacan's *objet petit a*, the object that stands in as a supplement of the absent cause or ground of desire. In a section that repeats all of the topics we have discussed so far, Žižek recalls the end of *City Lights*, when Charlie Chaplin, playing the tramp, finally appears to the woman who had earlier fallen in love with a misleadingly idealized image of him. In this scene, we find

> the very moment of this absolute undecidability when, confronted with the other's proximity as an object, we are forced to answer the question, "Is he worthy of our love?" or, to use the Lacanian formulation, "Is there in him something more than himself, *objet petit a*, a hidden treasure: far from realizing a predestined telos, this moment marks the intrusion of a radical openness in which every ideal support of our existence is suspended. This moment is the moment of death and sublimation: when the subject's presence is exposed outside the symbolic support, he "dies" as a member of the symbolic community, his being is no longer determined by a place in the symbolic network, it materializes the pure Nothingness of the hole, the void in the Other (the symbolic order), the void designated, in Lacan, by the German word *Das Ding*, the Thing, the pure substance of enjoyment resisting symbolization. The Lacanian definition of the sublime object is precisely "an object elevated to the dignity of the Thing."[19]

Like Bultmann's κρίσις, love's moment of decision-without-guarantees in relation to the other is all at once a radical break with the past—the values articulated in the "symbolic" field—and a "leap" which invests that object with the full weight of significance. This moment of sublimation, or the emergence of the *objet petit a*, is the selection of a kind of fetish object, but not one that is easily dismissed as merely odd or peripheral. To speak in the language of hermeneutics that we discussed above, the emergence of the *objet petit a* is, in a

19. Žižek, *Enjoy Your Symptom!*, 8.

sense, the *elevation to the level of a global frame or horizon*, a something that might otherwise be a mere nothing, a nobody, any old thing. No wonder Žižek will find in Paul's reference to "the nobodies" in 1 Corinthians 1 a perfect repetition of the psychoanalytic scene.[20] In the Lacanian world without metalanguage, sublimation, mad love, or *objet petit a precedes, grounds, or constitutes* the significance of the interpretive frame, or horizon of meaning, rather than the other way around.[21]

Were this line of thinking about identity formation to be followed, there would thus be a kind of Žižekian improvement on the older axioms of E. P. Sanders and the new perspective on Paul.[22] Recall that Sanders wanted to invert modern and largely German/Lutheran readings of Paul, whereby Paul's crucified Jesus effectively answers an imagined Jewish problem of legalism. In this older interpretive model, in other words, the "plight" (problems of conscience in relation to law, legal justifications in relation to God's goodwill) leads for Paul to a crisis and "solution" (in the form of Jesus, who dies for our sins). Sanders himself hoped to save Pauline interpretation from the anti-Judaism implicit in this earlier model, a model that seemed to need to imagine a widespread ancient legalism or economic transactionism as a "Jewish" foil for the (Christian) "solution" of Paulinism.[23] Hoping to liberate the interpretation of Paul from this self-serving Christian anti-Judaism, Sanders simply reversed

20. See also very useful discussion of this topos in John D. Caputo, "The Perversity of the Absolute, the Perverse Core of Hegel, and the Possibility of Radical Theology," in *Hegel and the Infinite: Religion, Politics, and Dialectic*, ed. Slavoj Žižek, Clayton Crockett, and Creston Davis, Insurrections: Critical Studies in Religion, Culture, and Politics (New York: Columbia University Press, 2011).

21. While it would take us too far afield to explain now, it is worth comparing this aspect of *jouissance* and the *objet petit a* as a "little piece of the real" with the rogue (post-)Kantianism in the New Testament interpretation of the (apocalyptic) Jesus and the (mystical interventionist) Paul in the extraordinarily significant writing of Albert Schweitzer. For discussion, see my chapter on Schweitzer in *Displacing Christian Origins*, where I develop the themes without explicit reference to Žižek and Badiou. For Žižek, see the interest in Paul primarily linked with 1 Corinthians and the assertion that it is "the nothings" that bear the power of revolutionary transvaluation, linked with the notion of a kind of antiwisdom or countercultural scandal as the mode of truth's revelation. See, for example, "Of Eggs, Omelets, and Bartleby's Smile," in *Parallax View*, 375-85, or "Christ's Uncoupling," in *The Fragile Absolute: Or, Why is the Christian Legacy Worth Fighting For?*, 123-29 and "Responses to the Event," in *In Defense of Lost Causes*, 386-97. See as well as more popular statements like "The Only Church that Illuminates is a Burning Church," *ABC Religion and Ethics*, August 8, 2011, http://www.abc.net.au/religion/articles/2011/08/08/3287944.htm.

22. Those wishing for an excellent overview of the rise of the "new perspective on Paul" should consult Stephen Westerholm, *Perspectives Old and New on Paul* (Grand Rapids: Eerdmans, 2004). For the work of Sanders, see initially the short summary of his more extensive writings in *Paul: A Very Short Introduction* (Oxford: Oxford University Press, 2001).

the poles of the earlier formula, saying that it was rather the "solution" (a crucified Messiah) that must have shocked Paul into imagining retroactively that there had been a "plight" in the first place (namely, an inability of law to secure salvation).

Perhaps you see already how there could be a Žižekian twist on Sanders's work. In these psychoanalytic efforts to articulate an immanent *enjoyment* that precedes all formal or metaphysical grounding of the self, the psychoanalytic tradition invites a new perspective on the new perspective. In this new formula, identity formation would move neither from plight to solution nor from solution to plight, but *from enjoyment to solution.* One could explore this formula in many new ways as a historical hypothesis that might unseat the way both the "old" and the "new" perspectives tend to operate within a history-of-ideas trajectory.[24] For example, when Paul becomes furious in a letter like the one to the Galatians, what is the underlying *enjoyment* that has been occluded, denigrated, or challenged? In a provocative recent book on the meal as a practice within Pauline communities, Hal Taussig proposes that we see the meal itself—as an experiential field of social experimentation—as a driving force in the development of Pauline *theological representations* of these communities. In Lacanese, such representations would be figures of the "symbolic" sphere,

23. While the new perspective has evoked a remarkably reactionary ire among North American evangelicals, little has been done in the way of a social or cultural history that situates it in an illuminating way, a labor that will be increasingly important in coming years. See, however, the excellent work of Denise Buell and Caroline Johnson Hodge, "The Politics of Interpretation: The Rhetoric of Race and Ethnicity in Paul," *Journal of Biblical Literature* 123 (2004): 235–51; James Crossley, *Jesus in an Age of Neoliberalism: Quests, Scholarship and Ideology,* Bibleworld (London: Equinox, 2012); and Brent Nongbri, *Paul without Religion: The Creation of a Category and the Search for an Apostle Beyond the New Perspective* (New Haven: Yale University Press, 2011).

24. While some early reactions against the new perspective might have imagined that they made an early history of Pauline doctrine into a sociological story, note the extent to which a story like James Dunn's remains almost entirely oriented by a fairly straightforward history of ideal entities existing and changing over time. This, ironically, is what strikes me about Dunn's *refusal* of the (largely evangelical) accusation against him, namely, that he explains away the significance of Paul's grand theological dualisms, making them merely sociological or rhetorical categories. Dunn, for me, rather does not go far enough. Paul is provoked by conflict in Dunn's work, sure, but ultimately Dunn himself remains an exegete of an ideal theological system that is itself an unquestioned object of analysis, for example, in the very interesting chs. 1 and 7 in *The New Perspective on Paul* (Grand Rapids: Eerdmans, 2005). In this light, I think we should note as well the sometimes intense reactions against "history of religions" approaches that one gets from prominent figures among the new perspective coterie. In place of modes of analysis like Franz Cumont's wonder about religion moving like weather patterns across collective psychic agencies constituting culture, the new perspective attempts to maintain a focus on the history of Christian ideas that becomes almost indistinguishable from a two-testament biblical theology.

precisely the organized or representational state of affairs that is *not* the sufficient cause of the explosion of transformative or sublimating desire. To repeat Taussig in this Žižekian light, Taussig's work would thus invite us to consider how the "meals became a laboratory in which a range of expressive nonverbal 'vocabularies' explored alternative social visions. The vocabularies consisted of alternative social relationships at the meals, complex ritual gestures, body postures, and actual food elements." [25] In this sense, the phenomenon of the collective event was itself the "spiritual experiment" whereby self-representations as "'the realm of God,' 'the body of Christ,' '*koinonia* with God,' 'the heavenly court,' or 'the heavenly city'" anchored their significance.[26]

Taussig's suggestions invite a comparison with our Žižekian formulation: *from enjoyment to solution.* For example, note that it is almost always some violation of a rather diffuse and inchoate *sense of the significance* of the meal that evokes Paul's fury (e.g., 1 Corinthians 11; Galatians 2). Differently put, the *investment* in the meal as a phenomenon seems to greatly exceed the meal's functional and ideational rationales, and it is this *excess* of significance, the way this particular issue so quickly becomes *the* issue on which all else is judged, that invites comparison to Žižekian enjoyment. Read this way, we might say that Sanders's reversal of the old Lutheran axioms still remains too centrally within the history of ideas, still assumes too tight a link between what Žižek calls "symbolic" logics and the radical investment of certain topics, practices, concepts. The Lacanian category of enjoyment—as precisely what is *not* explained or predicted very well by symbolic structures—encourages us not to miss the extraordinary seriousness of radical contingency, the solidarity-constituting investments in things that could have been very different. In other words, the axiom *from enjoyment to plight* encourages us to imagine the development of community forms and formulations against the backdrop of a radical openness of potential, but also in light of explosive *events* of love (and antipathy) in which *particular* people, moments, images, or tropes emerge as the

25. Hal Taussig, *In the Beginning Was the Meal: Social Experimentation and Early Christian Identity* (Minneapolis: Fortress Press, 2009), 54. Much more could be said about Taussig's work, which is—as here—very rich in its suggestiveness for an effort to understand the *materialities* of early Jewish and Christian community formations. Here, for example, what cultural theory is it that allows us to stay with the phenomena in question, namely, the one in which "vocabularies" "explore" (so to speak?) a mode of "vision"? Taussig's work invites a politically and sociologically infused history-of-the-senses approach that would leave behind the still-entrenched history of ideas models. Ideas and representations are there, but they are subtended or upheld by more subterranean driving forces, a field of force Lacan metaphorized as "enjoyment."

26. Ibid.

great mobilizing or memorializing names by which subsequent communities organize themselves. In the Žižekian universe, one moves *from* such intense moments *to* more ideational, representational, or identitarian modes of reflection, rather than the other way around.

The work of biblical scholars could expand on any number of things (tropes, *topoi*, themes, gestures, experiences of time in terms of affective intensity, forms of funding and organization, both explicit and inchoate forms of anti-imperialism, alterations of inherited economic and sexual roles, and so on) in order to contribute to our understanding of the multiplicity of modes in which this movement moved "from enjoyment to solution," from a kind of material phenomenality to structured ideational representations and self-descriptions. As I have already mentioned, this kind of focus would afford a counternarrative to stories of Christian origins that still tend to be affairs of the history of ideas. We should point out as well, however, that such an approach would greatly improve on some of the formulations of Paulinism in thinkers like Žižek and Badiou inasmuch as they—sometimes despite themselves—remain stuck in earlier forms of "Christian origins" stories whereby Paul is imagined to constitute a break with Judaism and the invention of Christianity. In part, they remain stuck in this mode of narration because they inherit Paul largely from a German philosophical tradition that was both informed by, and inspirational for, histories of ideas as we see them in, say, Hegel's lectures on history or on the history of religion.[27]

Developing within biblical studies an approach to identity formation in which representational forms *follow from* a material substratum of signification in which signs are more visceral agents than tokens of ideas existing elsewhere would also afford very important comparative resources for other more contemporary Žižekian and Lacanian projects of thinking through Paul. For example, in an important development of Lacanian categories, Eric Santner has developed Pauline riffs on psychoanalytic motifs, finding in some Pauline formulations exemplary indications of political, cultural, and theoretical

27. One should always pay attention to the general outline or chapter arrangements of Hegel's lectures on religion, aesthetics, or history, keeping these in mind when tracing the arguments in, say, *The Phenomenology of Spirit*. As Žižek and Jacques Derrida have both spent so much time showing to such good effect, Hegel is at once the worst sort of clunky, hierarchical systematizer while also remaining one of the most acute illuminators of negativity, remainders, loose ends, difference. Cf. Žižek's *Less than Nothing: Hegel and the Shadow of Dialectical Materialism* (New York: Verso, 2012); to Derrida's *Glas*, trans. John P. Leavey Jr. and Richard Rand (Lincoln: University of Nebraska Press, 1990). Illuminating discussion of Derrida's encounter with Hegel may be found in Mark C. Taylor, *Altarity* (Chicago: University of Chicago Press, 1987).

deadlocks of late modernism.[28] Broadly echoing some of Žižek's interests above in the excess of investment in the *objet petit a*, Santner locates Paul within a broader theologico-political history in which the actual rulers or mechanisms of power within a society find themselves doubled or haloed by a kind of aura of authority, a phenomenon Giorgio Agamben has recently glossed as an almost surrealist excess over the material he calls "glory."[29]

Playing off of Ernst Kantorwicz's classic study *The King's Two Bodies*, Santner shows how the society of the spectacle—in which power is diffuse, dispersed, decentralized—seems to solicit repetitions of Pauline tropes. Importantly, unlike Badiou and Žižek (and echoing important readings of Jacob Taubes and Giorgio Agamben), Santner does not locate this repetition so much in visions of a Lutheran Paul overcoming or universalizing inherited Jewish *nomos* discourse but rather visions of a Paul who appropriates and subverts Roman discourses of the political body. This shift in focus would, of course, be an important way to move beyond the more clunkily traditional reading of Paul as an index of a "Christian origins" story, more in keeping with the broad swath of more recent Pauline scholarship often glossed as "the new perspective." Reading Paul against the backdrop of Roman imperial discourse is a task that remains to be carried through, and Santner's work should be paired with Dale Martin's *The Corinthian Body* as perhaps theoretical and historical readings that would mutually electrify.[30] In Santner's work, the society of the spectacle receives from the religious archive something of the utmost necessity: a comparative name for the obsessive persistence or "stuckness" of everyday life in its fractured certainties, its stupidly everyday (though perhaps ignored) facticities or as ifs. Despite the implausibility of foundationalism, we continue to live oriented lives as if they were founded on certainties. Žižek will describe this as the repressed aspect of "belief" in contemporary culture.[31] In Santner's

28. See, e.g., Eric Santner, *The Royal Remains: The People's Two Bodies and the Endgames of Sovereignty* (Chicago: University of Chicago Press, 2011) following from Santner, *On the Psychotheology of Everyday Life* (Chicago: University of Chicago Press, 2001). Compare the excellent engagements with readings of Paul and Renaissance materialities in Jonathan Goldberg, *The Seeds of Things: Theorizing Sexuality and Materiality in Renaissance Representations* (New York: Fordham University Press, 2009). See also Julia Reinhard Lupton, *Citizen Saints: Shakespeare and Political Theology* (Chicago: University of Chicago Press, 2005).

29. Note that Agamben reads "glory" in keeping with questions of "surplus" value and sur-reality coming from the cultural theory of Guy Debord, making Agamben's reading of Paul absolutely central to his understanding of the society of the spectacle. See Giorgio Agamben, *The Kingdom and the Glory: For a Theological Genealogy of Economy and Government* (Stanford: Stanford University Press, 2011).

30. See also the work of Brigitte Kahl on Galatians, Robert Jewett on Romans, or Lawrence Welborn on Corinthians (see his essay in Blanton and de Vries, eds., *Paul and the Philosophers*).

language, the society of power via spectacle, immanence, or the "special kind of obviousness" that endows everyday life with its sense of being *really* real receives from Paul a notion of "the flesh." For Paul, Santner writes, "*the flesh is the thorn in the body*, the dimension of embodied subjectivity that registers an excess of the normative pressures that inform and potentially 'deform' a life lived in relation to agencies of authority and authorization."[32] Santner wants to find in Paul an indication of the way that reality as such guarantees, authorizes itself by way of a kind of sublime excess *within* everyday, banal reality. Note that Santner goes on to write (by way of a Paulinist tradition in Ephesians) that the problem of deformation as "the flesh" is precisely this: "The complex symbolic dynamic of the constitution of kingship itself comes 'to a head' precisely when the *body* of the king is posited as the *head* of the body politic."[33] Put differently, once the "special kind of obviousness" will become increasingly detached from causal institutional functions, the question of *autonomia* becomes all the more strangely opaque, soliciting a return of comparative tropes, metaphors, and structures of thinking that are able to keep pace with the peculiar intensity, aporia, and alterity endemic to self-grounding identity as such. Santner will name the set of issues as the problem of "a surplus of immanence within immanence."[34]

A great deal remains to be said about Santner's attempt to rewire discussions of Paul and the disclosive "event" to a history of the body and its excessive ticks and quirks and desires, all those "thorns in the flesh."[35] For the

31. See, e.g., Slavoj Žižek, *On Belief* (New York: Verso, 2001).

32. Santner, *Royal Remains,* 39.

33. Ibid.

34. Ibid., 27.

35. Above all, I would, in this context, like to discuss the relationship between older discussions of a factical horizon and the steering of this phenomenological tradition toward a focus on specific techniques and technologies of self-making, the specificity of which I find to be a good way of interacting with the focus of Santner. See Giorgio Agamben, *What Is an Apparatus? And Other Essays* (Stanford: Stanford University Press, 2009). Incidentally, I find that, from start to finish, the question of this specificity of technique is a much better way to engage the peculiar aura that attached to the Pauline movement than more holistic modes of thinking about a new covenant, new religion, new organizational mode. The surplus of immanence within immanence emerges from quirks in our *practices* of the everyday, the body's (un)rootedness in the symbolic identities on offer, and it will ultimately be important to engage this issue with more patient readings of the believing body in Pauline texts than have emerged to this point. Santner's statement is no less true for the ancient contexts than the medieval and modern ones: "What is missed in . . . all efforts to deflate the force of political metaphors by 'deconstructing' their metaphoricity, their status as fictions or rhetorical figures, is the difference between symbolic fiction and fantasy. What is missed is precisely the fact that such fictions get a grip on the imagination of individuals and collectives because they are ultimately sustained by the 'real stuff' of fantasy, by the dimension I have been calling the flesh" (42–43). Put differently for the sake of the Pauline conversations, this implies that all readings

moment, it is worth noting that it is precisely in the context of *this* juxtaposition of Paul and the excess of reality within everyday reality that someone like Žižek's or Stanislas Breton's central reflections on the kenotic, emptying, or hollowing "call" that is a Pauline proclamation of a crucified Messiah become significant as a mode of subverting the otherwise always-already effective link between power and facticity. In their philosophical appropriations of Paul is a scandalously unsettling, even "stupid" (cf. μωρία in 1 Corinthians 1) identification with the crucified Messiah that names a potential detachment, unhinging, or bracketing of the "special kind of obviousness" by which our world, or any world, solicits our participation, incites affirmation, thereby becoming what it is. Eric Santner explores the topic of obtrusive, excessive, or self-grounding enjoyment as a key for unlocking a contemporary political theology, as it were, of (the unconscious) God, the undying forcefulness of earlier theological motifs even after these theologies have ceased to seem convincing as systems of reflection.[36]

FUTURE PROSPECTS 1: RETHINKING DISCIPLINARY FORMATIONS

The (Paulinist or Lacanian) sense of frustration that I have confided about some of the "early statements" about Paul and philosophers like Slavoj Žižek could also be expressed in a more directly historical mode. Here I would want to be as positive as possible, as to say that it is possible to do so is already to transform a frustration about self-protectively invested limitations of recent thought into a story about how our disciplinary histories in these fields already contain a richness (and, yes, an "excess") of intellectual potential that affords a (kairological) chance to do better than our fields have done more recently. In that sense, for example, the specific *forms of scarcity* in what seems possible to think about in some of the early discussions are directly tied to the histories of, say, philosophy, New Testament studies, religious studies, psychoanalysis, as academic disciplines, as publishing venues, and as cultural roles. All of these

of the ancient collective imaginaries that are premised entirely on epochal, economic, or forensic distinctions between a "Jewish" and "Christian" mode of thinking about law, patrimony, etc., necessarily obscure important aspects of the mechanics of finding oneself, in the Pauline language, *in* Christ, crucified *as* Christ, etc.

36. See Eric Santner, *On the Psychotheology of Everyday Life: Reflections on Freud and Rosenzweig* (Chicago: University of Chicago Press, 2001); and Santner, *Royal Remains*. Santner's work, a rethinking of categories of the messianic in relation to a kind of surplus immanence within immanence, is very important, and I will return to it.

different histories constitute a prefabricated and preexistent staging for all of our comments. These histories, or these different economies, equip us with certain capacities (rather than others), load us up with some pressures and expectations (rather than others). Consider some of the ways recent explosion of fascination with the figure of Paul among Continental philosophers highlights the historical rootedness of recent interdisciplinary conversations.

Note two or three important disciplinary benchmarks. Friedrich Schleiermacher was the first professor of New Testament studies at the newly established University of Berlin, a model for a modern program in biblical studies that was extraordinarily influential. This New Testament scholar published widely on Platonic dialogues, on the critical philosophy of Kant, the authenticity of the Pastoral Epistles, on theories of culture and linguistic signification, and on a new way of studying religiosity within post-Kantian university contexts. Even the landmark topic that Schleiermacher basically invented as a modern university course—the course on the historical Jesus—emerged from his "interdisciplinary" reflections on how to understand a *bios* or singular form of life in relation to larger structures of culture, politics, and language.[37] New Testament scholars tend to understand the development of the disciplinary conversation from Schleiermacher (1768–1834) to the equally famous David Friedrich Strauss (1808–1874) in terms of a development of historical-critical method or in terms of discrete technical decisions (about, say, the prioritizing of the Gospel of John or the Synoptics in relation to the historical Jesus). But, of course, the shift represented by Strauss in relation to Schleiermacher could also be described in terms of the fact that Strauss was a self-styled disciple not of Immanuel Kant but of the philosopher G. W. F. Hegel.[38]

In other words, just as initial indications, it is worth saying that the disciplinary links between biblical studies and Continental philosophy are currently *not at all* what they once were. In fact, these days we have to do a lot of "additional" reading and "interdisciplinary research" just to begin to understand earlier moments in the life of the discipline in which modern

37. All of these topics are explored best in the recent work of Halvor Moxnes, *Jesus and the Rise of Nationalism: A New Quest for the Nineteenth Century Historical Jesus* (London: I. B. Tauris, 2011). Moxnes's book is a landmark of its own, nothing less than an intellectual breakthrough or paradigm shift regarding the significance of the modern social history of biblical studies in relation to more general histories of collective identities.

38. As a site for interdisciplinary articulations of the significance of biblical studies, the shift from Kant to Hegel is profound. I try to make clear some of the implications for the nature of biblical studies as a form of cultural criticism in the first two chapters of *Displacing Christian Origins*.

philosophy and biblical studies were produced in a vibrantly competitive or mutually influential struggle to define a holistic worldview or a university-wide engagement with "religion." Again, not to be overly critical of their engagements, consider the sometimes remarkable awkwardness of one of the earliest of the extraordinarily important recent encounters between Pauline scholars and Continental philosophers, that staged by John D. Caputo as *St. Paul among the Philosophers*. In the conference from which this collection of essays emerged, some august lights within biblical studies did not seem to be able to stop tutting at the "anachronistic" or "ahistorical" reading of Paul by Badiou and Žižek.[39] Fair enough. But never in any of these confident denunciations of the untimely or ana-chronistic interpretations of the philosophers do we get the sense that the biblical scholars present were interested to relate what *they* were saying about time (e.g., about timely speech concerning Paul, or about the proper limits of our—or Paul's—being located *within* our respective proper times) to the fact that both Badiou and Žižek themselves make a living thinking, talking, and writing *about time and historical change!*[40] Again, assertions of mastery became all the more forceful in the face of an evident weakness or *lack of mastery*. On this occasion, biblical scholars wanted to police appropriate boundaries and proprietorial limits, all the while failing to say nothing *illuminating* about the very constitution of the very laws they wanted to enforce. In this case, they said almost nothing about how the same questions about time, about being, about reality and time, are construed, not only by the discipline of Continental philosophy, but also in the actual writings of their interlocutors.

39. One hesitates even to begin to formulate long lists of references. *All* of the New Testament scholars involved seem to orient their interventions in relationship to philosophy almost entirely under the rubric of some cliché of an undergraduate classroom. Paula Fredriksen says, without reference to two hundred years of hermeneutical or historiographical reflection on the plural and displaced nature of "the present": "But the frame of reference for historical interpretation is not and cannot be the present. . . . Our frame of reference is the *past*" (61). E. P. Sanders begins similarly, though with disarming discussion of finitude and limits of knowledge that do not immediately translate into justifications for disciplinary divisions of labor. He just never makes a comparative turn to engage the radically postfoundational or nonrepresentational modes of thinking about "universalism" in the writings of Žižek and Badiou.

40. Some exceptions: Dale Martin's reading of historical criticism as a form of "asceticism" (94), his serious initial encounter with the nonrepresentational or purely inventive notion of a "universal" in Žižek or Badiou (101–2); Boyarin raises useful questions about the relation of systematicity and particularity (110-12, 167–68). He also, while claiming simply to differ from the Platonism of Badiou, invites us to reflect on the relationship between a subtractive universalism in Badiou and sophistic stratagems in Paul. This line of comparison could be explored in relation to Badiou's discussions of "forcing" the truth. All references from John D. Caputo and Linda Martin Alcoff, eds. *St. Paul among the Philosophers*. (Bloomington & Indianapolis: Indiana University Press, 2009).

Which is a shame really: Žižek and Badiou are both extraordinarily interesting theorists of time, being, and transformative encounters with the unplanned and unexpected.[41]

Interestingly, however, when read in light of earlier moments in the life of the discipline, it is almost like contemporary New Testament scholars have almost entirely forgotten their own disciplinary history, one wherein being-in-time was a topic that emerged from a period of scholarship when it was often very difficult to distinguish, say, the New Testament interpretation of Albert Schweitzer or Rudolf Bultmann from philosophical reflections on temporality and being by Ernst Cassirer or a young Martin Heidegger.[42] And having forgotten the cultural moment wherein biblical studies and Continental philosophy struggled both with and against each other, this more recent encounter staged an encounter that no one understood any longer, within which no one had much to say except to repeat the way they had grown accustomed to speaking within their own disciplines and then to reassert these disciplines themselves as the power that justifies their lack of capacity to say much that is provocative, productive, *going anywhere*. So I have started, then, with a question that the young Heidegger—and Bultmann with him—imagined as once hermeneutic, philosophical, and a repetition of the Pauline topic of a temporal *event* (καιρός): when you compare and contrast Paul and a philosopher, do you in fact already know what you are doing, or is there a surprising issue gurgling up through the oddly interspersed books on your bookshelf?

FUTURE PROSPECTS 2: COMPARATIVE ANALYSIS OF (MESSIANIC) INTENSITIES

To witness Žižek in full flight is a wonderful and at times alarming experience, part philosophical tightrope-walk, part performance-art marathon, part intellectual roller-coaster ride. Most startling of all are

41. Žižek speaks of a "terroristic" aspect to the "historicist" desire for closure, for territorial limits, for the posited and exhausted nature of the given (164).

42. Note chs. 3 and 4 of *Displacing Christian Origins*.

the nervous tics which accompany his every utterance: the constant wiping of his beard and lips, the incessant dabbing of his furrowed brow, the closed eyes, clenched fists and the strange guttural noises that punctuate his speech.[43]

I bear on my body the marks of Jesus.[44]

But let's start our comparative wheels turning with another simple but fundamental question: What are we to compare when we compare Paul and Žižek? Sometimes it seems to me that our comparative labors tend to be too cerebral, too idealistic, as if life and thought occurred between the leaves of an encyclopedia of the history of ideas. But it is not just from the disciplinary *past* that an excess of comparative matters emerges to overload containable categories. Let us pause for a moment, for example, over two speaking bodies, two itinerant voices, two individuals who seem unquestionably to be *driven*.

Playing a good psychoanalyst *avant la lettre*, the second-century satirist Lucian jokes that the great boast of philosophers—namely, that they are cosmopolitan travelers and therefore "at home in all cities the world over"—is really just a sublimation of the fact that they didn't get their jobs of choice back home.[45] Joining in the deflationary insight, Seneca imagines that itinerants should be read as trying desperately to escape themselves.[46] Both ancient thinkers invite us to wonder about our own doggedly determined itinerants, Paul and Žižek, their often grueling schedules or periods of travel. In both cases, would it be interesting to wonder about the relation between this intensively expansionistic orientation (see Rom. 15:19, 23), a kind of excessive itinerancy, and the way both Paul and Žižek are occasionally plagued with gossip about lack of recognition and prospects at the initial home base of choice, whether Žižek's Llubjana or Paul's Jerusalem?[47]

43. This is a very common thing to hear about Žižek. This particular instance, one of many, comes from Sean O'Hagen, "Slavoj Žižek: Interview," *The Guardian*, June 27, 2010.

44. Gal. 6:17 RSV.

45. See numerous variations on the motif in Lucian's "Philosophies for Sale," in *Lucian IV*, trans. A. M. Harmon, Loeb Classical Library (Cambridge, MA: Harvard University Press, 1996).

46. See Seneca's "On the Tranquillity of Mind" (2.13), in *Moral Essays II*, trans. John W. Basore, Loeb Classical Library (Cambridge, MA: Harvard University Press, 1996).

47. One can find references to life in Llubjana in numerous places within Žižek's writings. Very interesting also is the insightful, provocative, but understated exploration of these motifs in conversations with Astra Taylor in *Žižek!* (ICA Films, 2008), a feature-length documentary about the philosopher.

To stay with the comparative wonders, is it ever a *merely* incidental spur to the life of itinerancy that the second-best or newly acquired "home base" abroad is always more problematic than anyone would have hoped? No doubt some of the nastiest things to be said about Žižek emerged from Paris, where Žižek had gone to train in psychoanalysis and during which he wrote the first books that would eventually appear in English. Paul was (happily) allowed to "go the Gentiles" by the devotees of Jesus in Jerusalem, and he ended for a time in a vibrantly experimental Antioch. No doubt, however, some of the best anti-Paulinist yarns ever spun we produced among the Antioch devotees of John Mark after Paul's polemical split with him.

You can see how such experimental comparisons might begin to evoke very intriguing—and surprising—questions of both Paul and Žižek. In this case, we could elaborate the spurs to itinerancy, or wonder about the peculiarly complex intertwining of the "old and the new" in their respective writings. Did Paul "break with Judaism," and, if so, which ancient opinions should be taken as the real authority on such a matter? All of the complexities of the Pauline story, all the usual "problems" we point to in our historical reconstructions, could also be articulated at the level of controversies around Žižek. Consider the significance for situating Paulinism in relation to big differences of opinion among different ancient Jewish sects, or their differences about what would count as important shibboleth issues concerning practice. Or, why not compare the way Žižek's life and legacy are also constituted by sometimes unexpected and explosively polemical moments in which differences between groups or thinkers become polemical sticking points invested with profound significance, marking out Žižek (or Paul) as either "in" or "out" of this or that grouping? Is Žižek a Marxist, a Communist, a capitalist playboy masquerading as something else? Is he a fossil from an old Soviet utopianism that should be disavowed for a more up-to-date, less problematic philosophy in keeping with the structures of viability governing life amid the potential converts to the West of the old home base? (Is his messianism dead?) In keeping with the always sticky relationship between Paul's assumptions about ethnic particularity and his statements about "everyone," is Žižek engaging problems that really are *general*, or is he only working out his own backwater nationalist problems of an evidently failed communism? Tell me what you think of the one, and I'll predict what you'll say about the other.

One of the most interesting points of comparison is in the way both Paul and Žižek can both be fetishized or dismissed as "mere localists." In any case, both itinerants are caught up in a funny game of radical fidelity to a tradition that is itself also sometimes ruthlessly criticized by them.

No doubt, such dramas are enough to make one want to live indiscreetly among the problematically barbarous, all those territories that will really give the lackluster home crowds something to talk about. *Cosmopoliteis* are not just world travelers; they are travelers with attitude. Paul wants to visit the heart of empire in Rome, but preemptively declares that he wants to do so really only to collect money to get to the heart of barbarian territory in Spain (Rom. 1:15). That he is engaged in this performance even as he anxiously collects money and kudos to shore things up back home is, simply, the life of the cosmopolitan Lucian might have tried to deflate as another form of agonistic display of "making it big." Žižek went West as well, and perhaps to the exemplary seat of late capitalist state power, taking stints as visiting scholar in some of the finest American academic institutions. Paul never attained the crown jewel of living life among the barbarians of Spain. Žižek moonlighted by writing hilarious captions for photographs in an oversexed (because perhaps underaged) Abercrombie and Fitch catalog.[48] Pressured travels toward westward seats of power couple with willful self-presentations involving "barbarous" associations that, precisely, the seats of power are supposed to question. Both itinerants know something about the geography of telling truth as a "scandal."

Nor would we know, ultimately, where or how to distinguish between willful self-presentation as an outsider to power—that beloved costuming of philosophical cosmopolitanism—and repetitions of ways and manners of the outsider to these new cities that are less conscious and more unstudied. One thinks of Žižek's affirmations of Stalin, his fondness for bucolic dirty jokes from Poland (he tells us), or to never-sheepish references to new directions in the porn industry. That Žižek's philosophical and psychoanalytic insights often emerge directly from a reflection on these topics not characteristic, say, of North American academicism is itself to name the singular blend of insider/ outsider academic discourse for the itinerancy of Žižek. On the other hand (and to remain with Romans), consider how Paul announces his arrival at the center of power, loading his letter with polished forms of rhetorical sophistication and presenting himself as a classic philosophical cosmopolitan, someone who shows up from abroad in order to impart wisdom. Paul even warns them that, speaking with boldness (παρρησία), he comes as the bold speaker who refuses to submit to local decorum—a mode of self-presentation they would have loved, appearances of dogged criticism notwithstanding. Sometimes presenting oneself as critical outsider is the best way to get "in" with the insiders. And what are we to do with the almost comically out of sync pride in the (failed

---

48. See Žižek's (very funny, deflationary) captions in the twenty-third Abercrombie and Fitch catalog (Back-to-School 2003, "The Sex Ed Issue").

but sublimated) Jewish Messiah, the rapt attention to the Jewish patriarchal narrative as the key to the problem of desire, or the immediate accusation that the masculinity-obsessed military power of empire was deeply afflicted with a homoeroticism the man from the East believes to be caused by a primordial idolatry? Like nostalgia for bygone Communist regimes or problematically sexist or racist jokes from behind the North American lectern, we just could not know what the edges are between watchful self-performance and inadvertent missteps. Such is the comedy of life, for the apostle or the philosopher. Here we would have returned to our hermeneutic realization that the mind of the philosopher, and the mind of the apostle, are not interior spaces like the inside of two safes. These minds contain so many resonances with geographies of contestation, limitation, and hegemony; and we can intuit something about the slips, jokes, outbursts, confessions, and hesitations of the texts they produce if we attend to these spaces, these maps, these territories and terrains.

10

The Philosophers' Paul and the Churches

Neil Elliott

The occasion for this volume is one of the most remarkable recent developments in scholarship on the apostle Paul: the surprising attention being paid to Paul by a number of European and North American philosophers who find the apostle a model for their politically radical but nontheistic programs. The development is all the more surprising when we recall how some earlier philosophers, chief among them Friedrich Nietzsche, presented themselves as the cultured despisers of Paul's form of Christianity.[1]

Each of the other essays in this volume has addressed a particular philosopher who has engaged the apostle's legacy. The focus in those essays has been to describe and to evaluate diverse appropriations of the apostle, asking whether one or another philosopher has offered new insight into Paul's thought. My purpose here is different. I wish to shift attention from "the philosophers" and their interpretation of Paul to the Church and to Christian responses to the philosophers.

Such a prospect confronts several challenges. The first is bound up with that reference to "the Church," capitalized rather audaciously to indicate a single coherent entity—a common enough usage in theology, but one that must appear to beg the question today. I mean that, amid contemporary US churches, denominational differences pale in comparison with the metastasizing diversity of alternatives, from storefront missions to "emergent" coffee houses and full-service Christian megaplexes. Those "mainline" denominations that remain are often polarized by campaigns and agendas conceived in think tanks and driven by lobbying groups and full-spectrum Christian broadcasting, especially vibrant on the right. Protestants are now outnumbered by people affiliated with no

---

1. On Nietzsche, see the essay above by Peter Frick.

religious faith.[2] Mainline congregations compete for the adherence of their own members with the cultural axiom that religion is a matter of intensely personal preference. The enormous growth of what we may call "spirituality" industries manifests the triumph of capitalist values, as religious symbols are transformed into the infinitely customizable commodities of consumer style. To speak in such a context of "the Church" as a coherent and singular reality must seem wistfully nostalgic, perhaps even retrograde.

Further, until now, the subject of this volume has been of interest chiefly to individual scholars and, perhaps, their advanced students in philosophy, theology, and biblical studies, individuals who have been drawn to the topic by their own personal and professional interests. "The philosophers' Paul" appears as the subject of analysis at the narrow intersection of these academic disciplines, not beyond it. I am unaware of official ecclesiastical responses to the work of any of the philosophers discussed here, or of any prospect that such statements might be forthcoming. Even if a number of the scholars involved in recent discussions of this topic have been self-consciously doing theology on behalf of "the Church," broadly defined, or working in ecclesiastically affiliated institutions of higher learning, the diversity of their responses—ranging on occasion from enthusiasm, to condescension, to alarm toward one or another of the philosophers in question—points up the fallacy of construing them together as a single, univocal "Christian response."

Finally, although in recent years I have ventured to respond to one or another aspect of a philosopher's reading of Paul,[3] I readily concede that I am neither fluent in contemporary philosophy nor, although I am a priest in the Episcopal Church (U.S.A.), do I hold any sort of ecclesiastical or academic rank that would qualify me to do anything as audacious as speak broadly for "the Church."

My purpose here is necessarily more modest. I wish to point again to the wider radical project in which several of the contemporary philosophers are currently engaged as the proper context in which their appropriations of Paul must be understood and evaluated. Further, I propose that the failure, or at least reluctance, of some theologians to enter into that context, to step, so to

2. "'Nones' on the Rise: One-in-Five Adults Have No Religious Affiliation," Pew Forum on Religion and Public Life, Jan. 9, 2013, www.pewforum.org/unaffiliated/nones-on-the-rise.aspx.

3. See Neil Elliott, "Ideological Closure in the Christ Event: A Marxist Response to Alain Badiou's Paul," in *Paul, Philosophy, and the Theopolitical Vision*, ed. Douglas Harink (Eugene, OR: Cascade, 2010), 135–54; and Elliott, "Marxism and the Postcolonial Study of Paul," ,in *The Colonized Apostle: Paul through Postcolonial Eyes*, ed. Christopher D. Stanley (Minneapolis: Fortress Press, 2011), 34–50 (esp. 49–50).

speak, onto the philosophers' home turf, is symptomatic of a wider presumption of privilege on the part of Christian theology. That presumption is itself a case in point of the perilous contemporary ideological situation to which the philosophers wish urgently to draw our attention. At last, I wish to suggest that the apostle Paul himself offers, mutatis mutandis, a way out of the presumption of epistemic privilege that so dominates and distorts much Christian theology today.

THEOLOGICAL CRITIQUE BY DISMISSAL

In a spate of conferences and publications over the last decade, groups of theologians, philosophers, and biblical scholars have gathered to interact with selected works by Jacob Taubes, Giorgio Agamben, Alain Badiou, Slavoj Žižek, Walter Benjamin, and others grouped under the category of Continental philosophy.[4] This energetic activity suggests that the work of "the philosophers" has become a sort of cause célèbre for some in these circles—and the bête noir for others—which René Girard's work on "sacred violence" presented, beginning in the 1990s.[5] The reaction has not been uniformly enthusiastic. Alain Gignac points out the potential for a certain professional resentment when he playfully describes Taubes, Badiou, and Agamben as "poach[ing] in the hunting grounds of theologians and exegetes"; and sure enough, others have observed a note of "indignation" among theologians and exegetes posing as Paul's ecclesiastical defenders.[6]

4. See David Odell-Scott, ed., *Reading Romans with Contemporary Philosophers and Theologians* (New York: T&T Clark, 2007); John D. Caputo and Linda Martín Alcoff, eds. *St. Paul among the Philosophers*, Indiana Series in the Philosophy of Religion (Bloomington: Indiana University Press, 2009); Harink, ed., *Paul, Philosophy, and the Theopolitical Vision*.

5. Girard's works (*The Scapegoat*, trans. Yvonne Freccero [Baltimore: Johns Hopkins University Press, 1977]; *Violence and the Sacred*, trans. Patrick Gregory [Baltimore: Johns Hopkins University Press, 1986]; and René Girard, J. M. Oughourlian, and G. Lefort, *Things Hidden from the Foundation of the World* [Stanford: Stanford University Press, 1987]) inspired James G. Williams, *The Bible, Violence, and the Sacred* (San Francisco: HarperSanFrancisco, 1991) and, in particular connection with Paul, Robert Hamerton-Kelly, *Sacred Violence: Paul's Hermeneutic of the Cross* (Minneapolis: Fortress Press, 1992). The Colloquium on Violence and Religion (COV&R) was founded in 1990 to explore implications of Girard's theory and continues its work today in part through its journal *Contagion*; see also http://www.uibk.ac.at/theol/cover/aboutcover). For an early response especially to Robert Hamerton-Kelly's book, see Neil Elliott, "Paul and the Lethality of the Law," *Foundations and Facets Forum* 9, nos. 3–4 (1993): 237–56.

6. Alain Gignac, "Taubes, Badiou, Agamben: Contemporary Reception of Paul by Non-Christian Philosophers," in Odell-Scott, ed., *Reading Romans*, 154–211 (here 156); similarly Jerome Robbins, "The

The implication of metaphors like "poaching" or "expropriation" is that Paul is *properly* interpreted by the theological "insiders," indeed, that he is their property. It follows that atheists, no matter how erudite, can have no "proper" claim on the apostle. It is this proprietary presumption, this note that Paul "belongs" to the theologians, that I want here to contest; not because I think the theologians' interest in the apostle is illegitimate, but because the rush to defend Paul from dialectical materialists and their ilk appears to me a symptom of the very predicament that the dialectical materialists are laboring to diagnose. My purpose here is to point in the direction of a more fruitful interaction with the philosophers on the part of "the Church."

Some theologians have argued not only that the philosophers in question should not claim to interpret Paul because he is not properly their subject but also that the effort is doomed from the start; they *cannot* understand him. On this account, the philosophers fail to grasp fundamental and central aspects of Paul's thought because they cannot comprehend a reality in which, because of their lack of faith, they do not participate. So Jens Zimmermann has argued that "unbelieving" philosophers inevitably "fail to grasp" the irreducibly theological categories that are "the very fabric of Paul's thinking": concepts like "Christology," "transcendence," and "new creation" in Christ. Zimmermann insists he is not raising a mere "matter of interpretive preference"; the choice of these *theological* categories is grounded in the Christian's "ontological participation in" the new creation and new humanity that have been opened up in Christ.[7] In earlier essays, Paul J. Griffiths and Daniel M. Bell argued that precisely because the philosophers are not Christians, they have consistently failed to recognize as a fundamental truth that the only satisfactory answer to their quests is "the peace given by explicit knowledge of the God of Abraham," available only through communion with the Church, through which humanity is "taken up into the divine life of the Trinity." The only true and worthy

Politics of Paul," *Journal for Cultural and Religious Theory* 6 (2005): 89–94, describes a certain "territoriality" on the part of theological and biblical scholars defending "their" Paul against interlopers. Stephen Fowl, "A Very Particular Universalism: Badiou and Paul," in Harink, ed., *Paul, Philosophy, and the Theopolitical Vision*, 119–34 (here 119), has observed "a rather indignant attitude" toward the philosophers among Paulinists; and Paul J. Griffiths, "The Cross as the Fulcrum of Politics: Expropriating Agamben on Paul," in Harink, ed., *Paul, Philosophy, and the Theopolitical Vision*, 179–97 (here 180), invokes the analogy of "despoilers of the Egyptians" to describe Giorgio Agamben as reading Paul "from without" or "from outside"—"insiders" here being identified with church theologians and New Testament scholars.

7. Jens Zimmermann, "Hermeneutics of Unbelief: Philosophical Readings of Paul," in Harink, ed., *Paul, Philosophy, and the Theopolitical Vision*, 227–53 (here 235–36).

radicality, they asserted, is to be found in the familiar embrace of the Church's liturgical and charitable practices.[8]

Alas, this argument is made more often on cozily theoretical than on empirical grounds. One is left to wonder whether the philosophers (and others) might be more amenable to persuasion if "actually existing" Christian worship on any given Sunday morning gave just a bit more evidence of its alleged revolutionary potential. In the absence of such evidence, the theological critics seem, to my ear at least, to protest too much. Indeed, such theological critiques of the philosophers resemble a sort of defensive action, rather like that of a body's immune system rushing to guard against a foreign contaminant. But, as anyone who has suffered from hay fever knows, the body's allergic and defensive mobilizations can sometimes be out of any proportion to the actual danger posed by a foreign body.

Similarly, the nervous zeal with which some have rushed to demonstrate that, at one or another point, the philosophers have misinterpreted the apostle's thought, or that they have not kept up with the latest developments in the professional exegetical literature, seems misplaced. Admittedly, I have offered my own criticism elsewhere of Alain Badiou's appropriation of Paul in his book *St. Paul: The Foundation of Universalism*, arguing that Badiou relies on an untenable essentializing of "Jewish" and "Greek" discourses that theological and exegetical scholars still struggle—quite rightly—to disavow. I also argued, quite apart from questions of the historical veracity or verifiability of the resurrection of Jesus, that in its original apocalyptic context, the symbolization of the Messiah's resurrection bore far more *political* potential than Badiou recognizes.[9] But my goal in that effort was to *augment* the relevance of Badiou's argument, not to deny or disqualify it from the outset as insufficiently "theological."

Those who strive to make the latter case appear to miss the point. The philosophers neither claim nor aspire to give a comprehensive account of Paul's *theological* thought. Rather, they are trying to describe, and if possible to model, a radical militancy appropriate and necessary to our present situation. To reduce

8. Paul J. Griffiths, "Christ and Critical Theory," *First Things*, August/September 2004, 46, 50, 54–55; and Daniel M. Bell, "Badiou's Faith and Paul's Gospel: The Politics of Indifference and the Overcoming of Capital," *Angelaki* 12 (2007): 108. Both express a certain amount of condescension toward the benighted non-Christians, Griffiths naming them objects of "Christian pity and concern." Creston Davis, "Subtractive Liturgy," in John Milbank, Slavoj Žižek, and Creston Davis, *Paul's New Moment: Continental Philosophy and the Future of Christian Theology* (Grand Rapids: Brazos, 2010), expresses a similar enthusiasm for the eucharistic liturgy as an "Incarnational" reality through which union with the Trinity is achieved. Surprisingly, he attributes these thoughts to the apostle Paul.

9. Elliott, "Ideological Closure"; see also Ward Blanton's essay in this volume.

this to a matter of "theology" is to evade the greater responsibility to which the philosophers seek to call us all.

From the start of his book on Paul, Alain Badiou makes clear that he is indifferent to the more sublime dimensions of the apostle's theology. The resurrection of the Messiah, admittedly central to Paul (for it is to this single statement that, Badiou cheerfully admits, Paul "reduces Christianity"), is "precisely a fable" in which it is "rigorously impossible to believe."[10] For his part, Slavoj Žižek makes clear that his interest in Christianity is not in any of its dominant contemporary expressions but in its "perverse core," which he finds crystallized in Jesus' cry of dereliction from the cross (Mark 15:34).

> When Christ dies, what dies with him is the secret hope discernible in "Father, why hast thou forsaken me?": the hope that there *is* a father who has abandoned me. The "Holy Spirit" is the community deprived of its support in the big Other. The point of Christianity as the religion of atheism is not the vulgar humanist one that the becoming-man-of-God reveals that man is the secret of God (Feuerbach et al.); rather, it attacks the religious hard core that survives even in humanism, even up to Stalinism, with its belief in History as the "big Other" that decides on the "objective meaning" of our deeds.[11]

What Žižek here calls the "point of Christianity" is a "perverse core" because it is a perversion of the "core" of Christianity as most Christians historically have understood it. Indeed, in Žižek's own words, the "core" he poses as the proper object of philosophy is the substitution of a "religion of atheism" in the place of a belief in God. This "core," Žižek continues, can be redeemed "only in the gesture of abandoning the shell of [Christianity's] institutional organization (and, even more so, of its specific religious experience). The gap here is irreducible: either one drops the religious form, or one maintains the form, but loses the essence. That is the ultimate heroic gesture that awaits Christianity: in order to save its treasure, it has to sacrifice itself—like Christ,

10. See Alain Badiou, *Saint Paul: The Foundation of Universalism,* trans. Ray Brassier, Cultural Memory in the Present (Stanford: Stanford University Press, 2003), 4–5.

11. Slavoj Žižek, *The Puppet and the Dwarf: The Perverse Core of Christianity,* Short Circuits (Cambridge, MA: MIT Press. 2003), 171. He introduces this paragraph by declaring it is "the point of this book."

who had to die so that Christianity could emerge."[12] Evidently, then, Badiou and Žižek are chiefly interested in selected elements of Christian, and especially Pauline, theology because they perceive there elements of a radical subjectivity that they wish to extricate from the deadening context of contemporary Christianity, rather as one might pull smoldering embers from the cool bed of a dying fire to fan them into flame. Just as evidently, neither philosopher imagines contemporary Christian churches as providing the tinder (to extend the metaphor) for the fire they wish to see cast upon the earth. In the face of Žižek's call for renunciation, for "dropping the religious form," it seems hardly to the point to protest that Badiou or Žižek (or others of the philosophers) have failed to be adequately Christian in their theologizing. Theology—as a separate domain only circumstantially related to the political—is not the point.

THE COMMUNIST IMPERATIVE

What Badiou and Žižek wish (to limit ourselves to these two, though a similar argument could be extended to others of the philosophers) is to inspire a truly "revolutionary subjectivity." As he has described it in other writings, Badiou's goal is the performative revival in our day of "the communist hypothesis": "What is the communist hypothesis? In its generic sense, given in its canonic *Manifesto*, 'communist' means, first, that the logic of class—the fundamental subordination of labour to a dominant class, the arrangement that has persisted since Antiquity—is not inevitable; it can be overcome. The communist hypothesis is that a different collective organization is practicable, one that will eliminate the inequality of wealth and even the division of labour."[13] It is wrong, Badiou argues, to regard this hypothesis as "utopian." It is just as wrong to judge the value of the Communist hypothesis by the relatively brief and ultimately failed experiments of authoritarian Eastern bloc governments in the twentieth century; its legacy is much older.[14] "As a pure Idea of equality, the communist hypothesis has no doubt existed since the beginnings of the state. As soon as mass action opposes state coercion in the name of egalitarian

12. Ibid. Žižek returns to this interpretation of the cross in Slavoj Žižek, "A Meditation on Michelangelo's *Christ on the Cross*," in Milbank, Žižek, and Davis, *Paul's New Moment*, 169–81.

13. Alain Badiou, "The Communist Hypothesis," *New Left Review* 49 (2008): 29–42 (here 34–35).

14. "Utopian" aspects of Paul's thought were the subject of a special joint session of the Paul and Politics and Pauline Soteriology groups of the Society of Biblical Literature at the annual meeting in 2011. Papers by myself, Douglas Harink, Douglas Campbell, and Theodore Jennings will be published in a forthcoming volume. I thank Susan Eastman and Ross Wagner for their energy in pulling together this session.

justice, rudiments or fragments of the hypothesis start to appear."[15] The agenda to which Badiou calls us "during the reactionary interlude that now prevails" includes recognizing that conditions in our own day more nearly resemble the prerevolutionary nineteenth century than the twentieth. That is, we today confront "vast zones of poverty, widening inequalities, politics dissolved into the 'service of wealth,' the nihilism of large sections of the young, the servility of much of the intelligentsia." Given these realities, Badiou seeks "to renew the existence of the communist hypothesis, in our consciousness and on the ground."[16]

For his part, borrowing a (pseudo-)Pauline phrase from Eph. 6:12, Žižek declares, at the outset of a lengthy discussion of "living in the end times," that today, "our struggle is not against actual corrupt individuals, but against those in power in general, against their authority, against the [capitalist] global order and the ideological mystification which sustains it."[17] It is necessary, Žižek argues, always to "maintain the precise reference to a set of social antagonisms which generate the need for communism." This understanding of Communism is "still fully relevant": "Marx's good old notion of communism not as an ideal, but as a movement which reacts to actual social antagonisms." It is further necessary not only to recognize but also to participate in those conflicts: "It is not enough to remain faithful to the communist Idea—one has to locate it in real historical antagonisms which give to this Idea a practical urgency. The only *true* question today is: do we endorse the predominant naturalization of capitalism, or does today's global capitalism contain antagonisms powerful enough to prevent its indefinite reproduction?"[18] If Žižek uses the term "communist" somewhat less readily than Badiou, it may be, in part, because he, too, does not want his cause to be confused with the centralized state experiments of Eastern Europe in the last half of the twentieth century[19] and, in part, because he insists we must be not less but *more* radical than Marx.[20] The critique of the political economy of our age remains an urgent task, but according to

15. Badiou, "Communist Hypothesis," 34–35.

16. Ibid., 41-42.

17. Slavoj Žižek, *Living in the End Times* (New York: Verso, 2010), xv.

18. Slavoj Žižek, "How to Begin from the Beginning," in *The Idea of Communism*, ed. Costas Douzinas and Slavoj Žižek (New York: Verso, 2010), 209-26.

19. Ibid., 218–19 (though just here Žižek speaks frankly of the need today to "reactualize the communist Idea" and participating in "the communist struggle"). See also Terry Eagleton, *Literary Theory: An Introduction*, 2nd ed. (Minneapolis: University of Minnesota Press, 1996), 195.

20. Ward Blanton compares Žižek's "peculiarly complex intertwining of the 'old and the new'"—particularly with regard to the Marxist heritage—with that of Paul: see his essay earlier in this volume.

Žižek, Marx's tendency to represent the future as unfolding according to an inexorable materialist determinism not only has been disproved by history but is also theoretically too reliant on the mechanistic claims of nineteenth-century capitalism itself.[21] On this point, Žižek is taking part in an intense, wide-ranging, and long-standing deliberation carried on amid the political Left today. But this is a conversation of which all too few theologians and church leaders are aware and with which still fewer are conversant. This is unfortunate. The social moment that Žižek describes is also where the Church lives, and moves, and has its being.

> The Left entered a period of profound crisis—the shadow of the twentieth century still hangs over it, and the full scope of the defeat is not yet admitted. In the years of prospering capitalism, it was easy for the Left to be a Cassandra, warning that our prosperity is based on illusions and prophesizing [sic] catastrophes to come. Now the economic downturn and social disintegration [that] the Left was waiting for is here; protests and revolts are popping up all around the globe—but what is conspicuously absent is any consistent Leftist reply to these events, any project of how to transpose islands of chaotic resistance into a positive program of social change.[22]

It is just this aspect of the philosophers' contemporary work that demands and deserves the serious attention of US churches, whether or not that attention takes the form of engagement with the philosophers themselves. In the United States today, in the absence of a coherent and compelling narrative of our situation issuing from a well-arrayed Left, that ideological vacuum has been filled by competing arguments about how the capitalist machinery can best be carbureted to achieve "job creation," "deficit reduction," and "financial stability" without interfering with the sovereignty of a putative "free market." Challenges to the fundamental axiom of capitalism's necessity—that it is the *only* imaginable mechanism for "wealth creation"—now generally go unmentioned and appear to have become unthinkable. Indeed, our atmosphere has become so choked

21. "What Marx conceived as Communism remained an idealized image of capitalism, capitalism without capitalism" (Slavoj Žižek, *The Year of Dreaming Dangerously* [New York: Verso, 2012], 134. In his essay earlier in this volume, Lawrence Welborn argues that Walter Benjamin's similar repudiation of an "antiquarian approach" to history informed Jacob Taubes's reading of Paul.

22. Žižek, *Year of Dreaming Dangerously*, 133.

with the doctrinal assertions of neoliberalism that hardly anyone bothers to pose the question empirically, as a proposal for genuine controlled experimentation. (The "case study" provided by history, that is, by decades of virtually unchecked neoliberal policies, is presumably irrelevant to the question, for example, whether corporate profits fueled by tax breaks and federal subsidies should not already have rallied the "private sector" to its alleged mission of "job creation.") Instead, as Immanuel Wallerstein has observed, those exerting the most control over the machinery of contemporary capitalism have also taken the most care to protect it from political evaluation or from the sort of modification ("reform") that might make the stuff of campaign promises actually feasible. They appear more interested in securing their own privilege through ongoing structured inequality, rather like train robbers who weight down the throttle of a runaway locomotive before leaping free with their ill-gotten loot.[23]

We should, with Žižek, perceive here the "shameless cynicism of the existing global order," which perpetuates both the ongoing immiseration of the world's majority, not least through the imposition of "austerity" measures and the constant ideological obfuscations of its true nature under the guise of "news" and "information." That world order is now so pervasive as to seem *natural* to us.[24] It is difficult to imagine a concerted popular effort to stand against the tide; or perhaps we should say, it is difficult to imagine that such efforts, when they *do* take organized form as they have, for example, in the Occupy movement, will escape being framed by corporate media as the pointless antics of the idle and self-absorbed.[25]

23. Wallerstein observes that in the present moment of "structural crisis," "those in power will no longer be trying to preserve the existing system (doomed as it is to self-destruction); rather, they will try to ensure that the transition leads to the construction of a new system that will replicate the worst features of the existing one—its hierarchy, privilege, and inequalities. They may not be using language that reflects the demise of existing structures, but they are implementing a strategy based on such assumptions" (Immanuel Wallerstein, "New Revolts against the System," *New Left Review* 18 (2002): 29–39. The train robber analogy is my own contribution.

24. On the "naturalizing" function of ideology, with appropriate discussion of the heritage of Antonio Gramsci and Louis Althusser, see Terry Eagleton, *Ideology: An Introduction*, 2nd ed. (New York: Verso, 2007); and Jan Rehmann, "Ideology Theory," *Historical Materialism* 15 (2007): 211–39.

25. In the course of 2011 and 2012, left-leaning journals like *Mother Jones* and *The Nation* published a number of articles attempting to discern the future of the Occupy movement. Social anthropologist David Graeber proposed that Occupy Wall Street "allowed us to start seeing the system [of the financial industry] for what it is: an enormous engine of debt extraction. . . . 'Financialization,' then, is not just the manipulation of money. Ultimately, it's the ability to manipulate state power to extract a portion of other people's incomes"; it follows that a debt resistance movement would strike at the very heart of the mechanism ("Can Debt Spark Revolution?," *The Nation*, Sept. 24, 2012, 22).

My purpose here is not to offer a detailed diagnosis of our situation at this stage of hypercapitalism, as the overheated mechanism threatens to come unmoored and fly apart (to borrow just one of Žižek's vivid images for our time). It is to name the context of political struggle in which Badiou and Žižek seek to engage us as the "proper" context in which their references to the revolutionary subjectivity of the apostle Paul must be understood.

In their preference for a more safely distant and hagiographic approach to the apostle, various exegetes and theologians may gallantly protest that Paul simply was not *that* kind of fellow! But it would be much more to the point of the conversation to which Badiou and Žižek invite them for exegetes and theologians to propose a *better* social site than Pauline studies where truly revolutionary subjectivity may instead be found. For Badiou and Žižek, Paul is a *pointer*, like a finger pointing at the moon. To focus on the pointer—rather than the target at which it points—is to miss their intention.

That, alas, is a challenge that too few theologians appear interested in taking up. There are important exceptions, of course, as some of the essays in this volume demonstrate. For another example, Creston Davis begins a volume of essays drawn from a 2002 international conference by observing,

> At a point when the capitalist world is coming apart at the seams, we may pause and ask ourselves: what has happened to serious leftist protests against the unjust and dehumanizing logic of global capitalism? For the last few decades, any attempt to criticize the inner dark logic of capitalism has been simply dismissed as passé (or un-American). But now, as we perch precariously on the brink of total financial-capitalistic collapse, we may wonder why and under what cultural conditions true critique from the Left have been systematically marginalized into non-existence.[26]

How can such a "critique from the Left" be revived and nourished? Davis's own answer is that "theology (and the Christian tradition) serves as a wellspring capable of funding a materialist politics of subjective truth." He intends through his project "to challenge the American bourgeois interpretation of Christian faith that simply hands over the world to the corporation without a fight."[27]

---

26. Creston Davis, introduction to Milbank, Davis, and Žižek, *Paul's New Moment*, 1.

27. Ibid., 4.

Such combative language will seem the appropriate register of response to any reader who recognizes our current era as a time of unremitting class warfare being waged from the top. But for just that reason, Davis's positive proposal is all the more perplexing. He continues simply by referring his reader to the Church's eucharistic practice: "The liturgy is the material participation in the active ontological movement of the world's mediation of itself through which the world returns nonidentically to itself in the everlasting glow of God's glory."[28] However moving some Christians may find such descriptions of the liturgy, infused as they are with Orthodox tropes of mystical participation in the divine life of the Trinity, others may well ask whether the insatiably aggressive and irreducibly material corporate domination of "the world," which Davis has already invoked as his concern, has really met its match here. One may as well ask whether Davis has met his own stated theological criterion of "incarnational materiality," according to which "without the material . . . all simply remains in the ether of speculation."[29]

I name Davis because he explicitly recognizes the challenge posed to theology by Badiou and Žižek. He seeks to bring the theological resources of the Church's tradition into engagement with the material struggle being waged around us. (This is a struggle, we should note, in which the world's poor majority have been hard pressed, long before some of us who are more comfortable in the first world suffered imperiled mortgages and deteriorating retirement funds.) I also refer to Davis because the key of his response—a quasi-mystical description of the eucharistic liturgy—appears, despite his intentions, more fogbound in speculative abstraction than another time-honored, venerable, and doughty response to capitalism offered, not really so long ago, from within many churches.

The Strange Silence in Contemporary Churches

That other response, in a word, is socialism.[30] Almost a century ago, before his appointment as archbishop of Canterbury, William Temple could declare, "Socialism is the economic realization of the Christian Gospel."[31] It is some

---

28. Davis, "Subtractive Liturgy," 167–68.

29. Ibid., 150.

30. This would be an appropriate place for a lengthy excursus distinguishing "socialism" from "communism"; I ask the reader instead to settle, for purposes of my argument, for a rough interchangeability of terms in which either embodies Badiou's minimal criteria for a "communist hypothesis": the refusal of the "logic of class" wherein labor is subordinated to the interests of a dominant class.

measure of our current situation that "socialist" is no longer a banner carried by church leaders, but a term of reproach to be hurled against any of them who dare to deviate from "free-market" orthodoxy, as did Archbishop Temple's successor, Rowan Williams, for example, when he opposed harsh austerity measures that were presented as "welfare reform" in Britain.

The history of socialist movements is of course much larger than the history of Christian involvement in those movements. Nor should the history of socialism be construed as the history of a particular philosophy or viewpoint. It is rather one side of the history of class struggle; the other side is the history of massive, systematic opposition to and repression of even moderate social-democratic impulses.[32] The history of socialist movements in and alongside Christian churches is well documented;[33] it is often rehearsed along one or the other of two dominant narratives. The first often reads as a rather self-satisfied narrative of progress, describing how—despite a series of failures on the part of self-styled Christian socialists to stand, at crucial points, alongside working-class movements—many of their professed values nevertheless helped to ameliorate the worst upper-class antagonisms, to inform the eventual platforms of parties like Labor (UK) and the Democratic Party (US), and thus to indirectly shape the eventual construction of state welfare in the twentieth century.[34] The second narrative, more popular on the right, is an admonitory tale in which the history of Christian socialism is remembered through its decisive repudiations by towering theological intellects such as Karl Barth and Reinhold Niebuhr. For such defenders of the faith, this narrative tells us, theological liberalism, the social gospel, and other social-ethical impulses in Christianity were too optimistic, idolatrously arrogant about human capacity to reshape the world, and insufficiently "realistic" about human depravity.[35] It seems not to matter in such rehearsals that these repudiations are routinely exaggerated and unmoored from their historical contexts; that the continuing and equally comprehensive critiques of capitalism offered by these same theologians are downplayed or

31. See John C. Cort, *Christian Socialism: An Informal History* (Maryknoll: Orbis, 1988), 169-72.

32. Howard Zinn, *A People's History of the United States: 1492–Present*, rev. ed. (New York: Harper Perennial, 1995).

33. E.g., John C. Cort, *Christian Socialism: An Informal History* (Maryknoll, NY: Orbis, 1988); for the Anglican Left, Bernard Kent Markwell, *The Anglican Left: Radical Social Reformers in the Church of England and the Protestant Episcopal Church, 1846–1954* (Brooklyn: Carlson, 1991); on the legacy of the social gospel movement in the United States, Gary J. Dorrien, *Soul in Society: The Making and Renewal of Social Christianity* (Minneapolis: Fortress Press, 1995).

34. So, with regard to the Anglican Left, Markwell, *Anglican Left.*

35. The debate about Niebuhr's legacy is long and intricate; a helpful recent entrée is Larry Rasmussen, "Was Reinhold Niebuhr Wrong about Socialism?," *Political Theology* 6, no. 4 (2005): 429–57.

ignored; or that the so-called free market seems to have its own checkered track record, at best, so far as offering any restraint on human depravity is concerned. In these ways, the question, *What might a contemporary Christian refusal of the logic of class or the inevitability of inequality look like?* may be studiously avoided.

The contestations over these theological legacies, like the repeated rebukes of liberation theologians issuing from the Vatican, appear to be something other than academic disputes after all.[36] They replicate much larger systematic efforts in Western capitalist societies not only to criticize the effectiveness of "actually existing" socialist experiments but also to announce their fundamental unthinkability. Those efforts are observable in higher education generally. Historians have documented the decisive influence of Fordist industrial capitalism in shaping and redirecting academic institutions and curricula toward the production of an efficient managerial class, dedicated to the smooth function of expanding industry and generally as unmoved by the interests of the poor as they have been hostile to the organized efforts of the working class.[37] Steven Friesen has convincingly applied these observations to explain the otherwise mysterious absence of poverty in general, and poor people in particular, in the New Testament scholarship produced during the twentieth century. Friesen has proposed we identify the resulting scholarship—no less shaped by ideological commitments than "feminist" or "postcolonial criticism"—as "capitalist criticism."[38]

In the demise of the Berlin Wall and the collapse of the Soviet Union, some Westerners saw the "end of history," meaning its culmination in the triumph of a single world order so inevitable that meaningful alternatives could no longer be imagined. Terry Eagleton has chronicled the corresponding retreat, through the 1990s, of the humanities and social sciences from describing an alternative politics to theorizing the diversity of ethnic and gender identities.[39] Similarly, the rise of postcolonial theory, often regarded in biblical studies as at

36. Key texts are helpfully gathered in Alfred T. Hennelly, ed., *Liberation Theology: A Documentary History* (Maryknoll, NY: Orbis, 1990); and David J. O'Brien and Thomas A. Shannon, eds., *Catholic Social Thought: The Documentary Heritage* (Maryknoll, NY: Orbis, 1992).

37. Steven Friesen, "The Blessings of Hegemony: Poverty, Paul's Assemblies, and the Class Interests of the Professoriate," in *The Bible in the Public Square: Reading the Signs of the Times*, ed. Cynthia Briggs Kittredge, Ellen Bradshaw Aitken, and Jonathan A. Draper (Minneapolis: Fortress Press, 2008) points to the studies by Lois Menand, "The Marketplace of Ideas," in *American Council of Learned Societies Occasional Paper* 49 (New York: ACLS, 2001), http://www.acls.org/op49.htm; and Richard Ohmann, *Politics of Knowledge: The Commercialization of the University, the Professions, and Print Culture* (Middletown, CT: Wesley University Press, 2003).

38. Friesen, "Blessings of Hegemony"; see also Friesen, "Poverty in Pauline Studies: Beyond the New Consensus," *Journal for the Study of the New Testament* 26 (2004): 323–61.

the forward edge of progressive thought, has also been criticized as a convenient place where analytical tools and perspectives developed in genuinely revolutionary movements have been "parked" at a safe distance from political conflict. The effect, Aijaz Ahmad has written, has been "to domesticate, in institutional ways, the very forms of political dissent which those movements had sought to foreground, to displace an activist culture with a textual culture, to combat the more uncompromising critiques of existing cultures of the literary profession with a new mystique of leftish professionalism, and to reformulate in a postmodernist direction questions which had previously been associated with a broadly Marxist politics."[40] The aggressive formation of a reactionary corporate-capitalist ideological regime has deformed the life of the churches as well. Decades ago, lawyer and Episcopal theologian William Stringfellow observed that in US civil polity,

> the church becomes confined, for the most part, to the sanctuary and is assigned to either political silence or to banal acquiescence. Political authority in America has sanctioned this accommodation principally by the economic rewards it bestows upon the church. The tax privilege, for example, to which the church has acceded, has been a practically conclusive inhibition to the church's political intervention save where it consists of applause for the nation's cause. Furthermore, the tax preference, or political subsidy, the church has so long received has enabled, perhaps more than anything else, the accrual of enormous, if unseemly, wealth. In the American comity, the church has gained so huge a propertied interest that its existence has been overwhelmingly committed to the management of property and the maintenance of the ecclesiastical fabric which that property affords.[41]

39. Terry Eagleton, *After Theory* (New York: Basic, 2003), noting the irony of the academic focus on marginality, remarks that, for the socialist, "the true scandal of the present world is that almost everyone in it is banished to the margins. As far as the transnational corporations go, great masses of men and women are really neither here nor there" (20).

40. Aijaz Ahmad, *In Theory: Nations, Classes, Literatures* (New York: Verso, 1994), 1; see also Eagleton, *Literary Theory*, 205; and Leela Gandhi, *Postcolonial Theory: A Critical Introduction* (New York: Columbia University Press, 1998). On the fateful break of the former triangular bond between Marxist political action, theory, and historiography, see Göran Therborn, *From Marxism to Post-Marxism?* (New York: Verso, 2008).

41. William Stringfellow, *Conscience and Obedience* (Dallas: Word, 1977), 102–5.

Stringfellow wrote before the rise of the "neoconservative" policies of Reagan and Thatcher or the "neoliberalism" of the "Washington Consensus." He wrote before the rise of a well-funded and politically aggressive religious Right in the United States, devoted to "taking the country back" for a Christian quasi-theocracy and to demonizing even moderate gestures toward social democracy through institutions like the notorious Institute for Religion and Democracy. In the ensuing decades, the dynamics Stringfellow described have only been magnified. Denominational social service and public-policy advocacy agencies have suffered attrition, due in significant part to the withdrawal of funds by disgruntled congregations. (To be sure, even sympathetic observers have questioned their efficacy, given the structured indifference of the systems from which they sought ameliorative reforms.)[42] Especially after the financial crisis of 2008, church and denominational budgets are severely constrained, their real estate and investment portfolios so eroded that what Stringfellow called "the management of property" and the "maintenance of the ecclesiastical fabric" has become a matter of triage in many places. Meanwhile, the ideological atmosphere has become so poisonous that right-wing pundits can identify even the language of "social justice" as the hallmarks of socialism and Christian heresy, claims no less influential for being absurd.[43]

Such popular demagoguery is an easy target for ridicule. The fact remains, nevertheless, that while Stringfellow could observe that the churches were left room only to champion "the nation's cause," today the nation's cause is fused with the cause of corporate capitalism.

The effects of these ideological currents on even self-identified progressive or liberationist academic theological disciplines bear sober reflection as well. For example, theologian Catherine Keller has pointed out that postcolonial theory can be deployed in theological work "to relativize any revolutionary impulse, to dissipate the political energy of transformation, to replace active movements of change with clever postures of transgression."[44] Similarly, theologian Ivan

42. The authors in Timothy Sedgwick and Philip Turner, eds., *The Crisis in Moral Teaching in the Episcopal Church* (Harrisburg, PA: Morehouse, 1992) describe a "crisis in moral teaching in the Episcopal Church" in which moral teaching had come to mean resolutions directed to government, advocating specific policy recommendations, rather than moral reasoning directed to the faithful. Their theological critique corresponds in important ways with the political analysis of "nonhegemonic" anarchist thinkers like Richard J. F. Day, *Gramsci Is Dead: Anarchist Currents in the Newest Social Movements* (Ann Arbor: Pluto, 2005), who argues that the liberal impulse to petition hegemonic structures for "reform" simply reinforces the hegemony of those structures.

43. One notorious example is Fox News mouthpiece Glenn Beck's broadcast, "The State of Religion in America," July 2, 2010, http://www.foxnews.com/story/0,2933,595806,00.html.

Petrella observes a withdrawal from materialist politics in the present profusion of "contextual" liberation theologies, where preoccupations with ethnic and gender identities and with "hybridity" have often obscured the more fundamentally determinative fact of economic deprivation.

As Petrella points out, liberation theologians around the world (along with all other theologians) share a single material context—the poverty of the majority of the world's people—and a single theological context—the failure of liberation theologies (along with all other theologies) to deal successfully with that material reality. Despite their profusion, contextualized theologies remain "powerless to face the spread of zones of social abandonment. They're powerless because the upsurge of race, ethnicity, gender, and sexuality as organizing axes for liberation theology has blurred the fact that *material deprivation, that is, the deprivation that comes from one's class standing in society, remains the most important form of oppression.*"[45]

It is a perverse irony of our time that not only is so basic an assertion rare in liberation theology, but also that the realities of class antagonism, the exploitative nature of capitalism, and the mystifying power of "market" ideology are also virtually unspeakable in much Christian theological discourse, including theological discussion of "the philosophers." This is particularly ironic because, long before the rise of modern ideological criticism, Jesus of Nazareth did not hesitate to declare that one "cannot serve both God and mammon" (Matt. 6:24).[46]

AN ETHIC OF RELINQUISHMENT

I do not mean here simply to argue that more Christians, and especially Christian theologians, should embrace socialism (not that there would be anything wrong with that; it is simply an argument for another occasion).

44. Catherine Keller, *God and Power: Counter-Apocalyptic Journeys* (Minneapolis: Fortress Press, 2005), 103.

45. Ivan Petrella, *Beyond Liberation Theology: A Polemic* (London: SCM, 2008), 80–81; emphasis added.

46. It bears at least passing notice that, writing earlier in the twentieth century, F. Hauck could describe μαμωνᾶς as conveying "the demonic power immanent in possessions, surrender to [which] brings practical enslavement," art. "μαμωνᾶς" in *Theological Dictionary of the New Testament*, ed. Gerhard Kittel and Gerhard Friedrich, trans. Geoffrey W. Bromiley [Grand Rapids: Eerdmans, 1967], 4:389); at the century's end, M. Wilcox could simply generalize that "'mammon' is not inherently evil" and restrict his observations on Jesus' words to their linguistic derivation and consistency across the Synoptic tradition ("Mammon," in *The Anchor Bible Dictionary*, ed. David Noel Freedman [Garden City, NY: Doubleday, 1992], 4:490).

234 I Paul in the Grip of the Philosophers

Neither do I mean to argue that the writings of philosophers (or "antiphilosophers") like Alain Badiou, Giorgio Agamben, or Slavoj Žižek are only comprehensible when they are read by others who share their dialectical-materialist convictions. The latter argument would simply invert the insistence, mentioned above, that the philosophers cannot understand *Paul* without becoming Christians; but either argument surrenders faith in the capacity of human language and understanding to the pseudo-logic of doctrinal assertion.

I mean simply to deny the claim made by some theologians (and, I suspect, harbored implicitly by others) that the philosophers are doing something *improper*, something illegitimate, when they approach Paul from the perspective of dialectical materialism, as if they are wrenching Paul from his "proper" place—the domain of Christian theology. Badiou refers to this premise when he mentions a "Church dialect" governing the interpretation of Paul and repudiates it, one might say, from the outside.[47]

It is from *within* the theological "guild," however, that Mark Lewis Taylor has offered the most trenchant argument for exposing and disavowing this distinctive "Church dialect." Taylor distinguishes "Guild Theology" from what he seeks to articulate as "the theological." Guild Theology "is usually marked by some discourse of transcendence, that is, a thinking across (*trans-*), which involves a going above, a climbing (*scandere),* beyond the finite, somehow to another dimension above world and history."[48] The traditional and enduring hallmark of theology is precisely the claim to be dealing with the transcendent, with a reality categorically unlike all "merely" immanent, "merely" historical, "merely" material reality. This hallmark is evident in most contemporary affirmations of the relevance of Christian symbols, and in most of the ways in which those guild members whose professional responsibility it is to manage the interpretation of those symbols seek to represent their usefulness. What Corey D. B. Walker has written regarding so-called Radical Orthodoxy might be applied more generally to other streams of liberal and postliberal theology as well—namely, that theological projects are often "indebted to and predicated on historical and traditional flows of *conceptual certainty, epistemic privilege* and *theoretical imperialism* that mask the exploits and consolidations of political and intellectual power." This "masking" takes place precisely by means of these theological projects being endowed with an aura of the unassailably transcendent.[49]

47. Badiou, *Saint Paul*, 28.

48. Mark Lewis Taylor, *The Theological and the Political: On the Weight of the World* (Minneapolis: Fortress Press, 2011), 14.

The claim to epistemic privilege is evident in every protest that theological truth cannot and must not be "reduced" to merely secular or political truth. Such protests effectively fracture truth, polarizing the theological and the political as fundamentally different domains. The claim to epistemic privilege is evident, Taylor suggests, whenever ecclesiastical voices protest the encroachments of a perilous "secularism," or express a longing to perpetuate Christian beliefs and practices "within some Christian haven, thinking them protected from the challenges of secular thought, of other religions, or of the plurality of other Christian cultural readings."[50]

The fundamental error in such longing is precisely the assumption that "the theological" may be preserved by insulating it from the political, when in fact the opposite is the case. In our contemporary situation—the context of global capitalism and the corresponding ideological representations in which we live, move, and have our being—the categorical polarization of the theological and the political functions to protect the political sphere from the disruptive potentialities of religious symbols (i.e., those symbols traditionally assigned to the domain of theology). Theology is thus rendered politically irrelevant, *reduced*, precisely to a zone carefully demarcated and ideologically policed as *nonpolitical*. (It is also ironic that this happens just as some members of the theological guild struggle to reassert their cultural relevance in university humanities departments and other sites of public deliberation. Surely such relevance can only be purchased, if it is still available, at a price.)

Taylor's analysis allows us to predict that Guild Theology will be best received when it conforms to the ideological constraints of late capitalist culture. Equally predictably, in the present environment, those forms of Christianity will thrive that continue to truck in the rhetoric of free enterprise, individual initiative, and an economic version of double predestination in which humanity is neatly divided into those who (through personal virtue) prove themselves worthy of a share in the world's material resources and those who are deemed unworthy. If present ideological trajectories continue, just as predictably, the "liberal" extreme for church and theological academy alike will consist in advocating equality and tolerance amid a plurality of diverse identities. To the extent that state and civil-societal structures already manage the competition among identities within acceptable limits, liberal Christianity may be able to demonstrate its *congeniality* to liberal society, even if it is increasingly hard pressed to demonstrate its *necessity* even to its own members.[51]

49. Corey D. B. Walker, "Theology and Democratic Futures," *Political Theology* 10 (2009): 199–208; emphasis added.

50. Taylor, *The Theological and the Political*, 2.

But a Christian theology whose sails are carefully trimmed to tack with the prevailing ideological winds will not play a significant role in the history of class struggle in the twenty-first century. And the presumption of such a theology to stand in judgment of "the philosophers," without engaging the urgent contemporary context in which the philosophers seek to make their intervention, seems more than ungracious: it seems, in the worst sense of the word, merely academic.

The posture of claiming the epistemic high ground in the name of the apostle Paul has a long history (and, we may expect, an enduring-enough future). But it is not the only way to remember or engage the apostle's legacy. At what we may, in retrospect, recognize as a climactic point in his career, Paul wrote to the non-Jewish majority in the ἐκκλησίαι in Rome to warn them against "boasting" over an apparently defunct Israel (the "branches" that had apparently been "broken off": Rom. 11:13-25).[52] New Testament scholars increasingly recognize that this passage comes at the rhetorical climax of the letter, a climax that begins with a sudden, intensely emotional self-disclosure in Rom. 9:1-4.

What is less often observed is that the poignancy of Paul's words in Rom. 9:1-4 derives in no small part from the emotionally reassuring tone of his previous comments in 8:15-39. Paul has assured his (predominantly non-Jewish) readers that they are recipients of the love of God, that the Spirit testifies that they are true children (υἱοί) of God, that "nothing can separate" them from God's love. Now—abruptly—he invokes the same testimony of the Spirit in his own heart, but goes on to express his earnest wish that he might be "cut off" from Christ for the sake of his kinfolk. "They are Israelites," he declares, and to them belong—rightfully and first—all the benefits that Paul has just assured his readers were also *theirs*.[53]

---

51. The perceived decline of "liberal" or "mainstream" Christianity as compared to a resurgence of evangelical Christianity, especially in the United States, is a major concern to congregations, seminaries, denominational structures, and theological publishers alike. My comments here are meant to apply to the *theological* academy. On Terry Eagleton's analyses of the humanities academy more generally, see his *Literary Theory*, 169–208, and *After Theory*.

52. I have argued elsewhere that Paul is here confronting a perception among non-Jews in the ἐκκλησίαι that was shaped by the contemporary themes of Roman imperial ideology, especially concerning the supremacy of the Roman people over others and the evident status of Jews as *victi* (Neil Elliott, *The Arrogance of Nations: Reading Romans in the Shadow of Empire*, Paul in Critical Contexts (Minneapolis: Fortress Press, 2008), chs. 3 and 4.

53. On the force of this single rhetorical unit across Romans 8–9, see Neil Elliott, *The Rhetoric of Romans: Argumentative Constraint and Strategy and Paul's Dialogue with Judaism*, Journal for the Study of

I draw from this evocative passage a model to which Paul's theological guardians might well aspire as they warily contemplate the approach of the nontheistic philosophers. We know from this same letter that Paul himself was not shy when it came to claims of epistemic privilege. He declared a "mystery" to the Romans concerning God's plan toward Israel and the nations (11:25-27)—a mystery, one presumes, not given to any other mortal until Paul shared it. But that transcendent knowledge concerns the priority in God's purpose of those who are not presently "in Christ," who indeed "shall be saved" apparently *without* being incorporated "in Christ." By wishing *himself* outside of Christ, *for their sake*—more broadly, for the sake of a world now held in subjection (8:18-25)—Paul provides an even better prototype for Žižek's vision of Christianity's "perverse core," the necessary renunciation of privilege, than Žižek himself offers. "It is possible today," Žižek writes, "to redeem this core of Christianity only in the gesture of abandoning the shell of its institutional organization (and, even more so, of its specific religious experience). . . . That is the ultimate heroic gesture that awaits Christianity: in order to save its treasure, it has to sacrifice itself—like Christ, who had to die so that Christianity could emerge."[54] Such flourishes are unlikely to endear Žižek to the guild of professional theologians, for whom the "shell of institutional organization" includes the role of expert in a carefully protected field of knowledge. But Žižek's plea for a Christian renunciation of privilege does have a precedent, and a Pauline precedent at that. The assertion that Christ "had to die so that Christianity could emerge" is possible only in theological retrospect. But Paul was explicit enough in his own rhetoric, however imaginary the "heroic gesture" he made, and this allows us some poetic license. Might professional "Paulinists" follow Paul best by following just such a gesture of renunciation, abandoning their claims to transcendent knowing for the sake of a wider human and cosmic solidarity—as we, along with an imperiled world, face "the end times"?[55]

the New Testament Supplement series 145 (Sheffield: JSOT Press, 1990), 261–64, and Elliott, *Arrogance of Nations*, 114–19.

54. Žižek, *The Puppet and the Dwarf*, 171.

55. Žižek, *Living in the End Times*.

Bibliography

Agamben, Giorgio. *Altissima povertà: regole monastiche e forma di vita (Homo Sacer, IV, I).* Vicenza: N. Pozza, 2011.

———. *Homo Sacer: Sovereign Power and Bare Life.* Translated by D. Heller-Roazen. Stanford: Stanford University Press, 1998.

———. *Homo Sacer 3. Remnants of Auschwitz: The Witness and the Archive.* Translated by D. Heller-Roazen. New York: Zone, 1999.

———. *Idea of Prose.* Translated by M. Sullivan and S. Whitsitt. Albany: State University of New York Press, 1995.

———. *Infancy and History: the Destruction of Experience.* Translated by L. Heron. New York: Verso, 1993.

———. *Language and Death: The Place of Negativity.* Translated by K. E. Pinkus and M. Hardt. Minneapolis: University of Minnesota Press, 1991.

———. "Non à la Biométrie." *Le Monde diplomatique*, December 6, 2005.

———. "Non au tatouage biopolitique." *Le Monde diplomatique*, January 10, 2004.

———. *Opus Dei: archeologia dell'ufficio (Homo sacer, II, 5).* Torino: Bollati Boringhieri, 2012.

———. *Potentialities: Collected Essays in Philosophy.* Translated by D. Heller-Roazen. Stanford: Stanford University Press, 1999.

———. *Stanzas: Word and Phantasm in Western Culture.* Translated by R. L. Martinez. Minneapolis: University of Minnesota Press, 1993.

———. *State of Exception.* Chicago: University of Chicago Press, 2005.

———. "Terrorisme ou tragi-Comédie." *Libération*, November 19, 2008.

———. *The Sacrament of Language: an Archaeology of the Oath (Homo Sacer II, 3).* Translated by A. Kotsko. Stanford: Stanford University Press, 2011.

———. *The Kingdom and the Glory: for a Theological Genealogy of Economy and Government.* Translated by L. Chiesa and M. Mandarini. Stanford: Stanford University Press, 2011.

———. *The Time That Remains: A Commentary on the Letter to the Romans.* Translated by P. Dailey. Stanford: Stanford University Press, 2005.

———. *What Is an Apparatus? And Other Essays.* Stanford: Stanford University Press, 2009.

Ahmad, Aijaz. *In Theory: Nations, Classes, Literatures.* New York: Verso, 1994.

Badiou, Alain. *Being and Event*. Translated by Oliver Feltham. London: Continuum, 2005.

———. *Saint Paul: The Foundation of Universalism*. Translated by Ray Brassier. Stanford: Stanford University Press, 2003.

———. "The Communist Hypothesis." *New Left Review* 49 (2008): 29–42.

———. *The Incident at Antioch*. Translated by Susan Spitzer. New York: Columbia University Press, 2012.

Barth, Karl. *Die kirchliche Dogmatik*. Vol. 2.2. Zürich: Evangelischer Verlag Zollikon, 1942.

Bassler, Jouette M., ed. *Pauline Theology*. Vol. 1, *Thessalonians, Philippians, Galatians, Philemon*. Minneapolis: Fortress Press, 1991.

Becker, Jürgen. *Paulus. Der Apostel der Völker*. Tübingen: J. C. B. Mohr, 1989.

Bell, Daniel M. 2007. "Badiou's Faith and Paul's Gospel: The Politics of Indifference and the Overcoming of Capital." *Angelaki* 12 (2007): 97–111.

Benjamin, Walter. *Reflections: Essays, Aphorisms, Autobiographical Writings*. Translated by E. Jephcott. New York: Schocken, 1978.

———. *Selected Writings*. Vol. 2, *1927–1934*. Translated by R. Livingstone. Edited by M. Jennings, H. Eiland, and G. Smith. Cambridge, MA: Belknap Press of Harvard University Press, 1999.

———. *Selected Writings*. Vol. 4, *1938–1940*. Edited by H. Eiland and M. W. Jennings. Cambridge, MA: Belknap Press of Harvard University Press, 2003.

———. *The Arcades Project*. Translated by H. Eiland and K. McLaughlin. Cambridge, MA: Belknap Press of Harvard University Press, 1999.

———. "Theses on the Philosophy of History." In *Illuminations*. edited by Hannah Arendt. Translated by Harry Zohn. Glasgow: William Collins Sons, 1979.

Bennington, Geoffrey, and Jacques Derrida. *Jacques Derrida*. Chicago: Chicago University Press, 1996.

Benson, Bruce Ellis. *Pious Nietzsche. Decadence and Dionysian Faith*. Bloomington: Indiana University Press, 2008.

Berder, Michel, et al. "Saint Paul au croisement de la philosophie et de la théologie aujourd'hui: table ronde." *Transversalités* 114 (2010): 67–90.

Bewes, Timothy. *Reification: Or the Anxiety of Late Capitalism*. New York: Verso, 2002.

Bird, Michael F., and Preston M. Sprinkle, eds. *The Faith of Jesus Christ: Exegetical, Biblical, and Theological Studies*. Peabody, MA: Hendrickson, 2010.

Blanton, Ward. *A Materialism for the Masses: Saint Paul and Other Philosophers of of Undying Life.* Insurrections: Critical Studies in Religion, Politics, and Culture. New York: Columbia University Press, 2012.

———. *Displacing Christian Origins: Philosophy, Secularity, and the New Testament.* Chicago: University of Chicago Press, 2007.

———. "Disturbing Politics: Neo-Paulinism and the Scrambling of Religious and Secular Identities." *Dialog* 46 (2007): 3–13.

———. *Jesus: A Philosophical Companion.* Religion and Postmodernism. Chicago: University of Chicago Press, 2012.

Blanton, Ward, and Hent de Vries, eds. *Paul and the Philosophers.* New York: Fordham University Press, 2012.

Boer, Roland. *Criticism of Heaven: On Marxism and Theology.* Historical Materialism. Leiden: Brill, 2007.

———. *Criticism of Religion: On Marxism and Theology II.* Historical Materialism. Leiden: Brill, 2009.

———. *Criticism of Earth: On Marx, Engels and Theology.* Historical Materialism. Leiden: Brill, 2012.

———. *Criticism of Theology: On Marxism and Theology III.* Historical Materialism. Leiden: Brill, 2011.

———. *In The Vale of Tears: On Marxism and Theology V.* Historical Materialism. Leiden: Brill, 2013.

Boeve, Lieven. *Interrupting Tradition: An Essay on Christian Faith in a Postmodern Context.* Louvain Theological and Pastoral Monographs 30. Leuven: Peeters, 2003.

Bornemark, Jonna, and Hans Ruin, eds. *The Ambiguity of the Sacred.* Stockholm: Södertörn Philosophical Studies, 2012.

Borradori, Giovanna. *Philosophy in a Time of Terror: Dialogues with Jürgen Habermas and Jacques Derrida.* Chicago: University of Chicago Press, 2003.

Boyarin, Daniel. *A Radical Jew: Paul and the Politics of Identity.* Berkeley: University of California Press, 1997.

———. "Paul among the Antiphilosophers; or, Saul among the Sophists." In Caputo and Alcoff, eds., *St. Paul among the Philosophers*, 109–41. Indiana Series in the Philosophy of Religion. Bloomington: Indiana University Press, 2009.

Breton, Stanislas. *A Radical Philosophy of Saint Paul.* Insurrections: Critical Studies in Religion, Politics, and Culture. New York: Columbia University Press, 2011.

Britt, Brian. "The Schmittian Messiah in Agamben's The Time That Remains." *Critical Inquiry* 36 (2010): 262–87.

Brockman, James R. *Romero: A Life.* Maryknoll, NY: Orbis, 2005.

Calarco, Matthew, and Steven DeCaroli. *Giorgio Agamben: Sovereignty and Life.* Stanford: Stanford University Press, 2007.

Caputo, John D. *Heidegger and Aquinas: An Essay on Overcoming Metaphysics.* New York: Fordham University Press, 1982

———. "Introduction: Postcards from Paul." In Caputo and Alcoff, eds., *St. Paul among the Philosophers*, 1–23.

———. Caputo. *More Radical Hermeneutics: On Not Knowing Who We Are.* Studies in Continental Thought. Bloomington: Indiana University Press, 2000.

———. *The Prayers and Tears of Jacques Derrida: Religion without Religion.* Bloomington: Indiana University Press, 1997.

Caputo, John D., and Gianni Vattimo. *After the Death of God.* New York: Columbia University Press, 2007.

Caputo, John D., and Linda Martín Alcoff, eds. *St. Paul among the Philosophers.* Indiana Series in the Philosophy of Religion. Bloomington: Indiana University Press, 2009.

Castelli, Elizabeth A. "The Philosophers' Paul in the Frame of the Global: Some Reflections." *South Atlantic Quarterly* 109 (2010): 653–60.

Cort, John C. *Christian Socialism: An Informal History.* Maryknoll, NY: Orbis, 1988.

Crockett, Clayton. "Piety, Power, and Bare Life: What in the World Is Going On in the Name of Religion?" *Journal for Cultural and Religious Theory* 4 (2003): 1–8.

Crowe, Benjamin. *Heidegger's Phenomenology of Religion: Realism and Cultural Criticism.* Bloomington: Indiana University Press, 2008.

———. *Heidegger's Religious Origins: Destruction and Authenticity.* Bloomington: Indiana University Press, 2006.

Davis, Creston. "Subtractive Liturgy." In Milbank, Žižek, and Davis, *Paul's New Moment*, 146–68.

Day, Richard J. F. *Gramsci Is Dead: Anarchist Currents in the Newest Social Movements.* Ann Arbor: Pluto, 2005.

De la Durantaye, Leland. *Giorgio Agamben: A Critical Introduction.* Stanford: Stanford University Press, 2009.

Depoortere, Frederiek. *Badiou and Theology.* Philosophy and Theology. New York: Continuum, 2009.

De Meyere, Job. "The Care for the Present: Giorgio Agamben's Actualisation of the Pauline Messianic Experience." *Bijdragen* 70 (2009): 168–84.

Derrida, Jacques. *Edmund Husserl's Origin of Geometry.* Translated by J. P. Leavey. Stonybrook: Nicolas Hays, 1978.

———. *Acts of Religion* Edited by Gil Anidjar. New York: Routledge, 2002.

———. *De la grammatologie.* Paris: Minuit, 1967.

———. *L'écriture et différence.* Paris: Seuil, 1967.

———. *Le Voix et la Phenomena.* Paris: PUF, 1967.

———. *Of Grammatology.* Translated by G. Spivak. Baltimore: Johns Hopkins University Press, 1976.

———. *Speech and Phenomena.* Translated by D. B. Allison. Evanston: Northwestern University Press, 1978.

———. *The Truth in Painting.* Translated by by J. Bennington. Chicago: University of Chicago Press, 1987.

———. *Writing and Difference.* Translated by A. Bass. 1978. Reprint, New York: Routledge, 2001.

Derrida, Jacques, and Gianni Vattimo, eds. *Religion.* Stanford: Stanford University Press, 1998.

Derrida, Jacques, and Hélène Cixous. *Veils.* Translated by J. Bennington. Stanford: Stanford University Press, 2001.

Dickinson, Colby. *Agamben and Theology.* Philosophy and Theology. New York: T&T Clark, 2011.

———. "Canon as an Act of Creation: Giorgio Agamben and the Extended Logic of the Messianic." *Bijdragen* 71 (2010): 132–58.

Dorrien, Gary J. *Soul in Society: The Making and Renewal of Social Christianity.* Minneapolis: Fortress Press, 1995.

Dunn, James D. G. "Once More, PISTIS CRISTOU." In Hay and Johnson, eds., *Pauline Theology,* 4:61–81.

———. *The New Perspective on Paul. Collected Essays.* Wissenschaftliche Untersuchungen zum Neuen Testament 1/185. Tübingen: Mohr Siebeck, 2007.

———. "The New Perspective on Paul." *Bulletin of the John Rylands Liberary* 65 (1983): 95–122.

Eagleton, Terry. *Literary Theory: An Introduction.* 2nd ed. Minneapolis: University of Minnesota Press, 1996.

———. *After Theory.* New York: Basic, 2003.

———. *Ideology: An Introduction.* Rev. ed. New York: Verso, 2007.

Elliott, Neil. *The Rhetoric of Romans: Argumentative Constraint and Strategy and Paul's Dialogue with Judaism.* JSNTSup 145. Sheffield: JSOT Press, 1990.

———. "Paul and the Lethality of the Law." *Foundations and Facets Forum* 9, nos. 3–4 (1993): 237–56.

———. *The Arrogance of Nations: Reading Romans in the Shadow of Empire.* Paul in Critical Contexts. Minneapolis: Fortress Press, 2008.

———. "Ideological Closure in the Christ Event: A Marxist Response to Alain Badiou's Paul." In Harink, ed., *Paul, Philosophy, and the Theopolitical Vision,* 135–54.

———. "Marxism and the Postcolonial Study of Paul." In *The Colonized Apostle: Paul through Postcolonial Eyes,* edited by Christopher D. Stanley, 34–50. Minneapolis: Fortress Press, 2011.

Engberg-Pederson, Troels, ed. *Paul in His Hellenistic Context.* Minneapolis: Fortress Press, 1995.

Feltham, Oliver. *Alain Badiou: Live Theory.* New York: Continuum, 2008.

Feuerbach, Ludwig. *The Essence of Christianity.* Translated by George Eliot. New York: Harper, 1957.

Fortin, Anne. *L'annonce de la bonne nouvelle aux pauvres: une théologie de la grâce et du Verbe fait chair.* Montréal: Médiaspaul, 2005.

Fiorovanti, David. "Language, Exception, Messianism: The Thematics of Agamben on Derrida." *Bible and Critical Theory* 6 (2010): 1–18.

Fowl, Stephen. "A Very Particular Universalism: Badiou and Paul." In Harink, ed., *Paul, Philosophy, and the Theopolitical Vision,* 119–34.

Franck, Didier. *Nietzsche and the Shadow of God.* Studies in Phenomenology and Existential Philosophy. Translated by Bettina Bergo. Bloomington: Indiana University Press, 2012.

Fredriksen, Paula. "Historical Integrity, Interpretive Freedom." In Caputo and Alcoff, eds., *St. Paul among the Philosophers,* 61–73.

Frey, Christiane. "Klēsis/Beruf: Luther, Weber, Agamben." *New German Critique* 35 (2008): 35–56.

Frick, Peter. *Divine Providence in Philo of Alexandria.* Texts and Studies in Ancient Judaism 77. Tübingen: Mohr Siebeck, 1999.

———. "The Means and Mode of Salvation: A Hermeneutical Proposal for Clarifying Pauline Soteriology." *Horizons in Biblical Theology* 29 (2007): 203–22.

———, ed. *Bonhoeffer's Intellectual Formation: Theology and Philosophy in His Thought.* Religion in Philosophy and Theology 29. Tübingen: Mohr Siebeck, 2008.

Friesen, Steven. "Poverty in Pauline Studies: Beyond the New Consensus." *Journal for the Study of the New Testament* 26 (2004): 323–61.

———. "The Blessings of Hegemony: Poverty, Paul's Assemblies, and the Class Interests of the Professoriate." In *The Bible in the Public Square: Reading the Signs of the Times*, Edited by Cynthia Briggs Kittredge, Ellen Bradshaw Aitken, and Jonathan A. Draper, 117–28. Minneapolis: Fortress Press, 2008.

Fugle, Sophie. "Excavating Government: Giorgio Agamben's Archaeological Dig." *Foucault Studies* 7 (2009): 81–98;

Gandhi, Leela. *Postcolonial Theory: A Critical Introduction.* New York: Columbia University Press, 1998.

Genel, Katia. "Le biopouvoir chez Foucault et Agamben." *Methodos* 4 (2004).

Gignac, Alain. "Taubes, Badiou, Agamben: Reception of Paul by Non-Christian Philosophers Today." In Odell-Scott, ed., *Reading Romans with Contemporary Philosophers and Theologians*, 155–211.

Girard, René. *The Scapegoat.* Translated by Yvonne Freccero. Baltimore: Johns Hopkins University Press, 1977.

———. *Violence and the Sacred.* Translated by Patrick Gregory. Baltimore: Johns Hopkins University Press, 1986.

Girard, René, J. M. Oughourlian, and G. Lefort. *Things Hidden from the Foundation of the World.* Translated by Stephen Bann and Michael Metteer. Stanford: Stanford University Press, 1987.

Goldmann, Lucien. *Lukacs and Heidegger: Toward a New Philosophy.* New York: Routledge, 2009.

Griffiths, Paul J. "Christ and Critical Theory." *First Things*, August/September, 2004, 46–55.

———. "The Cross as the Fulcrum of Politics: Expropriating Agamben on Paul." In Harink, ed., *Paul, Philosophy, and the Theopolitical Vision*, 179–97.

Grimshaw, Mike. "Ruptured Romans: A Theological Meditation on Paul, Cultural Theory, and the Cosmopolitan Rupture of Grace." *Stimulus* 17 (2009): 32–40.

Guariano, Thomas G. *Vattimo and Theology.* New York: T&T Clark, 2009.

Hägglund, Martin. *Radical Atheism: Derrida and the Time of Life.* Stanford: Stanford University Press, 2008.

Hallward, Peter. *Badiou: A Subject to Truth.* Minneapolis: University of Minnesota Press, 2003.

Hamerton-Kelly, Robert. *Sacred Violence: Paul's Hermeneutic of the Cross.* Minneapolis: Fortress Press, 1992.

Handelman, Susan A. *The Slayers of Moses: The Emergence of Rabbinic Interpretation in Modern Literary Theory.* Albany: State University of New York Press, 1982.

Hansen, Ryan L. "Messianic or Apocalyptic? Engaging Agamben on Paul and Politics." In Harink, ed., *Paul, Philosophy, and the Theopolitical Vision,* 198–223.

Harink, Douglas, ed. *Paul, Philosophy, and the Theopolitical Vision.* Eugene, OR: Cascade, 2010.

Hart, Kevin, and Yvonne Sherwood, eds. *Derrida and Religion: Other Testaments.* New York: Routledge, 2005.

Hatab, Larry J. *Nietzsche's Life Sentence: Coming to Terms with Eternal Recurrence.* New York: Routledge, 2005.

Hay, David M., ed. *Pauline Theology.* Vol. 2, *1 and 2 Corinthians.* Minneapolis: Fortress Press, 1993.

Hay, David M., and E. Elizabeth Johnson, eds. *Pauline Theology.* Vol. 3, *Romans.* Minneapolis: Fortress Press, 1995.

———. *Pauline Theology.* Vol. 4, *Looking Back, Pressing On.* Atlanta: Scholars Press; Minneapolis: Fortress Press, 1997.

Hays, Richard B. "PISTIS and Pauline Christology: What Is at Stake?." In Hay and Johnson, eds., *Pauline Theology,* 4:35–60.

Heidegger, Martin. *Gesamtausgabe,* vol. 2. *Sein und Zeit.* Frankfurt am Main: Vittorio Klostermann, 1977. ET: John Mcquarrie and Edward Robinson. *Being and Time.* New York: Harper and Row, 1962. Cited as *Sein und Zeit.*

———. *Gesamtausgabe.* Vol. 5, *Holzwege.* Frankfurt am Main: Vittorio Klostermann, 1977. ET: Julian Young and Kenneth Haynes. *Off the Beaten Track.* Cambridge: Cambridge University Press, 2002. Cited as G 5.

———. *Gesamtausgabe.* Vol. 9, *Wegmarken.* Frankfurt am Main: Vittorio Klostermann, 1976. ET: William McNeill. *Pathmarks.* Cambridge: Cambridge University Press, 1998. Cited as G 9.

———. *Gesamtausgabe.* Vol. 26, *Metaphysische Anfangsgründe der Logik im Ausgang von Leibniz.* Frankfurt am Main: Vittorio Klostermann, 1978. ET: Michael Heim. *The Metaphysical Foundations of Logic.* Bloomington: Indiana University Press, 1984. Cited as G 26.

———. *Gesamtausgabe.* Vols. 56/57, *Zur Bestimmung der Philosophie.* Frankfurt am Main: Vittorio Klostermann, 1987. ET: Ted Sadler. *Towards the Definition of Philosophy.* London: Athlone, 2000. Cited as G 56/57.

———. *Gesamtausgabe.* Vol. 58, *Grundprobleme der Phänomenologie.* Frankfurt am Main: Vittorio Klostermann, 1993. Cited as G 58.

———. *Gesamtausgabe*. Vol. 60, *Phänomenologie des religiösen Lebens*. Frankfurt am Main: Vittorio Klostermann, 1995. ET: Matthias Fritsch and Jennifer Anna Gosetti-Ferencei. *The Phenomenology of Religious Life*. Bloomington: Indiana University Press, 2004. Cited as G 60.

———. *Gesamtausgabe*. Vol. 61, *Phänomenologische Interpretationen zu Aristoteles. Einführung in die phänomenologische Forschung*. Frankfurt am Main: Vittorio Klostermann, 1985. ET: Richard Rojcewicz. *Phenomenological Interpretations of Aristotle: Initiation into Phenomenological Research*. Bloomington: Indiana University Press, 2001. Cited as G 61.

———. *Gesamtausgabe*. Vol. 63, *Ontologie (Hermeneutik der Faktizität)*. Frankfurt am Main: Vittorio Klostermann, 1988). ET: John Van Buren. *Ontology—The Hermeneutics of Facticity*. Bloomington: Indiana University Press, 1999. Cited as G 63.

———. *Gesamtausgabe*. Vol. 66, *Besinnung*. Frankfurt am Main: Vittorio Klostermann, 1997. Cited as G 66.

———. *Nietzsche I–II*. Pfullingen: Neske, 1961.

———. *Nietzsche*. Translated by David Farrell Krell. San Fransisco: Harper & Row, 1979–1987.

———. *Poetry, Language, Thought*. Translated by A. Hofstadter. New York: Perennial Classics, 2001.

Hennelly, Alfred T., ed. *Liberation Theology: A Documentary History*. Maryknoll, NY: Orbis, 1990.

Horkheimer, Max, and Theodor W. Adorno. *Dialectic of Enlightenment: Philosophical Fragments*. Translated by E. Jephcott. Stanford: Stanford University Press, 2002.

———. *Dialektik der Aufklärung: Philosophische Fragmente*. 1947. Reprint, Gesammelte Schriften 3. Frankfurt am Main: Suhrkamp, 2003.

Hübner, Hans. *Nietzsche und das Neue Testament*. Tübingen: Mohr Siebeck, 2000.

Jaspers, Karl. *Nietzsche und das Christentum*. 2nd ed. Munich: R. Piper, 1952.

Jennings, Theodore W. *Reading Derrida / Thinking Paul*. Stanford: Stanford University Press, 2006.

Jewett, Robert, Roy David Kotansky, and Eldon Jay Epp, *Romans: A Commentary*. Hermeneia. Minneapolis: Fortress Press, 2007.

Keller, Catherine. 2005. *God and Power: Counter-Apocalyptic Journeys*. Minneapolis: Fortress Press, 2005.

Kisiel, Theodore. *The Genesis of Heidegger's* Being and Time. Berkeley: University of California Press, 1995.

Kroeker, P. Travis. "Living 'As If Not': Messianic Becoming or the Practice of Nihilism?" In Harink, ed., *Paul, Philosophy, and the Theopolitical Vision*, 37–63.

———. "Whither Messianic Ethics? Paul as Political Theorist." *Journal of the Society of Christian Ethics* 25 (2005): 37–58.

Langton, Daniel R. *The Apostle Paul in the Jewish Imagination.* Cambridge: Cambridge University Press, 2010.

Lüdemann, Gerd. *Paulus und das Judentum.* München: Kaiser, 1983.

Madden, Deborah, and David Towsey, "Derrida, Faith and St Paul." *Literature and Theology* 16 (2002): 396–400.

Malherbe, Abraham J. *Paul and the Popular Philosophers.* Minneapolis: Fortress Press, 1989.

Markwell, Bernard Kent. *The Anglican Left: Radical Social Reformers in the Church of England and the Protestant Episcopal Church, 1846–1954.* Brooklyn: Carlson, 1991.

Martin, Dale B. "Teleology, Epistemology, and Universal Vision in Paul." In Caputo and Alcoff, eds., *St. Paul among the Philosophers*, 91–108.

Mesnard, Philippe, and Claudine Kahan. *Giorgio Agamben à l'épreuve d'Auschwitz témoignages, interprétations.* Paris: Éd. Kimé, 2001.

Milbank, John. "The Christ Exception." *New Blackfriars* 82 (2001): 541–56.

Milbank, John, Slavoj Žižek, and Creston Davis. *Paul's New Moment: Continental Philosophy and the Future of Christian Theology.* Grand Rapids: Brazos, 2010.

Miller, Nichole E. "The Sexual Politics of Pain: Hannah Arendt Meets Shakespeare's Shrew." *Journal for Cultural and Religious Theory* 7 (2006): 18–32.

Mills, Catherine. *The Philosophy of Agamben.* Continental European Philosophy 11. Montréal: McGill-Queen's University Press, 2008.

Moxnes, Halvor. *Jesus and the Rise of Nationalism: A New Quest for the Nineteenth Century Historical Jesus.* London: I. B. Tauris, 2011.

Müller, Denis. "Le Christ, relève de la Loi (Romains 10, 4): la possibilité d'une éthique messianique à la suite de Giorgio Agamben." *Studies in Religion/ Sciences religieuses* 30 (2001): 51–63.

Murray, Alex. *Giorgio Agamben.* Routledge Critical Thinkers. New York: Routledge, 2010.

Murray, Alex, and Jessica Whyte. *The Agamben Dictionary.* Edinburgh: Edinburgh University Press, 2011.

Nancy, Jean-Luc. *Being Singular Plural.* Translated by R. Richardson. Stanford: Stanford University Press, 2000.

Nietzsche, Friedrich. *Beyond Good and Evil.* Translated by Rolf-Peter Horstmann and Judith Norman. Cambridge Texts in the History of Philosophy. Cambridge: Cambridge University Press, 2003.

———. *Daybreak: Thoughts on the Prejudices of Morality.* Translated by R. J. Hollingdale. Texts in German Philosophy. Cambridge: Cambridge University Press, 1982.

———. *Human All too Human.* Translated by R. J. Hollingdale. Cambridge: Cambridge University Press, 1996.

———. *Menschliches, Allzumenschliches.* Kritische Gesamtausgabe 2. 2nd ed. Edited by Giorgio Colli and Mazzino Montinari. Berlin: de Gruyter, 2002.

———. *On the Genealogy of Morality.* Edited by Keith Ansell-Pearson. Rev. ed. Translated by Carol Diethe. Cambridge Texts in the History of Political Thought. Cambridge: Cambridge University Press, 2007.

———. *The Anti-Christ, Ecce Home, Twilight of the Idols, and Other Writings.* Translated and edited by Judith Norman and Aaron Ridley. Texts in German Philosophy. Cambridge: Cambridge University Press, 2005.

———. *Writings from the Late Notebooks.* Edited by Rüdiger Bittner. Translated by Kate Sturge. Texts in German Philosophy. Cambridge: Cambridge University Press, 2003.

Nongbri, Brent. *Paul without Religion: The Creation of a Category and the Search for an Apostle Beyond the New Perspective.* New Haven: Yale University Press, 2011.

Norris, Andrew. *Politics, Metaphysics, and Death: Essays on Giorgio Agamben's Homo Sacer.* Durham: Duke University Press, 2005.

O'Brien, David J., and Thomas A. Shannon, eds. *Catholic Social Thought: The Documentary Heritage.* Maryknoll, NY: Orbis, 1992.

Odell-Scott, David, ed. *Reading Romans with Contemporary Philosophers and Theologians.* New York: T&T Clark, 2007.

Ohmann, Richard. *Politics of Knowledge: The Commercialization of the University, the Professions, and Print Culture.* Middletown, CT.: Wesley University Press, 2003.

Petrella, Ivan. *Beyond Liberation Theology: A Polemic.* London: SCM, 2008.

Räisänen, Heikki. *Paul and the Law.* 2nd ed. Tübingen: J.C.B. Mohr, 1987.

Rasmussen, Larry. "Was Reinhold Niebuhr Wrong about Socialism?" *Political Theology* 6, no. 4 (2005): 429–57.

Rehmann, Jan. "Ideology Theory." *Historical Materialism* 15 (2007): 211–39.

———. "Nietzsche, Paul and the Subversion of Empire." *Union Seminary Quarterly Review* 59 (2005): 147–61.

Ricoeur, Paul. "Paul apôtre. Proclamation et argumentation. Lectures récentes." *Esprit* (2003): 85–112.

Robbins, Jerome. "The Politics of Paul." *Journal for Cultural and Religious Theory* 6, no. 2 (2005): 89–94.

Robert, William. "Human, Life, and Other Sacred Stuff." *Journal for Cultural and Religious Theory* 10 (2009): 1–23.

Rohls, Jan. *Philosophie und Theologie in Geschichte und Gegenwart.* Tübingen: Mohr Siebeck, 2002.

Rosen, Stanley. *Hermeneutics as Politics.* New Haven: Yale University Press, 2003.

Ross, Alison. *The Agamben Effect.* Special issue of *The South Atlantic Quarterly* 107, no. 1. Durham: Duke University Press, 2008.

Rovère, Maxime. "Le grand récit du biopolitique." *Laviedesidees* 6 (2008).

Ruin, Hans. *Enigmatic Origins.* Stockholm: Almqvist and Wiksell, 1994.

———. "Faith, Grace, and the Destruction of Tradition: A Hermeneutic-Genealogical Reading of the Pauline Letters." *Journal for Cultural and Religious Theory* 11 (2010): 16–34.

Sanders, E. P. *Paul and Palestinian Judaism: A Comparison of Patterns of Religion.* Philadelphia: Fortress, 1977.

Santner, Eric. *On the Psychotheology of Everyday Life: Reflections on Freud and Rosenzweig.* Chicago: University of Chicago Press, 2001.

———. *The Royal Remains: The People's Two Bodies and the Endgames of Sovereignty.* Chicago: University of Chicago Press, 2011.

Schmitt, Carl. *Political Theology: Four Chapters on the Concept of Sovereignty.* Translated by George D. Schwab. Cambridge, MA: MIT Press, 1985.

———. *Politische Theologie. Vier Kapitel zur Lehre von der Souveränität.* Berlin: Duncker & Humboldt, 9th ed., 2009 [1922].

Scholem, Gershom. *Major Trends in Jewish Mysticism.* Jerusalem: Schocken, 1941.

———. *On Walter Benjamin: Critical Essays and Reflections.* Edited by G. Smith. Cambridge, MA: MIT Press, 1991.

———. *Sabbatai Sevi: The Mystical Messiah, 1626–1676.* Translated by R. J. Zwi Werblowsky. Princeton: Princeton University Press, 1973.

———. *Walter Benjamin: Die Geschichte einer Freundschaft.* Frankfurt: Suhrkamp, 1975.

Sciglitano, Anthony, C. "Contesting the World and the Divine: Hans Urs von Balthasar's Trinitarian 'Response' to Gianni Vattimo's Secular Christianity." *Modern Theology* 23 (2007): 525–59.

Sharpe, Matthew. "Only Agamben Can Save Us? Against the Messianic Turn Recently Adopted in Critical Theory." *Bible and Critical Theory* 5 (2009): 1–26.

Somner, Christian. *Heidegger, Aristotle, Luther. Les sources aristotéliciennes et néotestamentaire d'être et temps.* Paris: Presses Universitaires de France, 2005.

Standhartinger, Angela. "Paulus als politischer Denker der Gegenwart: Die Pauluslektüre von Jacob Taubes, Alain Badiou und Giorgio Agamben aus neutestamentlicher Sicht." In *Politische Horizonte des Neuen Testaments*, edited by Eckart Reinmuth, 68–91. Darmstadt: Wissenschaftliche Buchgesellschaft, 2010.

Stendahl, Krister. "The Apostle Paul and the Introspective Conscience of the West." In *Paul among Jews and Gentiles.* Philadelphia: Fortress Press, 1976.

Stringfellow, William. *Conscience and Obedience.* Dallas: Word, 1977.

Taubes, Jacob. *Abendländische Eschatologie.* 1947. Reprint, Berlin: Mattes & Seitz, 2007.

———. *Die Politische Theologie des Paulus.* Munich: Wilhelm Fink, 1993.

———. *The Political Theology of Paul.* Translated by D. Hollander. Stanford: Stanford University Press, 2004.

Taxacher, Grigor. "Messianische Geschichte: Kairos und Chronos: Giorgio Agambens Paulus-Auslegung weiter gedacht." *Evangelische Theologie* 7 (2010): 217–33.

Taylor, Mark C. *After God.* Religion and Postmodernism. Chicago: University of Chicago Press, 2007.

Taylor, Mark Lewis. *The Theological and the Political: On the Weight of the World.* Minneapolis: Fortress Press, 2011.

Terpstra, Martin, and Theo de Wit. "'No Spiritual Investment in the World As It Is': Jacob Taubes' Negative Political Theology." In *Flight of the Gods: Philosophical Perspectives on Negative Theology*, edited by Ilse N. Bulhof and Laurens Ten Kate, 319–52. New York: Fordham University Press, 2000.

Therborn, Göran. *From Marxism to Post-Marxism?* New York: Verso, 2010.

Tillich, Paul. *Systematic Theology.* Vol. 2. Chicago: University of Chicago Press, 1957.

Vattimo, Gianni. *A Farewell to Truth.* Translated by William McCuaig. New York: Columbia University Press, 2011.

———. *After Christianity.* New York: Columbia University Press, 2002.

————. *Belief.* Stanford: Stanford University Press, 1999.

————. *Beyond Interpretation: The Meaning of Hermeneutics for Philosophy.* Translated by David Webb. Stanford: Stanford University Press, 1997.

————. *Nietzsche: An Introduction.* Stanford: Stanford University Press, 2002.

————. *The Adventure of Difference.* Translated by Cyprian Blamires. Baltimore: The Johns Hopkins University Press, 1993.

————. *The End of Modernity: Nihilism and Hermeneutics in Postmodern Culture.* Baltimore: Johns Hopkins University Press, 1991.

Vattimo, Gianni, and Santiago Zabala. *Hermeneutic Communism: From Heidegger to Marx.* New York: Columbia University Press, 2011.

Vedder, Ben. *Philosophy of Religion.* Pittsburgh: Duquesne University Press, 2007.

Vries, Hent de. *Philosophy and the Turn to Religion.* Baltimore: Johns Hopkins University Press, 1999.

Walker, Corey D. B. "Theology and Democratic Futures." *Political Theology* 10, no. 2 (2009): 199–208.

Wallerstein, Immanuel. "New Revolts against the System." *New Left Review* 18 (2002): 29–39.

Washington, James M. *A Testament of Hope: The Essential Writings and Speeches of Martin Luther King.* New York: HarperCollins, 1986.

Weber, Samuel. *Benjamin's -abilities.* Cambridge, MA: Harvard University Press, 2008.

West, Cornel. *Prophesy Deliverance! An Afro-American Revolutionary Christianity.* Louisville: Westminster John Knox, 1992.

Westerholm, Stephen. *Perspectives Old and New on Paul.* Grand Rapids: Eerdmans, 2004.

————. *Understanding Paul: The Early Christian Worldview of the Letter to the Romans.* 2nd ed. Grand Rapids: Baker Academic, 2004.

Williams, Stephen. *The Shadow of the Antichrist: Nietzsche's Critique of Christianity.* Grand Rapids: Baker Academic, 2006.

Wright, N. T. *The Climax of the Covenant: Christ and the Law in Pauline Theology.* Minneapolis: Fortress Press, 1992.

Zarader, Marlène. *La dette impensé. Heidegger et l'héritage hébraïque.* Paris: Seuil, 1990.

Zerbe, Gordon. "On the Exigency of a Messianic Ecclesia: an Engagement with Philosophical Readers of Paul." In Harink, ed., *Paul, Philosophy, and the Theopolitical Vision,* 254–81.

Ziesler, John. *Pauline Christianity.* New York: Oxford University Press, 1986.

Zimmermann, Jens. "Hermeneutics of Unbelief: Philosophical Readings." In Harink, ed., *Paul, Philosophy, and the Theopolitical Vision*, 227–53.

Žižek, Slavoj. "A Meditation on Michelangelo's *Christ on the Cross*." In Milbank, Žižek, and Davis, *Paul's New Moment*, 169–81.

———. *Enjoy Your Symptom! Jacques Lacan in Hollywood and Out.* New York: Routledge, 1992.

———. "How to Begin from the Beginning." In *The Idea of Communism*, edited by Costas Douzinas and Slavoj Žižek, 209–26. New York: Verso, 2010.

———. *In Defense of Lost Causes.* New York: Verso, 2008.

———. *Less than Zero: Hegel and the Shadow of Dialectical Materialism.* New York: Verso, 2012.

———. *Living in the End Times.* New York: Verso, 2010.

———. *On Belief.* New York: Routledge, 2001.

———. *Tarrying with the Negative: Kant, Hegel, and the Critique of Ideology.* Durham: Duke University Press, 1993.

———. *The Parallax View.* Short Circuits. Cambridge, MA: MIT Press, 2006.

———. *The Puppet and the Dwarf: The Perverse Core of Christianity.* Cambridge, MA: MIT Press, 2003.

———. *The Ticklish Subject: The Absent Centre of Political Ontology.* New York: Verso, 1999.

———. *The Year of Dreaming Dangerously.* New York: Verso, 2012.

Žižek, Slavoj, Creston Davis, and Clayton Crockett. *Hegel and the Infinite: Religion, Politics, and Dialectic.* Insurrections: Critical Studies in Religion, Culture, and Politics. New York: Columbia University Press, 2011.

Žižek, Slavoj, and John Milbank. *The Monstrosity of Christ: Paradox or Dialectic?* Edited by Creston Davis. Cambridge, MA: MIT Press, 2009.

Index of Subjects

alterity, 9, 130, 133, 137, 208

anti-philosophy, 21–22

anxious concern, 42, 44–46, 49, 52–53, 56

apocalyptic, 58, 101, 119, 137, 139–41, 167, 203, 221, 233

atheism, 32, 41, 103, 131, 197, 199, 222

authentic, 40, 49, 52–53, 65, 129, 138, 200–201, 210

author, 1, 7–9, 11–13, 51–53, 70, 73, 80, 84, 86, 91, 139, 147, 163, 166, 169

being, 2, 9, 12, 23–28, 32, 34–36, 45, 46–47, 49–50, 52–53, 65–66, 77, 79, 87, 94, 100, 103–4, 107–9, 111, 114, 119, 121–24, 126–27, 129, 132, 134, 138–40, 144, 146, 149–52, 154–57, 160, 162, 165–66, 169–70, 172–73, 178, 182, 186–87, 189, 195–98, 200–202, 208, 211–12, 217, 220, 225–26, 228, 232, 234–35, 237

Being and Time, 45–46, 49, 100, 111, 126, 138, 198, 200

Berlin Wall, 3, 4, 9, 169, 230

biblical studies, 167, 194, 196, 200, 206, 210–12, 218, 230

Bild, 63, 177

biopolitics, 172, 174, 183, 187

biopower, 174

capitalism, 4–5, 9–10, 16, 152, 158, 200, 224–30, 232, 233, 235

caritas, 118, 128, 134–37, 139

Catholic/ism, 39–40, 70, 75, 117–21, 137, 230

Christ, 5–6, 10–11, 20–24, 28, 36–37, 53–56, 58, 61–62, 64, 72, 85–87, 96, 99, 102, 108–9, 114, 131, 134, 136,

153–54, 159–61, 166–69, 183–87, 189–91, 193, 198, 205, 209, 218, 220–23, 236–37

Christianity, 16–20, 22–25, 27, 31, 33, 36–37, 39, 41, 45–49, 52–53, 61–62, 71, 87, 96–98, 100–101, 108–9, 118, 120, 123–24, 126–38, 140, 145, 156, 175, 189, 197–201, 206, 217, 222, 223, 229, 235–37

Christology, 62, 165, 169, 187, 190, 220

Church, 6–7, 39–40, 44, 46, 48–54, 70, 75, 117–20, 130, 169, 183–84, 189, 203, 217–18, 220, 225, 229, 231–35

circumcision, 93, 95, 105–10, 112–13, 179

communism, 4–5, 110, 118, 120, 194, 215, 224–25, 228

conscience, 17, 19, 21, 24–27, 30–35, 203, 231

culture, 23, 48–49, 52, 97, 101, 113–14, 117, 119, 122, 124, 128–29, 134, 139, 164, 170, 173, 194–95, 203–4, 208, 210, 230–31, 235

Dasein, 45, 47

deconstruction, 8, 15, 92–95, 100–105, 115, 125, 195

denominations, 217

Enlightenment, 3, 62, 96, 104, 110–11, 114, 128

Epicureans, 2, 28

epistemological, 3, 122, 125, 143

event, 25, 39, 43–44, 51, 56, 77–78, 80–81, 83–84, 86, 92–93, 101, 103, 106, 108–9, 111, 119, 121–27, 129–30, 136, 138–39, 143–44, 146, 151–56, 158–63, 177, 184, 186, 190,

198, 201, 203, 205–6, 208, 212, 214,
218, 224–25, 229
existential, 7, 10, 26, 28, 34, 43, 72, 89,
99–100, 102, 114, 137, 182, 198, 201

facticity, 45, 98, 112, 208

Gentile, 6, 19, 27, 32, 53–54, 72, 74–76,
88, 154, 156, 161–62, 180, 199, 214
grace, 11, 45, 61, 72, 96–97, 154, 156,
158–60, 162, 184–85, 188–9, 191,
199, 201
Greek, 2–3, 27, 61, 64, 85, 93, 98–99,
101–2, 111, 136, 139, 147, 152–55,
160–62, 167, 172, 180, 184, 193,
201, 221
guilt, 17, 21, 23, 26, 30–35, 37, 87, 199

hermeneutics, 3–4, 7, 9, 20, 40, 45,
99–101, 122–25, 128–30, 136,
140–41, 163, 167, 194–95, 197, 203,
220
Homo Sacer, 170–74, 178, 180–81, 183,
186–87, 191
humanity, 4–5, 24–25, 28, 30–32,
35–36, 48, 76, 79, 109–10, 113, 138,
173, 201, 220, 235

immortality, 22–23
inauthentic, 49, 129
inoperativity, 175, 184–85, 189
Israel, 72–76, 80, 88–89, 114, 120, 131,
161–62, 178, 180–81, 191, 236–37

Jesus Christ, 6, 10–11, 20, 28, 102, 131,
134, 136, 169, 184, 189
Jetztzeit, 58, 64, 67, 177
Jew, 2, 18–20, 27, 32, 69–77, 80–81,
85–88, 91, 93, 101–2, 106–10, 112,
114, 119, 128, 132–33, 139–40, 147,
150, 152–56, 158, 161–62, 166, 168,
180, 181, 184, 191, 193, 198, 203–5,
207, 209, 214–16, 221, 236

kairological, 99, 209
kenosis, 117, 128, 136–37

La Bastille, 3
Latin America, 6, 10
left versus right, 5
liberation theology, 6, 10, 230, 233
life, 2, 8, 11–12, 15, 17–18, 20–24, 28,
30–31, 34–37, 39–40, 42–56, 62, 70,
72–74, 76, 82, 92, 95–99, 103, 127,
133, 138, 140, 149, 156–59, 167,
170–75, 180, 182, 184–85, 187, 191,
193–97, 199–201, 203, 205, 207–16,
218, 220, 228, 231
love, 10–11, 22–23, 47, 52, 54–56, 67,
72–73, 75, 85–88, 117, 119, 131–38,
140–41, 151, 159–60, 178, 184, 189,
193, 195, 197, 199, 201–3, 205–7,
209, 211, 213, 215–16, 236

Marxism, 4, 58–59, 143, 145, 147, 177,
218, 231
messianic, 16, 57–58, 60–64, 66, 71,
76–84, 86, 88–89, 101–2, 104, 162,
165–69, 174–91, 209, 213
messianism, 57–58, 94, 104, 109, 166,
168, 171, 174–75, 190, 214
metaphysical, 17, 29–30, 97–100, 102,
110, 112, 114, 121, 123–24, 129–37,
139–41, 166, 194, 204
militant subject, 145, 147, 155, 158
modernity, 3, 39, 78, 108, 118–20,
122–24, 130, 132, 137, 148, 170,
172, 174, 189
Moses, 63, 72–75, 87, 101, 108, 111,
114, 153, 156, 162, 186

neighbor, 10–11, 55, 85–8
neoliberal, 4–5, 168, 170, 204, 226, 232
nihilism, 23, 78–79, 81, 84–85, 118,
123–24, 127, 135–37, 174–75,
187–88, 224
nothingness, 22–23, 202

ontic, 28

ontological, 3, 28, 30, 34, 87, 104, 117, 123, 126, 129–32, 139–40, 166, 201, 220, 228

orthodoxy, 6, 179, 199, 229, 234

orthopraxis, 6

Other, 20, 96, 105, 167, 191, 194, 202, 209, 222

Paulinist, 69, 71, 73, 75, 77, 197, 199, 208–9, 214, 220, 237

phenomenological, 29, 41–44, 51–52, 56, 92, 98, 105, 122, 200, 209

philosophy, 2–12, 16–18, 20–22, 25, 28, 35, 39–42, 56, 58–59, 78, 82, 92, 94–99, 102–5, 110–11, 118, 120, 122, 125, 128, 131, 141, 143–44, 147, 149, 161, 163, 167–68, 171, 177, 181, 184, 188, 191, 194–96, 198–201, 210–12, 214, 218–22, 229

pluralisation, 147, 149

political theology, 17–18, 25–26, 31, 34, 65, 69–72, 74–81, 83–89, 207, 209, 229, 235

postmodern, 1, 4–5, 8–9, 118, 124, 133, 147–48, 194, 198, 231

poststructural, 5, 92, 195

prejudice, 1, 10–11, 18, 97, 110,

Protestant/ism, 3, 33, 48, 70, 163, 217, 229

psychoanalytic, 195, 197, 203–4, 207, 215

Reformation, 3

religion, 11, 15, 19, 22, 32, 40–43, 45–46, 48–49, 51, 57–59, 70, 87, 95, 98, 100, 102–5, 107–8, 118, 120, 126, 128–30, 133–34, 140, 145, 161, 166, 168, 184, 188–89, 194–95, 198, 203–4, 206, 209, 211, 218–19, 222, 232, 235

remnant, 137, 170, 172, 176–77, 180–81, 185, 188–89

resurrection, 2, 28, 37, 53, 62, 145, 153–55, 158–59, 186, 221–22

revelation, 75–76, 117, 125, 131–32, 134–39, 203

Seinsgeschichte, 119, 123–24, 134, 139

sin, 5, 17–18, 21–37, 97, 121, 128, 136, 157–58, 189

sinfulness, 23–24, 29–30

singularity, 66, 109–10, 146, 149, 155, 160

social liberation, 6

socialism, 40, 228–29, 232–33

sola scriptura, 3, 128

Stoics, 2, 28

symbol, 97, 107, 123

temporality, 92, 99, 101–2, 138, 165, 168, 176, 185, 212

text, 1, 8, 16, 40, 52, 58–61, 63–64, 66, 75–76, 78, 81–82, 87, 92–93, 106, 110–14, 132, 134–35, 137, 161, 163, 165, 199

Theologico-Political Fragment, 76–79, 81, 86

theology and philosophy, 2–3, 7, 9, 11

Torah/law, 2, 19, 27, 72, 168, 180, 183

Tornada, 67, 176–77

transcendence, 21, 23, 101–2, 110, 130–34, 150, 167, 179, 220, 234

truth, 6, 15, 21, 25, 43, 97–98, 111–14, 118, 120–23, 125–30, 132, 134–35, 137, 139–41, 134–35, 137, 144–46, 148–50, 154–55, 159–60, 164, 179, 184, 197, 199, 203, 211, 215, 220, 227, 235

universalism, 15, 71, 93, 109–10, 113, 143–44, 150, 196, 211, 220–22

unveiling, 111–12, 114, 140

veil, 91, 93, 95, 110–14, 140, 187

weak messianic power, 61, 82

weak thought, 118–19, 121, 123–24,
118

Zeitgeist, 121, 131

Index of Names

Adorno, Theodor W., 3, 62

Agamben, Giorgio, 15–16, 57–67, 70–71, 78, 81–82, 89, 95, 165–91, 207, 209, 219–20, 234

Ahmad, Aijaz, 231

Aitken, Ellen Bradshaw, 230

Alcoff, Linda Martin, 161–62

Altizer, Thomas, 131

Anidjar, Gil, 103

Ansell-Pearson, Keith, 30, 97

Anselm of Canterbury, 3

Aquinas, Thomas, 3, 40, 122, 128

Arendt, Hannah, 82, 167

Aristotle, 2, 85, 129–30, 166, 198

Assmann, Aleida, 69–70, 74, 80

Assmann, Jan, 69–70, 74, 80

Augustine, 1, 25, 26, 33, 44, 51, 93, 106, 135, 186

Badiou, Alain, 4, 7, 15, 22, 70–71, 143–64, 167, 178, 195–200, 203, 206–7, 211–12, 218–24, 227–28, 234

Balthasar, Hans Urs von, 70, 122, 131, 141

Barth, Karl, 1, 3, 75, 84, 168, 229

Barthes, Roland, 4, 8

Bassler, Jouette M., 169

Beck, Glenn, 232

Becker, Jürgen, 28

Bell, David M., 220–21

Benveniste, Émile, 57

Benjamin, Walter, 57–67, 76–79, 81–86, 89, 100, 103, 166, 170, 175, 177, 219

Bennington, Jeffrey, 93, 106, 112

Benson, Bruce, 103

Berder, Michel, 168

Bewes, Timothy, 200

Biemel, Walter, 48

Bird, Michael F., 169

Blanton, Ward, 116, 103, 144, 168–69, 193–94, 198, 207, 224

Blochmann, Elisabeth, 45

Bloesch, D.W, 11

Bloom, Allan, 4

Boer, Roland, 57, 62

Boeve, Lieven, 147–49, 158

Boff, Leonardo, 10

Bonaventure, 130, 135

Bonhoeffer, Dietrich, 8, 11

Bornemark, Jonna, 102–3

Borradori, Giovanna, 104

Bosteels, Bruno, 196

Boyarin, Daniel, 70–71, 161, 163, 211

Breton, Stanislas, 195, 200, 208

Britt, Brian, 177

Brockman, James R., 82

Buell, Denise, 204

Bulhof, Ilse N., 80

Bultmann, Rudolf, 1, 7, 40, 51, 95, 99, 168, 185, 199–202, 212

Burke, Séan, 8

Burtness, J. H., 11

Calloud, Jean, 187

Caputo, John D., 40, 105, 107, 122, 132–35, 137, 161–62, 194, 195, 203, 211, 219

Carman, Taylor, 49

Castelli, Elizabeth, 70–71

Causse, Jean–Daniel, 189

Celan, Paul, 93, 106, 108–11

Cixous, Hélène, 93, 110–11, 113

Colli, Giorgio, 15, 17, 82

Cort, John C., 229

Crockett, Clayton, 184, 203
Crossley, James, 204
Crowe, Benjamin, 100, 103
Crowell, Steven, 43

Davis, Creston, 198, 203, 221
Day, Richard J. F., 232
de Maeseneer, Yves, 179
de Vries, Hent, 105, 194, 198, 207
de Wit, Theo, 80, 84
Derrida, Jacques, 4, 8, 16, 58, 91–96,
    100–13, 115, 174, 206
Descartes, 93
Dickinson, Colby, 58
Diethe, Carol, 30, 97
Dilthey, Wilhelm, 125, 128, 131
Dorrien, Gary J., 229
Draper, Jonathon A., 230
Dreyfus, Hubert, 46
Dunn, James D.G., 168, 169, 204
Dutschke, Rudi, 69

Eagleton, Terry, 224, 226, 230–31
Ebeling, Gerhard, 40
Eiland, Howard, 58–59, 66, 89
Elliott, Neil, 6, 217–19, 221, 236–37
Ers, Andrus, 110

Feltham, Oliver, 144
Feuerbach, Ludwig, 3, 131, 222
Fiorovanti, David, 58, 174
Folkers, Horst, 69
Fortin, Anne, 187, 191
Foucault, Michel, 8, 9, 91, 170, 172, 187
Franck, Didier, 198
Fredriksen, Paula, 163, 211
Freedman, David Noel, 233
Freud, Sigmund, 87–88, 91, 93, 100,
    103, 209
Frick, Peter, 1, 11, 15, 217
Friesen, Steven, 230
Fukuyama, Francis, 4

Gadamer, Hans-Georg, 1, 4, 128, 167

Gethmann-Siefert, Annemarie, 41
Gignac, Alain, 16, 70, 71, 165, 167, 178,
    187, 219–20
Girard, René, 219
Goldberg, Jonathon, 207
Goldmann, Lucien, 200
Grelet, Stany, 166, 173
Grenholm, Cristina, 75
Griffiths, Paul J., 58, 168, 181, 183, 187,
    220–21
Grimshaw, Mike, 187–88
Guarino, Thomas G., 118
Guignon, Charles, 49
Gutiérrez, Gustavo, 10

Hägglund, Martin, 103
Hallo, William W., 73
Hallward, Peter, 143–44
Hamerton-Kelly, Robert, 219
Handelman, Susan A., 101
Hansen, Ryan, 58, 167
Harink, Douglas, 58, 167–68, 188,
    218–20, 223
Hart, Kevin, 105, 107
Hartwich, Wolf-Daniel, 69, 70, 74, 80,
    85
Hatab, Larry, 35
Hay, David M., 169
Hays, Richard B., 92, 169
Hegel, G. W. F., 3, 91, 93, 129, 185,
    194, 196–201, 203, 206, 210
Heidegger, Martin, 3, 7, 16, 17, 39–53,
    55–56, 93, 95–96, 98–103, 105,
    110–12, 122, 124, 126, 136, 138–40,
    170, 194–95, 198–201, 212
Heitmüller, Wilhelm, 48
Hennelly, Alfred T., 230
Hodge, Caroline Johnson, 204
Horkheimer, Max, 62
Hübner, Hans, 18–19, 21–22, 36
Hume, David, 127
Husserl, Edmund, 41–43, 93

Jaspers, Karl, 17, 48

Jennings, Theodore, 16, 94, 105, 223
Jennings, M. W., 58, 66
Jewett, Robert, 168, 207
Johnson, Elizabeth, 169
Jüngel, Eberhard, 40
Justin Martyr, 2

Kafka, Franz, 93
Kahan, Claudine, 166
Kahl, Brigitte, 207
Kant, Immanuel, 3, 17, 93, 104, 120–22,
    126, 196, 210
Kasper, Walter, 190
Kate, Laurens Ten, 80
Keller, Catherine, 232–23
Kelly, Geffrey, 11
Kierkegaard, Søren, 3, 16, 40, 98–99,
    102, 199
King, Martin Luther, 82
Kisiel, Theodore, 40–41, 48, 198
Kittredge, Cynthia Briggs, 230
Klein, Naomi, 5
Kroeker, P. Travis, 168, 188

Langton, Daniel, 70–71
Leavey, John P., Jr., 92, 206
Lévi-Strauss, Claude, 91
Levinas, Emmanuel, 8–9, 12, 94, 102,
    110, 127
Lilla, Mark, 69–70
Lukacs, Georg, 200
Lupton, Julia Reinhard, 207

Madden, Deborah, 94
Marcuse, Herbert, 69
Markwell, Bernard Kent, 229
Marongiu, Jean-Baptiste, 170
Martin, Dale, 161–62
Marx, Karl, 59, 84, 118, 194, 224–25
McLaughlin, Kevin, 59, 89
Mesnard, Philippe, 166
Meyere, Job, 58, 167, 181
Milbank, John, 191, 198–99, 221, 223,
    227

Miller, Nichole E., 167
Montinari, Mazzino, 15, 17
Moxnes, Halvor, 210

Nancy, Jean-Luc, 109
Niebuhr, Reinhold, 229
Nietzsche, Friedrich, 3, 15–37, 48, 61,
    85, 93, 95–98, 100, 102–3, 122–24,
    126, 133, 135–36, 198, 217
Nongbri, Brent, 204
Norman, Judith, 20, 35, 96

O'Brien, David, 230
Odell-Scott, David, 16, 71, 167, 219–20
Ohmann, Richard, 230
Ojakangas, Mika, 58
Origen, 2
Oughourlian, J. M., 219
Overbeck, Franz, 40, 48

Pasolini, Pier Pablo, 169
Patte, Daniel, 75
Pearson, Keith Ansell, 30, 97
Peterson, Erik, 70
Petrella, Ivan, 233
Philo of Alexandria, 2
Plato, 17, 93, 104, 122
Pope Benedict XVI, 40
Potte-Bonneville, Mathieu, 166, 173

Rahner, Karl, 40, 51
Räisänen, Heikki, 19, 189
Rand, Richard, 206
Reasoner, Mark, 188
Rehmann, Jan, 16, 226
Reinach, Adolf, 41
Reinhard, Kenneth, 86–88, 207
Ricoeur, Paul, 166
Ridley, Aaron, 20, 96
Robert, William, 167
Rohls, Jan, 17
Romero, Oscar, 82
Rorty, Richard, 127
Rosato, Philip J., 75

Rosen, Stanley, 194
Rosenzweig, Franz, 73, 209
Rousseau, Jean-Jacques, 92–93
Ruin, Hans, 16, 91, 110
Rushdie, Salman, 151

Salecl, Renata, 151
Sanders, E. P., 32, 168, 203–4, 211
Saner, Hans, 48
Santner, Eric, 207–9
Schleiermacher, F. D., 40, 210
Schmidt, Christoph, 69–70
Schmitt, Carl, 71–72, 74–76, 79, 81,
    170, 174
Scholem, Gershom, 65–66, 76–77, 166
Schweitzer, Albert, 203, 212
Sciglitano, Anthony, 16, 117, 13
Sedgwick, Timothy, 232
Shannon, Thomas A., 230
Sharpe, Matthew, 58, 166
Sheehan, Thomas, 40
Sherwood, Yvonne, 105, 107
Siegumfeldt, Inge-Birgitte, 107
Sobrino, Jon, 10
Somner, Christian, 198
Spinoza, 3, 128
Spitzer, Susan, 144, 197
Sprinkle, Preston M., 169
St. Arnaud, Guy-Robert, 190
Standhartinger, Angela, 70–71, 74
Stanley, Christopher D., 218
Stanley, Timothy, 3
Stendahl, Krister, 19, 32–34, 75–76, 88
Stringfellow, William, 231–32
Svennungson, Jayne, 110

Taubes, Jacob, 16–18, 25–26, 30–32, 34,
    65, 69–81, 83–89, 166–67, 170, 175,
    178, 207, 219–20, 225
Taussig, Hal, 204–5
Taxacher, Grigor, 58

Taylor, Astra, 214
Taylor, Carman, 49
Taylor, Mark C., 198, 206
Taylor, Mark Lewis, 234–35
Temple, William, 228
Terpstra, Martin, 80, 84
Tertullian, 2–3
Tillich, Paul, 1, 7, 28
Towsey, David, 94
Troeltsch, Ernst, 42
Turner, Philip, 232

Van Buren, John, 40
Vattimo, Gianni, 16–17, 95, 103,
    117–41, 194
Vedder, Ben, 103

Walker, Corey D. B., 234–35
Wallerstein, Immanuel, 226
Washington, James M., 82
Weber, Samuel, 89, 171, 179
Welborn, Larry (Lawrence), 16, 69, 207,
    225
West, Cornel, 199
Westerholm, Stephen, 33, 203
Williams, James G., 219
Williams, Rowan, 229
Williams, Stephen, 36
Wright, N. T., 186

Zarader, Marlène, 101
Zerbe, Gordon, 168, 188
Ziesler, John, 27
Zimmerman, Michael, 39, 49
Zimmermann, Jens, 9, 167, 220
Žižek, Slavoj, 16–17, 162, 193–209,
    212–15, 219, 221–27, 234, 237
Zohn, Harry, 82
Zupančič, Alenka, 151, 159
Zvi, Sabbatai, 77

Index of Biblical References

Hebrew Bible

Genesis
17:10......107

Exodus
6:12......108
6:30......108
20......66
32:10......72
34......73

Leviticus
6:41......108

Judges
12:6......105

Habukkuk
2:4......77

New Testament

Matthew
6:24......233
26:28......28

Mark
1:4......28
12:29-31......85
15:34......222

Luke
1:77......28
3:3......28
24:47......28

John
14:25-26......129

Acts
2:38......28
5:31......28
10:43......28
13:38......28
26:18......28

Romans
1:1-7......176
1:1......176, 178
1:5......52
1:14-17......176
1:15......215
1:16......183
2:9-16......176
2:25......107
2:25-29......176
2:28-29......180
3......33
3:9-12......176
3:9......27
3:19-24......176
3:20......189
3:21......177, 184, 190
3:22......168
3:27-31......176, 183
3:27......184
3:29-30......156
3:31......190
4:2-3......176
4:10-22......176
4:11......107
5:6-11......86
5:8......86
5:12-14......176
5:12......27

5:14......58, 63, 177
5:19-21......176
5:19......214
5:23......214
6:1-5......54
6:6......27
6:10......28
6:14......72
6:17......27, 52
7......25, 26
7:6......183
7:7-24......176
7:7......189
7:8......158
7:8b-11......157
7:12......159, 189
7:14a......159
7:15-20......157
8:6......156
8:15......55
8:15-39......236
8:18-29......84
8:18-25......237
8:19-25......176
8:19-23......65
8:20-23......78
8:26-27......55
8:38—9:2......72
9–11......75
9......180
9:1-4......236
9:2-3......72
9:3-9......176
9:3......73
9:4......75
9:24-28......176
10:2-12......176
10:4......183
10:6-10......184
11:1-16......176
11:11-26......180
11:13-25......236
11:25-27......237

11:25-26......176
11:26......75, 76, 88
11:28......75
11:29......75
12:1-2......188
12:2......188
12:13......55
12:21......84
13......78, 84, 86, 167
13:1-7......188
13:8-10......85, 86, 88, 176
13:8-9......184
13:8......88
13:9-10......55
13:10......10, 159
14:1—15:3......88
14:13......88
15:7......88
15:16......56
15:19......214
15:23......214

1 Corinthians
1......197, 203, 208
1:22-29......176
1:22......153
1:24......88
1:26-27......44
1:26-28......88
1:28......183
2:1-5......176
4:17......53
7:1......64
7:17-32......178
7:17-24......176
7:18-21......179
7:20-29......176
7:20......44
7:29-32......84, 176, 178
7:29......170, 181
7:31......63, 177
9:19-22......176
10:1-6......176
10:6......177

10:16-17......54
10:21......54
11......205
11:1......53
11:2......53
11:4......111
11:5......112
11:16......53
11:18-22......54
11:23......53, 54
12......191
12:13......54
13......10, 55
13:1-13......176
13:1-3......55
14......191
14:26-36......54
15......197
15:3-5......53
15:7-9......176
15:20-28......176
15:24......183
16:1-4......56
16:14......55
16:24......10

2 Corinthians
1:10-11......54
3:1-3......176
3:6-7......175
3:12-18......176
5:16-17......176
5:17......36, 179
8:2......56
10:4......100
12......62
12:1-10......176, 177
12:7......66
12:9-10......58, 61, 82
12:9......183

Galatians
1:11-17......176
2......205

2:1-14......176
2:2-9......53
2:2......53
2:16......168
3:5......183
3:10-14......176
3:10......189
3:13......191
3:19......189
3:22......27
3:24......189
3:28......85, 102, 147, 160
4:21-26......176
5:6......159, 183
6:10......64
6:17......213

Ephesians
1:9-10......176
1:10......58, 177
2:15......36
3:7......183
4:15-16......127
5:16......64
6:12......224

Philippians
1:3-4......54
2:4-11......55
2:5-11......176, 191, 129
3:3-14......176
3:12......190
3:21......183
4:6-7......55
4:13-17......176
5:1-3......176

Colossians
1:14......28
1:29......183
4:5......64

1 Thessalonians
1:5-7......138

1:6......139
1:9-10......139
2:14......53
4:9-10......55
4:15......181
5:17......55

2 Thessalonians
2:3-11......176

Philemon
1:15-16......176

Hebrews
1:1-2......129, 130